West -
Colo -
OKLA

Glenn F. Sanford

1st ed

Sagg 382
8272

Fine in adj. which
has small taped repairs -

114

The Great Plains

IN TRANSITION

The Great Plains

IN TRANSITION

by Carl Frederick Kraenzel

University of Oklahoma Press : NORMAN

Library of Congress Catalog Card Number: 55-9628

Copyright 1955 by the University of Oklahoma Press, Publishing Division of the University. Composed and printed at Norman, Oklahoma, U.S.A., by the University of Oklahoma Press. First edition.

To the rural residents
of the Great Plains,

with the hope that other United States citizens, in and out of the region, will find in these pages the ways and means to help build a satisfactory way of life for the Plains.

Preface

The Great Plains form a distinctive region. In the
United States this semiarid land is clearly distinguished from the humid area to the east and the arid area to
the west. An attempt is made to present this geographic distinctiveness in Chapters II and III.

The Plains find further distinction in that there have emerged
even a degree of unity. But this historical unity was destroyed
by the invasion of a humid-area way of life. These historical facts
give an understanding of the invasion of the Plains by unadapted
ways, and an appreciation of the possible institutional adaptations that may be made. This social history is presented in Chapters IV through XI.

The plains find further distinction in that there have emerged
certain characteristic problems, accompanied by erratic efforts
to adapt certain institutional and social ways to conditions in the
region. This social and economic distinctiveness is set forth in
Chapters XII through XV.

Finally, the region is distinctive because it has been an exploited hinterland and remains so today. In self-defense, the
residents have developed a set of attitudes and behavior patterns
best described as minority conduct. These psychological and
social aspects are described in Chapters XIV through XX.

There is a solution to this difficulty in the Plains: adapt or
get out. Some progress has been made in technological, economic, and social-institutional adaptations. Unfortunately, this
progress is chiefly in the area of agriculture. Such adaptation
needs to occur in all other phases of life. The nature of the current adaptation is set forth in Chapters XXI through XXIV.

The final solution to the difficulties in the Great Plains is to be found in regionalism, so that the area can become a unity once again, and can function for the welfare of the residents through democratically constructed channels. These opportunities and this challenge for regional unity are described in Chapters XXV through XXVII.

And not only will the residents of the Plains benefit from such regionalism. All citizens in the United States and many people in other semiarid lands will profit therefrom. There will be national and global significance to this development in the Plains, if steps are taken to make the area a full partner in the democracy of the United States.

Though the emphasis in this book is largely sociological, an attempt has been made to assign some measure of importance to all other operative factors affecting the Plains—geographical, psychological, economic, historical, technological, and social. A task of these proportions can only induce a sense of humility. This becomes all the more apparent when we realize that there are here countless problems for the solution of which we do not yet have full and scientific information. But, since the march of social events waits for no man, an obvious choice was made: to analyze the problems of the Plains *now,* with the factual information at hand. The author is well aware of the deficiencies and shortcomings of this information.

Information about the region is often fragmentary, and is included incidentally in texts. Public school teachers have had at their fingertips only limited and highly specialized information about the region. Agency personnel, administrators, and business people, often newcomers to the region, frequently have no information about the peculiarities of the Plains to assist them in shaping their programs. Moreover, agencies and business concerns, located in cities on the periphery of the region and extending their influence into it, have not generally understood the problems of the region. For these reasons, this book is an attempt to bring together certain pertinent but not generally available information about the area, so arranged as to provide a meaningful frame of reference. The product of much study, reading, research, and discussion, its contents have been used in undergraduate and graduate college classes. Above all, it was written in the Plains, about them, by one who is a part of them. From these facts arises its major bias—namely, its Plains-centered premise.

Acknowledgment is here gratefully made to many for their direct and indirect help. This book could not have been written without benefit of countless prior research projects undertaken by others. The bibliography will make clear the great range and importance of these contributions, whose authors have my warm thanks.

Some of the inspiration for this effort was provided by certain persons who left their marks, not always recorded, in and about the region. Among them are M. L. Wilson, formerly of Montana State College and former director of the United States Extension Service; and E. A. Starch, formerly of Montana State College, now on leave from his position as secretary of the Great Plains Agricultural Advisory Council to assist in shaping an agricultural program for the Near East and the Orient. In a similar manner, encouragement came from Walter Prescott Webb of the University of Texas; from Lois Payson, formerly librarian at Montana State College, now serving at the University of Wyoming; from Don Chapman, the Great Plains wheat farmer who has since been president of the Montana Farmers' Co-operative and Educational Union; from James G. Patton, president of the National Farmers' Co-operative and Educational Union, who has been striving for the general welfare of all in the Plains and the nation; and from Lyman Brewster, rancher, formerly of the Quarter Circle U and now the X Diamond from near Birney, Montana. Others, too numerous to name, have also lent encouragement.

The following merit very special mention. Miss Anna Zellick of Lewiston, Montana, edited much of the manuscript at an intermediate stage and made many valuable suggestions. Mrs. Frances MacDonald read some of the manuscript critically and offered constructive suggestions. M. A. Bell, assistant director of the Montana Agricultural Experiment Station, superintendent of field stations at Havre, Montana, and Woodward, Oklahoma, is the natural scientist of the Plains by whom the farm and field data were checked. Maurice Kelso, formerly head of the Department of Agricultural Economics and Rural Sociology, now director of the Experiment Station and Extension Service, Montana State College, served as an inner conscience for the sifting of the agricultural economics and the statements of fact in the social sciences. Robert Dunbar, professor of history, also of Montana State College, served in this capacity for the history of the Plains. Finally, Mr. and Mrs. Richard Shipman, who farm near Brooks, Montana, served as patient analysts of reader interest. To all these fine friends, many thanks for their efforts and encouragement.

The Great Plains in Transition was written outside the job. There was no financial help from foundations outside the region. Montana State College provided stenographic, editorial, and other assistance. For these latter aids the author extends his appreciation.

Carl F. Kraenzel

Tehran, Iran
July, 1955

Contents

Tables and Figures

FIGURES

The Great Plains

IN TRANSITION

CHAPTER 1

The Great Plains in National and Global Perspective

The Great Plains make up one-fifth of the land area of the United States. Extending from the foothills on the eastern slope of the Rockies (the 4,500-foot contour), the Plains reach eastward to the ninety-eighth meridian, a distance of about 750 miles at the widest point. They extend from the Canadian border on the north to the Mexican border on the south, a distance of more than 1,600 miles "as the crow flies." They include portions of ten states: the eastern sections of Montana, Wyoming, Colorado, and New Mexico; and the western expanses of North and South Dakota, Nebraska, Kansas, Oklahoma, and Texas (Figure 1).

This area encompasses 586,461 square miles of land, or 20 per cent of the nation, and 53 per cent of the land area of the ten Plains states. About five and one-half million people lived in the Great Plains proper in 1950, the equivalent of one-third of the total ten Plains states' population, but only 3.7 per cent of the nation's population. There was an increase in population (14.9 per cent) in this region between 1940–50, slightly greater than the 14.5 per cent increase for the nation as a whole (Table 1). The rural segment of the population of all the Great Plains states, however, had significant decreases during the forties and fifties. The Great Plains have always had a proportionately larger rural and agricultural population than any other region in the nation, with the exception of the Great Basin, between the Rockies and the Sierras.

The Great Plains are a semiarid land, which makes them strikingly different from the subhumid and humid land to the east and the arid land to the west. The Canadian Prairie Provinces to the north and some of Mexico to the south are similarly semiarid. In fact, about 15 per cent of the world's land area is classified as semiarid.

These semiarid lands, the American Plains included, offer hope to an overcrowded and hungry world, for they represent potential settlement opportunities and some of the potentially most fertile soils of the globe. But to make possible successful living in these lands requires greater knowledge of their problems and better efforts at solution than have heretofore been known or made. It has not yet been demonstrated that civilization can thrive, or even survive, in the American Plains without subsidy. Especially is this true of a civilization that is shaped preponderantly by humid-area institutions and values.

The basic assumption behind this study, as a matter of fact, is that a humid-area type of civilization cannot thrive in the semiarid American Plains without constant subsidy, or, lacking this, without repeated impoverishment of the residents. Nor would America want to test this proposition, for the cost in human suffering and destruction of morale would be considered too high. The forces that motivate most Americans, including the readiness to migrate, would come to the rescue before the test was actually made. The task, then, is to understand the semiarid American Plains and to make the necessary adaptations for institutions and social organizations.

The semiarid Great Plains of the United States, as is true of similar lands elsewhere, have offered many attractions to settlers. In the United States, the first homesteaders, like the earlier mountain-plainsmen and cattlemen, were enticed by the vast and open nature of the grasslands. Treeless, these Plains promised rich crops and grass fodder, without the backbreaking and tedious tasks of grubbing stumps, digging roots, and burning slash.

For people from a forested country, who once before had been tempted by the fertile Mississippi prairies and had found a rich country, the attractions of the Plains grasslands could not be dimmed by the earlier rumors that it was a "Great American Desert." And the prospect of riches seemed even more probable after inventions and improvisations such as the revolver, the sod house, the barbed-wire fence, the windmill, the steel plow,

4

TABLE 1. Population for the United States, the ten Great Plains states, and the Great Plains proper, classified by rural, urban, and total for the years 1930, '40, and '50. * (Population and area figures in thousands)

Item	1930 United States	1930 Great Plains States	1930 Great Plains Proper	1940 United States	1940 Great Plains States	1940 Great Plains Proper	1950 United States	1950 Great Plains States	1950 Great Plains Proper
Area (sq. miles)	2,977.1	1,107.6	586.5	—	—	—	—	—	—
Total Population	122,775.1	15,075.7	4,538.4	131,699.3	15,618.3	4,808.6	150,697.4†	17,335.6	5,524.2
Per cent Change‡	—	—	—	7.2	3.6	6.0	14.5	10.9	14.9
Density	41.3	13.6	7.7	44.2	14.1	8.2	50.6	15.7	9.4
Rural Population	53,820.2	9,526.7	3,415.8	57,245.6	9,196.9	3,109.3	61,769.9	7,785.5	2,787.4
Per cent Change‡	—	—	—	6.4	-3.5	-9.0	7.9	-15.3	-10.3
Rural as Per Cent of Total	45.0	63.2	75.3	45.0	58.9	64.7	41.0	44.9	50.5
Urban Population	68,954.8	5,549.0	1,122.6	74,423.7	6,421.4	1,699.3	88,927.5§	9,550.1	2,736.8
Per cent Change‡	—	—	—	7.9	15.7	51.4	19.5	48.7	61.1
Urban as Per Cent of Total	55.0	36.8	24.7	55.0	41.1	35.3	59.0	55.1	49.5

* Taken from the United States Census of Population
† Exclusive of 481,545 abroad in the armed services
‡ These changes are from 1930–40 and from 1940–50
§ Number by the old definition. The new urban definition gives a figure of 96,467,686 for the urban

5

the grain drill, the reaper, and the early railroads had made their appearance.

But these homesteaders brought with them their humid-area way of living, which had not yet been tested in a land of recurring drought and flood. They may have known rust, but not dust—insects, but not hordes of grasshoppers. These forest people knew deep snow, but not blizzards—sleet, but not grassland hailstorms. They brought with them their forest-land ways of farming and town building, their humid-area school organization and local government, their forest-land ideas of home and hearth, their experience of permanent residence on the farmstead. Vernon L. Parrington's *Main Currents in American Thought* contains possibly the most easily understood explanation of those pressures which caused the more adventurous early settlers to move westward, bringing with them, from their "fixed abode and familiar acres," their traditional humid-area institutions and conceptions.

From the beginning, the homesteaders of the Plains experienced great suffering, many finding it necessary to return home to the humid land. They blamed their misfortunes on the climate (drought, hail, blizzards, dust) and its attendant rigors (leaf rust and grasshoppers). Inexperienced in the conditions that make for the uniqueness of a semiarid land, they did not look for the explanation of their hardships in the inappropriateness of their forest-land way of living. They failed to see the need for fitting their institutions and their philosophy to the facts of semi-aridity in the Plains. And there was no help to be found in any of the customary, traditional patterns of contending with environment. Western civilization, nurtured by humid-area and forest-land influences, did not possess knowledge of this kind of living.

In addition, the humid-area civilization continued to push into the Great Plains through the cities that bordered the Plains on the eastern edge and through the avenues of communication that spanned the region.

This invasion is today still unchecked. Cotton growers of the humid South, cornbelt farmers of the humid Midwest, and small grain, feed, and dairy men of the "wet" Red River country of the North constantly press west into the Great Plains. Supported by Midwestern cities, newspapers, radio, tanker trucks, streamliners, and financial ties, this westward thrust of a humid-area civilization exerts a constant pressure upon a now defenseless semiarid land—a land almost without large cities and universities, a land with only a handful of residents, a land without adequate communication to explain its peculiar conditions and needs.

The residents of the Plains are, therefore, like pawns. Twice, in the last two world wars, the residents of the region have patriotically overextended themselves to raise bumper crops, each time with the help of more than the usual amount of rainfall. At present, these residents are in the second postwar period of painful readjustment to the decline in such production, a decline made more pronounced by a reduced precipitation. Since the economy of the Plains is chiefly agricultural and without local controls to govern price or volume of production as there are in the case of many industrial areas, the residents are at the mercy of forces outside the region.

Various climatic and natural hazards cause the semiaridity in the Plains, including unpredictable variations in precipitation about a norm that is always relatively low. This results in wide income fluctuations for the residents, and, therefore, severe contractions in living standards and institutional services. These climatic factors will be dealt with later.

But there is emerging a new hazard in the Plains, one arising from today's higher standard of living with the resultant increased demand for "boughten goods." Since demand for and prices of Plains production are governed by forces outside the region, fluctuations in these are not always synchronized with the fluctuations brought on by the special hazards in the region. Higher and more rigid living and production costs intensify this situation, pressing with especial urgency upon these Plains residents because of their economic dependence.

There was a time, earlier, when people lived in a more self-sufficient manner. Then, when income was low, reductions could be made in living and farm operating expenses with prospects for readier recovery. Today, a "pulling in of the best" spells severe contractions in living and farm operating outlay. What was once a temporary setback, today assumes the dimensions of a calamity.

Related to this is still another misfortune, one yet to be ex-

7

perienced by the region as a whole, when suffering on the Plains may be more extensive than ever before. That is drought on a wide scale, while the rest of the nation lives in prosperity. Individuals in the region have had this experience. So have ranchers and farmers in small dispersed localities throughout the region, as recently as the forties and the early fifties. The year 1953 gave a foretaste of what may be in store for Plains residents during the present decade. The gambling odds that the severe droughts of 1953–54 will recur soon are clear.

A depression of major proportions, resulting from this cause at a time when the rest of the nation enjoys plenty, is likely to be even more demoralizing than the events from 1873 to the end of the century or the events of the thirties. In addition to continued high operating and living costs, there would be certain expenses not borne formerly: rural electrification services would demand continued direct cash outlays; prepaid hospital and medical payments would continue; social security deductions would still be compulsory. To drop out of the prepaid hospital and medical-care program, having been a long-time member and with increased chances that the services will be necessary, would foster a resentment not easily dispelled.

Today the residents of the Plains are, therefore, faced with a gigantic task. They must fit their basic institutions and social values to the conditions of semiaridity. The entire social, economic, and institutional pattern—from church and schools, through hospitals, to local government—must undergo a change similar to that which has taken place in the realm of mechanical gadgets. In social and economic matters, adaptations have been few and accidental.

The change incident to this task will tear at the emotions of the plainsmen. There will be frustrations and enmities—times when people will not think clearly but act from impulse. Yet there is a rational way of fitting the institutional life of the region to the semiaridity of the Plains. It is to be found in regionalism. By this is meant the unique but democratic ordering and programing of the economic, social, and living activities of the residents of a common area, through political and all other avenues, so that the greatest possible advantages can accrue to these residents and to the entire nation and the world as well.

To participate in the development of an adapted way of life

8

for the Great Plains, the residents must recognize that the region has a rich history, entirely capable of making citizens into patriots. Opportunities for employment and investment must be created within the region and controlled by residents of the region. Builders of the region must reside in the area permanently, rather than exploit it as nonresidents. The residents must invent the kind of institutional patterns that are suited to the prevailing environmental forces. This means region-centered cities and communication facilities. It means the development of a spirit of self-criticism and self-discipline, not bordering on sectionalism, but based, instead, on co-operation with other parts of the nation. Only in this way can the Plains achieve a status of equality with other regions.

The analysis that follows is a study in cultural adaptation— or lack of it—for the semiarid Great Plains. There is already evidence of adaptations, especially in the area of agriculture. It is in the non-agricultural population of the region—the people on Main Street, in the professions, and in the ranks of labor—that these adaptations have little meaning. Constantly alert to the tempo of economic, social, and political forces outside the region, this segment of the population is uninformed and confused about native issues at stake. Yet, unknowingly, these people bear the responsibility for the future of their land. When it is realized that the residents of the Plains face this task of developing a suitable way of living without the help of region-centered cities and modern two-way communication, the job appears almost hopeless.

But the Great Plains are a frontier, and American history has demonstrated that the frontier has consistently influenced the formation of American institutions. The Plains could provide an experiment in true regionalism—an approach by which both the United States and the Plains could achieve fuller development than now prevails.

However, more peoples than those of the United States would gain from such an experiment. There are global implications here. The American Plains reach beyond the borders of the United States and extend into Canada and Mexico. Similar agricultural products are grown throughout the entire region. The people of both Canada and Mexico are watching the progress in irrigation in the U. S. portion of the Plains, and there are, un-

fortunately, international jealousies concerning the use of bor-
derland waters—the scarcest of all commodities. Production
plans of these neighbors are closely geared to the course of U. S.
agricultural production and policy.

The world-wide significance of experimentation in the Great
Plains is emphasized further when it is realized that fully one-
seventh of the world's surface is semiarid: the rainshadow slopes
of the Andes, including the Pampas of Argentina, Paraguay, and
Bolivia; the border country of the Great Australian Desert, about
29 per cent of Australia; the northern and southern margins of
the Sahara, and much of the Kalahari Desert (in all, 20 per cent
of Africa); the basins of the Spanish Meseta and the Mediterra-
nean coastal area of Spain; a great deal of southeastern European Russia; one-fifth of the land area of Asia, especially Asia
Minor, eastern Manchuria, and the borders of the Thar Desert
in India.

These semiarid lands include extensive "underdeveloped"
parts where increased production could not only feed and clothe
the natives more adequately but could also fill the granaries
of the hungry peoples in overcrowded humid areas.

The task is to develop social organization in these semiarid
lands so that knowledge, skill, inventions, and finances can cir-
culate among their peoples. Coupled with man power and
adapted practices, these lands could produce plentifully. But
foreign relations and business activities first need to be made
more just and honorable than they have been.

Steps towards these goals have already been taken through
the creation of a UNESCO Advisory Committee on Arid Zone
Research. The committee was created in January, 1951, after
the problems had been considered by several subcommittees
and by the General Conference of UNESCO, starting with its
third session held at Beirut, Lebanon, in 1946. A committee of
experts found that many countries were interested in reclaim-
ing their arid and semiarid lands and in building defenses against
the extension of such conditions. It was thought that basic and
applied scientific research could aid greatly in bringing to light
techniques for the resource development of such lands. The
World Health Organization, at its seventh session in January,
1951, passed resolutions to support UNESCO in this effort.

The Great Plains residents have some of the necessary knowledge, skill, and inventions to produce efficiently under conditions of semiaridity. But they do not have all the answers to the needs. They, too, must observe and learn. There must, now, be a courageous willingness to experiment in those matters that pertain to fitting the social organization, institutions, and values of living to the conditions of semiaridity. In these respects, the semiarid lands, wherever they may be, may have models that are worth studying, modifying, testing, and applying to conditions in the American Plains.

Above all, the American Plains have the opportunity of building regionalism into a practical model, not only for Plains residents but for citizens in any part of the United States. Regionalism of this order is an emerging need both here and abroad.

CHAPTER 2

The Climate of the Great Plains

The Great Plains are more nearly unique than most people realize, and, therefore, their problems and needs are not fully appreciated. They are not an arid land; were that the case, their place in the American scene would be readily understood. An arid or desert condition is quickly recognized by even the least observing. They are not a humid or subhumid land; were that the case, they would stand shoulder to shoulder with the American Midwest, the South, and the East in fully benefiting from the preponderantly urban and industrial civilization that prevails in the United States today.

Instead, the Plains are a semiarid land. They are not semiarid in that the climate is halfway between humid and arid. They are not half dry and half wet; rather, some years they are dry and even arid; other years they are very wet; and still other years they are wet or dry at the wrong times from the standpoint of agricultural production and yields. It is this undefinable aspect of semiaridity that gives the Plains their distinctiveness.

The climate of the Great Plains is distinctly continental in character. The interior location of the region, the great distance from oceans, and the position of the Rocky Mountains influence the combination of the four weather-producing factors—temperature, air pressure, winds, and moisture.

The continental character of the climate is, in part, the result of three large sweeps of air masses into the region. Those coming from Canada and Hudson Bay are of the colder and drier type. Those crossing the Rocky Mountains from the Pacific may range from warm to cold, and from dry to moist. Those from the Gulf of Mexico tend to be warm moisture-laden currents.

The accidental collision of the first of these air masses with either of the other two, especially the last, results in most of the precipitation for the region. Generally, the tropical maritime air currents from the Gulf come up the Mississippi Valley and then turn eastward, missing the Great Plains. Sometimes, however, these moisture-laden currents move farther north and west, entering the Plains. It is then that the Plains receive more than the minimum of precipitation. The collision of this air mass with the polar air produces violent rainstorms and heavy precipitation. That is the explanation for the unusual rains in Kansas in the flood year of 1951, or the late but heavy rains in the Northern Plains in the spring and summer of 1953, while the southwestern part of the region was in a drought stage.

At other times the warmer and drier winds from the southwest, and from west of the Rockies, collide with the polar air and produce only a minimum of precipitation, or none at all.

The semiaridity of the Plains is then accounted for, in large measure, by the presence of moisture-deficient air currents. Only occasionally do the more humid air masses enter the region. Furthermore, at least two of these air masses must collide if there is to be precipitation. These conditions contribute not only to semiaridity, but to variability and unpredictability in the amount and kind of precipitation. The location of potential precipitation is also variable and unpredictable. The topography of the Great Plains, it must be remembered, is not broken by high mountains or by large bodies of water which might assist in directing the flow of these air masses. Thus even the low precipitation potential does not have a predictable location, because of the physical characteristics of the Plains.

The resulting combinations of temperature, air pressure, winds, and moisture content cause the changeable, highly versatile weather. The rain may be spasmodic and of cloudburst or gentle drizzle proportions. Weather may also be in the form of chinook winds or blizzard-like blasts. It may take the shape of hail or of dry, searing drought. A good, early growing season may be followed by a late spring frost or by leaf rust. An early fall frost may be followed by a long Indian summer. These are all highly unpredictable weather variations, induced by the large sweeps of air masses that flow unimpeded over an extensive plain.

The climate of the Plains is continental in another sense. The major amount of the precipitation falls from May through July, the growing season. If the limited moisture fell in the nongrowing season, the region would, of course, be a desert. In contrast, a typical West Coast climate, in addition to being humid, has its highest precipitation from October to April. Another humid-area type of moisture situation, contrasting strongly with that of the Plains, is found in the Great Lakes region where there is no striking variation in precipitation from month to month.

Evaporation is still another important influence on Plains climate. With the long-time average annual precipitation varying around twenty inches or less, a high rate of evaporation can contribute to a critical situation. Studies have shown that "warm season" evaporation from an open pan is slightly more than the equivalent of thirty inches of water in the northern part of the region, and about sixty inches in the southern part. This is the equivalent of a difference of ten inches of annual rainfall, and represents the need for an additional inch of precipitation for every 150 miles in a southerly direction.

This greater amount of evaporation in the southern part of the region is of striking significance for the agriculture, compared with the northern part, especially when coupled with the longer warm season there. It is the chief factor that distinguishes the High Plains, extending from the Pecos in Texas to about the Platte River in Nebraska, from the rest of the region. It is, perhaps, the major reason why the Dust Bowl reached its full climax during the thirties in western Kansas and in the panhandle areas of Oklahoma and Texas, with lesser and more spotted intensity in the northern part of the region. It is also a factor in explaining why drought in 1953 reached newsworthy and political importance in the Southern Plains, but the yield deficit in the north was less newsworthy.

Temperature, aside from its relation to evaporation, is a weather phenomenon that has much effect upon growing conditions and on human behavior. Its lines of gradation, unlike so many other characteristics of the Plains, tend to travel in an east-west rather than north-south direction. The reasons are that the elevation for the region is relatively uniform, with a westward inclined up-slope, and that distance from the equator and the pole tend to govern temperature. Temperature, in addition to

14

affecting evaporation, also determines the length of the growing season. The growing season in the Southern Plains may be longer by as much as two or three months, compared with the northern part.

Temperature variations are more extreme in the Plains than in other parts of the nation, with the exception of that northern tier of states east of the Plains and extending to the Atlantic. Some areas in the nation have average monthly temperature hotter than that of the Plains, but these areas tend to be warmer the year around. Few areas get as cold as the Plains, with the exception of certain Great Lakes and New England areas.

There are striking variations of temperature in the Plains during the same season and even shorter periods. For instance, a blizzard may vanish in a matter of hours, to be followed by a warm wind that melts the snow everywhere. A beautiful growing day may be transformed into a chilly one with hailstones the size of hens' eggs or larger, coating the fields at a depth of several inches. A cool, dewy morning may be transformed into a disease-breeding heat wave by midmorning. The truly initiated resident of the Plains is always prepared for the chinook, the blizzard, the sleeter, the hailstorm, and the norther, for these have wrecked much havoc upon the unwary.

The famous painting by Charles Russell, depicting a starving, hunched-up cow standing in the snow with her back against the wind and a coyote in the near vicinity awaiting her death, reflects the nature of the climatic hazard in the region. Known by two titles, "Waiting for the Chinook" and "The Last of 5,000," the picture was inspired by the havoc wrought by the winter storm of 1886. The original was on a postal card which bore the report that Russell, as cowhand, addressed to his boss at Helena, Montana, following that fateful week. The range had been clear all fall and early winter by virtue of little snow and the chinook winds. This was followed by a heavy snow and a chinook which melted the top. Overnight, this was followed by heavy freezing weather, then by more snow, which achieved its climax in a raging blizzard. This was the year which ruined the open-range cattle industry in the Northern Plains, forcing the ranchers to adopt a winter feeding system in order to survive. Something similar happened in the Southern Plains a year earlier, in the winter of 1885–86. The feeding practices now in vogue saved the northern ranchers from a similar catastrophe in the winter of 1948–49.

The final (and now obvious) major characteristic of the Great Plains climate to be described is its semiaridity—namely, an average of twenty inches or less of precipitation annually. C. Warren Thornthwaite, chief of the Climatic and Physiographic Division, Office of Research of the Soil Conservation Service, summarized the significant aspect of a semiarid climate as follows: "In a desert, you know what to expect of the climate and plan accordingly. The same is true of the humid regions. Men have been fooled by the semiarid regions because they are sometimes humid, sometimes desert, and sometimes a cross between the two. Yet it is possible to make allowances for this, too, once it is understood."

The ninety-eighth meridian, the eastern border of the Great Plains, approximates the twenty-inch total annual precipitation line in the northern part of the region. West of this the total annual moisture is less than twenty inches, on the average, over a series of years. In the southern part, the twenty-inch annual average precipitation boundary is considerably to the west of the ninety-eighth meridian. Here the thirty-inch precipitation line is closer to the vicinity of the ninety-eighth meridian. But the higher evaporation reduces the effectiveness of this added ten inches, so that there appears to be considerable justification for including the twenty- to thirty-inch precipitation area in the southern part as belonging to the Great Plains.

In any case, the boundary between the semiarid Plains and the subhumid and humid area to the east must be thought of not as a thin line, but as a zone or belt, which shifts at times from semiarid to lower subhumid and back again to semiarid. It is interesting that the residents of this border country look east, and shun the country to the west of them. They seem to take pride in their closeness to the humid region and to feel no loyalty or responsibility towards the semiarid area. This attitude and its results are like "cutting off the nose to spite the face," for it is exactly this transition zone—that area in which people prefer to use the expression "subhumid" rather than "semiarid"—that the more disastrous consequences follow upon conditions of semiaridity. This is because the people of this area, and their institutions, are not prepared for such an eventuality.

The western border of the Plains is a more arbitrary one than the eastern border. The foothills of the Rockies provide a reasonable delineator, since, above them, temperature conditions and shorter growing-season prospects begin to limit crop production. Whether or not certain mountain extensions into the Plains should be included in the Great Plains is again a matter of convenience and choice, depending upon local conditions and attitudes. One major difference, other than lower rainfall, soil, and native plant differences and a less level topography for the mountain area, is the greater prevalence of irrigation for both pasture and crop production, and reliance upon forest cover and mountain elevation to serve in lieu of reservoirs for a supply of irrigation water. These conditions result in a more spotty and island-like distribution of agriculture and settlement in the mountain area.

The significant thing for the Plains region is the low average crop season rainfall, at or below the margin of successful agriculture as practiced under humid-area conditions. In short, the cropping practices change from a humid to a dry-land system. Coupled with this is the great variation in growing-season precipitation from year to year and within the same year. Almost everywhere the driest year brings less than ten inches of rainfall, and the wettest brings more than three times the lowest amount. This makes the seasonality of the rainfall almost as important as the amount in order to have reasonable yields. It places a premium on field and range practices that cut down on moisture runoff and evaporation.

These critical conditions of variability and seasonality are further intensified by the unpredictable occurrence of the precipitation. If the variations were predictable, adjustments in the way of living might be readily made. The added fact of unpredictability increases the climatic hazard significantly.

Figure 2 shows the probable history of precipitation in the vicinity of Havre, Montana, 1784–1949. The chart shows the growth of tree rings in one sixtieth of an inch, and was prepared by M. A. Bell, formerly superintendent of the Northern Montana Experiment Station Branch at Havre. These data illustrate the facts of semiaridity, variability, and unpredictability for the Plains. During this period, precipitation appeared to have varied from one-fourth of the average to double the average.

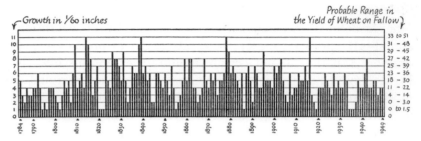

FIG. 2.   Tree ring growth, 1784–1949, in Havre, Montana, area showing probable history of seasonal cropping conditions. (*Source:* M. A. Bell.)

During the span of 165 years, there apparently was a severe drought after 1784 when twenty out of twenty-four years had less than average precipitation. Apparently Lewis and Clark, on their trek through the Plains, noted these drought conditions. Again, seventeen out of twenty-one years (1917–38) had less than average precipitation. Also, twenty-two of the thirty-three years between 1917 and 1950 had less than average precipitation.

During this entire period of 165 years, there were eight occasions, varying from four to nine consecutive years each, during which precipitation was probably not below the average. There were also eight occasions, varying from three to eleven consecutive years each, during which precipitation was probably below average.

Two warnings are in order. Tree-ring growth does not measure timeliness of precipitation or the amount of moisture carry-over from the previous year. Probably the fortunate yields since 1938 were the result of improved dry-land farming methods, plus timeliness of precipitation, and the presence of moisture reserves. But there have been partial crop failures in this area since 1938.

A similar study, published by the North Dakota Agricultural College and Experiment Station, shows comparable results. The author, George F. Will, is a businessman at Bismarck, North Dakota, chiefly interested in the seed and nursery business. Under his direction, a master tree-ring growth chart has been compiled covering a period of 535 years. The data came from a master oak tree near Bismarck, and from other trees living at

TABLE 2.   Wet and dry periods, by duration in years, based on a study of tree rings for a master burr-oak stump and related data, found near Bismarck, North Dakota, by George F. Will, covering the period 1406–1940.*

Dry years	Wet years	Dry years	Wet years
(9)	1406–15		1649–54 (5)
	1415–33 (18)	(9)	1654–63
(2)	1434–35		1663–1702 (39)
	1435–37 (2)	(1)	1703
(15)	1437–52		1703–06 (3)
	1452–71 (19)	(13)	1707–20
(14)	1471–85		1720–23 (3)
	1485–88 (3)	(7)	1728–35
(13)	1488–1501		1735–38 (3)
	1501–05 (4)	(2)	1738–40
(13)	1505–18		1740–44 (4)
	1518–25 (7)	(8)	1744–52
(6)	1525–31	(9)	1752–86† (10)
	1531–39 (8)		1786–1802 (16)
(4)	1539–43	(7)	1802–1830† (7)
	1543–47 (4)		1830–36 (6)
(6)	1547–53	(15)	1836–51
	1553–62 (9)		1851–63 (12)
(14)	1562–76		1865–67 (2)
	1576–96 (20)		1870–76 (6)
(15)	1596–1611	(14)	1877–91
	1611–23 (12)		1891–93 (2)
(2)	1623–25	(6)	1894–1900
	1626 (1)		1900–02 (2)
(1)	1627	(3)	1902–05
	1627–31 (4)		1910–20 (10)
(16)	1633–49	(15)	1922–37
			1937–40 (3)

* "Tree Ring Study in North Dakota," Agricultural Experiment Station, North Dakota Agricultural College, *Bulletin No. 338.* (April, 1946), 21–22. The years not shown (1631–33, 1723–28, 1863–65, 1867–70, 1876–77, 1893–94, 1905–10, and 1920–22) were average years.
† The period 1752–86 varied almost from year to year and totaled ten wet years, nine dry years, and fourteen average years. Similarly, the period 1802–30 varied from year to year with many of average rainfall and seven of drought in the series.
   "Although the number of dry periods over seven years long is four greater than the number of wet, the longest periods are wet ones. There is one wet period of thirty-nine years, one of twenty years, one of eighteen years, and one of nineteen years. The longest dry period is of sixteen years, but there are seven periods of thirteen to sixteen years inclusive and only one wet one. This does not give the complete picture as there are dry and wet periods both interrupted by periods of the opposite kind lasting one to four years."

the time of the study. Also, these data were fitted into timbers excavated and salvaged from the ruined sites of the Mandan Indian villages. The growth period of some of these timbers dates back to some time between A.D. 1200 and 1300. These data were compared with known climatic records and yields, and corrections were made so that the accuracy of the master tree-ring chart is reasonable. Mr. Will warns that the data come from one small area, and that the records of tree-ring growth will naturally be "smoother," with less variation from year to year, than the actual rainfall would be.

Table 2 is a reproduction of this information. Mr. Will points out that the 534-year record (1406–1940) shows that "years of drought and moisture seem to run in series, sometimes separated by from one to several years of average rainfall. . . . It appears impossible to work out any definite pattern as to the number of years in succeeding series. The number varies greatly, from one year to a maximum of thirty-nine wet years and twenty dry years. At certain points in the graph there are very short successions of one to three wet years followed by an equally small number of dry years. . . . For the most part, however, the periods are considerably longer, most of them not less than five years."

A similar study by Harry E. Weakly showed like conditions for the Plains of Nebraska. The sample of red cedar and ponderosa pine, including living specimen and buried stumps, covered a period of four hundred years (1539–1939). The tree-ring data for the last sixty-four years of the period were compared with the known rainfall records at the North Platte Weather Bureau Office. In this case the annual volume of wood produced, rather than the width of the tree ring, was used as the measure of growth and was thought to be "a better indicator of rainfall than the width of ring, which naturally becomes narrower as the diameter of the tree increases." The data were summarized as showing "a very significant degree of relationship between annual rainfall and tree growth. . . . This is still more true if the correlation is based on rainfall from October 1 to September 30 rather than for the calendar year." The author points out that a single dry year in a group of moist years has little effect on tree growth due to the presence of subsoil moisture. Therefore, the study does not single out the shorter periods of moisture fluctuation.

20

TABLE 3.* Alternate periods of fertility and drought (of five years or more) during the past four hundred years, as shown by the annual growth-ring of trees in western Nebraska.

Droughts of 5 years or more		Periods between droughts	
Period	No. of Years	Period	No. of Years
1539–64 (inclusive)	26	1565–86 (inclusive)	22
1587–1605 "	19	1606–25 "	20
1626–30 "	5	1631–67 "	37
1668–75 "	8	1676–87 "	12
1688–1707 "	20	1708–27 "	20
1728–32 "	5	1733–60 "	28
1761–73 "	13	1774–97 "	24
1798–1803 "	6	1804–21 "	18
1822–32 "	11	1833–57 "	25
1858–66 "	9	1867–79 "	13
1880–95 "	16	1896–1905 "	10
1906–12 "	7	1913–30 "	18
1931–39 "	9		
Total	154		247
Average	12.85		20.58

* Harry E. Weakly, "A Tree Ring Record of Precipitation in Western Nebraska," *Journal of Forestry*, Vol. XLI, No. 11 (November, 1943), 816–19.

Table 3 shows the results of the study. There were thirteen drought periods of five or more years during this span of four hundred years, totaling 154 years, or an average duration of 12.85 years. The longest drought period continued for twenty-five years (1539–64). Long drought periods also occurred 1587–1605, 1688–1707, 1761–73, 1822–32, and 1880–95. This represents six long drought periods. The other seven periods were of five- to nine-year duration, with the last one extending for eight years (1931–39).

There were twelve wet periods, totaling 247 years, or an average of 20.58 years. The average wet period was of longer duration than the average dry period by about eight years. None of the wet periods was less than ten years, and seven were of twenty-one or more years' duration. The longest wet period extended for thirty-six years (1631–67). Since 1804 there were five wet periods, the last of seventeen years' duration (1913–30).

The three studies emphasize the unpredictability and irregularity in the major climatic rhythms of the Plains from dry to wet. The data are of little use in forecasting. Their value lies in the fact that they show a long record of climatic conditions, covering a span of many human generations, that defines the Plains as a semiarid land.

One final set of factual data is offered to give some evidence on degree of drought. This information was prepared by T. Lommasson of the United States Forest Service, District One, Missoula, Montana. The study is entitled "The Influence of Rainfall on the Prosperity of Eastern Montana," and the results are shown in Figure 3. The data extend from 1878 to 1946.

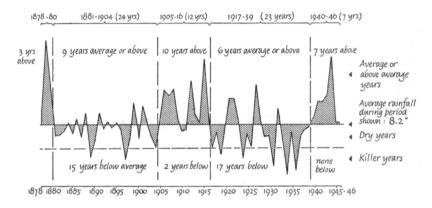

FIG. 3.   Rainfall in eastern Montana, 1878–1946. (*Source:* T. Lommasson.)

During the period 1881–1904, twenty-four years in all, nine years had average, or more, rainfall, and fifteen years had below average. Lommasson characterizes 50 per cent of the years as dry and 12.5 per cent as "killer years," the latter being years when drought was so severe that it killed grass on the range.

Of the twelve years, 1905–16 inclusive, ten had average or above rainfall. Only 16.7 per cent of the years are described as dry years, and there were no "killer years." This was the period when much of eastern Montana was settled by homesteaders.

The period 1917–39 was again a time of hardship for eastern Montana. Only six of these twenty-two years had average or above rainfall. In this case Lommasson characterizes 39.1 per cent of the years as dry and 34.8 per cent as "killer years."

The six years, 1940–46, all had above average rainfall. It

should be noted that the sixty-eight year average was only 8.2 inches annually.

Another interesting fact, already pointed out, is that the two favorable periods for eastern Montana, in this study, were 1905–16 and 1940–46, coinciding in part with World War I and II and the high prices of those periods. In this area, the years of good production on the range and in the fields have continued beyond 1946, with some recent years of spotty drought conditions, but with the favorable prices of the Korean incident as a backdrop.

Most farmers and ranchers of the Great Plains are seriously worrying about what the climate during the remainder of the fifties will have in store for them.

CHAPTER 3

The Soils, Plants, and Animals
Native to the Plains

Climate, coupled with the native plant life, is one of the most important factors in the creation of soil. Only parent material and topographical slope may be more influential. One would expect, then, that the Plains climate, since it is distinctive, would produce a unique soil, and the evidence shows that this is the case.

The top earth strata of the Plains are laid down on a base of marine-rock sheets which has a general uniform westward incline or up-slope. Thus, the Plains have a higher elevation in the west than in the east. This marine-rock incline became severely eroded, for a time, and then was covered with a mantle of debris.

The mantle of debris is an apron-like outwash from the Rocky Mountains and from the ice age debris from the North. It constitutes the present surface strata of the region, and was carried onto the Plains by an instance of that kind of stream action which often picks up much of the accumulated debris in the uplands and deposits it on the level plain below. Here the stream is slowed in its movements, and, therefore, the deposit builds up the land area as the stream meanders on its course, often changing channels until the plain becomes relatively level. This is what the Missouri and the other streams of the region are doing even now at flood stage.

In parts of the region the debris mantle has a lesser depth than in other parts; and sometimes there are uplifts of the marine rock and other parent strata to form elevations higher than the debris outwash. The Black Hills in South Dakota are such an uplift, as are the Bear Paws in Montana, but such formations are the exception. Otherwise, the debris strata have a westward-sloping incline like the marine-rock strata.

The building of the debris apron is dated, in geological terms, from anywhere near the middle of the Tertiary Era to the early Pleistocene Age. The beginning of the present degradation, or erosion, stage dates back to that period of climatic variation in the Pleistocene period which, in the Great Basin of Utah and Nevada, gave rise to repeated floodings of large areas and the creation of lakes. This alternate flooding and drying-out phase in the evolution of the Great Basin, with a spilling over at the top of the Rockies onto the Plains, apparently occurred at the time of the alternate invasion and recession of glaciers to the north of the High Plains, in the mountains, and in the Norther Plains area itself. This accounts for the increased stream flo and the mantling of the Great Plains with an apron of debris

The High Plains, extending from the Pecos north to Platte in Nebraska, stand up as an area of constant upbuild by river deposit, whereas the remainder of the Plains, to north, were more severely degraded or eroded by glaci and the more immediate action of streams at the head of glaciers.

Thus, time, interacting with climate, was a significant tor in building and shaping that part of the parent materia the Plains soils which is classified as a debris apron. Climate elief, and plant activity since the last glacier, again involvi time, have shaped the topsoil of the region into its present acture. Other factors operating through this period included volcanic action and deposition, wind erosion, cloudbursts, te erature changes, and other eroding processes, together with e action of vegetation.

The entire erosion process in the Great Plains ha roceeded at a slower pace and is of a different character m that in the humid regions. The geological formation of the reat Plains is clear evidence of a basic contrast between the ins and the humid Midwest and East. The surface topograp to the east of the Plains is the result of stream erosion and dgradation, the consequence of surplus moisture. The topograp of the Great Plains is the result of stream deposit or aggradtion, the result of moisture deficiency.

The factors that develop soils—time, parent material, climate, relief, and botanical and biological activity—have produced a distinct soil region for the Plains. Figure 4 is a reproduction of the distribution of Plains soil types. These soils, at maturity, have two characteristics that distinguish them from other soil types: the presence of a horizontal zone of alkaline salt accumulation (which is usually, though not exclusively, a lime carbonate on some horizon of the soil), and the relatively dark color f the soil. Both of these conditions are caused by the lack of nough moisture in the Plains to bring about the leaching of the

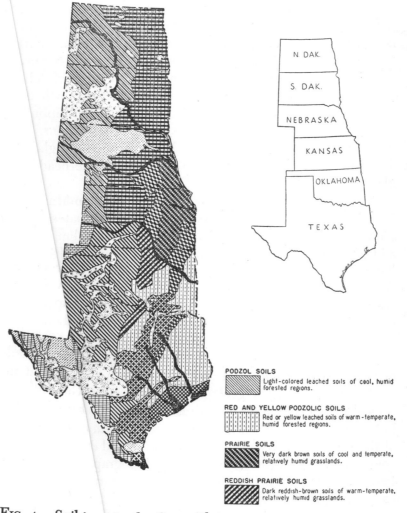

PODZOL SOILS
Light-colored leached soils of cool, humid forested regions.

RED AND YELLOW PODZOLIC SOILS
Red or yellow leached soils of warm-temperate, humid forested regions.

PRAIRIE SOILS
Very dark brown soils of cool and temperate, relatively humid grasslands.

REDDISH PRAIRIE SOILS
Dark reddish-brown soils of warm-temperate, relatively humid grasslands.

FIG. 4.   Soil types in the Great Plains.

soil, a process whereby the excess moisture seeps down into the underground water channels.

Outside the Plains, these two characteristics do not appear side-by-side. The alkaline salt accumulation zone, the result of nonleaching, extends west of the Great Plains into the mountainous and arid western portions of the nation; however, it is not accompanied by the dark color, except in island-like instances. The dark-colored soils extend eastward beyond the Great Plains into the prairies and forest lands of the Midwest and eastern United States, but are not accompanied by the carbonate zone. The Plains can, therefore, be clearly distinguished from the other soil areas of the nation.

Though the soils of the Plains possess two general characteristics in common, they differ within this classification in degree. There are many explanations for the minor differences that are to be found, but these differences are within the bases of the first two characteristics that have been set forth. It is possible to subdivide the Plains soils into four belts, as is shown: the Black belt along the eastern edge of the region, the Very Dark Brown belt, the Dark Brown belt, and the Brown belt on the western rim, up against the mountains. The Black and the Dark Brown belts are again subdivided into several minor classifications.

These soil-color differences are chiefly associated with depth of soil and variations in minor characteristics of the carbonate zone. Generally, the closer to the surface the carbonate zone,

CHERNOZEM SOILS
Dark-brown to nearly black soils of cool and temperate, subhumid grasslands.

CHESTNUT SOILS
Dark-brown soils of cool and temperate, subhumid to semiarid grasslands.

REDDISH CHESTNUT SOILS
Dark reddish-brown soils of warm-temperate, semiarid regions under mixed shrub and grass vegetation.

BROWN SOILS
Brown soils of cool and temperate, semiarid grasslands.

REDDISH BROWN SOILS
Reddish-brown soils of warm-temperate to hot, semiarid to arid regions, under mixed shrub and grass vegetation.

RED DESERT SOILS
Light reddish-brown soils of warm-temperate to hot, arid regions, under shrub vegetation.

PLANOSOLS
Soils with strongly leached surface horizons over claypans on nearly flat land in cool to warm, humid to subhumid regions, under grass or forest vegetation.

RENDZINA SOILS
Dark grayish-brown to black soils developed from soft limy materials in cool to warm, humid to subhumid regions, mostly under grass vegetation.

WIESENBÖDEN (1), GROUND WATER PODZOL (2), AND HALF-BOG SOILS (3)
(1) Dark-brown to black soils developed with poor drainage under grasses in humid and subhumid regions.

(2) Gray sandy soils with brown cemented sandy subsoils developed under forests from nearly level imperfectly drained sand in humid regions.

(3) Poorly drained, shallow, dark peaty or mucky soils underlain by gray mineral soil, in humid regions, under swamp-forests.

BOG SOILS
Poorly drained dark peat or muck soils underlain by peat, mostly in humid regions, under swamp or marsh types of vegetation.

SANDS (DRY)
Very sandy soils.

LITHOSOLS AND SHALLOW SOILS (ARID-SUBHUMID)
Shallow soils consisting largely of an imperfectly weathered mass of rock fragments, largely but not exclusively on steep slopes.

ALLUVIAL SOILS
Soils developing from recently deposited alluvium that have had little or no modification by processes of soil formation.

27

the lighter the soil color. Soil colors also differ, in minor details, by virtue of the structure and type of deposit and the kind of vegetation present.

Generally speaking, the soils of the Great Plains are among the most fertile to be found anywhere. According to some authorities, they are potentially the most fertile, with inadequate moisture being their only limiting factor. This soil condition is related to the climatic conditions that have given rise to the Great Plains. To the east of the Plains, the humid climate has led to leaching of the soil. The surplus moisture can only seep downward into the underground water courses and wash all the fertility out of the soil. The eastern edge of the Plains begins at that point where such leaching has not taken place. The greater moisture on the eastern edge of the Plains, compared with the more westerly parts of the region, has carried the chemicals and the carbonate zone to a greater depth, but still within reach of the plants. The subsoil is deeper and the color darker. Along the western edge of the Plains, the chemicals and the carbonate zone are nearer the surface, making for a subsoil of lesser depth and lighter color.

Clearly, then, Great Plains soils represent special types. Products of a semiarid climate, these soils coincide with the climatic area of the Great Plains. The fact that they are on the threshold of very high fertility, the limiting factor being moisture, makes it apparent that adapted farming techniques that assist in retaining the limited precipitation will add to the productivity of the region. But this takes dry-land farming techniques that are not readily learned by people who have their roots in a humid-area way of living. Soil blowing has often been thought of as decreasing the fertility of the Plains. Within limits, this is not the significant reason for insistence upon the control of soil blowing in the Plains. The real reason for controlling soil blowing in the region is to insure maintenance of the thin topsoil. By doing so, it is possible to maintain the conditions for plant anchorage and support, a medium for holding the roots of the plant, and to store the limited moisture that does occur.

Not all the elements in the carbonate zone are useful for plant growth. Some are actually harmful to plants, and to animals, and to the productivity of the soil itself. Because of the absence of leaching, an increase in soil moisture may release these elements and bring them to the surface within ready reach of the plants, thus killing or stunting them, or changing the nature of the vegetation complex entirely. This is the condition that also accounts for the alkali and other "slick spots" that dot the region in island-like fashion.

NATIVE PLANT LIFE

Walter Prescott Webb describes the Great Plains and the area west of the ninety-eighth meridian, except for parts of the Rockies and the West Coast, as the treeless and timberless part of the nation. The absence of trees, except along the water courses, is, perhaps, the most striking feature to the man from

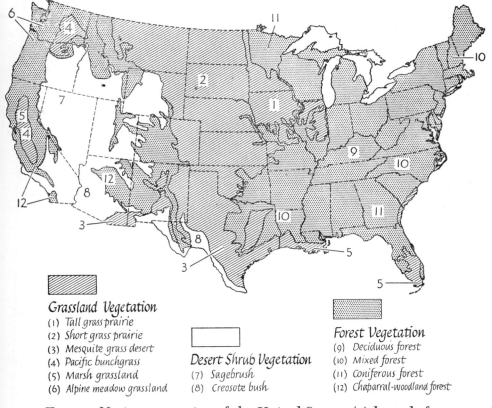

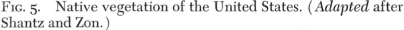

Grassland Vegetation
(1) Tall grass prairie
(2) Short grass prairie
(3) Mesquite grass desert
(4) Pacific bunchgrass
(5) Marsh grassland
(6) Alpine meadow grassland

Desert Shrub Vegetation
(7) Sagebrush
(8) Creosote bush

Forest Vegetation
(9) Deciduous forest
(10) Mixed forest
(11) Coniferous forest
(12) Chaparral-woodland forest

Fig. 5. Native vegetation of the United States. (*Adapted* after Shantz and Zon.)

the humid land as he enters the region. But it is more appropriate to describe the region in positive terms, identifying it as the "short-grass country." Figure 5, a reproduction of the natural vegetation complex of the nation, isolates the major vegetation associations in the Plains as being of a distinct type. It identifies

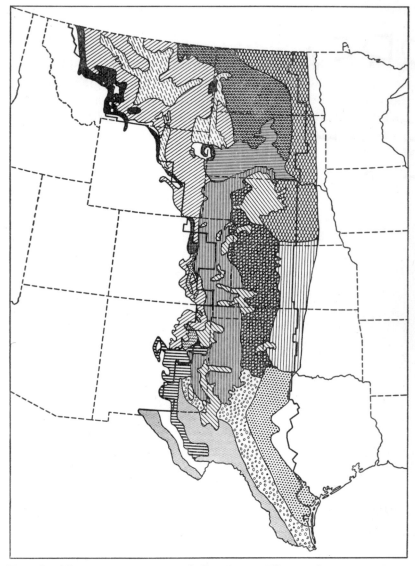

FIG. 6   Native vegetation of the Great Plains. (*Source:* H. L. Shantz.)

30

the short grass, the tall grass, and the mesquite and desert-grass savanna in the Plains.

The eastern border of the short-grass country is somewhat west of the ninety-eighth meridian and the twenty-inch precipitation line. Put another way, the tall-grass vegetation, typical of subhumid conditions, projects into the twenty-inch precipitation zone at certain points, and into areas west of the ninety-eighth meridian. This is especially true in northern North Dakota and in Nebraska. Undoubtedly, the lower evaporation rate in North Dakota accounts for the invasion of the taller grasses west of the ninety-eighth meridian. In the case of Nebraska, it is the prevalence of a certain type of sandy soil and the availability of underground water which contribute to this westward invasion of the tall grasses.

Actually, the dividing line between the vegetation of the Great Plains and that of the true prairie, or humid, area to the east is farther east than the short-grass line indicates. It is in the vicinity of the ninety-eighth meridian, in reality, and includes a strip of what is defined as the tall-grass vegetation. Closer study of the evidence, according to some ecologists, shows that the taller grasses just west of the ninety-eighth meridian are not true tall-grass prairie associations. All typical Plains vegetation associations take on some tall-grass characteristic when favorable moisture conditions prevail. Many short-grass species then grow more luxuriantly, giving a false impression to observers who do not take the long view.

Short Grass (plains grassland)

	Grama & Western Needle Grass
	Wire Grass
	Western Wheat-grass
	Grama and Buffalo Grass
	Grama Grass
	Grama Grass & Mountain Sage
	Grama and Muhlenbergia

Sage Brush (Northern desert shrub)

	Sage Brush & Western Wheat-grass

Tall Grass (prairie grassland)

	Needle Grass & Slender Wheat Grass
	Bluestem Bunch Grass
	Sand Grass & Sand Sage or Shinnery

Mesquite & Desert Grass Savanna

	Thorn Bush & Mesquite Grass
	Mesquite & Mesquite Grass

Mesquite Grass (Desert Grassland)

	Black Grama
	Desert Shrub

31

Figure 6 shows the distribution of the principal grass communities of the Great Plains region as described by H. L. Shantz.
His eastern border closely approximates the ninety-seventh meridian. He argues that the disappearance of the carbonate zone
in the soil is the true indicator of the eastern limits of the Great
Plains vegetation associations. This termination of the carbonate
zone occurs when the soil contains more moisture than is extracted by evaporation and by plant growth. West of this point,
mineral elements and plant nutrients are not leached into underground water streams. It is at this point that the true Great
Plains vegetation associations meet the humid-area associations.

The significant point here is that moisture consumption or
evaporation, through plant growth and atmospheric evaporation, consume all the moisture that falls, thus giving rise to a
soil type. Thus the associations between native plants, soils, and
climate are inextricably interrelated. Thus, again, all three—
native plants, soils, and climate—converge to define the Great
Plains as a distinctive area.

Minor variations in the conditions that make for plant growth
account for the type and distribution of the principal plant communities identified in Figure 6. The short-grass communities
tend to prevail in the western part of the Plains. On the very
western edge, the gramas and buffalo grasses are associated
with sagebrush in the north and some mesquite grass and Muh-
lenbergia in the south. The simple short-grass communities consist largely of grama and buffalo grasses. To the east of these,
the simple short grasses are found in association with other
grasses, such as western needle grass, wire grass, and western
wheat grass. These latter are generally somewhat taller and,
in very favorable years, may be reasonably tall and thick so that
they overshadow the grama and buffalo grasses. This, however,
is still a short-grass association.

These taller short-grass communities are occasionally found
in favorable spots in the short-grass area, but are largely confined to the eastern portion of the Plains, north of the Canadian
River. They border on and readily invade the grama and western
needle grass communities, the wire grass communities, and the
western wheat grass communities. In Texas, the eastern portion
of the Plains is predominantly occupied by mesquite and mesquite grass, which tend to give way to the thorn bush and mes-

quite grass. Shantz describes the appearance of the Plains grass-land association as "a closely pastured meadow. Except during years of more than normal rainfall, the taller growing plants are almost entirely absent and the vegetation presents the appearance of extreme monotony. . . . The transition to the tall grass formation is gradual in the east where many of the taller plants occur. . . . In spring the short grasses start growth as soon as temperature conditions are favorable. Many flowering plants vary the monotony of the short grass cover. If the season is unusually dry, these plants are usually inconspicuous and even the short grasses may fail to put up flower stalks. If the season is unusually moist, annuals and herbaceous perennials often become a prominent component of the vegetation."

ADAPTED CHARACTERISTICS OF
PLAINS VEGETATION

The native grasses of the Plains have become adapted to semiarid conditions by selection. Some quickly absorb the limited surface moisture during dry periods by extending the flexible root system to the surface. Some have the ability to extend roots quickly to the subsurface if moisture is lacking.

Many plant varieties have the ability to become dormant during drought periods and then revive with the coming of the late-summer or fall rains. Again this is an example of flexibility. Some have the ability to grow taller or remain short, to flower and mature quickly, or to postpone this maturing process, depending upon the moisture conditions. These, again, are examples of the flexibility of native plant life.

If climatic conditions are right, some native plants have the ability to continue growth throughout a long season. This, too, is an example of flexibility. Some plants can produce many or only a few seeds, depending upon the climatic conditions. Many plants, to survive, have enhanced means of mobility in the form of wind-borne assists. For others, survival is enhanced by the ability of the seed to withstand great vicissitudes for many years, even for numerous decades.

In addition to having drought-sustaining or drought-evading characteristics, as exemplified above, some semiarid plants have drought-resisting traits. They have the ability to roll their leaves, thus exposing less surface to the sunlight and evaporation influences. This makes for a husbanding of the moisture in the plant and in the soil. Some plants have a grayer color and a more oily coating. Both are devices for protection against excessive evaporation. Thus, Plains vegetation often appears to have less of a green hue than that in humid areas. These characteristics of a grayer color and a thicker skin, often bordering on a hard growth, and of the more oily and waxy outer coating are drought-resisting or reserve-building traits.

In summary, it might be stated that plant ecologists have spent far too little time in identifying the peculiar plant traits that make for survival in a semiarid region—traits of flexibility, mobility, and reserve. These appear to be typical, in various degrees, of hardy semiarid plants, native to the Plains. Knowledge of these traits has been sought by plant breeders who have tried to import and improve other plants for Plains conditions. But these traits have not been effectively identified. A basic description of these survival traits of native semiarid plants would assist in accelerating the breeding of adapted plant varieties.

NATIVE ANIMAL LIFE

Animals, in their native state, appear to prefer a specific habitat unless crowded out by numbers, inadequate food, or other forces. We may expect this in areas where nature exercises more rigid selection. There are fewer varieties of color and species among native animals in a more rigorous and demanding climate, such as that of the semiarid Plains, than in the warmer, more humid climates.

Something about the semiarid Great Plains apparently has made for selection of animals that possess certain characteristics. These traits are not uniformly present in all species. If one were to establish a list of traits that enhance the survival of animal life in the semiarid Plains, all species native to the region would have one or several, but not all, nor necessarily the same kind of, traits.

Abundant description exists of every form of animal life on the Plains. But physiologists and zoologists have described each form separately and independently. Too few studies have been undertaken either to determine and evaluate the kind of traits that are essential to the survival of all animals in a semiarid land or to note the prevalence of such characteristics among all forms of native animals.

For these reasons, there is a need to be more cautious in assigning specific provinces to animal communities and in describing an association of animals than is the case for native plants. Animals have greater flexibility of habits than plants. Ecologists have described the animal population of dry, open lands in only a very general way. In an attempt to define the bio-ecology of the North American grasslands, ecologists have been rather imprecise and have depended more on plant than on native-animal evidence. There are two principal reasons. First, it is more difficult to demonstrate that animals have a natural habitat, because of their greater mobility and adaptability. Secondly, animal ecologists have not been forced to experiment with adaptations to environment in the same degree as the plant ecologists.

Selective plant breeding for semiarid conditions is much further advanced than is selective breeding of animals for such conditions. Animal ecologists are, therefore, less aware of the characteristics that augment survival of animals under conditions of semiaridity.

It remained for the historian of the Plains, Walter Prescott Webb, to point the way in describing the survival traits of native animals. What he has done may be challenged by animal ecologists, but they, perhaps, cannot offer scientific evidence at this time to prove that he is wrong. The simple description of Plains animal life by Webb might have been more effective had he couched it in terms of principles, as well as details.

The brief review which ends this chapter will not be exhaustive, but will be an attempt to describe some of the major features that appear to insure greater chances of survival, features that are, in reality, adaptations evolved by natural selection. Generally, these survival traits are likely to be of the kind that increase mobility, make for flexibility in habits, or are incident to great and sustained effort or stamina, here called the capacity for reserve. It is to be understood that no animal necessarily possesses all these traits.

More specifically, the important survival qualities to be

looked for, at least in the larger native animals of the Plains, include: a peculiar limb structure to facilitate jumping or hopping and to gain fleetness and great mobility; the instinct to move uphill when in flight; wide range of vision and keen sense of hearing and smell; the instinct for being on guard, as exemplified by posting sentinels and the ability to signal and send warnings; and the burrowing habit, a defense often as effective as mobility. Flexibility is assured, moreover, by strong mastication apparatus to consume a wide range of forage; changes in protective coating, either in terms of color adaptation or weather acclimation; and by the instinct to live as a scavenger and to be omnivorous. And, finally, the reserve power of these animals of the Plains is owing to their unusual stamina and endurance; the ability to slow down on water consumption or to manufacture the necessary water supply; and the instinct for gregariousness as exhibited in the colonization and flocking habits and in the formation by the males of protective circles around the weak and the young. Here also should be included the fact of precociousness or self-sufficiency of the young, and the instinct of facing into the weather.

The peers of the animal life of the Great Plains, in terms of number, colorful history, and contact with the white man, were the *bison*. Though they roamed from west of the Rockies to the Great Lakes and the Mississippi, the Great Plains were their true home. Webb says that the bison's "occupation of the forest and mountains was merely incidental, an overflow from their natural habitat."

Having poor eyesight and little fear of sound, the bison traveled in large herds. They were slow of gait and, at times, clumsy, but they could occasionally summon great speed, especially during the "running season." They were often described as stupid, but this is hardly fair, judging by their conduct in their natural abode. Among the traits that fitted the bison for the Plains were great size, stamina, and endurance; a certain insensitivity to hazards; and clannishness. They could endure both extreme heat and cold, though there was a tendency to migrate with the weather. The bison seasonally shed their heavy winter coats, thus adjusting to extreme climatic variations, although they were probably bothered by insects. They were grass eaters, but could go for a long time without either feed or water. Their chief means of survival was mobility. They learned to travel trails that exhibited considerable engineering skill.

One special trait of the bison, not possessed by domestic cattle, was the habit of facing into the storm or not traveling at such times. Thus, the bison avoided the death resulting to cattle from their tendency to drift with blizzards, becoming stalled in coulees and creeks covered with drifts, or being precipitated over ledges and embankments and trampled. But the bison were ruthlessly pursued by white hunters, almost to the point of extinction by the 1880's.

The pronghorn "antelope" is the one animal, perhaps, truly indigenous to the Great Plains in origin and habit. Not a true antelope, the pronghorn is the unique representative of a distinct family. Its habitat reaches from the Missouri to the Rocky Mountains, from Mexico to Saskatchewan, and northwest into Oregon and Washington. Pronghorns have horns like cattle but annually shed the horn's external covering or sheath. The pronghorns have the curiosity of a goat but the timidity of a deer.

The young of the pronghorn antelope are precocious, being self-sufficient at an early age. The adults are the swiftest runners among the wild animals of the continent, known to have traveled at speeds of sixty-five and seventy miles an hour. Their sense of sight is highly developed and so, apparently, is that of hearing. They have a signal system by means of the tail, known as the "flag," which communicates danger over considerable distances. Accompanying the flagging, a characteristic odor is emitted to aid in warning the herd. Their endurance is great. They feed on grass and small shrubs when necessary.

Again, as in the case of the bison, the chief traits for survival of the pronghorn are speed, mobility, and tremendous endurance. They travel great distances to feed and water, are gregarious, and readily make adjustments to climatic variations.

Jackrabbits, especially the prairie hare and the blacktailed varieties, have their natural home in the western United States, including the Great Plains. They are best adapted to open country or nonforested conditions. They depend upon their sight, hearing, and speed, especially uphill, for survival. The long ears assist them in hearing, and they combine a running and a bounding gait, assisted by highly developed hind legs and short fore-

37

legs. In flight, they seek open ground and avoid refuge in holes, bushes, or hollow trees. Jackrabbits do not burrow, and their young are born full-coated in open nests and with open eyes. With exceptions, the species in the north have two annual molts, and those in the south have one. The adults in most species have a darker or buff coat in warm seasons and are almost all-white in winter.

Rabbits eat virtually any vegetation, including bark and brush. They have been so destructive to grain crops that people have organized large-scale drives as a sport and as a measure of control. Rabbits are tasty as food when properly prepared, though occasional severe epidemics caused by improper cooking of them have decreased the extent of their use for this purpose.

A typical Plains animal, the jackrabbit has many of the traits required for survival in the region, among them mobility and speed, change in protective coloring, and flexible food habits.

Prairie dogs, in reality a species of squirrel, are the sedentary burrowing animal of the Plains. Their habitat is almost exclusively restricted to the region. They live in colonies in intricately constructed burrows, with a funnel-like protrusion to shed the rain. Frequently, as many as several hundred, or even several thousand, live in a single prairie-dog town. Several "guards" are always stationed at the hole. The prairie dog's vision is highly developed, and the warning bark results in a scampering for the burrows. It takes a skilled marksman "to get his dog."

These ground squirrels represent an interesting adaptation to the Plains, from the standpoint of feeding habits. Prairie dogs require no moisture, having the metabolism facility to produce their own. Neither do they require variety in their diet, which consists almost exclusively of grass, green or dried, including the roots. Limited in mobility, these marmots are nevertheless oriented by virtue of their town habits, the ability to create their own moisture needs, and their intensive utilization of the entire plant. They are as well adapted to their environment as the hare and the pronghorn antelope but by virtue of entirely different qualities. Rather than being mobile, they are home builders, utilizers of the means at their disposal, and depend on reserves.

The coyote is the scavenger, marauder, and coward of the Plains. Except for the prairie wolves, coyotes are the chief Carnivora. Living on insects, rodents, jackrabbits, prairie dogs, and the helpless young or the dead carcasses of larger animals, the coyote has been described by Horace Greeley as "a sneaking, cowardly little wretch of dull or dirty-white color, much resembling a small, short-bodied dog set up on pretty long legs." By some, but notably by J. Frank Dobie, he has been characterized as "Don Coyote." Dobie thinks of the coyote as extraordinary. "Extraordinary folklore develops only around extraordinary characters, though not all extraordinary characters inspire it. . . . While such folklore is often false as to fact, it is oftener true in character, illuminating instead of betraying truth. . . . The coyote is extraordinary in another way. He is extraordinary as a character quite aside from economic, political, and like importances. He has something in common with Abraham Lincoln, Robin Hood, Joan of Arc, Br'er Rabbit, and other personalities— something that sets popular imagination to creating."

Whatever his morals, the coyote has become adapted because he is mobile and has great speed. He burrows and is a good hunter. He migrates with his prey. Since many of his victims go to areas where there is food and water, he himself is always provided for. In addition to that, he is smart enough to fit into a variety of situations, even new ones; he does not live by instinct alone.

The grasshopper, an ever present pest, and not to be classed with the animals in this chapter, is also a scourge of the Plains, coming, at times, in migrating hordes that dim the sun. These invasions are most likely to occur when climatic hazards are severe. At such times grasshoppers are reputed to have attacked ravenously even fence posts and hardwood pitchfork handles.

Whatever their pestlike attributes, these Rocky Mountain grasshoppers have adaptations for survival under the most rigorous of climatic conditions. As their name implies, they are hoppers. They migrate in hordelike fashion and for great distances. They reproduce in large numbers so that the species survives in spite of the vulnerability of the individual. Very sensitive to climatic conditions, they appear to thrive most satisfactorily under conditions of semiaridity and aridity. Aside from their

39

great mobility, the characteristic that stands out in the grass-hoppers, considering their size, is the extent and the effective-ness of their mastication apparatus.

For colorful history and drama among the Indians and whites of the Plains, the *horse* has no equal. With its help the whites eventually conquered the Indians, handled the cattle, pushed settlement across the Plains, carried the mail, and, finally, broke the sod and harvested the grain. Today the horse is still the core of much of the recreation of the region.

The horse, which originated and evolved in the grasslands of North America and then spread to other continents, became extinct here, apparently because of some epidemic. From these other countries, the horse, including the Barb, a descendant of the Arab, was again introduced to America, first through the Plains and later by way of the humid East. The first of these re-introductions, obviously by the Spaniards, was followed by a lengthy process of diffusion extending over a period of two cen-turies. By 1784 the horse was known to most of the Indians of the Plains.

What are the characteristics of this horse that became so use-ful on the Plains? Among others is the trait of mobility. The horse can travel rapidly and for long distances. It has stamina and reserve. It is a grasseater, but feeds upon other vegetation as well and has the characteristic mastication and digestive ap-paratus to cope with this range. Its young, coming usually in single births, are precocious. The horse travels in herds and establishes garrisons for the protection of the young and helpless in the face of marauders. It can acclimate itself to temperature extremes. It paws through snow for feed and faces with the storm, but does not drift with the helpless abandon typical of cattle. It communicates danger by a sharp whistle and posts sentinels. It is an intelligent animal and adaptable for survival in many ways. For all these reasons the horse became the chief ally of the Indian and the white in the Plains.

It is interesting to note that many of the animals native to the Plains have acquired misnomers: the present "pronghorn antelope" is not a true antelope, the "buffalo" is in reality a bison, the "jackrabbit" is a hare, and the "prairie dog" is a mar-mot. Webb states that "this is suggestive of what happened when a people having their background in a humid, forested region came out into a new environment. The point is not important except as a symptom of the Easterner's misunderstanding of the West."

In conclusion, we repeat the fact of the uniqueness, in the United States, of the climate of the Great Plains due to its semiaridity. Distinctive soil and plant life, which interact and are both the products of climate, also assist in defining the region as separate and different.

Although more unpredictable in regard to habitat, the native animals, like the soil and plant life, are unique, and these animals possess ready mobility, flexibility of habits, and capacity for reserve building. The native plants, too, possess one or several of these traits, traits which we might well recognize as keys for successful living in the region.

CHAPTER 4

An Old and Forbidding Land

The Great Plains are generally identified as the last of America's frontiers, and as an area without a spirit of unity. This is the case only because humid-area man believes this to be so. In reality, the region's history is old, and there was a time when there was unity in the events on the Plains.

History grants St. Augustine, Florida, the distinction of being the oldest white settlement on the East Coast, having been established in 1565; but Coronado had visited the Southern Plains more than twenty years before. Although Jamestown, Virginia, founded in 1607, is famous as being the first permanent English settlement in the New World, Santa Fé was established about the same time—some say about 1605, some say in 1609. And Santa Fé was not the earliest settlement in New Mexico, for it came after San Juan on the Río Grande, established by Don Juan de Oñate about 1598.

In 1681, La Salle began the journey to the Mississippi, reaching the Gulf of Mexico in April, 1682. Thus the French laid claim to the whole of the interior of North America, including the Plains. Spain proclaimed Texas a province in 1691, in defense of its claim to the Plains, and established a number of missions, one of which was San Antonio. In the meantime, Henry Kelsey, an adventurous youth of twenty, carried the glory of the Hudson's Bay Company into the Plains west of Winnipegosis in the eastern part of Saskatchewan. All this was before the East Coast settlers dared to venture far inland from the sea and before William Penn brought his Quakers to Pennsylvania.

But these ventures into the Plains were on the periphery only, from the South, the East, and the North. The region was a forbidding land. It was not until 1739, when Pierre Gaultier de Varennes la Vérendrye, the French-Canadian explorer, set foot into North Dakota, that white man entered the heart of the region. La Vérendrye and his party spent that winter with the Mandan Indians on the Missouri. But this was early in the exploration of the interior of America, being only seven years after George Washington was born.

The Treaty of Paris, in 1763, concluded the French and Indian War, and temporarily eliminated France as a contender for the Plains. Spain was given all the territory west of the Mississippi, and England that to the east. Again, the Americans had no stake in the Plains, for all this happened before Daniel Boone, "ordained of God to settle the wilderness," had penetrated through the Cumberland Gap in 1769, and even before Captain James Smith of Pennsylvania, about 1766, had himself traversed the Gap.

It is clear, then, that the recorded history of the white man along the Atlantic Coast is not significantly older than the recorded history of the white man in the Plains. Long before the Americans established their claim by means of the Louisiana Purchase of 1803, there had been much activity in the region on the part of the French, the English, and the Spaniards. This early and dramatic history of the Plains, briefly summarized in this and the following chapter, is yet to be generally known and understood; a true knowledge of such a history would modify the assumption of many that the Plains are a recent frontier.

The period 1527–1803 was one of exploration in the Plains. The first visitors during this period were the Spaniards. In 1582, Cabeza de Vaca and his fellow survivors, marooned on the Texas Gulf Coast, began their adventures, and wanderings, and after crossing the Plains of Texas, they finally reached Mexico City some eight years later. Shipwrecked on the eastern coast of Texas, they made their way across to the Río Grande. During the journey they saw the bison, which they described as the "hump-backed cow," and the Plains Indian, neither of whom had hitherto been seen by white men.

The first official Spanish expedition to the Plains was undertaken in 1540–42 by Coronado, starting with 225 mounted cavaliers, 62 foot soldiers, 800 Indians, 1,000 Negroes, plus herds of horses, oxen, cows, sheep, and swine. Coronado had been ordered by the governor of northern Mexico to visit the Seven Golden Cities of Cibola (Zuñi villages) which had been re-

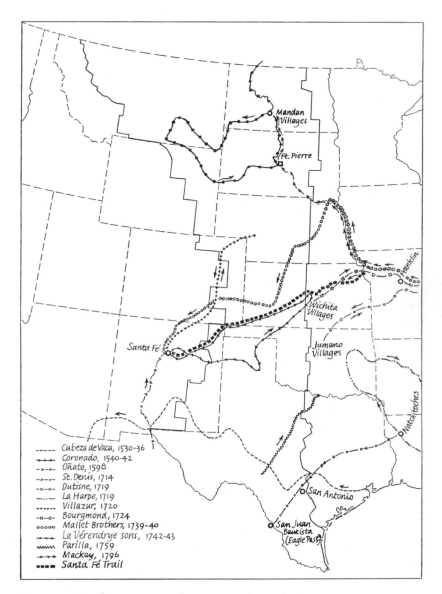

FIG. 7.   Explorations in the Great Plains before 1800.

ported for their wealth by Friar Marcos de Niza, who stated that he had been in that vicinity only a year earlier.

After his conquest of the Zuñi in New Mexico, Coronado led his forces eastward, into the Plains proper, and on south as far as the Brazos River in western Texas. From there he traveled perhaps as far east as the hundredth meridian and as far north as the Arkansas River near what is now Dodge City. Then he turned northeast, going possibly as far as the Wichita villages on the Kansas River.

In 1582, Antonio de Espejo and Bernardino Beltrán made a trip up the Río Grande to rescue some priests. Later, in 1591, Castaño de Sosa, with wagons and settlers, went as far north as Taos to establish a settlement. He was escorted home to Mexico by an armed force because he had no license for such a project. A few years later two other Spaniards, Captains Leyva de Bonilla and Juan de Humaña, set out into the Plains for Quivira, but were killed by Indians.

In 1598, Don Juan de Oñate, with four hundred men, eighty-three wagons, and seven thousand cattle, set out on a private settlement enterprise, with the blessings of the viceroy of Mexico. He went down the Conchos and up the Río Grande, past El Paso and into Pueblo country. He did not found the city of Santa Fé, but built his capitol on the Río Grande near the pueblo called San Juan. Oñate himself explored a part of the Plains in 1601 (going down the Canadian River and, perhaps, as far east as Wichita) and then returned.

Other settlements were soon established. Among these was Santa Fé, probably not founded until 1609. By 1630, New Mexico had become a Spanish province, with a civil and military organization of 250 Spaniards and 500 Indians. Hereafter, there were numerous expeditions into the Plains, having as their origin New Mexico or other bases south of the Río Grande. No settlements occurred within Texas until 1685.

What prompted the Spaniards to come to the Plains? Spain was interested in gold. The expeditions of Coronado, De Vaca, and De Oñate, for instance, were motivated by the hope of finding precious metals and stones. There was also the religious factor: the desire to convert the Indians. Spain's first agents in the Plains, therefore, were the explorers and the friars. The work of the latter was performed in the missions where Indians were

45

given religious instruction and guidance. Usually, these missions were protected from attack by a garrison of soldiers known as the presidio.

THE FRENCH EXTEND THEIR
EXPLORATIONS INTO THE PLAINS

The Spaniards, always the first to arrive, soon had competitors. The French, their curiosity nourished by Indian rumors of a western sea, a western river, and shining mountains, pushed ever westward. Combined with their desire for adventure was the hope of profit from fur trade.

The French entered the Plains in large numbers from the east. In 1693 three deserters from La Salle's expedition reached Santa Fé, and in 1698 the padres from Santa Fé ransomed two little French girls from the Navajoes. In 1700 a French force was in western Texas, and perhaps in western Kansas, where they destroyed a town of Jumano Wichita Indians. Probably the first to explore the Missouri was Étienne Venyard Bourgmond who went as far up the river as the Platte in 1714. Claude du Tisné started out from the Missouri River in 1719 and traveled to the Jumano villages on the Arkansas in present-day Kansas. In the same year, Bénard de la Harpe explored the middle Red River, and proceeded to the Arkansas and the Canadian rivers. His object was to open trade with the Plains Indians.

But trouble was in the making between the Spaniards and the French in the Plains—the Spaniards operating out of Santa Fé, and the French out of New Orleans, established in 1718. The appearance of the French greatly disquieted the Spaniards. The latter had been seeking gold and converting the Indians. Now they had a third incentive, the necessity of checking the French who could wedge themselves between the Spanish hold in Florida and that in Mexico. Spain, therefore, proclaimed Texas a province (1691) and established a number of missions on the eastern edge of the Plains. This was not all. Beginning with Pedro de Villazur, the Spaniards undertook a number of expeditions for the express purpose of winning over the Indians.

De Villazur, with his force, started out from Santa Fé, crossed the Arkansas, and got as far as the junction of the North and

South Platte rivers in the present state of Nebraska, where the expedition was destroyed by the Pawnee Indians. Other expeditionary forces were little more successful. Esteem for the Spaniards fell to a low ebb among the Indians. "Every Plains tribe," wrote a historian, "deserted to the French or sent its war parties to molest the enfeebled Spanish defenders."

Immediately, the French seized upon this opportunity with an expedition under the leadership of Étienne de Bourgmond. He was delegated to build a fort opposite the present town of Waverly in Caroll County, Missouri, in 1723. Along with forty traders well equipped with goods, he proceeded from the Missouri the next year to the Padouca Comanche villages near present Ellsworth, Kansas. There he spread presents before the eager-eyed natives. All these and more, he said, would be theirs if they promised only to trade with the Frenchmen. In 1727 the French had a force at Cuartelejo, out on the Plains, northeast of Santa Fé.

The whites of this period also traversed other parts of the Plains. In 1739, desiring to establish trade with Santa Fé, the French brothers, Paul and Pierre Mallet, led a party of six from the Illinois country up the Missouri as far as Yankton, South Dakota, then along the Platte, and then southwestward, across Kansas and southern Colorado, until they reached Santa Fé. In 1739, after leaving Santa Fé, four of the party followed the Canadian River and the Arkansas to the lower Mississippi. However unsuccessful they may have been in obtaining a license to trade from the officials at Santa Fé, their venture was not a total failure. The people in New Mexico expressed a strong desire for goods—a desire that attracted many traders from the Missouri to Santa Fé. In the same year another party of Frenchmen came to Santa Fé by way of Taos.

But hostility developed among the Indians east of the Mississippi, and both the French and the British became involved in the subsequent outbreaks. So France had no time to follow up her advantage in the Plains, and nothing further was done by the French in arousing the Plains Indians against the Spaniards.

Farther north, the Hudson's Bay Company had received its royal charter in 1670. In 1690, Henry Kelsey led an exploring party for the Hudson's Bay Company into the Great Plains. He was the first Englishman to venture any great distance inland, and he explored farther westward in Canada than had any white man before him. He was the first of his countrymen to hunt bison and to visit with the Plains Indians, with whom he spent some two years.

A more colorful character in the central and northern part of the Plains was Pierre Gaultier de Varennes la Vérendrye. A fur trader and explorer, his thirteen-year quest for the western sea and the shining mountains was filled with anguish, hardship, and disappointment. By the time he reached the present site of Winnipeg, his expeditionary forces, including his three sons Jean, Pierre, and François, and fifty voyagers, had already spent seven long years exploring westward from Montreal along the border waters of what is now Canada and the United States. From Winnipeg, La Vérendrye turned south late in 1738, stopping near the site of present Bismarck, North Dakota, among the Mandan Indians on the Missouri.

Unfortunately, the Mandans could not direct La Vérendrye to the western sea, and the creditors of the undertaking, back in Montreal, were annoyed. Returning to reckon with them, La Vérendrye left to his sons the unfinished task of finding the mountains and the river draining into the western sea. Turning south and west from the Mandan villages, the sons of La Vérendrye in 1742 proceeded west and south along the Little Missouri to the Black Hills, then northwest to the Yellowstone River. They had entered what are now the states of South Dakota, Wyoming, and Montana. On New Year's Day of 1743, they came within sight of the snow-capped Big Horn Mountains.

From here, the expedition turned east to the Missouri. Apparently, they camped on this river near the site of what is now Fort Pierre in South Dakota. Many years later a plaque was unearthed there with the inscription *March 30, 1743*.

By 1747 the sons of La Vérendrye had entered Canada and established a post, Fort Dauphin, on the south side of Lake Winnipegosis, and another post, known as Fort Bourbon, near the mouth of the Saskatchewan River. By 1750, sons Pierre and François had ascended the Saskatchewan to the mouth of the Pasquia and erected Fort La Pas. From there they continued westward to the forks of the Saskatchewan, in the heart of the Canadian Plains, where they erected another fort.

To show that the French, who were so diligently exploring the Northern Plains, were at this time all over the region, it can be pointed out that a party of Frenchmen, in 1748, sold some muskets to an Apache tribe of Indians northwest of Santa Fé. And in the years between 1727 and 1755, the French made various attempts—along what later became the Santa Fé Trail—to establish regular trade with the Spaniards.

THE HUDSON'S BAY COMPANY

CLAIM TO THE PLAINS

In the meantime, the British had to maintain their claim to the Plains. Anthony Hendry, in 1754, in the name of the Hudson's Bay Company and accompanied by some Assiniboin Indians, pressed into the Plains in the area between the North and the South Forks of the Saskatchewan. He was the first Englishman to come in contact with the Blackfeet, with whom he spent the winter.

By 1770, the French Canadians, backed by Canadian financial interests, organized a company known as the Pedlars. These *voyageurs* offered stiff competition to the Hudson's Bay Company traders for the inland fur trade. This forced the traders of the grand old company into a new and more aggressive policy.

The accounts of these expeditions and explorations show that the French entered the Plains from the north, the east, and the southeast. While their chief interest was fur trading, they were also explorers. However, the international conflict between European powers, known as the French and Indian War of 1754–63, resulted in the Treaty of Paris. It was at this time that France lost control of the New World. Spain was given all the territory west of the Mississippi, and England that to the east. France was no longer a threat to Spain in the latter's attempt to establish herself on the Plains.

THE GREAT PLAINS DURING SPANISH

CONTROL OF LOUISIANA TERRITORY

Following Spanish acquisition of Louisiana in 1763, the roles of New Orleans, the Texas settlements, and Santa Fé underwent a change. There was no longer the need for the Spaniards to protect themselves against the French threats centered along the Mississippi. A concerted attack upon the Plains could be directed now from Santa Fé, as well as from the Mississippi.

It was in this period, 1763–1800, that St. Louis, Santa Fé, and New Mexico grew. So did San Antonio and its environs. However, only a single citizen of the United States came to Santa Fé during this time. He had been captured by the Spaniards in the Gulf of Mexico and imprisoned in a dungeon near the Palace in Santa Fé. He escaped and returned to St. Louis in 1774. The absence of Americans in the Plains then was to be expected, for this was the period of the Revolution.

But the Spaniards expected to be friendly with the Americans. Afraid of the English, they made it possible for Americans to settle west of the Mississippi. As an inducement they offered eight-hundred-acre homesteads to the Americans for the sum of $40. However, this attracted few settlers, since the demand for Spanish citizenship and adherence to the Catholic religion were strictly enforced.

The Spanish holdings in the Mississippi Basin were tied to her provinces in Mexico and New Mexico by the San Antonio Road, which spanned the Southern Plains, reaching from Eagle Pass (San Juan Bautista) on the Río Grande through San Antonio to the Red River at Natchitoches, and was mainly the highway for priests and soldiers upon whom Spain relied to hold her empire. There was little trade, since the established missions were few and largely self-sufficient, as will be explained. Spain continued to keep only a military guard on the Red River as a protection against the Indians.

San Antonio did not grow as rapidly as Taos and Santa Fé. But all three were the northernmost outposts of the Spaniards. According to Leah Carter Johnstone (*San Antonio*), hardly five hundred Europeans lived in San Antonio in 1744. This settlement and four other missions had farms on which the settlers grew grain, cotton, flax, sugar cane, and other vegetables and fibers. They also raised cattle, sheep, goats, and horses. Irrigation being practiced extensively, they had fine orchards and grew considerable fruit. The settlements were concentrated and protected by high walls, but the fields and pastures were located outside the settlements proper. For these reasons, these mission settlements very nearly "ran" themselves. However, by 1790 the era of this particular type of mission was coming to an end.

North of the San Antonio Road was the Santa Fé Trail. It crossed the Southern Plains, too, establishing a strong tie between the Mississippi and the Spanish settlements to the west of the Plains. Santa Fé and Taos were the focal point of much trade between the French, the British, and the Americans, on the one hand, and the Spaniards and Mexicans, on the other. According to R. L. Duffus (*The Santa Fé Trail*), the Trail "was sprinkled with blood and sweat and bones long before the dawn of the nineteenth century."

Taos and Santa Fé of this period, Duffus continues, attracted the trade that moved along the Santa Fé Trail, despite continued smuggling by the French. During the latter half of the eighteenth century, Taos was the leading trade center, with Pecos ranking second. The white population of San Fernandez de Taos grew from 160 in 1760 to 1,351 in 1799. The temporary population, at the time of the great annual fairs in July and August, was much greater. Duffus points out that Taos attracted the Comanches, the Arapahoes, the Pawnees, the Utes, and other Indians of the Plains and the mountains. They traded their furs and skins for trinkets, cloth, food, and drink. To Taos, also, came the trappers with their furs and skins. Up from Chihuahua rode the merchants from Mexico with goods and wines. This, proclaimed Duffus, was "the Golden Age of Taos. . . . The crown was soon to pass to Santa Fé."

It was during this time that St. Louis, far to the north on the Mississippi, came into being. Pierre Laclède Liguest, a French trader, had been granted trading privileges at and around the mouth of the Missouri River. Unaffected by the transfer of the whole of Louisiana to Spain, the project continued under the guidance of the French. Liguest chose the site and entrusted the founding of the settlement of St. Louis to his agent, Auguste Chouteau. This happened in 1764, and the French continued to supervise until Spain took over in 1770. St. Louis and a few lesser posts in this vicinity were the chief bases of operation for the fur trade of the time. In the footsteps of the French came the British traders, who continued their operations even after the Revolutionary War.

Following the Revolutionary War, the country east of the

Mississippi became American territory. The Americans, rather than the British, then became a threat to Spain's security west of the Mississippi. The British, at first, and the Americans, later, made severe inroads upon the Indian trade west of the Mississippi. Therefore, the Spaniards attempted to extend more forceful control over the Louisiana Territory.

For those whose history of the Missouri and the Plains begins with the Lewis and Clark Expedition, it may be of interest to learn that Spanish traders pushed up the Missouri from St. Louis immediately after the close of the Revolutionary War.

The Spaniard, Juan Munier, acquired the exclusive privilege to trade with the Ponca Indians on the Niobrara River in northern Nebraska in 1789. Jacques d'Église opened trade with the Mandan Indians in North Dakota in 1790. Jacques Clamorgan and other traders from St. Louis organized the Company of Commerce for the Discovery of the Nations of the Upper Missouri, also known as the Missouri Company, in 1794. Jean-Baptiste Truteau led the first expedition of the Missouri Company up the Missouri, starting on June 7, 1794, from St. Louis. He traded with the Arikaras in South Dakota and that year built the first house in South Dakota, in what was later to become Charles Mix County.

The second expedition of the Missouri Company, in 1795, was unsuccessful. A third expedition, led by James Mackay, a Scotsman who had become a naturalized Spaniard, started up the Missouri the same year for a proposed six-year period. While Mackay erected a fort at the mouth of the Platte among the Omaha Indians, one of his aides, John Evans, continued up the Missouri. In 1796, he arrived at the Mandan villages and took possession of the British fort located there. He was in contact with British traders from the Assiniboin and Souris rivers in Canada. In the same year, Régistre Loisel built a trading post on Cedar Island between the town of Pierre and the Big Bend River in South Dakota.

However, the Spaniards had lost control of the Upper Missouri by then. The British from the Great Lakes and the Hudson Bay areas were more effective traders with the Indians. The expedition led by Mackay and Evans was a failure. Then came the Louisiana Purchase.

THE SPANIARDS ARE HALTED IN THEIR
ATTEMPTS TO OCCUPY THE PLAINS

Simultaneously with the attempts to hold the Louisiana Purchase area on the eastern side, the Spanish authorities were considering the extension of their influence over the western portion of that area. In the long run, was the Louisiana Purchase area a worthwhile possession to hold and to maintain? The answer was in the negative. Secretly, in 1800, therefore, Spain ceded the whole territory of Louisiana to France. Why was Spain willing to part with this large possession?

From the very beginning of her endeavors, Spain was headed for defeat in the Plains. Her explorers were unable to find gold, and her colonizers were unable to convert the Indians. Coronado and others wrote discouraging reports concerning the wealth and general physical characteristics of the areas. And, likewise, the experiences of the clergy were reported in disappointing terms.

The Plains Indian, when the Spaniards first came, was a nomad. The dog was his chief domestic animal. With the appearance of the Spaniards came also the horse. Learning from the Spaniards, the Indian soon became the horseman of the Plains. He was not interested in settling down on a mission to work for the white man and worship the white man's God. Instead, he became a constant threat to the Spaniard. In addition, the Spaniards had to face the problem of distance. To outfit and maintain far-flung outposts was extremely difficult.

These factors Spain took under serious consideration following the termination of the French and Indian War. In 1766, she sent El Marqués de Rubí on an inspection tour. His recommendations were that the frontier line should be moved farther south, with only Santa Fé in what is now New Mexico and San Antonio in Texas to remain as the two northernmost outposts. He also urged the abandonment of missions in eastern Texas and the extermination of the Apache Indians.

While Spain could not successfully carry out the recommendations, she made certain modifications in her policy. In taking over Louisiana in 1763, she retained the French system of fur trading. And, in 1772, Spain abandoned the use of the missions, relying thereafter upon the military. But, unfortunately, the soldier did not feel equal to the task. Frequently, he was afraid to leave the garrison, so terrifying was the effect of the Indians. Spain was willing to part with her possession to France in 1800.

This brief analysis of the history of the Plains from 1527 to 1800 demonstrates several important points. One is that recorded history for this region is, simply in point of chronology, as old, though by no means as full, as that of the Atlantic seacoast area. In the past twenty-five years important contributions have been made, by a growing number of scholars, to an increased knowledge and an improved understanding of American history as it has occurred in the Great Plains. One of the most significant of these contributions has been the editing and publishing of journals, diaries, notebooks, and other original records kept by explorers, traders, soldiers, and pioneers who traveled across the Plains on their various expeditions or who even lived on the Plains for a number of years.[1] A great many of the men who made early history on the Plains or who saw it being made by others kept careful account of their adventures, and these accounts give understandable significance and emphasis to the Plains as the scene of many historical events. All that is needed to make the history of the Plains a living history is to have existing published accounts read and digested by thinking citizens.

A second important point demonstrated in an analysis of Plains history is that the Plains were a forbidding land. Twice the French failed to conquer the region—once when they lost by provisions of the Treaty of Paris in 1763, and again when they sold their interest in the region to the Americans in 1803. But the many explorations into the region by the French illustrate that they strove heroically to possess the area. The Spaniards were rebuffed in their attempt to occupy the region, though they came earlier than any other whites. They disposed of their interest by a secret trade to France in 1800. The English, through

[1] Reuben Gold Thwaites (ed.), *Early Western Travels*. (Cleveland, Arthur H. Clark Co., 1905 *et seq.*).

The American Exploration and Travel Series. (Norman, University of Oklahoma Press, 1938 *et seq.*).

The Civilization of the American Indian Series. (Norman, University of Oklahoma Press, 1932 *et seq.*).

54

the Hudson's Bay Company, penetrated into the region from the north, but were satisfied to remain on the northern edge.

Thirdly, these whites did not have the institutions to conquer the semiarid Plains. The French and the English had a humid- and forest-area background. They stayed along the river courses and traveled by boat. They did not have the mobility to get inland and cope with the climate and the Indians. The Spaniards, better equipped to occupy a semiarid land than the French and the English, nevertheless were not able to conquer the region. Though they were mobile, they came to subjugate the natives and to extract tribute from them. But the Indian was even more mobile than the Spaniards, and the Spanish system was not sufficiently flexible to allow for quick adaptation to the Plains. So the Spaniards, too, lost the Plains. It remained for the Americans to conquer them.

CHAPTER 5

Plains History Immediately Following the Louisiana Purchase

Aside from the Lewis and Clark Expedition and the writings about the mountain-plainsmen, the Plains history immediately following the Louisiana Purchase, until about 1846, is far too little known. This is unfortunate, since the events of this period represent a unique experience in history. There are few situations in which a people from a humid land have extended themselves into a semiarid land under conditions similar to those that existed in the United States and Canada; for Australia and Argentina, the situation has been somewhat different. Also, the years 1803–46 have been the only period, thus far, that the Great Plains, from north to south, have been recognized in national considerations as a single economic and geographic unit. After 1846, except for the cattlemen's era, the region was dissected into southern, central, and northern parts by the attempts to cross the region and to settle it from humid-area bases.

The Great Plains—the larger portion of the Louisiana Purchase—offered a challenge to both the government and its individual citizens after 1820. Exploration and travel into and about the region had St. Louis as a focal point for a three-pronged attack. Looking west from St. Louis, and forced to make a choice about how to enter the region at that time, one could choose from three different available routes. One way was southerly and overland, on the Santa Fé Trail—diagonally across Kansas, across the Panhandle of Oklahoma, and into New Mexico. A second route was north and west, up the Missouri River. A third was centrally located, across country in a westerly direction, up the Platte River across Nebraska, via Fort Laramie in Wyoming, and into the Green River country. Somewhat later, this middle route offered several alternatives.

It was along these three routes that much of the early history of the area embraced in the Louisiana Purchase took place. There were numerous government and commercial expeditions

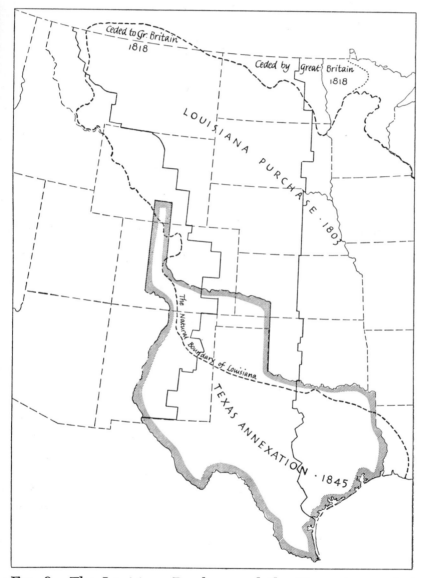

FIG. 8.   The Louisiana Purchase and the Texas Annexation of 1845.

57

into the region, and the mountain-plainsmen traveled along all
three routes, crossing from one to the other.

Expeditions beginning at St. Louis were being made into Louisiana even before Spain lost control of the territory to France
and before France sold the area to the United States. Toward

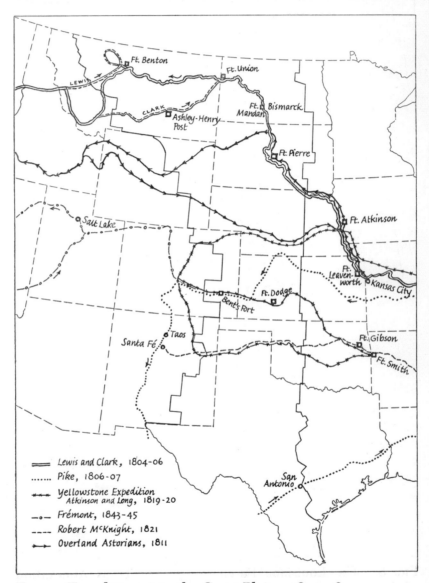

FIG. 9   Expeditions into the Great Plains. 1803–46.

58

the end of the eighteenth century, The Company of Commerce for the Discovery of Nations of the Upper Missouri sent out expeditions for the express purpose of capturing the peltry trade and of discovering, if possible, a southern transcontinental route. The first of the Missouri Company expeditions set out in 1794 under the direction of Jean Baptiste Truteau. Two more followed in 1795, one under the direction of Lécuyer and the other under James Mackay. In 1803, Régistre Loisel made a last expedition—an expedition recorded by Pierre-Antoine Tabeau[1]— for the Missouri Company, unaware when he did so that Louisiana had become the property of the United States. On his way back to St. Louis in May, 1804, Loisel met the Lewis and Clark expedition which had left St. Charles, Missouri, only a few days before, and it was from Loisel that Lewis and Clark secured much valuable information about the Upper Missouri country.

Immediately following the Louisiana Purchase, the United States government financed the Lewis and Clark Expedition to the West (1804–1806). The expedition traversed the Plains going and coming, by way of the Missouri River. In fact, the first winter (1804–1805) was spent at the Mandan villages, and the return trip, in 1806, was along much the same route. The journals of the expedition offer much information about drought in the Plains, measured by the seared nature of the vegetation and the poor condition of the native animals.

The history of this expedition is so familiar that the details will not be reproduced here. It was, however, one of the few early expeditions into the region that was equipped for the rigors it had to face, perhaps from accident rather than from design, since its route was by boat along the river courses which kept it in touch with game, water, and fuel. And, fortunately, it had the help of a guide, Sacajawea, an Indian woman who knew of the region and the mountains to the west. The expedition had a specific goal and a time limit. It was also fortunate in having the capable leadership of both Captain Lewis and Captain Clark, who were abundantly equipped by temperament and experience for their great task.

The next expedition, and perhaps one of the more successful, was that led by Zebulon Montgomery Pike, an army officer who

---

[1] Annie Heloise Abel (ed.), *Tabeau's Narrative of Loisel's Expedition to the Upper Missouri* (Norman, University of Oklahoma Press, 1939).

was given orders directing him to visit the Indian tribes west and southwest of St. Louis and determine the direction, length, and navigability of the Arkansas and Canadian rivers.

Setting out in July, 1806, with a party of twenty-three whites and fifty-one Indians, Pike started from the Missouri, crossed Kansas, and entered Colorado. From here he proceeded southward to the Upper Río Grande, where he and his party were arrested and taken by the Spanish officials to Santa Fé. After Pike was released and had returned to the States, he submitted a report.

Containing much valuable information, particularly with respect to trading conditions in and around Santa Fé, the report is of especial interest because it states that the Plains were uninhabitable; that they were a domain only for the Indian—not for the agriculturalists, who were advised to stay on the east sides of the Mississippi and of the Missouri. Thus, only six years after the transaction, the greatest part of the Louisiana Purchase was officially condemned.

The American public, in general, however, showed little interest in Pike's report or his warning, for the intense public interest in the Plains was not to come until several years later. In the interim came the War of 1812, and for the time being, the ordinary American continued to remain uninformed about the region beyond the Mississippi River.

Following the War of 1812, there was general unrest among the Indians; British influences continued to be felt; and American trade was in need of protection. For these reasons, it was believed necessary for the United States to show its strength and authority, and accordingly, Congress authorized another Louisiana Purchase expedition, which was to proceed as far as the Mandan villages.

This particular expedition was the Yellowstone Expedition of 1819–20, which was both a military and a scientific venture. Colonel Henry Atkinson was in charge of the former, and Major Stephen H. Long was in charge of the latter. As subsequent events proved, the expedition turned out to be almost a farce, although it started out in elaborate style. For the first time, an attempt was to be made to navigate the unpredictable Missouri by means of a steamboat, instead of by a keelboat, which at the time was the most satisfactory method of transportation.

Colonel Atkinson started his force with five steamboats from St. Louis. Two boats were not even able to enter the Missouri. One "gave out" thirty miles below Franklin, Missouri. The other two wintered at Cow Island, a little above the mouth of the Kansas, and were returned to St. Louis the following fall. The contract negotiated for materials and services was granted to an individual primarily interested in profit. At times, services not rendered were paid for at exorbitant prices. The entire management was weak. Troops suffered, and some hundred men died from scurvy. The absurdity of the affair called for a Congressional investigation which resulted in withdrawal of funds. The expedition thus was never carried out according to original plans. Instead, as a side show, Stephen H. Long with his scientific crew was authorized to explore in the Central Rocky Mountain region.

Yet the Yellowstone Expedition of 1819–20, in spite of its failure, is of especial interest to the historic-minded plainsman for two reasons. First, the expectations of the government with regard to the military; second, the report made in 1820 by Stephen H. Long. It was actually believed that in transporting and maintaining a thousand men on the Plains, the government would save $40,000 a year because of the presence of abundant game. If the soldier could shoot his own game, there would be a reduction in the cost of subsistence. Apparently it was believed that a professional soldier could, with ease, become an expert mountain-plainsman. The plan never came to fruition; nevertheless, a lack of understanding of the geographic conditions in the Plains, on the part of those who proposed the plan, is quite evident.

Major Long submitted a report based on observations made as he and his men proceeded from Fort Atkinson on the Missouri, along the Platte, over to the South Platte, and then cross-country down to the Canadian and Arkansas rivers. In this report Long said: "In regard to this extensive section of the country between the Missouri River and the Rocky Mountains, we do not hesitate in giving the opinion that it is almost wholly unfit for cultivation, and, of course, uninhabitable by a people depending upon agriculture for their subsistence." The map which accompanied the report designated the Plains area as "The Great American Desert."

It goes without saying that Long's report and map confirmed the observations of previous explorers from Coronado to Pike. It did even more: it prejudiced the American reading public. The "Great American Desert" became a reality in the minds of the American people.

Simultaneously with the government expeditions into the region, individuals, too, came to seek profit. Chief among these were the mountain-plainsmen, who were the fur traders of the region. During the period 1803–47, fur trading reached its prime in the Plains and mountain country, and constituted one of the most dramatic chapters in the history of the region.

One of the government's chief concerns in the West during this fur-trading era was the Indian. In dealing with him, the government planned a new policy—one of trading goods for furs at forts strategically located throughout the area. This was known as the factor system, and the rate of exchange was to be governed by the cost of the goods and the cost of maintaining the forts—not by profits. Yet another aspect of the new policy was the attempt at controlling the liquor traffic with the Indians.

On paper there was nothing wrong with these objectives. In actual practice, however, the program proved a failure, and the factor system was abolished in 1822. Liquor, instead of being eliminated from the scene, became the most powerful weapon used in the competition for the Indian trade. The traders, in their effort to outdo each other, dispensed it freely among the Indians. The enforcement of government controls became virtually impossible because the government did not monopolize the liquor business for itself. At the time the government was organizing its own program, it was also granting licenses to private individuals and parties interested in fur trading. In so doing, the government put itself in the role of a competitor with private individuals and groups who, beyond the reach of the law, would generally perform as they pleased.

The three fur-trading firms that dominated the Plains and the Rocky Mountain area were the Missouri Fur Company, the American Fur Company, and the Rocky Mountain Fur Company. By 1843 there were no fewer than 150 occupied or previously occupied posts west of the Mississippi, most of which were along the Missouri River.

Like the cowboy who followed, the fur trapper was the most

colorful figure roaming the Plains during his era. Known also as the "mountain man," and sometimes called the "plainsman," he is more correctly titled the mountain-plainsman. "In a beaver or a coonskinned cap and fringed buckskin suit gayly decorated with dyed porcupine quills or bright glass beads, the trapper was proudly dressed. . . . For money he had little need." His equipment consisted of a tipi for winter shelter, a buffalo robe for summer, and two horses. Often he lived with Indians, and sometimes he married their women. Thus equipped, he went in search of his game and met his fellow associates once a year—at the rendezvous.

Formerly, in the forest country, the fur-trade business was carried on at a post where the furs were bought and sold. But in the Plains area this system proved unsatisfactory because the Indians were mobile as well as antagonistic. To them the fort was a manifestation of the white man's intent to stay.

Confronted with this difficulty, William Henry Ashley, founder of the Rocky Mountain Fur Company, conceived a new idea. Instead of relying on the Indians for supply, his own men undertook the task of hunting and collecting furs. And his idea, after it had been tried for the first time in 1825, brought forth a routine that was used regularly for the next fifteen years. Each spring the mountain-plainsmen met at an agreed point. Here they procured their necessary supplies and disposed of their pelts. This became the rendezvous, a substitute for the fort. It was a time of excitement and great merrymaking.

Hiram Martin Chittenden, the classic writer on the subject of fur trading, described the highlights of the rendezvous as follows: "As soon as everyone expected had arrived, the business began. The parties belonging to the company turned over their furs and received their wages and new equipment. The free trappers and the Indians trafficked their furs on the best attainable terms, and purchased their equipment for the ensuing year. While all this business was going on, and while the cargoes were being made ready for the homeward journey, the heterogeneous assemblage went in for a good time. The flat alcohol kegs were broached, liquor flowed like water, and the wildest tumult at length ensued, ending not infrequently with fatal results. The debauch extended likewise to the Indians, many of whom were presently reduced to a state of the most abhorrent and revolting intoxication. Gambling was actively rushed during the whole time, and few were the trappers who did not pay a heavy tribute upon the altar of chance. In fact, with gaming, treating and feasting, most of the hard earnings of a year's toil found their way directly back into the pockets of the company at the enormous profit which these prices secured. The caravan then returned to the States, and the soreheaded trappers, after recovering from their dissipation, betook themselves with heavy hearts but light packs to their lonely retreats in the mountains, there to pass another 360 days in peril and toil, that they may spend five in drunken frolic."

These mountain-plainsmen were hardy characters. There was Jim Bridger, affectionately known as "Old Gabe," because he was reported to have escaped from death and the angel Gabriel so many times. There was John Colter, formerly of the Lewis and Clark party, who outran the Indians on the headwaters of the Missouri and traveled in the nude from Three Forks to Lisa's fort on the Big Horn, about 220 miles in seven days, and who was called the "great liar" because of his description of the Yellowstone wonders. Jedediah Smith was still another. He became interested in the Santa Fé trade after being a part owner in the Rocky Mountain Fur Company. He was killed by the Comanches in the south along the banks of the Cimarron. There was also Kit Carson, a mountain-plainsman whose jaunts carried him from the Southern to the Northern Plains, and who became immortal largely because of his activities as an emigrant and army scout.

Others were the Sublette brothers, Joe Meek, Thomas Fitzpatrick, David E. Jackson, James P. Beckwourth, Étienne Provost, and Robert Campbell. There were Old Bill Williams, Joseph Reddeford Walker, William and Charles Bent, and Ceran and Felix St. Vrain. The list, of course, is not complete.

The term "mountain men" by itself and as generally used by historians is a misnomer, because these men were also plainsmen. Much of their activity was in the Plains as well as in the mountains, and much in the foothills where the Plains and the mountains meet. These men knew the Plains chiefly because they were forever crossing them on their way to the mountains to hunt, to trap, and to trade. They again crossed the Plains on their way back from the mountains to their various bases of operations, frequently the forts located in the Plains area. Many of these men, later in their careers, became expedition guides and army scouts and crossed the Plains many more times—north and south, east and west—on a variety of missions. They learned to live and survive on the Plains, and perhaps one of their chief contributions to Plains history is their demonstration of an almost unique self-reliance in adapting to whatever environmental situations confronted them. The mountain-plainsman was a solitary figure, going alone across uncharted territory, many times into uninhabited regions of the West, depending upon himself alone for survival. He was a reconnaissance party-of-one who brought back to the frontier line the information and observations that stimulated frontiersmen to push farther westward, following where the mountain-plainsman had led.

The interrelation and intertwining of activity in the north and the south of the Plains region during the first half of the nineteenth century are revealed in a series of events. In 1804, William Morrison, a merchant of Kaskaskia, Illinois, entrusted a French Creole, named Baptiste La Lande, with a stock of goods and sent him to Santa Fé. La Lande arrived there, but appropriated the goods to his own purposes and remained in New Mexico. In 1805, James Purcell (Pursley), after misadventure among the Indians of the Plains, met up with the Comanches and the Kiowas who had been driven into Colorado by the warlike Sioux. He was asked by the Kiowas to go to Santa Fé and request the Spaniards to allow the Kiowas to stay in Colorado.

In 1807, Manuel Lisa, along with Auguste Pierre Chouteau, and in the company of John Colter, returning from the upper Missouri country, organized an expedition up the Missouri. On that expedition, Lisa built a fort at the mouth of the Big Horn River in Montana where it empties into the Yellowstone, a branch of the Missouri. That same year Lisa and a partner, Jacques Clamorgan, are said to have sent Louison Bàudoin to New Mexico via the Santa Fé Trail with a large quantity of goods. Lisa mentions further attempts at encouraging trade with Santa Fé in letters as late as 1812.

In 1809, while Manuel Lisa was organizing his St. Louis-Missouri Fur Company, three Missourians—James McLanahan, Reuben Smith, and James Patterson—under the guidance of a

Spaniard named Emmanuel Blanco, traveled the Santa Fé Trail. Taking the southern route of the Trail and reaching as far as the headwaters of the Red River, they were captured by other Spaniards, taken to Santa Fé, imprisoned in Mexico, and were not freed until 1812. That same year, 1812, Robert McKnight and his party went up the Missouri River and then across country to New Mexico. They were also captured and imprisoned at Santa Fé until 1821.

In the meantime, the overland portion of John Jacob Astor's Pacific Fur Company, under Wilson Price Hunt, traveled up the Missouri in the famous keelboat race with Manuel Lisa. Lisa won, and Hunt agreed to cross the mountains to the mouth of the Columbia in 1811. In 1812–13, Robert Stuart, one of the Astorians, came east, overland, crossing through South Pass. He erected the first post and cabins on the North Platte River, before Fort Laramie was founded.

Joseph Philibert and party hunted and camped on the upper Arkansas in 1814. Philibert returned to St. Louis for supplies in 1815, but was delayed in going back to his party. On his return to the Arkansas, he joined with Jules DeMunn and Auguste Pierre Chouteau, a name very familiar on the upper reaches of the Missouri. The three, when they reached the upper Arkansas, found that Philibert's companions had been captured by the Spaniards and taken to Taos. DeMun was sent to Taos to ask their release. He was successful in this mission, the success having, perhaps, been occasioned by the brewing revolt of New Mexico and all of Mexico against Spain. After the release had taken place, the entire party, including Chouteau, continued their trapping in the mountains north of Santa Fé. They were eventually ordered by the Mexicans to leave the area. However, winter hemmed them in, and, unable to leave, they were captured by the Mexicans and imprisoned in May, 1817. They were finally stripped of their goods and sent to St. Louis after an imprisonment of forty-eight days.

In 1819, David Merriwether, traveling across the southern Plains with the Pawnees, was captured by the Spaniards and taken to Santa Fé. There he was imprisoned, fined, stripped of clothing, and set free on the Plains, where he again met up with the Pawnees who re-outfitted him. Merriwether was the last American so treated on what is now New Mexico soil.

In 1821 a significant event occurred in the history of the southern part of the Great Plains. All of Mexico rebelled against the Spaniards, and Mexico became an independent republic. Thereafter American citizens migrated into Texas to settle there. It was during this time that the Santa Fé Trail achieved its greatest glory. Captain William Becknell, known as the "Father of the Santa Fé Trail," was the first to take wagons over the trail. It remained open continuously from then on until its end. In 1825 the United States government made money available to survey and mark the trail, and money was provided for some limited construction. With the appearance of Josiah Gregg's *Commerce of the Prairies* in 1844 interest in the Santa Fé Trail greatly increased. The mountain-plainsmen gradually became guides for emigrant trains and travelers, scouts for the army, hunters for the railroad workers, and Indian agents.

EXPLORATION OF THE REGION

RESULTED IN CHANGES

The period 1834–40 marked an era of climax in the Great Plains region. The army, which had been sent to pacify the Comanches and the Kiowas on the Santa Fé Trail in 1834, was sent north to the upper Missouri in 1835, to contain the Arikaras especially. Captain Benjamin Louis de Bonneville lost the fur trade of the Green River country to the Hudson's Bay Company after several years of intense struggle. On the other hand, in 1835, Rev. Samuel Parker and Dr. Marcus Whitman crossed the mountains through South Pass for the Congregational and Presbyterian Foreign Mission interests, to bring religion and medical care to the northwestern Indians. Dr. Whitman returned and made a second trip west in 1836, this time in company with two women and with wagon transport. At South Pass, they and their wagons were turned over to the leaders of a Hudson's Bay Company party and taken to the Pacific Coast. This marked the claim of the British over the Oregon Territory. It also marked the occasion when the first white women and wagons, going west beyond South Pass over what later was known as the Oregon Trail, made the entire difficult journey to reach the Northwest.

In the Southern Plains, on the other hand, the Americans in Texas rebelled against Mexico in 1836. They concentrated their attack on San Antonio and the Mexican Army stationed there. The Mexicans were finally subdued, but General Santa Anna then marched from Mexico to subdue the Texans in turn. In a one-sided battle, a small contingent of Texans was finally defeated at the Battle of the Alamo, and Santa Anna recaptured San Antonio. Later General Sam Houston defeated Santa Anna at the site of what is now the city of Houston.

At the time that Captain Bonneville lost his and the American fur-trade interests of the Far West to the Hudson's Bay Company, along with the Oregon Territory, the struggle between the Rocky Mountain Fur Company and the American Fur Company came to a crisis, with the latter absorbing the former. At this time, also, a small army was sent out to contain the Plains Indians following a series of uprisings, but the containment was not brought about. The Indians were temporarily subdued, but by disease and not by the army. This was the year 1837—the time of the smallpox plague, when Indians over the entire region died by the hundreds and thousands. The Mandans were wiped out practically to the last man, the few survivors being absorbed by other tribes. This was also the period of the decline of the great fur-trade activity—the beaver hat went out of fashion, the fur resources were almost exhausted, and the Indians were dissipated. The rendezvous system was coming to an end, and the mountain-plains fur trade was soon to be an enterprise of the past. From then on, trading was done at trading posts only, largely in the Plains, with emphasis upon the buffalo-robe trade, and with only small companies and small groups engaged in the business.

THE END OF AN ERA IN THE PLAINS

The period 1840–46 represented the end of one era in the history of the Great Plains and the beginning of another. Father DeSmet, the black-robed priest who had been long awaited by the Flatheads, finally came to live among them in 1840. John James Audubon, whose interest had been brought to high pitch by the collections and scientific information gathered by Thomas Nuthall and John Kirk Townsend in 1837, came to the Missouri in 1843, and collected specimens along the Missouri and the Yellowstone. Affairs on the Plains seemed to settle down, but only apparently so.

In 1842, John Charles Frémont returned from his second trip across the Plains and from the mountain region. Texas sent an expedition towards Santa Fé in 1841 with the intention of laying claim to the territory west to the Río Grande, but the New Mexicans destroyed the party. In retaliation, bands of Texans harassed the Santa Fé Trail until Captain Philip St. George Cooke drove the raiders off the Trail. Thereafter Santa Anna closed the forts of northern Mexico to trade flowing over the Santa Fé Trail.

Mexico was on the point of war with the United States. Units of the United States Army had been deployed among the Indians in the Plains, with an eye to holding the Great Plains against all comers. Fort Leavenworth was the main point of origin for army detachments that moved into the Plains area. The nation was poised to fight Mexico. Also, the nation was ready to "look John Bull in the eye" about the Oregon Territory. An empire was in the making.

It is interesting to examine the observations of historian Louis Pelzer concerning events up to this time. In his editorial remarks for *The Prairie Logbook*, a description of army life in the Plains, he says: "About two hundred and fifty years were required for settlement to spread from Jamestown to the Mississippi but a series of advancing frontiers caused the Trans-Mississippi West to become 'settled' in about five decades." Professor Pelzer has not overlooked the fact that Plains history begins as early as that of the Eastern seaboard and he is certainly aware that Plains history is almost coextensive with that of the Eastern Coast, but the quotation marks around the word *settled* in the passage above suggest to us the need for evaluating, as carefully as Professor Pelzer intended, the significance of his remarks. Settlement was largely in name only. Then, as now, the distance between some houses in the Great Plains may have been as much as thirty miles. Speaking historically, though the greatest amount of settlement of the Plains did occur in as brief a time as five decades, a slower, more sporadic, and less intense sort of settlement had been going on for many years prior to

69

the settlement push which took place in the last decades of the nineteenth century and early decades of the twentieth.

Moreover, "settlement" could never take a course on the Plains similar to that of the humid area. The East was settled, for the most part, in a community way. The wilderness of the first coastal frontier—the tidewater area—was approached not by the lone individual and then later by a few more pioneering spirits, but from the very first by whole groups of people operating as social, economic, and civic units. Settlement in the humid area was for the most part a matter of colonization, a far different process than the "squatter" settlement that took place west of the Mississippi. Of course, settlement in any one area of the United States was never limited either to corporate or to individual action. But to a very large degree, the advance of the frontier beyond the humid area was the result of individual initiative, the result of the trader or the scout or the trapper's going out beyond the frontier into unsettled areas, bringing back word of the land beyond to the frontier communities, encouraging one or maybe two families to move fifty or a hundred miles out into the region west of them. Gradually other families would follow. Then the whole frontier line would begin to move forward. Although the same may be said, in certain instances, about the Ohio Valley, certainly the western part of the Mississippi Valley, the entire Missouri Valley, the Great Plains, and the western mountain regions were, on the whole, settled in this manner—not initially by colonization, but by the gradual advance of the frontier, which involved the enterprising and adventurous individual who was always moving ahead of the frontier, pioneering the course the frontier might follow. The colonization which did take place in the West was late occurring—after a certain primary settlement of the region had already taken place—and was in many instances made possible only because the pathways to settlement in the West had already been opened.

But the Great Plains were not only settled differently than was the East; the growth of Plains population demonstrates a major difference between the development of the two areas. A great deal of the populating of the Plains was, actually, by default—something never true of the humid area. Population by default means simply that many people settled in the Great

Plains either because they were unable to get all the way across the Plains on their way to California, Oregon, or Washington, or because they had been to the Pacific Coast, had failed financially or otherwise, decided to leave, and fell back into the Great Plains region, never making it all the way back to their native East.

This brief summary of the Plains from 1800 to about 1846, conveys, even if telescopically, some of the events that lead the present-day historian to identify the Great Plains of the first half of the nineteenth century as a historical unit. The Plains have never been unified socially, economically, or culturally, but in the years following the Louisiana Purchase the Plains were thought of, for the first and perhaps only time, as an integrated unit and were so treated by humid-area leaders and consequently by the national government. For the first and perhaps only time there was public interest in the region as a whole. Commercial and military activity did not center in any one region of the Plains alone but extended throughout the area—north and south, and from the Mississippi to the Rockies. The mountain-plainsman, the army officer, the trader—anyone who had specific interests in the region was acquainted with both the northern and southern parts. What happened in any one part of the Plains was usually duplicated in other parts.

After 1846, this unified approach to and attitude toward the Plains began to disappear, and never since has the region been able to demand such national consideration as a geographical or historical unit. After 1846, the region was to experience—at least for a time—the full impact of having been so often defined as a desert. The Plains became a land to cross, at best a base of operation, little more than a barrier on the road to Empire. The war with Mexico, the attachment of California, and the settlement of the Oregon issue—interests beyond the Plains—now occupied the attention of the people.

The Americans had not yet conquered or really accepted the Plains. They had exploited the fur trade of the Plains and the mountains, had studied and examined the Plains only in order to fit them into a larger scheme of commerce and territorial acquisition. Now the Americans were ready to establish their interests farther to the west.

CHAPTER 6

The Adapted Ways of the Plains
Indian and the Texans

The origin of the Indian of the Plains is not fully known. Though some tribes arrived at a later time than others, as a group they had many similar traits and ways of living. In fact, the similarities are so striking that it has become customary for anthropologists to identify a particular body of traits as belonging to the Plains Indian group, as distinguished from those traits belonging to tribes from the mountain, woodland, tundra, seacoast, and lakeland parts of America. Included in this Plains Indian group are the Comanche, Kiowa, Apache, Arapaho, Cheyenne, Teton-Dakota, Crow, Assiniboin, Gros Ventre, Blackfoot, and Sarsi tribes.

No attempt will be made, here, to describe the customs and traditions that composed the way of life of the Plains Indians, or to contrast the differences among the several tribes. The writings by anthropologists on these subjects are plentiful.

The basic problem in the settlement and permanent occupation of the Plains has been the determination of the nature of the fundamental harmony between climate and civilization. Do the natural conditions of the semiarid Plains require the development of certain adapted techniques for the survival of civilization? What is the nature of these adaptations? What might the white man have learned from the Indian in order to establish a more secure civilization in the Plains?

The following treatment of the Plains Indian is an attempt to describe some of the basic traits that enhanced his opportunities for survival. The anthropologist, usually a newcomer to the Plains, has not emphasized this aspect of cultural adaptation. He has been satisfied with the description of what he has found, and the differences he has noted, among the several Plains tribes.

The Plains Indian tribes tended to have the following characteristics—which meant a measure of adaptation to the conditions of the Plains—in common: The Plains Indians were nomadic and non-agricultural in their way of life; they depended, for their subsistence, upon the wild animals of the region, especially upon the bison; they invented weapons and methods especially adapted to the hunting of big game, particularly the bison; they used a beast of burden for transportation, first the dog and then the horse, and this is evidence of their nomadic habits and their ingenuity; and they successfully adopted the horse and became expert horsemen long before the humid-area white man came into contact with the Plains Indian.

MOBILITY AS THE CORE OF THE
PLAINS INDIAN CULTURE

From the facts known about the Plains Indian's way of life, the one outstanding characteristic was his mobility, which had been developed to high perfection with the adoption of the horse, in place of the dog, as a beast of burden. In addition to being the basis for locomotion, the horse was important in other ways. The status of a brave or leader was measured by the number of horses he possessed, for often horses were acquired by raiding other tribes and camps, and thus were a measure of prowess and daring. Horses were used as a bid for the hand of a young woman in marriage. The horse assured greater success in the hunt and in war-making ability. The living conditions of the Indian were much improved after the transition from the dog to the horse as a beast of burden took place.

But, let it be emphasized, the use of the horse increased the mobility of the Indian on the Plains. Indian horsemanship proved to be the prime tactical hindrance to the humid-area white man who came to conquer the Plains. "Thus armed, equipped, and mounted," says Walter Prescott Webb (*The Great Plains*), "the Plains Indians made both picturesque and dangerous warriors—the red knights of the prairie. They were far better equipped for successful warfare in their own country

73

than the white man who came against them, and presented to the European or American conqueror problems different from those found elsewhere on the continent."

The Spaniards withdrew from the southern edge of the Great Plains about 1772 because their system of conquest and occu-

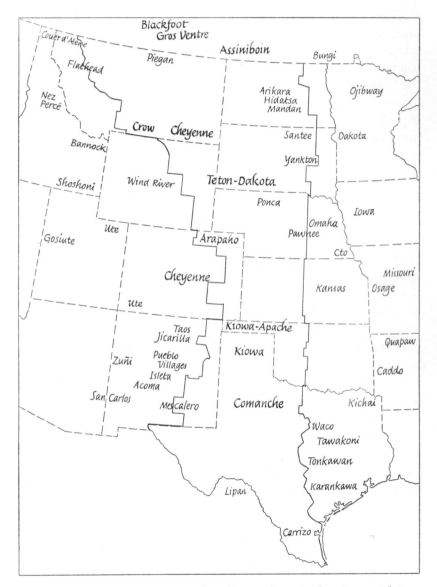

FIG. 10.   Original location of Indian tribes in the Great Plains.

pation was not adequately adapted to the mobility of the Plains tribes. This withdrawal was intended as a temporary measure, the hope being that soon other means might be found to conquer the Indian. But by the time the Spaniards were ready to resume colonization, the Indians had developed their horsemanship and warlike traits to such perfection that the Spaniards had lost the chance to subdue them.

Similarly, the whites from the humid-area East, in order to defeat the Plains Indians, had to learn how to use the horse in a way different from that dictated by humid-area customs. In fact, the whites had to dispose of their "forest guns" and adopt a new technique of warfare. This is best exemplified by the Texas Rangers, an organization with a unique and colorful history especially created by Texans for the purpose of mastering the Indian in his own environment, about whom more will be said later. In most ways the American whites were successful in their initial approach to the Plains. Unfortunately, however, the Americans did not study the Plains Indian culture, which they were about to destroy, with a view to learning the possible techniques that might assist them in living successfully on the Plains.

But of even greater importance to the Indian than the horse was the bison. The bison was the very core of the Plains Indian culture. Pté, the bison, provided the Indian with meat, parts of which the mountain-plainsmen considered the best of all meats. The bison was the source of the skin for tipis, clothing, blankets, footwear, and articles of decoration. Pté served as the center of the Indian's occupation, the division of labor between the sexes, and his war-making activities. The bison also served as the source of fuel and the wherewithal for tools, implements, needles, buttons, and household utensils. The bison, moreover, was the center of much of the Indian's recreational life; skill displayed in the bison hunt distinguished the brave from the youth. The bison was the core even of the Indian's religious life. The sacred white buffalo was a religious symbol of the highest order among many tribes. The lore and sagas of the Indian are full of Pté, who often had to be lured to come from long distances when the tribe was starving. The preparation for the hunt was a lengthy and dramatic affair, much of it dedicated to the bison. Finally, the hunt itself occupied much of the time of the Indians —as individuals, as braves, and as a colony of men, women, and children. Truly, there was no phase of Indian life that was not in some way influenced by the bison—one of the animals best adapted to Great Plains conditions.

The one most important characteristic that Pté had was, of course, that he was a traveler, a migrant. He roamed to grass and water. He even moved to the warmer climate and to the more protected parts of the terrain during the severe winter seasons. In the summer, when one range or water hole could not supply him, he moved to another. Mobility was the bison's great asset for survival in the Great Plains, and, since he was the very heart of Indian culture, this meant that the Indian was continually "on the go." The horse made such movement easier.

Some of the Plains Indians did live in permanent quarters and established non-migratory villages. But they were the exceptions, not the rule. Among these were the Mandans and the Pawnees, sedentary Indians who grew agricultural crops of a wide variety and perfected intricate ways of preserving and storing food. They had settled along streams which were constantly supplied with water, and their agricultural economy was stream centered, using the lowlands in a sub-irrigation manner.

But these sedentary Indians were also mobile. They hunted the bison herds that were established in the locality, or that passed the Indian villages in their migrations. Here, too, was an example of an ingenious adaptation to the conditions of the region. But again, the white man learned little from these Indians.

It was not the skin tent, the bone utensil, the buffalo robe, the white buffalo, or even the horse and its use that the Indian might well have bequeathed to the white man when he came to the Great Plains, but simply the idea of mobility. Instead, however, the white man not only denied himself the opportunity to study and analyze Indian culture, but almost exterminated Indians as a race.

The nation's Indian reservation policy spelled the doom and destruction of a culture—for two reasons. First, the bison disappeared, and in his place came slaughtered beef, meted out at the trading post. How was the Indian to make love to his maiden now, and to show his personal feats and abilities? How could the youth become the brave? Whom could one worship, and by what ritual? What would a strong male Indian do to occupy his time, and what were the responsibilities of the Indian woman? What was a man to tell his children so that they might be proud of him? How was a man to hold his family, his clan, and his tribe together? How could a brave become a chief, exert authority, exhibit leadership? Under these conditions could an Indian—male or female—be anything but a "ward" or a "cultureless creature"?[1]

The second destructive blow to the Indian was his confinement to a restricted area. The reservation limited mobility, and it placed severe restrictions on the use of a horse. It "fenced in" a large number of "cultureless creatures." It forced groups of human beings, whose culture had been suddenly destroyed, to live next to one another. No wonder the Indians rose in angry rebellion to defend their land against the whites. No wonder they raided the agency posts. No wonder they tried to escape from the reservation. And no wonder they just sat. In the face of such frustration, the use of opiates, especially as exhibited in Peyotism and the "Red Messiah" religion, became a favorite form of withdrawal behavior.

OTHER TRAITS OF THE
PLAINS INDIAN CULTURE

In addition to mobility, the Plains Indian revealed other traits that had been learned at the price of threatened extermination. He had learned to utilize the gifts of nature round about him. He made dyes and rich colors from plant and animal by-products and from the clay materials nearby. He utilized the berries and fruits of the land. He harvested the roots of many plants for his diet.

From dried meats, mixed with berries and roots, he made a preserved food called pemmican. This mixture was pounded and rolled and then placed in skins. In this dried form it was

---

[1] When the Indian uses the word "ward" he gives it the proper inflection and, therefore, does not mean what the white man means. Since the Indian already uses the word correctly and the white man does not, it is desirable to use the word "cultureless creature" so that the white man may better understand the Indian's plight. Other words that approximate the meaning implied in the expression are "marginal man," "protoplasm floating in limitless space," "nonentity," "spacelessness." These are the things the Indian means by the word "ward."

stored for future use—a form of hardtack and K ration not un-familiar to Americans today. This was the Indians' way of lay-ing aside a reserve from days of plenty for days of need. Al-though far less appetizing than fresh meats and fruits, pemmi-can was a form of preserved food readily adopted by the early mountain-plainsman. Until modern refrigeration came to farm and ranch homes, via rural electrification, food preservation by whites in the Plains was not basically superior, nutritionally, to that used by the Indian, and the diet of the farm and ranch home of the early period was at least as monotonous as that of the Indian. In addition, even periods of near starvation were as prevalent among whites as among Indians.

And the Indian had a form of housing that was especially adapted to living in the Plains. Though not developed by the Plains Indian until after his encounter with the white man and therefore a relatively recent addition to Plains Indian culture, the tipi, or lodge, is nevertheless a good example of the Indian's willingness to accept—at any time—whatever means he could find to a better adaptation to his environment. The Indian tipi, though differing in size from tribe to tribe, generally stood be-tween fifteen and eighteen feet in height and could accommo-date about twenty persons. It consisted of specially treated ani-mal hides, sewn together to form a conical structure when erected. This covering was draped over some twenty poles which were arranged in a circle at the bottom and were then leaned together to form the cone ribs. At the top was an open-ing with an especially arranged ventilator, for the escape of smoke and air. At the bottom, on one side was an opening with a flap for entrance and exit. Inside, the tipi was lined with an additional skin drop, to form an air space about the wall for protection against cold or heat. The bottom of the tipi could be raised for additional ventilation in summer. In the center, usual-ly, was the fireplace. The tipi, with a floor diameter of about fifteen feet, was a comfortable living quarter, with air-condition-ing superior to that offered by the shacks and huts of the early homesteader and rancher.

In addition, the tipi fitted readily into the mobile life of the Indian. The poles were used as a travois, the front end resting on the dog or the horse and the rear dragging on the ground. On the travois were placed the tipi hides and the remainder of the household possessions. Speed and economy of time were thus a part of setting up and dismantling the home, and being on the move.

CROW INDIAN LIFE TYPICAL OF

PLAINS INDIAN CULTURE

Other habits of life had been evolved to support the basic trait of mobility among the Plains Indian, and these habits are well illustrated by the Crow tribe. Among the Crow, for example, there was extensive use of smoke signals and a highly-developed sign language for communication over long distances or with alien tribes. Since the Crows had no boats, they waded or swam across rivers, transferring their property on improvised rafts of driftwood, lodge poles, and buffalo skins.

The Crows were not engaged in agriculture, except for the cultivation of small patches of tobacco. They made no use of the fish in the streams. Theirs was principally a meat diet, supplemented by wild berries and roots. The meats were generally boiled in rawhide vessels with the aid of hot stones, or baked in the ashes, roasted in holes, or broiled over an open fire. Their utensils were few and light and readily replaced.

The clothing of the Crow was made of the skins of mountain sheep, antelope, deer, elk, and bison specially treated to insure pliability. The men wore a breechclout, leggings extending to the hip, a fringed shirt richly decorated, and a buffalo robe with the hair inside. The women wore knee-length leggings, a sleeveless dress extending to the feet, a cape-like shoulder piece falling loosely over the arms, all highly decorated, and a small buffalo robe. On the feet, both sexes wore moccasins cut from a single piece of leather.

The customary division of labor was also governed by the fact of mobility. Among the Crow, the men did the hunting, the fighting, and the making of weapons. The women gathered the firewood, fruits, berries, and roots; did the cooking, the preparation of the skins and clothing, the decorating; and made, erected, and dismantled the tipis.

Community life was governed also by the facts inherent in mobility. There were, originally, thirteen clans, organized along matrilineal lines. Descent and inheritance followed the female line. Marriage was outside the clan. The clan was the basis for much of the allegiance among persons, including the responsibilities for child rearing, and caring for the ill and the incapable. In case of death of either parent, the responsibilities for the support of dependents and survivors were clearly defined duties of clansmen. Adulthood for the males was postponed to the middle twenties, unless proved at an earlier age by special exploits of bravery and courage.

Law and order among the Crows were informal but well defined. The chiefs, honored for the accomplishment of notable exploits, had limited powers, and a number of them usually formed an advisory council. They had little power. Ridicule and derision, generally expressed in public through stories and song, were the main agencies of social control. Personal vengeance and settlement of offenses were mandatory but within specific limits. Exile from the clan was an effective form of punishment.

For more complex administration of protective functions there were clubs or societies, membership having its basis not in exploits but in election. These clubs performed certain military and policing functions, certain ceremonials, and were responsible for general discipline in the camp and among clan members, as well as for interclan relations.

THE TEXAS APPROACH TO THE PLAINS

It is clear, then, that Plains Indian life was shaped, strikingly, to the fact of mobility. Indirectly, this meant also a high degree of flexibility in many aspects of life. Thus it followed that the Indian failed to lay aside liberal reserves for hard times, which in turn was the cause of much suffering, unless the bison were always at hand.

White man had centuries before become habituated to sedentary life centered in cities and towns and on the farmstead. Mobility, long since rejected as something undesirable, was estimated in slighting and sneering value judgments of, for example, the suitcase farmer and the sidewalk farmer until very recently, and the disparagement of farm tenancy and mobile labor generally. The values identified with homesteading were the kind that discriminated against mobility and formed an established home and hearth in the community. It was hard for the white man, therefore, to see any merits in mobility.

A more observant white man, one less prejudiced in favor of the peculiar values of his culture, might have learned how to live more successfully in the Plains had he recognized a value in mobility. This he could have learned from the Indian of pre-reservation days. Or he might have learned from the Texans, for they, too, could have bequeathed to the whites from the humid area a better adapted way of life.

Because of its historical background, Texas furnishes an interesting illustration of how the rest of the Plains might have been settled. This state, for a time, was a republic in its own right and was required to solve its own problems. Furthermore, it had a strong Spanish background which, in some ways, was better adapted to semiarid conditions than was that of the forest settler. The details are as follows.

Stephen F. Austin brought a colony of immigrants to Texas from the United States in 1821 and settled just east of the ninety-eighth meridian, in the timbered and well-watered area along the Brazos and the Colorado rivers, east of San Antonio. Other settlers established themselves nearby. Difficulties soon arose, however, with the Plains Indians, and Austin was forced to deal with their hostility as well as with the interference of the Mexican government in an essentially Anglo-American colonization movement. He and the people of his community therefore decided to provide for mounted rangers in order to protect themselves. This was an innovation and was the origin of the famous Texas Rangers, whose horsemanship and marksmanship proved to be decisive factors in controlling the Indians.

Then followed in 1836 the Texas revolution and the achievement of independence by Texas, which became a republic. Subsequently, Texas was under constant threat of war from Mexico, and the frequent partisan raids by the Mexicans added to the need for vigilance. A more formal organization of the Rangers had occurred by 1835–36, but, by 1840, the organization had become a well-known and highly-important institution in Texas government. The Rangers were respected for their versatility, and of their abilities it was said, "A Texas Ranger can ride like a Mexican, trail like an Indian, shoot like a Tennesseean, and fight like a very devil."

The settlements which Austin made, and those which followed, were at the junction of three cultures—Mexican, Texan, and Plains Indian. Such a junction provided a fertile situation for invention. And at this time, according to Webb, the need emerged for a weapon different from those used in the forest area, a weapon that fitted the peculiar needs of the plainsman. According to Webb, the answer to this need was the Colt revolver, invented by Samuel Colt in 1835, but which had not received general acceptance by the public. Instead, it had become a surplus on the market though cheap in price, and later, because of its "uselessness," went out of production. The gun then in demand was the long rifle, a convenient weapon for a man on foot hunting in wooded lands. The hunter, standing firmly on the ground, could rest his gun in the crotch of a tree. The hair trigger, the double sights, and the fine bead were features significant in a weapon that could be nicely adjusted and accurately aimed.

But to the man on a horse, this kind of small arm was awkward and cumbersome. It even proved to be a handicap when the rider met with a skilled Indian warrior, who, with his bow and arrow, lance, and riding skill, could easily demonstrate his superiority.

Therefore, the Texas Rangers, having tried the long rifle and found it wanting, turned to the Colt, which they purchased at bargain prices. The Rangers soon came forth with testimonials about the worth of the weapon; they suggested improvements and various names and terms. They found it indispensable in their wars with the Indians and the Mexicans.

The Colt revolver, however, did not come into general acceptance until General Zachary Taylor landed in Texas with his army in 1847. Seeing the Rangers in action with the revolver convinced him of its usefulness. Since there was none on the market, he requisitioned the government for a thousand revolvers, and so it was the Colt revolver began to play its historic role in American history.

The origin and acceptance of the Colt revolver is highly significant. It is a vivid illustration of how ideas could be developed on the Plains and adapted to the existing needs. The organization of the Rangers, the horsemanship and war-making skill of the Mexicans and the Plains Indians, mobility in moving armed units long distances across the open and coverless terrain of the Plains, and, finally, the revolver as a weapon—all these were woven into an effective instrument for conquering the Texas Plains. Only by the acceptance of these adaptations to Plains life was the area finally subdued.

The "Texas approach to the Great Plains" also included the public land policy of that state. When Texas became one of the states of the Union it retained control of its lands, a most significant fact concerning land policy in the Great Plains region. The Texas land policy, moreover, with its roots in Spanish and Mexican tradition, often provided the settler with some land along a stream, supplemented by grazing land away from the stream. Land was classified by its best use prior to alienation to homesteaders, and the size of the farm or ranch was considerably larger than that permitted the settler in the rest of the Plains.

So strongly was Texas land policy influenced by the semiarid conditions of the state that Texas had later to modify its own policy and make concessions to the conditions prevailing in the state's humid portions. Here was action quite the reverse of that which took place in the remainder of the Great Plains.

Following 1880, the remaining public domain of Texas, located primarily in the semiarid part of the state, was classified into three groups: (a) agricultural, (b) grazing, and (c) forest lands. The grazing classification was subdivided into dry grazing and watered grazing land. In accordance with state regulations, a purchaser could acquire one section of agricultural land or two of grazing land, or a combination of one section of each as a homestead. In other words, a homestead was not a free acquisition, as in other Plains states, but landholding secured by purchase and exempt from sale for any form of debt, except taxes.

In 1885 the stipulation was provided to permit a homesteader to purchase three sections of unwatered grazing land. After 1887, by legislative act, a homesteader was allowed to purchase four sections of dry grazing land. After 1906, the state law permitted a homesteader to purchase eight sections, or 5,120 acres. As a consequence, the family-sized ranches in the permanent ranching country ranged from four to twenty sections, or from 2,560 to 12,800 acres; whereas, the family-sized farms in the better farming areas ranged from 80 to 160 acres.

The significant thing here is that Texas had a public domain policy of her own. With few exceptions, it did not provide free homesteads, for the land had to be purchased. Such a policy avoided settlement by those who were not truly agriculturalists and cut down on speculation. Secondly, the disposal of the land was in large units—not in small acreages—that approximated the minimum requirements for a successful ranch or farm. Texas land policy proved to have roots that were well adapted to the peculiarities of the area and ultimately to the advantage of the settlers. Such was not true of land policy of the rest of the nation, where values were predicated on humid- and forested-area concepts of agriculture.

In summary it can be said that the various other land policies governing settlement of the Plains had a fine model available to their makers in the Texas example, and it would have been far better for the federal and state legislators to follow the Texas example than to follow the ill-adapted plans actually adopted. The Texas example suggests what might have been accomplished in the way of adapted community and settlement patterns for the entire region had the push from the humid and forested area not been so strong. Certainly the errors of institutional development in the Plains cannot be attributed to lack of sound models. The Indian way of life and the Texas settlement pattern were both available at an early date. The failure to consider these models is one more evidence of the overriding projection of humid-area ways onto the semiarid Plains.

CHAPTER 7

"The American Desert," a Land to Cross

The year 1846 has aptly been described as the "year of decision." All of the historical evidence sustains the view that it was, for many related actions carried out in earlier years—by presidents, congressmen, and orators—had shaped the course of empire; now it was necessary to make final decisions by which—for good or ill—empire could, in fact, be achieved.

The areas of decision were all in the West, extending from Texas in the Southwest to California on the Pacific Coast and to Oregon. Texas alone lay partly on the Great Plains, but the California and Oregon issues were to have a profound influence upon the Plains, as will be seen.

Though Congress had consented in 1845 to the admission of the Republic of Texas as a state, Texas itself did not become a state, in the sense of a change of government, until February, 1846. But admission prompted the Mexican War in May that year. After its declaration, the federal government moved an army into and across the Plains to prosecute the campaign against Mexico. A few weeks later, in violation of his orders, Captain J. C. Frémont encouraged American settlers to occupy Sonoma, California, and raise the "Bear Flag" of independence, a "revolution" which can be viewed only in relation to the Mexican War and its aftermath. Farther north, the great territory of Oregon had been at stake between Britain and the United States for more than three decades. Its ultimate fate was to be decided by a fast crowding immigration from the United States beginning as early as 1843, and by the determination of Democratic leaders to have it or to go to war—"Fifty-four forty or fight!"

The decisions before the country in 1846 were thus the final inclusion of Texas as a state, the War with Mexico, the attachment of California as a territory, and the settlement of the Oregon issue with Britain.

To set the stage for the fulfillment of these four objectives it had been necessary to do several things. First, Americans had to be encouraged to live and settle in the areas beyond the Plains, especially in California and Oregon. Secondly, it was necessary to have an armed force in readiness to back up the diplomatic negotiations involved in these issues, and so parts of the army had been deployed in the Plains. Finally, it was necessary to follow up the settlement of these issues by increasing the population in the areas acquired. This meant preparation for a great migration across the Plains.

The events above, in their national perspective, have been described in detail by scholars and orators. What has often been forgotten is the accompanying role of the Great Plains. Though the Plains at this time had the reputation of being "The Great American Desert"—a land to cross on the road to empire—there were important happenings in this vast area. A full accounting of them would lend drama to the history of the region and would aid in the making of patriots. But it is true that at precisely this time the region began to lose the cultural unity it once possessed. This was a necessary consequence of the fact that the Plains had become a land to cross.

STATEHOOD FOR TEXAS

During the ten year period from 1836 to 1846, Texas achieved its independence from Mexico, pursued its course as a nation, was admitted to the Union in 1845, but did not enter into it until after the year 1846 had dawned. Annexation transferred the problem of the southern boundary dispute with Mexico from Texas to the government of the United States. Was the Río Grande the boundary, as the Texans were asserting, or was it the Nueces River, as contended by the Mexicans?

Though President Polk favored the claim of Texas, he hoped the problem could be settled peacefully, for the Oregon issue was also in the balance. Accordingly, he sent John Slidell as minister to Mexico to settle the dispute. But Slidell was not received by the Mexican officials. To Polk, the settlement of the issue about Texas was paramount. Texas could be used as leverage for the acquisition of California, which was of great interest to him. If necessary, he was prepared to use force. The crossing of the Río Grande by a group of Mexicans, who killed or wounded sixteen Texans, served as the occasion for Polk's message to Congress that gave rise to war.

THE WAR WITH MEXICO

The Mexican War had a significant relationship to the Plains, as has been mentioned, in that the region served as the overland military route. The cross-country operation involved some 2,700 men under the command of one of the nation's ablest frontier officers. Colonel (later General) Stephen W. Kearny received orders to organize and lead an army from Fort Leavenworth to Santa Fé for what turned out to be a two-fold purpose: one, to protect the Santa Fé trade; the other, to secure New Mexico and California.

The bulk of this "Army of the West" was made up of young Missouri farm boys—volunteers, whose awkwardness, dislike of routine, usual army grouchiness, and lack of military demeanor annoyed some of the West Pointers. "It was the damndest army" ever to be organized, in the opinion of these officers. These volunteers, notwithstanding the fact that they were already outdoor men, had much to learn. Many things were strange and new. Jack rabbits, antelope, and buffalo were attractions. The country was "unimaginable." The Plains were on a scale the men had not dreamed of. Man was diminished to a dot that appeared to be traveling along the bottom of a bowl. Most devastating of all was the sun. It flattened the life in man, filled his eyes with the color of blood, and baked him to the bone. In addition, rattlesnakes, mosquitoes, buffalo gnats, alkali water, and the smell of fires made of buffalo chips made army life a hardship. Practically all the time the going was rugged. Of those less fit, some were sent home, and others died.

But Stephen Kearny, a capable army officer, was also a frontiersman who had formerly traveled over the Santa Fé and the Oregon trails. To accomplish his assignment, he disciplined his men and demanded daily marches of from twenty to thirty-two miles, rather than the customary fifteen.

After entering Santa Fé, he laid the groundwork for territorial organization, and Charles Bent, who had been one of the owners of Bent's fort, was named Governor of New Mexico. Kearny then split his forces into three groups. One, under the command of Colonel A. W. Doniphan, was to march south to Chihuahua and force the issue with Mexico. The second, with Colonel Sterling Price in charge, was to stay in New Mexico to maintain order. The third, under Kearny's personal command, was to march on to California.

THE CALIFORNIA INCIDENT

The acquisition of California involved another prominent figure who had explored in the Great Plains earlier. He was Captain John C. Frémont. Through his reports, which were published and read, he had become known for two expeditions involving the Plains and the West. One was to South Pass in the Rockies; the other was to Oregon and California. In 1845, he left St. Louis on his third expedition, this time to survey a new emigrant route to Oregon. With sixty armed men (most of them mountain-plainsmen) he broke a trail across the Salt Lake Desert and west of the Great Salt Lake, to Ogden or Mary's River, which he renamed the Humboldt. Then he went to California where, without authorization, he instigated the Bear Flag Revolt against Mexico and proclaimed the independence of California. With the help of Kearny's forces and those of Commodore John D. Sloat, California officially became a part of the United States.

THE OREGON ISSUE

In the interim, things were stirring in Oregon, jointly occupied by Great Britain and the United States since 1818. The issue there was the settlement of the boundary line. The issue came to a crescendo in 1844. The Americans up to this time had desired the forty-ninth parallel as the boundary, but now declared that they wanted all of Oregon—"Fifty-four Forty or Fight!" The British, who had formerly believed that the Columbia River should be the boundary, now offered the forty-ninth parallel. Late in 1845, President Polk asked Congress to inform Great Britain of the termination of the joint occupation agreement. But because of the Mexican War, the nation was hard pressed. Polk could not afford a war with Great Britain. So in June, 1846, the two nations compromised by establishing the forty-ninth parallel as the boundary line.

THREE ROUTES ACROSS THE PLAINS

The most important ingredient in the westward course of Empire and the push across the Plains was the pioneer. It was he, with his irresistible urge—whether based on the desire to acquire gold, or to establish a home, or to seek adventure—who defied all formal agreements and natural barriers. However, to reach Texas, California, or Oregon he had to cross the Great Plains. To the pioneer, as to the soldier, the Plains offered a means to an end.

There were three major routes across the Plains at this time: the Santa Fé Trail, the Oregon Trail, and the Missouri River. The pioneer route of them all was the Santa Fé. History gives us only incomplete information about its origins. It is known, however, that the French Mallet brothers went along the Upper Arkansas and into New Mexico in 1739 and that the Spaniard, Pedro Vial, in 1792–93, was requested to find a route between Santa Fé and St. Louis. Likewise, Zebulon Pike in 1806 crossed segments of it. From what is known of French and Spanish trading, it is safe to assume that during this early period, the Trail was traversed and known by many.

But it was not until 1821 that the Trail became a steady highway for commerce and travel. At that time, Mexico proclaimed its independence from Spain. This did away with the trading laws which, until then, had excluded foreign merchants from Mexico. New Mexico was now open to outsiders. Also in 1821, William Becknell, an American, traveled the Trail for the first time, and he is credited with the honor of being the first to cross the Cimarron Desert, establishing a shorter route, and the first to use wagons. Previously, pack animals were used.

With the introduction of wagons, trade grew from $35,000 in 1824 to $450,000 in 1843; and correspondingly, the number of wagons carrying the goods increased from 26 to 250. The

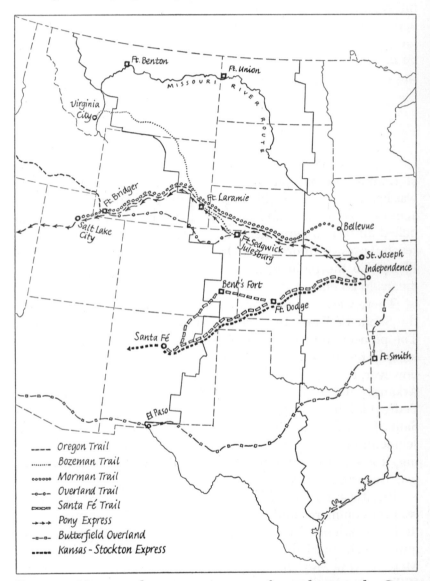

Fig. 11. Nineteenth-century avenues of travel across the Great Plains.

chief articles of freight to New Mexico were dry goods and hardware. Cotton was a very important item. From New Mexico came precious metals and furs, notably beaver skins and buffalo robes.

The westward trips on the Trail originated, first, at Franklin, Missouri, but soon thereafter at Independence. The route was composed of four rather distinct segments: the first extended from Independence to Council Grove; the second from Council Grove to the Arkansas Crossing; the third from the Crossing through the Cimarron Desert; and the fourth from the edge of the desert to Santa Fé. There was also a mountain cutoff stretching from the Cimarron Desert, along the Arkansas River as far as Bents Fort, and then, turning southwest, over Raton Pass.

While the Santa Fé Trail was initially a commercial highway only, it was used, later, by the military and by those pioneers interested in reaching Texas, New Mexico, and California. Its role as a military trail during the Mexican War has already been mentioned. In 1849–50 it was used again by the government, this time for military express and for mail which was delivered monthly from Independence to Santa Fé. In spite of its eight-hundred-mile length to Santa Fé, requiring forty-five to fifty days of travel, and though it traversed Indian country, travel on the Santa Fé was not especially difficult.

The pioneer historian of the Santa Fé Trail and the man who perhaps contributed most to making the Trail known and understood was Josiah Gregg—naturalist, traveler, and author. Gregg, who made many trips from Independence to Santa Fé, published in 1844, his *Commerce of the Prairies,* a veritable handbook of Western life based upon notes he had taken as a trader along the Trail from 1831 to 1840. The book has been accepted for over a century, now, as the most authoritative source of information available about pioneer life in the Southern Plains area and about the Santa Fé Trail itself.[1]

A second route across the Plains was the Oregon Trail. Though Lewis and Clark, as early as 1803, had travelled across the Rockies, and though fur traders and missionaries were, by

[1] Josiah Gregg, *Commerce of the Prairies,* 2 vols. (New York, H. G. Langley, 1844); Reuben Gold Thwaites (ed.), *Commerce of the Prairies,* Vols. XIX and XX in *Early Western Travels* (Cleveland, Arthur H. Clark & Co., 1905); Max L. Moorhead (ed.), *Commerce of the Prairies,* Vol. XVII in *American Exploration and Travel Series* (Norman, University of Oklahoma Press, 1954).

1812, journeying to the Pacific by canoe and keelboat, on horse-back, or afoot, the first person to find and follow a route from the Pacific to St. Louis that could be used by wagon trains was Robert Stuart. Robert Stuart's discovery, in 1812–13, of the route known as the Oregon Trail made possible the subsequent migration that was to populate the American Northwest. By mid-century the "great migration" was underway. In 1843, 1,000 men, women, and children of all ages, along with 5,000 oxen, set out from Independence, Missouri, following the trail that Stuart had pioneered. The practicability of travel having been demon-strated, traffic and trade increased significantly. In 1845, for example, 3,000 emigrants are said to have gone to Oregon, a number equal to all who had gone before. In 1846, only 1,650 persons reached Oregon, but 5,500 went there in 1847. With the discovery of gold in California in 1848, the volume of traffic increased. Of the 42,000 persons who reached California in 1849, 25,000 came by way of the Oregon Trail. And by 1852, it had served some 100,000 emigrants altogether.

The route itself was approximately two thousand miles long, and required six months to travel. Like the Santa Fé, it origin-ated at Independence, and for a stretch of forty miles the Santa Fé and Oregon trails were one and the same. At this point, the Oregon road proceeded to the southern bend of the Platte River where Fort Kearney was located. From there it continued up the Platte River, on up the North Branch as far as Fort Laramie. Following the remainder of the North Platte and the Sweetwater Fork, the Trail passed Independence Rock and Devils Gate and crossed through the famous South Pass, across the Great Basin, and on to California or into the Willamette Valley of Oregon.

Up to 1848, the history of the Oregon Trail was the history of fur traders, missionaries, and homeseekers. But with the dis-covery of gold, to the list of travelers could be added adven-turers, gamblers, gunmen, thieves, and prostitutes. The pioneer phase of the road had then ended; it was now a highway.

The third or northern route was that of the Missouri River. This was the route which was traced in its entirety (from St. Louis to the mouth of the Columbia River) by Lewis and Clark in 1803–06. And it was on the Missouri that Hunt and Lisa in 1811 had their famous keelboat race, with Lisa proving to be the winner. Unlike the Oregon Trail, the Missouri was mainly a commercial highway, used primarily by fur traders and gold seekers rather than by homesteaders. With the discovery of gold during the late fifties and the early sixties in Montana and Idaho, many (especially those headed for Montana) came via the Missouri.

The chief feature of river transportation at this time was the steamboat. As early as 1819–20 Major Long, with his exploration party, tried to use the steamboat on the Missouri but got no farther than Council Bluffs. The first successful trip was that made by the steamboat *Yellowstone,* which came as far as Fort Union at the junction of the Yellowstone and the Missouri in 1832. And in 1859, the first steamboat reached Brulé Bottom, fifteen miles below Fort Benton, Montana, which became the head of steamboat navigation. Goods were brought up every spring by steamboat, and furs and gold were taken down river. Many times the robes and peltries were taken to St. Louis in Mackinaw boats—fifty feet long and of four feet hold, capacity fourteen tons—propelled by a crew of twelve men.

The amount of steamboat travel for the later period can best be gauged from the following data:

Year	Number of Steamboats	Year	Number of Steamboats
1859	1	1868	35
1860	2	1869	24
1861	None	1875	11
1862	4	1876	21
1864	4	1877	25
1866	31	1878	46
1867	39		

THE HAZARD OF PLAINS TRAVEL

The pioneers, coming from a land of streams and forests, were never adequately prepared for the semiarid Plains conditions. Those taking the northern route found the Missouri very unpredictable. Being navigable only from spring until fall, the river was prone to change its course, and at times its water was shallow or its channel was filled with trees, dead animals, and snag bars. Those taking the Oregon Trail were forever pressed by the problem of sheer distance. For those taking the

Santa Fé, the obstacle could be the intense heat, or the Indians, or both.

Travel across the Plains proved to be an excruciating experience. Because of the length of time involved all the pains and pleasures of man were experienced on the trip—birth, marriage, death, family quarrels and feuds, mental illness, physical illness, hunger, pestilence, religious ministrations, dancing, singing, and gossiping. Psychologically, men and women experienced a great fear and dread as they left the forest lands and came on the Plains, which appeared to stretch out indefinitely, with only the ever-receding horizon ahead. The Plains dwarfed men to pigmy stature, and the fear of Indians, marauders, disease, death, and hunger ate away at their vitality so that many became inhuman in their relations with their fellows. With the break from their heritage behind them, the threat of insecurity ahead of them, and the necessity of constant vigilance ever present, many emigrants developed deep frustrations that ever after affected their lives. Only those who had a deep purpose and a disciplined organization, as the Mormons did, succeeded in living reasonably normal lives on the trails.

THE MORMON TREK

Of all the pioneers who made their way across the Plains, the Mormons in particular deserve special comment. The year 1846 found them on their way West. Starting at Nauvoo, Illinois, they crossed the Mississippi, and then proceeded on to the Missouri River opposite Council Bluffs, where they established winter quarters. Preparations and arrangements for the great trek took place during that winter. Early the next spring 146 members made up the first Mormon train to cross the Plains. They followed the north bank of the Platte, instead of the south, as far as Fort Laramie, from which point they traveled the wagon trail to Fort Bridger. They arrived in the Salt Lake Valley on July 23, 1847, and, two hours after their arrival, plows were breaking the soil, and groundwork for an irrigation system was being laid.

The second Mormon expedition left winter quarters late in the spring of 1847. Over fifteen hundred made this trip and they took with them a large number of cattle, sheep, horses, hogs, and chickens. Other expeditions followed. By the fall of 1847, some four thousand "Saints" had arrived at the Great Salt Lake.

For those with limited means who could not purchase wagons, but were nevertheless desirous of reaching Zion, Brigham Young devised a new scheme. Handcarts, two-wheeled and large enough to hold a settler's belongings, were made at the request of the Mormon church. The summer of 1856 saw the first "handcart brigade," made up of five hundred men, women, and children, push its way across the Plains to the tune of a song which went as follows:

> Some must push and some must pull
> As we go marching up the hill;
> As merrily on the way we go
> Until we reach the Valley, Oh.

Thus imbued with religious zeal and determination, the brigade traveled twelve hundred miles in the same time that it would have taken to travel by prairie schooner. When the handcart went out of use in 1861, a total of 662 had been pushed across the Plains, while some three thousand people walked the entire distance.

The Mormon contribution to the history of the Plains rests in the fact that they were able to accomplish more, on less, than other emigrants. With limited means, the Mormons were able to make their way across the Plains in less time and with fewer hardships because, for one thing, they were fortunate in having an efficient organizer for their leader—Brigham Young. And equally as important was their knowledge of the probable conditions they would encounter. They had made a study of the Plains before embarking on their mission.

SERVICES ACROSS THE PLAINS

The migration of people to the West called for services such as the transportation of mail, passengers, and freight. The provision of these services demanded ingenuity, capital, and federal subsidy.

Mail and transportation first spanned the Southern Plains with the aid of federal subsidy. The project to initiate this service had the support of the United States Postmaster General, A. V. Brown, who was a Southerner. In 1857, John Butterfield, William G. Fargo, and associates were awarded a contract to render mail service for $600,000 per year. The well-known mail route, Butterfield Overland Mail, began at St. Louis and ended at San Francisco, passing through Fort Smith, El Paso, and Fort Yuma. The Overland was 2,795 miles in length and required about twenty-five days for travel. Measured in terms of service, Butterfield Overland Mail was a success.

Across the Central Plains, similar activities were, for a time, supplied by private enterprise—Russell, Majors, and Waddell. In 1855, Alexander Majors, an experienced freighter on the Santa Fé, went into business with William H. Russell and W. B. Waddell. Three years later, they were operating 3,500 covered wagons, employed 4,000 men, and owned 40,000 draft oxen. They freighted goods to western mining towns and to army posts. Their freighting business was such a success that they decided to undertake two additional ventures, the Pony Express and the Pike's Peak Express.

The famous Pony Express had a short-lived existence, namely from April 3, 1860, to October 24, 1861. In anticipation of a federal subsidy, Russell conceived the idea of a Pony Express to demonstrate the feasibility of a central route. It was a semi-weekly service from St. Joseph to San Francisco. The mail was carried by pony riders, and stations, ten to fifteen miles apart (about 190 in total), were built where both the rider and the horse could be accommodated or exchanged. The complete trip took about ten days and utilized about seventy-five riders and ponies. The charges were five dollars per half ounce letter, later reduced to one dollar, plus ten cents postage for each letter.

The expenses of the service were tremendous during the last few months of its existence and had to be subsidized by the rest of the company's business. But Russell had made his point. Mail could be transported cross-continent—speedily and safely. With the completion of telegraph service from Missouri to California on October 22, 1861, the Pony Express went out of existence, its heavy cost being a factor in the eventual bankruptcy of Russell, Majors, and Waddell.

The Pike's Peak Express, also owned by William H. Russell, was his contribution to the Union cause. Russell was a Northerner, interested in a central, not a southern, route. His loyalty to the Northern cause hatched the idea of a Pike's Peak route, operating from Missouri to Denver. He believed it could be done without government subsidies. But the failure of the Colorado mines proved to be the undoing of the Pike's Peak Express, resulting in its financial failure.

To save the investment, Russell, Majors, and Waddell purchased another concern, reorganized it, and started daily stage service between St. Joseph and San Francisco. The newly reorganized Central Overland, California, Pike's Peak Express Company (C.O.C.&P.P.), however, was soon called "Clean Out of Cash and Poor Pay." It, too, proved to be an unfortunate business venture.

The hopes of the three owners were given an additional blow when Congress in March, 1861, awarded the long-hoped-for government mail and express contract to the Butterfield Overland Express, rather than to Russell, Majors, and Waddell. The contract was granted with the understanding that Butterfield was to operate his services between St. Joseph and Placerville, California, by way of the central route. Butterfield granted Russell, Majors, and Waddell the right to convey the mail from St. Joseph to Salt Lake City. But even this concession did not help, for the firm went bankrupt and the business was purchased at public auction by Ben Holladay, on March 22, 1862.

For the next five years, Holladay dominated western transportation. In that time he had a business entailing five thousand miles of stage route which extended into Idaho, Montana, and Colorado. "Over this empire he ruled with an iron hand, riding constantly over his lines, goading his men on, and overawing the cutthroats who manned his stations until he became a legendary figure in the West." The term "Napoleon of the Plains" was appropriate. Realizing that the railroads would sooner or later take over, Holladay sold his interests in 1866 to Wells, Fargo and Company. He acted none too soon, for within three years stagecoaching was superseded by the railroads.

THE RAILROADS CROSS THE PLAINS

In 1853, following the insistent national demand, the first of four railroad surveys was made with a view to building a road to the Pacific. But Congress appropriated no money for construction at this early date.

In 1862, President Lincoln signed the bill for federal assistance in the construction of the first transcontinental railroad. The Central Pacific started building from the West in 1863. The Union Pacific started to build from the East in 1865. The tracks were joined at Promontory Summit, Utah, in 1869. They had spanned the nation, and the Oregon Trail had become a thing of the past. Again the task of crossing the Plains had been accomplished.

South of the Oregon Trail, the Kansas Pacific Railroad, originating at Wyandotte, opposite Kansas City, started building westward toward Denver in 1863. It was reaching out for the cattle trails of the Great Plains. Dodge City, south of the line, later on the Santa Fé system, was to become one of the famous cattle shipping points of the Southwest.

Then farther south, the famous Atchison, Topeka, and Santa Fé Railroad was chartered in 1859. This route, which paralleled the Santa Fé Trail, extended from Topeka to Santa Fé. Thus, when the latter was reached in 1879, the Santa Fé Trail, as the Oregon Trail had been earlier, was relegated to history as a once important thoroughfare across the Plains.

To the north of the Oregon Trail, the railroads came considerably later. The Northern Pacific reached Bismarck in 1872. It spanned the rest of the northern Great Plains and reached the Pacific in 1883. The Great Northern, still farther north, became a transcontinental road in 1893.

The completion of railroad building marked the end of the historical unity of the Plains when the traders and mountain-plainsmen roamed from north to south as well as from east to west. The laying down of the tracks, as subsequent events proved, forever partitioned the Plains into three parts: North, Central, and South, for the obvious reason that all main routes were henceforth lateral, thereby crippling the north-south flow of traffic.

THE CIVIL WAR IMPACT UPON
THE PLAINS

While all this activity was going on in the Plains along the routes used in crossing it, something was happening on the eastern threshold of the Plains. The passage of the Kansas-Nebraska Act, in 1854, injected into the national political arena the slavery issue which hitherto had been silenced by the Missouri Compromises of 1820 and 1850. In 1854, once again, the national issue became: What is to be the status of the territories, slave or free? This time the issue could not be quieted.

The Missouri Compromise of 1820 specified that, excluding Missouri, slavery was to be prohibited in the Louisiana Purchase territory north of 36° 30". The Missouri Compromise of 1850 provided that California be admitted as a free state, and stipulated that Utah and New Mexico be organized as territories with the understanding that the voters decide the issue of slavery. The Kansas-Nebraska Act, signed by President Pierce on May 30, 1854, set up two separate territories: Kansas and Nebraska, both on the west side of the Missouri and including most of the Louisiana Purchase area. It stipulated that the people were to decide for themselves whether or not this should be slave or free country. This provision formally repealed the Missouri Compromise of 1820. And, as one writer expressed it, "The fat was in the fire."

With the creation of the Kansas and Nebraska territories, it was not the gold seeker or the home seeker interested in the Pacific who rushed to Kansas and Nebraska, but the ordinary settler of certain deep convictions and opinions. He was not interested in "crossing"; he came to stay. He was, at the same time, an instrument of a diplomatic offensive designed to increase the voting power of either the North or the South. And with him—whether he came from New England, from the South, or from neighboring states—he brought traditions and cultural practices which worked well "back home." But how would these practices fit into the general scheme of things in his new habitat? Only time could tell.

The Civil War, in the form of the Kansas-Nebraska Act, had such a decided impact upon the Plains that a few of the details must be listed. The drama of this period was played, not to the west of the ninety-eighth meridian but to the east of it—the humid-area threshold to the Plains. It was in this period that certain humid-area institutions established themselves in the humid part of the Nebraska and Kansas Territories, and later flowed out into the Plains to help sway it the humid-area way.

This was the period when pro-slavery men settled at Leavenworth, Atchison, and Lecompton, and anti-slavery men, many from New England, settled Lawrence, Osawatomie, Manhattan, Wabaunsee County, and Topeka to hold these territories for their respective causes. The Reverend Henry Ward Beecher, of Brooklyn, was one of those who aided the cause of the Abolitionists. Sharps carbines were sometimes packed in cases and marked with the word "Bibles"—hence they became known as "Beecher's Bibles." It is said that Beecher believed that "the Sharps Rifle was a truly moral agency and that there was more moral power in one of those instruments so far as the slaveholders were concerned than in a hundred Bibles." Even John Brown, no longer a young man and one who carried a Sharps rifle in one hand, a Bible in the other, and a bowie knife in his belt, came to Kansas to stamp out slavery. He "taught the Kansans to fight back" and to protect themselves against the slavery men. Thus, to the threshold of the Plains, came the early skirmishes of the Civil War—the raids of the Jayhawkers and the Freebooters, and the guerrilla activities in the "Burnt District" of Missouri.

The postwar period saw the rise of such outlaws as Jesse James, the Ford Brothers, and others. It was the continued raiding of such outlaw elements on the cattle herds from Texas, on the way to the St. Louis market—plus the continual interference on the part of the Indians in Indian Territory, and plus the general hostility of the white settlers in southeast Kansas and southwest Missouri to the trailing of Texas cattle through their area—which turned the cattle drovers westward and then north, into the grasslands of the Plains.

This epilogue of the Civil War demonstrates the push of the humid-area civilization into the semiarid Plains—the attempt to seek land for statehood in order to sway politics in favor of North or South; the settlement of humid-area people who shaped the constitutions of these territories which were later carved into several states.

STRANGE EMPIRE IN CANADA

The youth in the Plains, in the course of his formal education, may learn about the exploits of Kit Carson in the Plains, the fierce struggle of the Kiowa and Comanche Indians for their homeland, the colorfully depicted "runs" of the pioneers to settle the Cherokee Strip and other Oklahoma territory, the Texas Rangers, the Colt revolver, the fight at the Alamo, independent nationhood and eventual statehood for Texas with the condition that it might be sometime divided into four states. If he does learn about these things, his appetite is whetted for Plains history—the Southern Plains.

But in the Northern Plains, too, there was an empire in the making. About this the youth of the Plains knows little or nothing. This strange empire, despite its failure, had ingredients similar to those found in the Southern Plains in Texas. But its history has been made available only recently to the plainsman—the first full English version having been written only in 1952. The history of the Northern Plains empire is found between the covers of a book entitled *Strange Empire,* by the late Joseph Kinsey Howard.

What were the components of this strange empire? The dates range between 1870 and 1885. The story begins with the dispossession of the Métis (the Indian-French racial mixture) in the humid Red River country of the North. These people, following their leader, Louis Riel, were pushed out of their heritage, into the semiarid Canadian Plains. There, attempts were made to create a new nation. The attempts might have been successful had Chief Joseph, and his Nez Percés, been able to escape from the United States across the border into Canada, or had Sitting Bull and his Sioux been able to do so. The joining of the Métis, the Canadian Plains Indian, and the Plains Indian of the United States, might have formed the foundation for an empire.

And there were influences from the humid-area Twin Cities

of Minnesota and the Red River which contributed to the misunderstanding. Canada was forced to hew a road across the Laurentian Plateau, north of the Great Lakes, to get an army into the Plains of Canada; otherwise Canada faced the prospect of violating the peace with the United States by bringing armed troops around the southern tip of the Great Lakes.

The fact is that Louis Riel escaped to the Plains of the United States and lived for a time near Lewistown and Fort Benton on the upper Missouri in Montana. Whisky was trailed by traders into Canada, up the Whisky Trail from Fort Benton, to help debauch the Indians. The Canadian Red Mounties, like the Texas Rangers, helped bring peace and order to this Plains frontier. Finally Riel returned to his people in Canada to lead them in their last and futile effort at obtaining justice. It was called a rebellion and Riel was hanged in 1885. The Canadian Plains were securely attached to the Canadian humid-area East, to the chagrin of some people south of the border.

Here, then, on the northern rim of the Plains, was historical drama and intrigue, and nationhood—real or threatened—just as in the case of Texas and Mexico on the southern edge of the Plains. Between these two areas, Plains historical events have been treated as an orphan—pertaining to a desert and "a land to cross."

CHAPTER 8

The Adapted Ways of the Early Cattlemen

The first whites to attempt permanent settlement of the Plains were the cattlemen. Though of great influence in parts of the region today, the period of their domination was brief, lasting from the time of the Civil War to about 1900. The dates for the beginning of the decline of the cattlemen's influence are usually given as the winter of 1885–86 and that of 1886–87.

During the early part of this short era the cattlemen succeeded in developing a way of life that grew out of the conditions in the region. A close study of this way of life would have avoided much of the tragedy that followed the coming of the homesteader.

After the Civil War there developed a contest between two ways of life in the Plains. On the one hand was the cattlemen's way, with roots in the Plains but without cities and formal institutions, and without formal civil government to support it; on the other hand was the way of humid-area man with the support of cities, institutions, and government. It was inevitable that the latter won out.

It must be repeated, for the sake of emphasis, that in this struggle the humid-area values won the upper hand for the very reason that they had the support of authority from outside the region. Not only did the humid-area culture have its centers of creation and its authority for government outside the Plains, but its power to "push" was located in the humid area just east of the Plains. When to this was added the "push" of sheer numbers of people, this total "subsidy" from outside the region naturally gave the humid-area way of living the upper hand.

The cattlemen's way of living even lacked numbers of people to assist in its survival. Consequently the cattlemen, and what they stood for, were often and unfairly described as "the outlaw and the criminal element"—the antisocial forces which attempted to keep civilization (the humid-area way) from establishing itself. Then, as today, the humid-area culture was insisting that it was suitable for the Great Plains.

ORIGIN OF THE CATTLEMEN'S CULTURE

How did this cattlemen's culture originate? As the emigrant trains crossed the Plains, usually with oxen and frequently trailing livestock for foundation stock in the new home, the area along the trail became overgrazed. The footsore draft oxen frequently had to be exchanged at river fords or frontier posts for trail-hardened animals. In the mountains of Colorado, Wyoming, and Montana, the mining camp population required beef. Often there were greater profits in selling high-priced beef over the butcher's block than could be had from the pans of the placer miners. For these reasons it became profitable to establish cattle herds in the favorable valleys of the mountain region and on the Plains proper.

The firm of Russell, Majors, and Waddell wintered fifteen thousand head of cattle along the Oregon Trail, in the mountains, as early as the winter of 1857–58. Ranches along the trails made and sold hay to the emigrant trains as early as the sixties. J. W. Iliff, the first cattle king on the northern range, got his start, about 1861, by supplying cattle to the Colorado mining towns from his headquarters along the South Platte.

In the South, the Mexicans had established a stock-growing industry along the Río Grande and its tributaries prior to 1800. The earliest Spaniards always were accompanied by herds of cattle, sheep, and goats, when they migrated into new lands. Even Coronado had herds with his army as he started his trip to the Plains. Thus the cattle industry was early and well-established in the southern part of the region.

As early as 1866, Nelson Story trailed a herd of 600 Texas longhorns from Dallas, Texas, all the way up the Bozeman Trail to the Gallatin Valley in Montana. This was the first herd trailed all the way from Texas, into the North. But even so, Nelson

Story's trip north occurred in the twilight of open-range cattle history on the Great Plains—just before the Union Pacific penetrated into Wyoming, and only seventeen years before the Northern Pacific entered the city of Bozeman, in the Gallatin Valley.

In fact, the cattle industry and the cattlemen were already established in the mountains and in the Great Plains—in the North and the South—before the history of the trail herders moving north began. The possibility of expanding their herds, so as to utilize to full advantage the enormous pastoral resources on every hand, depended upon a supply of cheap cattle that could be used for stocking the empty ranges, and upon a connection with the eastern market. Texas was the source of the cheap cattle.

Texas, like all the South, was economically prostrate in 1865 as a result of the Civil War. But it had cattle in large numbers— the longhorn, a mixture of Texas and Mexican breeds grown wild while Texas cattlemen were serving in the Confederate Army. The returning veterans needed capital. They could round up the loose cattle and ship them north. Thus started the history of the cattle trailing industry.

THE GROWTH OF THE CATTLE INDUSTRY

IN THE PLAINS

Before 1866 cattle had occasionally been trailed to St. Louis, but the real trailing of cattle out of Texas started in that year. The trail's end for the herds was Sedalia, Missouri, the railhead for the northern markets. There was no attempt at this time to get into the Great Plains.

But the trail herds met disaster from armed mobs on the way to Sedalia. Some of these mobs represented thieves and robbers—border renegades from Civil War days who were entrenched in the Ozark Hills. Some were Missouri farmers who were afraid of Texas cattle fever. To avoid these hazards the drovers trailed west into the Plains before reaching the border of Kansas and then turned north. After trailing north some distance, some herds traveled east to St. Joseph, while others kept on going north into Wyoming.

The Kansas Pacific Railroad had built an extension west to Lawrence, Kansas, in 1865, and by 1866 had reached to Topeka and Junction City. The following year it was extended to Hays City. The Atchison, Topeka and Santa Fé Railroad also built west, reaching Hutchinson and Dodge City in 1872. Thus sprang

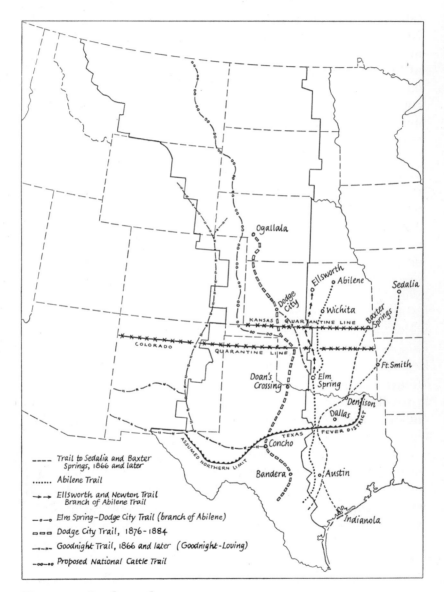

FIG. 12. Cattle trails.

up the trail cattle towns of the Plains—Abilene, Salina, and Ellsworth, along with Dodge City, a little south of the Kansas Pacific Railroad.

Joseph G. McCoy, a livestock shipper from Illinois, had dreams of bringing the cattle buyers and the Texas drovers together at the point where the cattle trails would reach the railroads. He selected Abilene for this purpose, soon after the rails got there. He tried to interest railroad men from the Kansas Pacific in financing a stockyard and the Missouri Pacific in giving favorable freight rates from the state line to St. Louis. Failing to get help from these sources, he at least obtained a contract from the Hannibal and St. Joseph Railroad for reduced freight rates from the Missouri River into Chicago. This is believed to be the reason why Chicago, rather than St. Louis, became the stockyard and slaughtering center for the cattle industry.

From this beginning the range cattle industry spread over the entire Great Plains region. Webb summarizes the situation as follows: "The first step was made when the Spaniards and Mexicans established their ranches in the Nueces County of southern Texas . . . ; the second step occurred when the Texans took over these herds and learned to handle them in the only way they could be handled—on horseback; the third step was taken when the cattle were driven northward to the market; the fourth came when a permanent depot was set up at Abilene which enabled trail driving to become standardized; the fifth took place when the overflow from the trail went west to the free grass of the Great Plains."

For a time the bison herds and the Indians were a hindrance to the growth of the cattle industry. But both were soon contained. The bison, in the Southern Plains, had been largely exterminated, or pushed into the area below the Arkansas River, by 1872. The army, with a surplus of generals who needed reputations and honor, succeeded in containing the Indians of the Southern Plains in 1874–75, chiefly the Cheyennes and the Comanches. In the north, the Sioux made their last stand at the Battle of the Little Big Horn in 1876.

Thus, after 1876, the cattle industry was free to move farther west and north—north beyond the southern railroads. Charles Goodnight moved into the Texas Panhandle in 1876. Large and small ranchmen moved north. Word of success spread to New

York, and Boston, and to England, Germany, Holland, and France. The story of 30 per cent profits attracted all kinds of capital, from speculators and titled persons as well as hard-fisted businessmen. Barbed wire was invented; railroad land grants could be purchased; and homesteads could be acquired.

Cattle were trailed north from Texas on the Goodnight-Loving Trail, starting in 1866. This route led west into New Mexico, then north along the Río Grande, and continued north-ward along the foothills of Colorado, into Nebraska and Wyoming. The Dodge City Trail extended from near Laredo in Texas, north to Dodge City, and then continued north to Ogallala.

There was, for a time, opposition to Texas cattle because of the possible diseases they might carry. This opposition came from Northern stockmen. Since the meeting of the Northern and Texas cattle occurred in the vicinity of the South Platte, Denver was the focal point for much of this expressed hostility. But the lure of profit soon overcame this obstacle, and the north-ern range in Idaho, Wyoming, and Montana became the stocker range—the area where Texas cattle might be fattened and ma-tured. In 1869, a million cattle and two million sheep were re-ported grazing in this northern area, over half this number in the area between Denver and the southern boundary of Wy-oming.

The Nelson Story herd of longhorns from Texas was followed by others. In the winter of 1867–68, Iliff went to New Mexico and purchased a herd from Charles Goodnight. He trailed them north to Cheyenne that winter. The Union Pacific, completed through this area in 1869, was now a means of transporting cattle to the Eastern market. The first cattle were shipped east out of Wyoming in 1870. During the later seventies, Ogallala and Sydney, Nebraska, and Pine Bluffs and Rock River in Wy-oming were leading livestock shipping points. In 1871, the ranges of western Nebraska and southern Wyoming received about 100,000 of the 630,000 head of cattle that crossed the Red River out of Texas.

The Wyoming cattlemen of the seventies were largely the men who had lived in the territory before the arrival of the Texas herds. They merely enlarged their operations and herds by the addition of longhorns. But some of the Texas drovers and cowhands stayed in Wyoming as ranch workers and as independent operators. Montana and the Dakotas also developed similar patterns.

Since Ogallala became the receiving point of the Texas cattle, it was here that the Northern and Southern stockmen met, and cattle herds shifted hands. From here cattle spilled over into Wyoming and on into Montana and the Dakotas. The fattened cattle were again trailed down to the Union Pacific, until the Northern Pacific was completed in 1883.

Typical of the large ranch operations on the Plains were the XIT and the Matador of the Texas Panhandle or those of Antoine de Vallombrosa, the Marquis de Mores in the Badlands of Dakota Territory. In a span of three short years, 1884–87, before he was thirty years of age, the Marquis controlled "hundreds of thousands of acres of grazing land in the Dakota Territory; became affiliated with the Mellon Brothers in financial enterprises; founded the Northern Pacific Refrigerator Car Company; launched a million-dollar packing plant in the wilderness (at Medora, North Dakota); established a newspaper, a hotel, and a town of several hundred people on the frontier; engaged in duels and had been acquitted of a charge of murder; and, finally, lost two million dollars in a co-operative ranching enterprise in the Dakota Territory." His rancher neighbors included a "four-eyed dude from New York" by the name of Theodore Roosevelt, later President of the United States; A. C. Huidekoper, founder of the famous H–T brand and a Harvard graduate; Pierre Wibaux, a Frenchman who later amassed a fortune in the cattle business but who just then lived nearby in a cave scooped out of the virgin earth. The Eaton brothers, founders of the first dude ranch enterprise, and C. B. Richards, who later established the Hamburg-American steamship line, were his neighbors. And there were others; small ranchers, cowhands, wolf hunters, the last of the buffalo hunters, and rustlers. There was also "Hell-Roaring" Bill Jones—often called "Foul-Mouthed Bill"—and Teddy Blue and Andy Adams who had come up the Trail. There also was Charlie Russell—the cowboy artist, who called himself an "average cowhand."

SETBACK FOR THE CATTLE INDUSTRY

The cattle industry soon became a highly speculative enterprise and was infiltrated by foreign influences. It became overextended. Cattle had become so numerous that prices fell drastically. The high profits had been squeezed out. The range had become overstocked and overgrazed. By 1886 the setting was ripe for disaster. E. S. Osgood (*The Days of the Cattleman*), states the situation this way: "With a rapidity that could almost be measured in months rather than years, every available bit of range in northern and central Wyoming was occupied; the country in eastern Montana, north of the Yellowstone to the southern boundary of the Indian reservation, was filled up, and herds began to look for favorable locations beyond the international boundary along the Saskatchewan River." Cattle crowded onto the market and the price fell from $4.25 cwt. in 1883 to $1.00 cwt. in the winter of 1887.

The only disaster yet to be experienced by the cattlemen, to destroy them, was winter blizzards on a large scale. These, too, came and added their havoc—the winter of 1885–86 in the Southern Plains and the winter of 1886–87 in the Northern Plains. The fences in the Southern Plains became barriers for drifting cattle which piled up, starved, trampled each other and, finally, froze to death. Cattle losses ranged from 40 per cent to 90 per cent of the herds. "Cowmen swore they could walk along the drift fence north of the Canadian River all the way from Indian Territory (in present Oklahoma) to New Mexico, and along another from Ellsworth to Denver—four hundred miles—without stepping off swelling carcasses of dead cows." Bankruptcy was general.

Until these winter tragedies occurred in both the Southern and the Northern Plains the open range system had prevailed. Cattle were not fed or sheltered in the winter. Only a few ranchers and cattle companies had established a more secure basis of operation, warned by the winter losses of 1880–81. For the most part, losses ranging from 5 to 10 per cent had already become a normal expectation—the wintering of cattle had never been more than a process of slow starvation. After the blizzards winter feeding of livestock became a more accepted part of range livestock practices.

DESCRIPTION OF
THE CATTLEMEN'S WAYS

What were the major practices of the range cattle industry that made it a separate way of life and what were some of the adapted traits that suited it especially to Plains conditions? Webb thought of the cattle industry as having arisen "in a natural manner and spread with amazing rapidity over the whole area to which it was adapted." He also described it as "new, without counterpart or analogy among the institutions of the humid country of the East. In short, it was an industry remarkably adapted to the country that it appropriated." Webb goes on to say that no sooner had the cattle kingdom been set up as a "natural institution adapted to its environment than the forces of the Industrial Revolution began to modify and destroy it. . . . From the East came the old institutions, seeking . . . to utilize the land after the manner of men in the humid timberlands. . . . Though the civilization of the cattle kingdom was as complete within itself as was that of the Old South, it was not independent, but subject to the general condition of the nation. It was affected by . . . the panics of 1873 and 1893, the boom of 1885, and the condition of the world market in general; it was affected by the railroad extension, the invention of barbed wire, and the adaptation of the windmill—things which altered the whole nature of the economy of range practice; finally, it was affected by the immigration of the small farmer, granger or nester, into the West."

Some of the separate institutionalized aspects of this original and adapted industry can be described in the terms in common use at the time. Mobility and flexibility were at the root of these adaptations. The unit of operation was the *ranch*, including the *home base* and the *range*, which were not always contiguous and required movement of the stock. The range was either *open* or *fenced*, and the former situation required rules very different from the latter. *Ranching*, very different from *farming*, was the activity of harvesting the natural vegetation by means of livestock. Those who handled the cattle were the *cowboys*.

In the beginning, all the range was *free* or *open range*, meaning unfenced. There was no ownership. *Control* was through appropriation in the sense of *first come*, first *use*. The ranch *headquarters* or base usually governed the location of the range.

Since water was scarce, the ranch headquarters were generally located along a river or creek and the land on either or both sides was the range for that base. This entitled the ranch headquarters to exclusive *control* of the range. The *customary range* was acquired by appropriation through notice in the nearest weekly newspaper, listing the *brand* and thus establishing, by personal decree, the extent, boundaries, and land marks of the particular range. This same definition of the customary range by each operator was on file in the *brand books* of the state or territory concerned. *Grass pirates,* those interlopers who had not established a base or customary range, were *trespassers* summarily dealt with by the established ranchers. *Rustling* and *brand blotting* early became heinous criminal offenses because they were methods used to encroach upon the open range property of those who had priority. The *cattlemen associations,* sometimes of the *vigilante* type, enforced the *range rules* with speed and dispatch, leaving no opportunity for doubt, discretion, or sympathy. The act of moving cattle from the customary range by others than the owner was clear evidence of rustling.

And these rules worked efficiently. Joseph Kinsey Howard (*Montana: High, Wide, and Handsome*) describes how many of these practices, rules, customary range definitions, and limits of ranch boundaries became part of the Montana statutes as early as 1877. He shows how John H. Conrad of Fort Benton "was socially and economically ostracized" when he brought a herd of cattle into the customary range claimed by the Niobrara Cattle Company in Central Montana in 1855. The *local cattleman's association* passed a resolution which read as follows:

> "WHEREAS, the custom of disregarding the prior rights of others on the range is becoming frequent, annoying and damaging in a high degree to range interests. . . .
> "RESOLVED, That we discountenance such action [as Conrad's] as unfair and injurious to the best interests of the country and that we refuse to recognize or work with any parties infringing upon the prior rights of others by turning on a range previously occupied and be it further
> "RESOLVED, That we refuse to work with or in any way handle the cattle of said J. H. Conrad."

So were the grass pirates treated. During the *roundup,* the *roundup boycott* was applied to offenders as in the case of Conrad. Sometimes the grass pirates retaliated by having a roundup sooner than the regular one, thus appropriating the unbranded *mavericks* into their herds. Such *sooner roundups* were forbidden by law, making it illegal to brand on the open range between December 1 and May 1.

The *divides* of watersheds were the significant *boundary lines* for ranch identification. One of the tasks of the cowboys was to *drift* a neighbor's cattle *across the divide*. This was a neighborly act. The roundup was staged twice a year, once in the spring and again in the fall. It was a community undertaking and the calves were *branded* and *earmarked*. When cattle were taken to a new range in the spring, *trailing* was the descriptive term for the activities involved. When they were taken to market in the fall, the *drive* was the customary descriptive term applied to the operations.

On the range, there were rules that applied to the *number* and *quality* of *bulls*, the time for *breeding*, and other stock improvement practices. These were usually *local association rules*, generally not written into law. Many of these extralegal rules are still in effect in *grazing districts* and on *forest grazing lands*. In spite of these range practices, the early cattlemen had difficulty in following an improved breeding program.

On the trail, at the roundup, or in his work on the range the cowboy usually had a *string* of horses assigned to him from the *cavvy* or *remuda,* by the wagon boss of the *outfit's* horses. The cavvy was handled by the *wrangler* and the *night hawk*. Trail and roundup supplies were carried in *the wagon,* usually driven by the *cook,* who had the night hawk as a *camp-helper* to assist with the chores. The cowboy's *gear,* including his dress and his *saddle,* were frequently his only possessions.

Rules concerning the handling of the roundup, the exchange of help, the handling of mavericks and the branding of stock were generally local association rules. The *local association* was an important institution for conducting the administrative business of the industry in a community. Some of these rules were incorporated into statutes by the legislatures of the individual states. Occasionally, for interstate affairs, there were rules and statutes promulgated by the various *state cattlemen's associations* in co-operation with one another. These were important in the period of trailing cattle and on the drive to market. For these purposes certain trails were officially designated as trails, with rules applying to *bedding, watering* and *feeding* enroute.

The problem of controlling the amount of grazing on the *public domain* was a difficult one to handle, especially when dry seasons occurred. In the mountain area, the added distinction between *winter* and *summer grazing lands* added other difficulties. The control of *water holes* and *streams* was the major means of prohibiting encroachment by others. Drifting the neighbor's cattle across the divide was another. Allowing adequate *reserve feed* for one's own stock was still another. Beyond that, the control was extralegal and often illegal in the eyes of humid-area law.

These individual methods of dealing with the problem of the control of grazing had to be finally submitted to *association rules,* and were a major factor in the organization and maintenance of the local association as an administrative instrument. These associations were first organized in Colorado as early as 1872, as Texas herds began to move north. Wyoming and the Dakota Territories soon followed with such associations. In addition to protection against trail cattle, these associations had to protect themselves and their herds against Indians, rustlers, land speculators, and sheepmen. They were forced to seek police protection for the entire community, and against disease among their cattle; provide for the control and extermination of wild animals which preyed on their herds; educate territorial governors who were usually imported from a humid and forested area; and study and promulgate their legislative needs as compared with those demanded by the miners and other vested interest groups.

The cattlemen also had to deal with the federal government in matters of controlling Texas fever, and meat inspection matters for the urban markets in the East and in foreign countries. Thus, a bill was passed for the creation of the Bureau of Animal Industry in the United States Department of Agriculture in 1884. The function of this bureau was expanded in 1890 to include meat inspection.

During the latter part of the cattleman's era, the rancher of the Plains found himself in difficulty concerning the control of land. His system of control did not involve ownership. The humid-area homestead program, on the other hand, placed the emphasis upon ownership. The coming of barbwire, the windmill, the reaper, and the railroad land grants all assisted the latter.

So the rancher had to make the transition from the free and open range to the fenced range, and the acquisition of sufficient land to round out his operations, usually through ownership, became a pressing need. He did this with reluctance. Sometimes he fought pitched battles with the farmers. Often he resorted to subterfuge by having his cowboys acquire the homestead and then turn it over to him. By strategy and devise, and with the help of some capital, some of the ranchers were able to hang on. Some were fortunate to live in or near areas not fit for agriculture and could survive by leasing public domain. Others emerged as ranchers after the first settlers had gone bankrupt. In the meantime much enmity had been built up between ranchers and farmers, and between ranchers and the federal government—enmity that still expresses itself as opposition to governmental agencies and bureaucrats.

Following the winters of 1885–86 and 1886–87, the cattle industry continued in less spectacular form, but still on the basis of some of the original development, modified in part only. The problems of size of operation are not yet solved. The relation of public domain to privately owned lands is still an issue today. The relation of the ranch base to grazing lands at some distance away is still an unsolved issue. The question of how to obtain adequate feed in an extended drought period is a major public policy issue today. Finally, the pros and cons of a beef support price, or an alternative, have been the subject of much discussion in recent years. Underlying all these issues is the question of an agricultural policy for ranchers that is shaped to cope with the conditions peculiar to ranching in the Plains region.

It is clear then that the basic element of the original cattleman's way of life had mobility at its very heart. There was flexibility too in many forms. The element of reserve was least prevalent. The coming of the homesteaders and a humid-area land settlement policy placed a premium on immobility. Thus the old cattleman's way was restricted and hemmed in. It became choked off by the facts of immobility and inflexibility.

Where it survived in its most typical form it did so only because it was allowed to keep some of its mobility and some of its flexibility, and eventually, was supplemented by the idea of reserves in the sense of controlled and regulated use of the public domain, rotation pastures, reseeding, and a permanent feed base.

It might have been wise public policy for the nation to stop and look at the early cattleman's way of life before settling on a land policy for the semiarid Plains. Having failed to do so, the nation can still look to this historical example as a guide for a policy today, for the issues are not yet settled. Not alone the ranchers, but the wheat and cotton farmers of the Plains would benefit from a revised and better-informed national attitude towards the control and use of land in the Plains area.

CHAPTER 9

Sheepmen's Days and Ways

The history of the sheepman on the Plains and in the West has not been recorded in as dramatic a fashion as that of the cattleman. However, the sheepman faced similar problems of adaptation and need for local invention. The industry illustrates more clearly than the cattle industry the role of mobility in the Plains.

The Western open-range system of herding and handling sheep represents a set of institutional patterns clearly of Western origin. The farm flock system of the humid East, imported from the humid areas of Europe, came to a halt near the ninety-eighth meridian. Edward Norris Wentworth (*America's Sheep Trails*) says the following in this respect: "Along the hundredth meridian, the states [the Dakotas, Nebraska, Kansas, Oklahoma, and Texas] characteristically developed farm flocks in their eastern sections and range flocks in the west. Beyond Fort Pierre, the expanse of territory, the ravages of predators, and the insecurity of operation under threat of homesteads made farm flock routines impossible, and the herding methods so distinctive of the Southwest imperative."

THE SPANISH ORIGINS OF
THE SHEEP INDUSTRY

The range sheep industry had its origin in New Mexico and the Southwest—a Spanish background modified by conditions in Mexico. The conquerors from Spain, in their travels in the New World, always had goats and sheep on their expeditions. These animals furnished fresh meat and by-products such as milk and cheese. Sheep were especially advantageous in that they could do with less grass and water than cattle, and had the flocking instinct rather than the individual roaming habit. They did, however, slow the rate of travel.

Cortez imported sheep and cattle into Mexico in 1519–21. Coronado, who traveled into the Plains in 1540 with an army supplied by a band of five thousand sheep, met up with the Indians, who recognized the significance of sheep apparently from their experience with the remnants of de Vaca's flocks. When Coronado left New Mexico in 1542 he apparently left a band of sheep with several of the friars who stayed with the Indians. This probably was the origin of the sheep industry among the Hopi Indians.

By 1595 sheep, horses, and cattle were numerous in the Spanish provinces just south of the Río Grande. It is recorded that two hundred thousand sheep were sent to Mexico City from this area in 1595. Captain Juan de Oñate took 483 wool sheep and 617 mutton sheep up the Río Grande to the vicinity of Santa Fé in 1598. The Texas Mission settlers also raised sheep. Wentworth says that, "The close of the eighteenth century saw Spanish flocks in eastern Texas, in the San Antonio region, in the mountains above Santa Fé and Taos, and throughout the New Mexico valleys, as far north as the Gila in eastern Arizona, in the Moqui Country, and up to San Francisco Bay on the Pacific." This was before Lewis and Clark went up the Missouri and before Lt. Zebulon Montgomery Pike took his trip to the Rockies and New Mexico. Pike records the fact that Don Francisco Garcia of El Paso del Norte owned 20,000 sheep and 1,000 cattle; and 300,000 sheep were traded annually from the area into Mexico.

The herding system grew up in this Southwest country among the Spaniards and the Mexicans. Remains and records indicate that shepherds congregated in small shepherds' villages on the Plains, and penned their flocks by night, usually within stone walls. The sheep furnished wool, meat, milk, and cheese for the herder while he was away from home. It was the practice to take the sheep from these feeding centers to the range beyond for several days, where there was no water but good grass, and then return them to the main camp for a short time. Burros were used to carry water and food for the herder.

Such a procedure made for extensive mobility of the flocks. Most of the flock owners lived in southern New Mexico, even in Mexico, but their herds roamed far and wide over the area, in the mountains, and on the plains. The Spanish governor of New Mexico, in 1800, was reported to have owned two million head of sheep, handled by 2,700 peons who ranged from super-intendents to herders and cooks. Don José Leandro Perea had over two hundred thousand in 1846, which he had farmed out in bands of 2,500 head to *partidarios*. These *partidarios* were herders with families, who had a few head of sheep of their own and were seeking to establish flocks of their own on a share-increase basis. The system of peonage provided many grades of labor, frequently on such an exploitative basis that poverty was general. The lands were grants from the crown, and thus the idea of the open range had its origin.

This is not the place to trace in detail the Spanish-Mexican system. It is sufficient to point out that the system of handling sheep was an indigenous development, based on trial and error and much hardship. The system found its way into Texas, where additional modifications were made. Together the Texan and the Mexican systems furnished a basis on which the Americans of the West could build the open range sheep system as it was finally developed in the Plains.

SHEEP TRAILS OF THE WEST

Starting in 1853 and running throughout the Civil War and immediately following, farm-flock sheep were trailed from the Midwest states across the Great Plains into California and Oregon especially. The trailing conditions required the de-velopment of new techniques of handling open-range flocks. Dr. Thomas Flint was among the first to be such a trail flockmaster. Between 75,000 and 100,000 sheep were trailed in this manner during the decade 1851–61. During this period New Mexico was also a source of sheep. About 550,000 head were trailed from New Mexico to California between 1860–70; another 100,000 were taken to Colorado, Kansas, Nebraska, and Wyoming.

Sheep were an effective way of utilizing the arid and also the forested portions of these far Western states. Soon, however, such areas were fairly well stocked. The wool could be marketed by rail to the East, but the disposal of the meat in the West represented a problem because of the small population resident there.

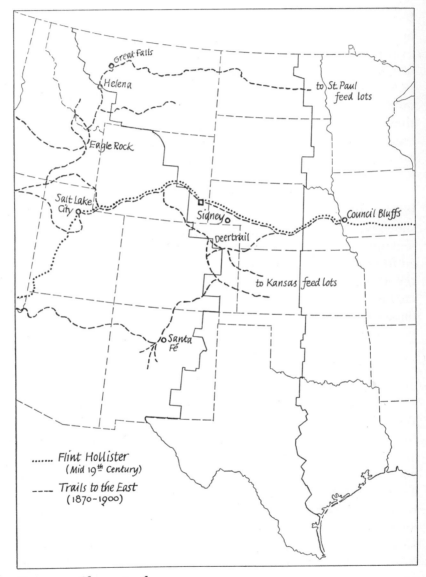

FIG. 13. Sheep trails.

120

Thus, starting in the late seventies and extending through the nineties, sheep began to move from west to east for purposes of stocking and grazing the Plains. Some of these sheep were also destined for rail heads and then to Eastern markets. Even when rail service was available, it was profitable to trail the wethers at a slow pace, allowing them to grow, mature, and take on weight while crossing the country, and then to ship them by rail the final stretch to feed lots or to slaughterers. The period of this trailing often lasted as long as seven or eight months.

Figure 13 gives the location of the major sheep trails leading from west to east. The major characteristics of the open-range sheep industry included the following: (a) the availability of public domain, (b) the trailing of sheep long distances while they matured and fattened, (c) the mobile character of the operations, and (d) the need to adapt the industry to the varying local conditions. These same characteristics typified the sheep industry for the non-trailing operators, except that distances covered were shorter than on the long trails. For example, the local sheepmen from the vicinity of Great Falls, Montana, would start their herds of ewes and lambs east in the spring after lambing and continue to graze them along the Missouri. En route, the ewes would be sheared and the wool shipped from railroad points along the way. The flocks would continue east into North Dakota. In the fall, the flocks would be sorted, the lambs sent to feeders and to market, and the ewes would be trailed back to the home range that fall and early winter.

THE SHEEPMAN'S WAYS

The characteristics of the range-sheep industry, in contrast with the farm-flock operations east of the ninety-eighth meridian, show a decided difference in organization. The farm-flock operations were based on the use of fences, and on intensive handling of each sheep. The industry thrived on the expectation of having twin and even triplet births; on non-seasonal breeding, lambing, and shearing so that the production would be great; and on a type of lamb that would yield the highest weight and greatest possible wool production.

The *open-range* system depended upon *herding*, and *for-*

aging over large areas, including *movement from winter to summer range and back to winter range.* A ewe could readily support only *one lamb,* and strains with that capacity were prized. Lambing took place in the open. *Breeding, lambing,* and *shearing* were of necessity limited to certain seasons only, in order to handle the *large bands* efficiently. Success for this type of operation depended upon numbers of sheep and less on quality of meat and wool. The type of wool covering desired was that which was open about the face to permit sight of danger, and *open about the legs* to permit cleaner wool.

Mobility of the band was at a premium in this herding system. Sheep could do without water for a time, but preferred running or live streams to standing water. They could subsist on snow or ice runoff and on the succulence of plants in bloom alone, if necessary. Thus, they could utilize range not used by cattle. Sheep would start to *graze* early in the morning, move as a flock, move while grazing, rest at noon, graze again later in the day, and then *bed down* for the night. On the trail they covered from seven to ten miles per day. All this required special techniques for handling sheep.

Other institutionalized patterns, invented and developed around the mobility of the herd, were the *herder* who had many duties and had to have the "patience of Job," *the wagon, the dogs, shearing, lambing, dipping,* and a host of other techniques. Recently, the Texans have developed the *fenced pastures* for sheep, thus changing these operations somewhat.

The early sheepman depended upon the *public range* as much as did the cattleman. He used the ideas of the *customary range, priority* in holding land, the *divide* as the boundary, and the *living stream* as headquarters in much the same way as the cattleman. In addition he had the patterns belonging to the *trailing system* and *rules governing trailing.*

The sheepman came into the Plains at a somewhat later date than the cattleman—usually by ten years or more. Therefore, the sheepman generally found himself without priority in established areas, and was considered a *trespasser.* If he utilized the farther reaches of the divide—the public domain proper which could be considered less of a customary range for the cattleman than the range close to the ranch headquarters—he was again considered a trespasser. Again, when he trailed his

122

sheep across the customary range to some more distant place, still unclaimed, or to market, the slow pace of the herd also put the sheepman into the category of a trespasser. Only when the sheepman arrived at *unclaimed range* was he able to invoke the same rules and privileges of the range as those possessed by cattlemen. Thus, there were frequent conflicts between sheepmen and cattlemen.

At first, in an established area, the sheepmen belonged to the same *livestock association* as the cattlemen, for purposes of *control* and *administration* of the range. Frequently the conflict between the two groups was so intense that the sheepmen formed their own associations. In a sheep area, the sheepmen had their own associations. Generally, however, they had weaker associations than the cattlemen, largely because, except in headquarter areas, they were far more mobile than the cattlemen.

SIMILARITIES BETWEEN THE WAYS
OF THE CATTLEMEN AND THE SHEEPMEN

The interests of sheepmen and cattlemen were, however, very similar. The problems of the range and the environmental conditions of the Plains exerted similar pressures, and the solutions were nearly alike. Mobility and flexibility were at the root of both sheep and cattle operations. Actually, many ranchers had both sheep and cattle, and the two were not in as much conflict as has been so often implied.

The problems created by the trespassing sheepman were the same as those created by the trespassing homesteader and the trespassing cattleman. Who had the right to the unfenced range? How much and under what conditions were those rights maintained? What system of land utilization should predominate—that created by humid-area legislative forces, or that created by the conditions in the region?

Like the cattleman's way, the sheepman's way consisted of local inventions on the Plains or in areas to the west. It was a highly developed system, created by trial and error, but adequate to the environmental conditions of the region. It filled a gap in the settlement of the Plains at a time when the westward-moving humid-area culture actually came to a halt on the ninety-eighth meridian for a period of forty years.

But the sheepman's institutions, adapted though they were, were finally disregarded and overcome—first by the speculation, introduced from the humid area, to which the sheepman, like the cattleman, had to yield, and secondly, by the onslaught of the homestead movement.

What might an adapted land control and settlement pattern have been like for the Plains had the ways of the sheepmen, like those of the cattlemen, become the accepted patterns for living in the region?

As in the case of the cattlemen, the ways of the sheepmen succeeded because of the mobility inherent in the system. When mobility was curtailed, the operations became less successful and the range was used less effectively. Flexibility was also prominent in the operations, best exhibited in the trailing arrangements of ewes and lambs on the road to market. Again, as in the case of the cattleman, practices having to do with reserves were least conspicuous in the sheep operations. Such practices have been of more recent origin, again in the form of controlled grazing on the public domain, in rotation pasturing and grazing, in reseeding, and in greater dependence upon feeding operations.

CHAPTER 10

Hesitation along the Ninety-eighth Meridian

For several decades prior to 1880, in spite of the Homestead Act, the westward push of settlement was almost stationary and came to a near halt along the ninety-eighth meridian. People from the humid and forested East crossed the Plains by the several trails but did not settle in the Plains in any large numbers. During the decade and a half following the Civil War, cattlemen established themselves in the region and sheepmen roamed about in it, but the agriculturists appeared to hesitate. For utmost accuracy, we may say that, while settlement did occur on the Plains, it was an arrested thing, lacking the drive of earlier and later movements.

And there were good reasons for such hesitation. That the climate was different was apparent. There were no trees and few stones for fencing, for marking off land boundaries, or for home building. Water for livestock and for humans was scarce. Railroads were few, and the prospects of having neighbors nearby were dim. Space was something of a threat. And in addition, the ninety-eighth meridian marked the eastern boundary of Indian territory, set aside for Indian use by a federal act in 1825. Indians from other parts of the nation had been relocated here.

THE COMING OF FIRST SETTLERS

The first significant movement of agricultural settlers into the borders of the Plains states occurred about 1854, incident to the passage of the Kansas-Nebraska Act. By 1880, both Kansas and Nebraska were well settled as far west as the ninety-eighth meridian, but not beyond it.

The situation was similar for the other states along the eastern edge of the Plains, with the exception of Texas. The first white settlement in South Dakota, for example, occurred in the eastern part, in the vicinity of Sioux Falls, Flandreau, and Medary about 1857. The next settlement was at Vermillion where a church society was organized and a school was built in 1860. And in 1868, Joseph Ward brought his bride and undertook to found a parish and a college at Yankton. West of there, settlement had not taken place by 1870.

The Selkirk Colony, founded in 1812 in Canada, attempted to project settlements along the full length of the Red River into North Dakota during the early fifties. Charles Cavalier attempted to establish a Protestant mission at St. Joseph in 1852, but it failed and the establishment of Fort Abercrombie in 1858 brought only a few whites into North Dakota. It was not until 1870 that a permanent white agricultural settlement was established in North Dakota.

Following these small protrusions, there were two settlement booms in the Dakota Territory, one during 1868–73, and the other during 1873–78. But with the exception of the invasion of the Black Hills, where gold was discovered in 1875, these "spurts" had no effect on the quiet western front west of the ninety-eighth meridian.

Then there was Oklahoma. It was the last of the eastern tier of the Great Plains states to be settled. Established as an Indian Territory in 1834, it was closed to white settlement and not until President Harrison opened the Oklahoma District, a relatively small area in the center of the present state, for homestead entry "at and after the hour of twelve o'clock noon, on the twenty-second day of April, 1889," was this central portion thrown open to whites. The remainder—most of the present state—remained under tribal jurisdiction until statehood in 1907.

In other words, the frontier line at the ninety-eighth meridian from 1850 to 1880 was stationary, not only because of the Indians on the Plains, but because of a basic recognition that this vast area was different from the humid and forested area through which the settlers had come.

The region did not become attractive for settlers until certain inventions had been introduced. These included transportation, fencing, water, housing, and certain new farm equipment. More specifically these inventions were the railroads, barbed wire, the windmill, the sod house, and the steel plow, the drill, and other equipment.

THE ROLE OF THE RAILROADS

It is readily apparent that the railroads were a significant factor in the settlement of the Plains. Not only were they the major means of transportation across the Plains, hauling people, raw materials, and manufactured products, but they were also the colonizing agents. Excluding the Great Northern Railway Company, the four major transcontinental roads received extensive land grants from the government.

The Union Pacific, for example, received twenty sections of public land and a government loan of $16,000, as a second mortgage, for each mile of construction on the Plains. The Northern Pacific, on the other hand, received twenty sections of public domain in the states and forty sections in the territories per each mile of construction. Likewise, favorable land grants were made to the Santa Fé and to the Texas and Pacific, which later transferred its land rights to the Southern Pacific. These lands were either leased or sold. But few settlers were willing to make a purchase unless they knew what they were buying; hence, it was necessary that they be shown the "good, rich productive lands."

Even the Great Northern—a transcontinental route not subsidized by land grants—engaged in the same vigorous sort of advertising. Its founder, James J. Hill, sincerely believed that the Plains could be thickly settled—one family to every 160 or 320 acres. "He would force this 'wasted' empire into the frame of his vision: his picture of little green fields and little white houses and big red barns, with lightning rods to deflect the shafts of the Northwest's primeval gods." Like the others, the Great Northern offered excursion rates, prizes for the best wheat grown, and provided emigrant and demonstration trains.

Aside from bringing settlers and hauling their products and consumer goods, the railroads served another important function. They helped save the remnants of the cattle industry. Ranchers, who foresaw that they could not long depend upon the vast public domain, purchased railroad land. It was reported, for instance, that in Wyoming the Union Pacific, in 1884, "sold in large, compact tracts (lands) . . . for grazing and ranch purposes. A prompt and ready sale . . . disposed of the great bulk of available land, the transactions aggregating 2,081,130 acres and representing an almost solid, continuous body from the eastern boundary of the territory west to the vicinity of the North Platte River at Fort Steele." This practice closed some of the lands to settlement by homesteaders.

But, the railroads brought unfortunate conditions and ways along with the good. In the East, they came subsequent to towns and settlements, but in the Plains they preceded the population. Townsites were laid out and named in arbitrary fashion. Speculation in townsites became extensive. Webb points out that soon after settlement began there were "ten times as many paper roads as there were real roads. These theoretical roads ran everywhere, arousing the most intense excitement in the scattered inhabitants and leading to ruinous competition in putting up houses, to rivalry between places that got the roads and the ones that failed to get them."

Secondly, the railroads, in the main, crossed the Plains in east-west directions, which in due time meant a loss of the former consideration given the area from north to south. In fact, it is only since the coming of the railroad that the region has lost its unity. The railroads definitely directed the course of settlement and prescribed the settlement pattern.

Thirdly, railroading made a hinterland of the Plains. Extensive settlement of the area had to wait until the railroads came. But to get them into the region, subsidization, credit, and finance were necessary. These, in turn, could be obtained only in the financial centers—the cities of the East—which, in turn, demanded the processing of the raw materials of the region. The railroads were the first major vehicle by means of which the humid-area influence made the Great Plains a colony of the humid East.

THE ROLE OF FENCING

In the early days, without fences, livestock wandered off or were killed by marauders or joined the herds of others.

Range cattle and horses, as well as wild stock, readily trespassed onto the farmer's grain fields. Since the Plains were short of trees and stones, materials were scarce for fencing. The practice of "chasing off" what one could legitimately call his own became most serious. At the same time, it was costly to transport the stakes and riders for a rail fence. Barbed wire was still unknown. Therefore, there was hesitation in settling the region.

These conditions became so severe that newspapers and magazines devoted much space to discussion of these matters. The subject of fencing became the object of concern and study by the United States Department of Agriculture. The Plains could not be settled until adequate materials for fencing became available.

Hedges such as Osage orange or bois d'arc, hyacinth, thorn locust, and mesquite were suggested as a solution to the fencing needs. There was much in the way of literature concerning the planting, cultivation, and final hedgerow treatment of hedge fencing, and nurseries were founded for the purpose of growing the seedlings on a commercial scale. But the Great Plains were a semiarid land where, under the best of conditions, hedges would grow only slowly, and where for countless centuries, nature had found it impossible to grow trees. Some other type of fencing device was necessary.

Inventors came forth with an answer to the problem—the barbed wire. One story is that there was a housewife in De Kalb, Illinois, who was much concerned about her garden flowers. She asked her husband to place a wire fence around them to ward off the dogs. But since the plain wire was no barrier, the husband, J. F. Glidden, wound small pieces of wire in the form of barbs around the main strands. According to another story, Glidden hit upon the idea of a barb as he was observing an exhibit at a local fair. The exhibit was a strip of wood through which long nails had been driven. The exhibit showed how the wood could be attached to a plain wire, and thus keep the stock from going through the fence.

Whichever of the two stories served as an inspiration, Glidden started to experiment. By accident one day, some wires became entangled, and, while picking them up, he became inspired with the idea that two wires could be twisted, one upon the other, in such a way that they could hold the barbs in place.

The idea worked. By using a small crank on a grindstone, he was able to twist the wire with greater ease than doing it by hand. Such is the origin of the barbed wire fence.

While there were others who were working on the problem independently, and while some may have been well on the way in their efforts in perfecting the barbs, Glidden, according to the scholars on the subject, was the first to be successful.

Though the need for something equivalent of barbed wire was great, many—including the U. S. Patent Office—had to be convinced that such a danger to stock and man was the answer. Glidden was forced to submit his application three times—the last application being almost identical with the first. The patent was granted in 1874. Two years later, in 1876, the Washburn and Moen Company, manufacturers of plain wire at Worcester, Massachusetts, came into possession of all the existing patents but one. And with this move, the manufacture of the barbed wire fence was started.

The estimated production and sale of barbed wire grew from 10,000 pounds in 1874 to 80,000,000 pounds in 1880. In 1874 the wire sold for $20 per hundred pounds compared to $1.80 per hundred pounds in 1897. To introduce the use of the barbed wire among farmers and ranchers was not the easiest task. It was difficult to overcome tradition and habit, but once it caught on, it spread like prairie fire.

The advent of the barbed wire was one factor in the decline of the range cattle kingdom. It speeded the disappearance of the free range, the open range, and the cattle trailing industry. Fence cutting became customary but was soon declared to be a crime. Barbed wire meant that the homesteader—the farmer—could settle on the Plains.

Again, with the good came the bad, particularly isolation. Oftentimes, fenced-in ranches and farms spelled a restricted and confined outlook—the points of view "bounded by the limits of the fences." Only recently, a true son of an old-time cattleman from eastern Montana, not a young man at that, expressed in conversation his deep bitterness and rancor about the sodbuster. Perhaps the barbed wire, if one gives consideration to what life might have been under conditions of the open range and the unfenced farm, brought isolation for rancher and farmer alike.

INVENTIONS TO MAKE WATER AVAILABLE

But the fencing of the homestead and the range was not enough to make settlement practicable. More serious still, for both the rancher and the farmer, the barbed wire fence often meant a shortage of water—more limited yet than before. Many a rancher or farmer found that the water hole he believed to be his was actually outside of his 160-acre homestead, encircled by a barbed wire fence. At times, the need for water became very acute. The struggle among ranchers and between ranchers and farmers for the use of the infrequent water holes or the limited stream sites represents one of the more tragic chapters in the history of the region. Harsh words, legal suits, physical violence, and sometimes gun war took place among neighbors and members of a community.

Water shortages and needs on the Plains cannot be overemphasized. Few creeks and rivers are live streams; most of them merely carry runoff from snow and cloudbursts. These are sometimes spanned by dams to hold water for a time. Lands nursed by springs and containing artesian water are limited. Therefore, the chief and most reliable source of water is the deep well, often drilled through a hard rock formation and operated by a pumping apparatus. The well development in the Plains had to await the creation of mechanized methods and the appearance of specialized well drillers—itinerants who drilled the wells and generally walled them with metal casings. It required a skilled artisan and one who had the equipment for the job. Once the well was dug, the task of raising water from great depths represented a problem in terms of time, labor, and power. The source of power was, at first, the windmill, and then later, the internal-combustion engine.

The self-governing windmill was apparently invented in 1854 by a "pump doctor" who manufactured the first ones at South Coventry, Connecticut. Because of the inconvenience and high cost of shipping to the West, where the windmills were in demand, the factory was moved from South Coventry to Chicago in 1862. One of the first buyers was the Union Pacific Railroad, which bought seventy windmills when it built its road across the continent. The windmill was also purchased by many small

towns for municipal uses. Beginning in the seventies, it was purchased by cattlemen, and still later by the settlers.

In addition to supplying water for livestock and home use,
the windmill made possible the irrigation of the garden and the
home lawn. Thus it assisted in supplementing the farm income
and added a bit of luxury about the home. Nature, in the form
of relatively constant winds, was harnessed to aid man in the
Plains. Settlement and the use of the windmill went hand in
hand. Here is an illustration of a technique whose widespread
use, if not invention, came about as the result of existing needs
on the Plains, for the windmill did not come into extensive use
until men started to settle in the Great Plains area.

SOD HOUSE AND TAR PAPER SHACK

Along any Plains highway the traveler occasionally
comes across a monstrosity of a home—a two-story house with
outside walls only partially finished, some of the shingles wind-
blown, and the exterior unpainted. It is not adapted to the Plains
by taste, looks, or comfort.

The Indian tipi was picturesque, and comfortable in winter
and in summer. The settler of the East and of the prairie country, too, had his own home and hearth traditions. The log cabin
or the stone house were made of native materials, and wood for
fire was near at hand. The building bees were among the more
colorful neighborhood and community activities of these forest
people. Occasionally, the homesteader on the Plains built a log
cabin or a stone house for his bride or the family to follow. The
cottonwood floor boards may have warped soon and the rafters
and ridge poles may have sagged readily but it was a cabin
home, nevertheless.

But for the most part, the Plains had neither forests nor stone
in quantity. It was necessary, therefore, to invent a new type of
home—the dugout, the sod house, and later, the tar paper shanty.
The women had to learn to live in these with the aid of an inconvenient stove, often a hay burner, and the smell of buffalo
chip smoke. Bugs and insects were numerous, as were snakes.
There was threat of loss from fire and the ruination of household
goods from leaks in the roof and penetration of water through

the sod walls. No wonder women went mad! It took courage to live under such conditions, and sometimes flight into the realm of mental images was a satisfying escape.

The experiences of Howard Ruede are typical. A bachelor, recently come from Pennsylvania and a printer by trade, he settled in Osborne County in the plains of Kansas in 1877. His family—father, brothers, mother, and sister—followed individually in the next years.

Upon his arrival he and a friend located their claim and then lived, for a time, with a neighbor who "thought he could make room for us until we had a place. . . . We have good fare, too, though Syd would turn up his nose at the side meat. . . . This is a sod house, plastered inside. The sod wall is about two feet thick at the ground, and slopes off on the outside to about 14 inches at the top. The roof is composed of a ridge pole and rafters of rough split logs, on which is laid corn stalks, and on top of those are layers of sod. The roof has a very slight pitch, for if it had more, the sod would wash off when there is a heavy rain."

Ruede, with the help of his partner, built a dugout on his own claim soon after his arrival. The hole for the dugout was "10 x 14 feet, and in front 4 feet deep; 4½ feet behind." The dugout was heightened by a sod wall, topped off with a ridge pole, boards, and straw and the whole covered with sod. The diary for April 7 reads, in part: "Used part of the straw on the roof, and covered the whole roof with a layer of sod, and then threw dirt on it and the 'House' was finished." The cost of the house, not including labor totaled as follows: "Ridge pole and hauling (including two loads of firewood), $1.50; rafters and straw, $.50; 2 lbs. nails, $.15; hinges, $.20; window, $.75; total cash paid, $4.05. Then there was $4.00 worth of lumber, which was paid for in work, and $1.50 for hauling it over, which, together with hauling the firewood, $.50, makes $10.05 for a place to live in and firewood enough to last all summer."

Ruede did without a stove for a considerable time. His meals were largely improvised and often were obtained at the neighbors. For April 17 the entry reads in part: "Made fire and got me some dinner. Bill of fare—mush and broiled ham. The meat flies have got at it, and it must be used soon. Send me a recipe for making johnny cakes. The corn-meal here is what you call

133

chop-hulls and all. Don't publish my diary entire. If you want any of it published, let Syd make up letters from it. I don't care to let everybody know how I live, though it might deter some from coming who would otherwise throw away their money. This is not a hightoned way of living, and I wish for some 'Ol Re' Bread. If I had a stove I could do better. My sod chimney would draw all right but the fire place leaks badly, and I have a hard time starting fire."

Insects, especially mosquitoes, were a bother. Ruede can be quoted as saying that the "people who live in sod houses, and, in fact, all who live under a dirt roof are pestered with swarms of bed bugs. . . . Where the sod houses are plastered the bed bugs are not such a nuisance. . . . You don't have to keep a dog in order to have plenty of fleas. . . . Just have a dirt floor and you have plenty of fleas, sure. . . . Another nuisance here is what people call 'Kansas itch,' which attacks nearly everybody within a short time after arrival here; few are immune."

Ruede, with the help of his father and a brother, built a second dugout on a different part of his claim a year later to welcome his mother. But for most settlers, if they stayed long enough, years of good yield followed years of drought, hail, or grasshopper invasion, while families grew in size, and when it became necessary to rebuild—three, ten or twelve years later—the new home was usually a frame structure, generally built from lumber out of what is now the cutover of the Great Lakes states.

But the important thing is that people had to learn to live in sod houses and dugouts for a time at least. No wonder there was hesitation of settlement along the ninety-eighth meridian.

NEW MACHINES

In 1862, the year of the Homestead Act, President Abraham Lincoln also signed the Morrill Act, and in 1887 the Hatch Act was passed, creating the system of experiment station research. These two acts provided land grants and income to assist in study, research, and teaching in those sciences that would assist farmers in improving their way of life. Before this, new discoveries in agriculture and its technology were entirely up to the individual farmer or some enterprising businessman.

134

It took a new technology to handle the sod of the Plains and the larger acreage necessary for making a living. John Deere, originally of Vermont, settled in Illinois and invented the steel plowshare in 1837, making it out of a handsaw blade. The walking plow came into prominence quickly on the prairie and the eastern Plains. Cyrus McCormick moved his reaper manufacturing plant to Chicago as early as 1847 to be nearer to the market. The Marsh Harvester came into being in the early seventies and was quickly converted into the wire self-binder in the late seventies. In 1880 the twine binder was invented and by 1885 the McCormick-Deering binder was standard equipment in the prairies and on the Plains.

The endgate seeder was in general use in the late seventies, but was then quickly replaced by the drill. The rotary-drop corn planter was in use at the end of the seventies, and the wire-check corn planter was invented by 1880. The simpler machines such as the harrow, the mower, and the hay rake, including the automatic-dumper feature, had been perfected during this time. By the eighties, the large red-wheeled, four-furrow gang plows were in general use. The thresher-separator was in general use by the mid-seventies, and the steam engine was a success by 1880. The traction engine was in general use after 1885.

Though the Homestead Act was passed in 1862, and the steel plow and the reaper—along with the harrow—had been invented by that time, a great deal of farm technology had not yet reached the stage that a settler could use it to farm the open grasslands of the nation. The newer and, in this respect, more helpful technology came into use only after the seventies. Even then, most of the early settlers did not have the money to buy equipment; many were unskilled in its use. Many settlers, therefore, even though eager to move on west, were forced by circumstances to halt, at least temporarily, along the ninety-eighth meridian.

Clearly then, there was hesitation in the push of settlement onto the Plains for a time. Unless the settler was willing to cross the Plains, it appeared wise to stay to the east of them. Certain technological inventions, pushed to completion by the industrial trend after the Civil War, were clearly related to demands in the prairie and in the Plains country. But before a practical application of these inventions had been made, the people hesitated—during the seventies and eighties—to settle in the Plains. Only after a technology had been developed that would make settlement under the Homestead Act more feasible and more possible in the Plains did the dam along the ninety-eighth meridian burst and settlement push on westward.

But technology is only part of a way of life. Were there like changes in institutions to make those institutions suitable for life on the Plains?

CHAPTER 11

The Settlement Era

The major homestead settlement of the Plains proper got under way in the early seventies. Once started, like prairie fire, settlement spread everywhere, then came to a gradual end about 1910. Thereafter, new settlement was chiefly a replacement of those who moved out. Small areas, still untouched, were filled in as late as the years following World War I. But the basic pattern had by then been long established.

SETTLEMENT PROCEEDS RAPIDLY

Everett Dick (*The Sod-House Frontier*) can be quoted as saying "in 1880 the population of Kansas was 996,096. In 1887, it was 1,518,552, an increase of 552,456 in seven years. The population of Nebraska, likewise, increased more than 600,-000 between 1880 and 1890. In Dakota, a great expanse of hitherto almost uninhabited territory became, in a decade, a sufficiently populous region to be admitted to the Union in 1889 as two states. During the eighteen-year period, ending June 30, 1880, the total number of homestead and pre-emption claims filed was only 44,122. The land office records show that in the following year and a half 16,718 claims were entered."

In a short span of fifty years, 1870–1920, population had increased twelve times in these seven states. There was a complete transition from open range cattle and sheep grazing to farming and ranching. In other parts of the nation a like transition lasted for two hundred or even two hundred and fifty years.

Perhaps it was this rapidity of settlement which, in large

measure, accounted for the push of humid-area ways of living upon the Plains. Perhaps it was the speed with which things were happening that made the settler forget all about the hesitancy of his predecessors, the peculiarities of the region, and the rumor that the Plains were a desert.

An over-all view showing what took place can be seen in Table 4.

TABLE 4. Population for certain Plains states for the period 1870–1920.*

States	1870	1880	1890	1900	1910	1920
Colorado	39,864	194,327	412,198	539,700	799,024	939,629
Kansas	364,399	996,096	1,427,096	1,470,495	1,690,949	1,769,257
Montana	20,595	39,159	132,159	243,329	376,053	548,889
Nebraska	122,993	452,402	1,058,910	1,066,300	1,192,214	1,296,372
N. Dakota	————	————	182,719	319,146	577,056	646,872
S. Dakota	————	————	328,808	401,570	583,888	636,547
Wyoming	9,118	20,789	60,705	92,531	145,965	194,402
Total	556,969	1,702,773	3,602,595	4,133,071	5,365,149	6,031,968

* Taken from the United States Census of Population.

Many reasons have been given for the settlement of the region. Among them are cited the lure for new land, the excitement found in settling a new country, the attractive land offerings made by the railroads, the promotion schemes of land settlement agencies, the colonization policy of foreign nations, and the "baiting" of settlers by those already in the Plains.

Often a combination of two or more of these factors determined the spot where a particular emigrant decided to locate. As an example, take William Rueb, Sr., who finally settled in St. Francis, Kansas. A German Russian, Rueb was a descendant of a German family who had emigrated to the Ukraine in the early nineteenth century to avoid compulsory military service. When the Russian Czar threatened to enforce military conscription, William—as so many of his friends and relatives—decided it was time to leave.

He chose America and arrived in this country in 1906. He went to the state of Washington to roam for three months in search of good agricultural land. Though it was for the asking, Rueb was not satisfied with what he saw. Hence, upon the urging of his friends and relatives, he joined them in northwestern Kansas near St. Francis. Upon arriving, he found that homesteads were not to be had. All of the Kansas public domain had been claimed. He had to purchase his own land—320 acres.

Later he was informed by other German friends and newspapers that good lands were available in Texas. Tempted, he went there to take a look. Apparently, he was not interested for he returned to St. Francis. But again he was tempted; this time, by the East. Going all the way to Maryland, to look at the land there, he returned fully convinced that St. Francis was the best yet! It was best because nowhere else was he able to acquire lands similar to those with which he was so familiar in the Ukraine. It was best because St. Francis was a large settlement of German Lutherans whose backgrounds paralleled his own. He was among friends.

St. Francis, however, was only one such settlement of foreign emigrants in the Plains. There were others representing Scandinavian, Finnish, Danish, Yugoslav, French, English, Bohemian, German, and Russian nationals. Many came, not as individuals like Rueb, following friends and relatives who had migrated earlier, but as colonizing groups, brought by their church, the railroads, or the settler agencies. Many, unlike Rueb who explored about, settled in an unknown land and stayed, to remain through drought and prosperity. It was their children, two and three generations later, who left the farmstead.

No matter where they came from, how they came, or when they came, the Plains settlers were people of little means. This was true in the beginning as well as later. Many times all they possessed, after some years of effort, was a team of horses, a wagon, a few farm tools, a crude barn, some personal belongings, and a shack.

THE HARDSHIPS START IMMEDIATELY

Settlers, whether arriving earlier or later, soon encountered hardships which, at times, were local in nature, and, at other times, were general throughout the region. There came the grasshopper scourge of 1874, followed by lesser numbers in 1875, 1876, and 1877. Immediately some states and communities were forced to provide relief measures. Another source of terror and destruction was the prairie fires. Cold and blizzards were another. The winter of 1880–81 was called the hard winter, but only until those of 1885–86 and 1886–87. The school children's storm of 1888 is also well-remembered, as are the dust storms of 1889 and the river floods of 1881.

There were repeated localized and general droughts. The drought of 1889–90 was of major proportions, extending over all the Plains, and the entire decade of the nineties caused suffering and misery. Other drought years in that decade included 1893, 1894, 1895, and 1896. The year 1894 was one of the driest ever recorded in eastern Kit Carson County (Colorado), with 8.42 inches of precipitation, comparable with the 7.76 inches in 1934.

A good description of the hardships suffered by the early settlers has been set forth by R. S. Dunbar in his description of events in Kit Carson County, Colorado. This county had been a cattle range prior to 1886, when the farmers began to move in. Dunbar points out that "the settlers experienced crop failure almost from the very start. The crop of 1888 was fair, but the next two suffered from hot winds and drought. The year 1889 was very dry, but 1890 was drier. The settlers reacted to the drought of 1889–90 in various ways. Many emigrated, some temporarily, others permanently. . . . Of those who stayed, some required relief to remain through the winter and spring of 1890–91. Shortly after the first of January, 1891, the destitution among the poor families became so acute that some of the more fortunate citizens of the county formed a relief organization. . . ."

The population of Kit Carson County decreased from 2,472 in 1890 to 1,580 in 1900, and a transition was necessary from grain farming to ranching in order to survive. Dunbar explains that "all who stayed gradually adjusted their agricultural techniques to the needs of the environment. Slowly, they came to realize the aridity of the region. Through repeated crop failure they learned that they could not farm as they had back in the wet country. . . . In short, they learned that eastern Colorado was not a corn or wheat farmer's country, but a cattleman's country, a great pasture land. And so they turned to livestock."

Vance Johnson (*Heaven's Tableland*) describes this migration of settlers into the southern portion of the Great Plains through the eyes of a cowboy, sitting by the fire at night expressing the following thoughts: "Farmers are allus goin' out there in times like these, and comin' back when it gits dry. Take me.

I went—and I'm comin' back. Y'know, you kin tell by the remains of their camps which way they're goin'. Goin' west, they leave cracker boxes and cans about; comin' east, all they leave is rabbit hair and fieldlark feathers." The cowboy continues: "Y'know they ain't nothin' but wind and sun upon them plains. Why, the wind blows so hard up there that if a man loses his hat he don't bother to go chasin' after it. He just waits to grab the next one comin' by."

The closing words of the cowboy are symbolic of values acquired by these people. "I wouldn't give a pair of boots for the best section up there. Matter of fact, just before I left, I swapped two sections of the best land you'll find anywhere on them plains for these boots I've got on." Still the settlers came, and perhaps even the cowboy returned to the Plains. After all, it was "some of the best land," and perhaps he could get two sections for a pair of boots when he returned.

Johnson points out that settlers came in large numbers from east and south, in 1886; even in 1886 they came before the stench of the rotten carcasses of the cowman calamity of 1885–86 had been entirely erased. They came with wagons, whitetops, brindle cows, towheaded children, a dog, moldboard plows, rope-bottomed chairs, a sickle or scythe, an axe—traveling fifteen to twenty miles a day. They first lived in dugouts, and used cow chips or twisted grass for fuel, often burned in a "hay-burner" patented stove. Most children went barefooted except during winter. Some settlers had difficulty with the cattlemen; others were in free areas. All had difficulty with the elements—downpours, drought, heat, dust, blizzards, hail, grasshoppers.

Some pushed out on the Southern Plains even while the effects of the drought of 1887 were still apparent. The sod was tough; only small acreages could be planted, often too late to make a yield. In the words of Johnson, "in less than three years more than 6,000,000 of the 7,246,000 acres of public domain in the Garden City land district of Kansas were pre-empted by homesteaders. Fifteen thousand claim holders made final proof under the Homestead Law. By 1890, most of the good farm homesteads in Kansas and Colorado were reported occupied. The census of that year revealed a population of 47,479 in the twenty-five western counties of Kansas—four times the population of 1880. . . . Population on the Colorado Plains more than trebled in the same period and in the thirty-one counties of the Texas Panhandle, six times more people were counted in 1890 than ten years previously. . . . Towns sprang up everywhere."

New counties were organized almost as rapidly as new town sites. Often more oxen, horses, and nonresidents (who had placed their names in some hotel register), even in far-off towns, voted for civic improvement than did actual residents.

ECONOMIC AND POLITICAL HAZARDS
TAKE THEIR TOLL

In addition to the hazards of climate, there were others, chiefly economic. In the eighties and nineties, the price of wheat was low and after payment for transportation, the settlers received very little. A scanning of a chronicle of events for North Dakota brings to light the following human experiences in the Plains. On June 6, 1890, North Dakota farmers began taking wheat into Manitoba, paying a duty of fifteen cents per bushel, yet receiving six or seven cents more than they could get at home. On March 2, 1891, the United States Senate passed an agricultural bill with an item providing seed wheat for the drought-stricken regions of North Dakota. Wheat fields were devastated by Rocky Mountain locusts on June 20, 1891. A week later the North Dakota Farmers' Alliance declared in favor of the People's Party. In September of that year, state officials attempted to inspect grain at Grand Forks under new rules, but were successfully resisted by the elevator operators. On April 26, 1892, the North Dakota Supreme Court decided that the legislature could fix grain elevator rates. In June of that year, the Farmers' Alliance, in convention at Valley City, nominated a full slate of state officers. On May 14, 1894, the United States Supreme Court decided in favor of state control of grain elevators in North Dakota. On August 23 of that same year, railroad representatives, after meeting with farmers, refused to reduce railroad rates, whereupon farmers started a movement to reduce wheat acreage by one-third. On July 6 and July 27 of 1895, farmers in certain sections of the state suffered extensive crop damage from hail. On October 14 of the same year they sustained heavy losses from prairie fires. In July of 1896 ex-

142

tensive damage from army worms was suffered by wheat fields in certain areas of the state. On August 7, hail damage was severe in other areas.

A decade later the following were some of the memorable events in North Dakota: In February, 1901, the state house passed a bill limiting the maximum interest to 10 per cent. On September 6 and 7, of 1903, farmers lost a million dollars because of heavy rain. Less than a week later, snow fell to a depth of two feet. A little more than a month later the first State Irrigation Convention in North Dakota was held at Bismarck. A permanent organization identified as the State Irrigation Congress of North Dakota was formed. On August 23, of 1904, it was announced in Washington, D. C., that in 1903 North Dakota led all the states in acreage patented under the Homestead Act, the amount being 1,798,551 acres and the cash receipts, $1,234,-218. It was also announced that in 1902, North Dakota had sixty-nine systems for irrigation, an increase of more than double. In February, 1905, the state house passed a stringent antitrust measure, and the state senate passed an irrigation bill. On June 9, 1906, the government began investigating charges of extensive homestead land frauds in North Dakota, while in August of that year, the State Board of Equalization succeeded in raising the railroad assessment by 20 per cent, placing the figure at nearly $28,000,000.

This chronicle of events in North Dakota is evidence of the basic struggle for survival, not alone against natural hazards, but against vested interests as well, from the beginning of settlement. In addition to drought, flood, hail, blizzards, and insect hazards, and interest in irrigation development, there were struggles, with corporations and monopoly interests, to protect the people of the state against high interest rates and high freight rates, against low prices for wheat, and against unfair grading of grain at elevators. The earlier record was for a drier period, while the second was for a period of higher rainfall. The experience was not different from that of other Plains states. Apparently, the collective action taken by farmers against equity foreclosure during the Farm Holiday period of the 1930's was not different from a similar threat in 1894 to cut wheat acreage by one-third to force the lowering of freight rates. Apparently, the motives for the Farmers' Alliance action of that earlier period were not very different from those that gave rise to the Non-Partisan League of a later day.

In Kansas, settlers early resorted to political action. The story can be read in William Allen White's *Autobiography*. His chapter entitled "I Become a Blind Leader of the Blind" depicts the conflict of interest aroused by the appearance of the Farmers' Alliance. He can be quoted as saying "I had a low opinion of the Farmers' Alliance credo, and a still lower opinion of the leaders of the movement. So my editorials in the *Republican* were biased. . . . I was satisfied, being what I was, that the whole Alliance movement was a demagogue's rabble-rousing, with no basis in sound economics. How intellectually snobbish I was about 'sound economics.' . . . But I was a young fool. I sat at night in the office of the Eldorado *Republican*, writing reactionary editorials about Sound Economics which I learned from Francis Walker's college textbook, just one of ten thousand other fools across the land who thought that classic economics could be fitted into the social and political upheaval that was closing a brilliant era in our national history."

This was in 1890. That fall the Farmers' Alliance got control of the House of Representatives in Kansas. In 1892 the Democrats and the Populists joined hands in "an unholy alliance" and then rose to power in politics until the climax in 1896 when Bryan won Kansas but McKinley was elected President of the United States—all because Mark Hanna used the editorial "What's the Matter with Kansas?" and spread it all over the land.

SETTLERS KEEP COMING
AFTER HARDSHIP PERIODS

While crises and hardships drove some settlers out of the Plains, many stuck it out, and during the good years others came in. For instance, the winter of 1885–86 resulted in a considerable exodus of settlers. So did the drought period of 1890–91, the grasshopper year of 1892, the panic year of 1893, and the drought period of 1894–96. But the rains of 1896 brought more settlers. By 1899, the boom was going strong again. By 1906, it was at its peak again, bringing farmers from Iowa and Missouri and from all the Midwest, the South, and the East.

Vance Johnson (*Heaven's Tableland*) suggests that "by 1909 it was estimated that 400,000 persons a year were pouring into the western states with the intention of buying land—and perhaps a majority of these were headed for the Southern Plains. . . . The census of 1910 revealed the population of sixty-one Southern Plains counties had increased nearly 350 per cent in ten years. . . . Wheat acreage increased nearly 600 per cent and the corn acreage was expanded nearly four times."

C. W. Post, the originator of cereals by that name, from a comfortable office in Battle Creek, Michigan, spent much money and manpower in an attempt to make rain by dynamiting and blasting the atmosphere during the period 1910–13 in the Southern Plains. He conducted twenty-one battles at a cost of about a thousand dollars each. He owned large farming operations in the vicinity of the Caprock in Texas. His plans were to build a model town and community. If he could not get water by digging wells, he planned to tunnel for it into the side of the Caprock. But dry weather had started in spots, with the year 1908. In 1910 the drought was general; but only spotty again in 1911. However, in that year, dust started to blow. Drought took a tighter grip in 1912, and dust blew in the early winter of 1913. But the battles brought no rain, and Caprock never developed into a model town.

THE RAILROADS BID FOR SETTLERS

Railroads were the great boosters of settlement. Never before had the Plains been subjected to such praise and flattery! Those loudest in their praises were the immigration bureaus established by the land grant railroads. They were heard not only in America but in such distant places as England, Russia, Germany, Holland, and the Scandinavian countries. The gist of their message was that only a fool would by-pass the Plains. The climate was depicted as most healthful. The valleys were described as "flowery meadows." The lands were counted as plentiful and rich. And, by virtue of the very fact that there were no trees, nature was described as having shown her kindness. The Plains were meant for the plow! They were meant for the one who wished to make good and become rich. Only will and determination were needed!

Once an interest was aroused, the next step consisted of details handled by the land departments of the railroads. Within their jurisdiction were the pricing of land, the providing of credit, the arrangement of excursion trips at special rates, and the provision of entertainment—all for those who were interested in undertaking a journey to the Plains.

The records show that W. P. Svash ran eighty-seven special trains, carrying 75 to 250 passengers each into Texas about 1906. By 1905, the Santa Fé alone had brought 60,000 Mennonites from the Ukraine. The Campbell system of dust mulch farming started to take hold before 1910. Johnson says: "That the period from 1896–1906 still stands as the wettest and most favorable crop years on record on the Southern Plains. A great reservoir of moisture was in the soil, and the rainfall from 1906 to 1910 was almost as plentiful as it had been in the previous five years." Nature co-operated gallantly to lend truth to the florid railroad advertising.

The story of settling the Northern Plains is not much different, except that there were fewer people involved. Jim Hill, of the Great Northern—the railroad without land grants—was the empire builder there. He had visions of putting settlers on every 160, at least every 320 acres. "One upstart scientist from Montana State College who ventured to differ with Jim's views on agriculture was told 'not to contradict Mr. Hill.'" Special fares for settlers—one-way—were $12.50 from St. Paul to points in eastern Montana along the Great Northern. It was frequently difficult to "scratch together" the return fare.

Jim Hill's vision was one of building an agriculture in the Northern Plains like that found in the humid Midwest. "That was his vision (in 1912); and Havre (Montana folks who heard him) looked at the powerful stocky little man with the huge head and admitted that if it could be done Hill would do it." Joseph Kinsey Howard recites that one year after Hill's speech in Havre, homesteaders stood for two days and two nights in front of the United States Land Office there, waiting for it to open. They were spelled by their wives and children. They were allowed to enter the offices in groups of twenty-five; 250 entries resulted on the first day. In March, 1913, entries totaled 1,600 in that office alone. In 1912, there were 12,597 homestead entries in Montana, compared with 20,662 in 1914.

Autos, introduced after 1900, helped to extend the promotion started by the railroads. Settlers arriving by trains at various depots were met by representatives of land and real estate companies who took them by car to see the agricultural lands. One central Montana local paper stated that "every available automobile, some thirty or forty in number, has been in use for the last week whisking hundreds of prospective homeseekers." The newcomers, upon arriving, were first shown the luxuriantly growing fields and then the agricultural lands that were for sale or subject to homesteading.

Then came World War I in Europe, some more rain, and good prices. This brought the era of the tractor and extensive expansion—expansion beyond the margin of reasonable land use. "Between 1914 and 1919, the United States' wheat production had been expanded 27,000,000 acres, of which nearly 22,000,000 acres were winter wheat. More than half of the increased winter wheat came out of the good, rich grasslands of the Great Plains."

The average yearly rainfall in the Southern Plains—based on a forty year record at Amarillo, Texas—is about 20.96 inches. In 1918, it was 18.86 inches, and in 1919, about 21.20 inches. But a blizzard in the Texas Panhandle in 1917, and grasshoppers in Kansas in 1919, were signs of difficulty ahead. Spotty drought occurred in the Northern Plains in 1919 and 1921. Then came the agricultural depressions of 1919 and 1925. Following this came the big machines and the great plow-up. The thirties brought even more depression, more drought, and dust storms.

THE PLAINS HAVE LEADERS

Hard times and suffering produce leaders. The Plains were no exception. Some of the leaders were early settlers seeking a solution to the problems they faced in the new land; others were native sons. The list of such leaders is long and their accomplishments are diverse and manifold. Therefore, reference will be made to only a few.

Medicine Lodge, in semiarid Barber County, Kansas, was for a time—as was, also, Guthrie, the onetime capital city of Oklahoma Territory—the home of Carrie Nation, the hatchet-wielding exponent of temperance who gained nationwide repute.

147

Medicine Lodge was also the home of "Sockless Jerry" Simpson, the Great Lakes sailor who became the leader of the Populist Revolt in Kansas in the nineties.

Isaac Newton Gresham, a newspaper man of Point, Texas, in Rains County, was the originator of the Farmers Educational and Co-operative Union of America. H. W. Campbell of Brown County, South Dakota, became the exponent of the dust mulch method of dry-land farming. And Arthur C. Townley of North Dakota, a native of Minnesota, was the father of the Non-Partisan League.

Others with some claim to residence and fame in the Great Plains states, if not the Plains proper, are "Cactus Jack" Garner of Uvalde, Texas, once Vice-President of the United States; "Pa" and "Ma" Ferguson, the husband-wife governor's team of Texas; "Pappy" O'Daniel, onetime Texas politician; the Cappers of Kansas; Will Rogers, resident of Oklahoma and of the world; and "Panhandle Puck" Howe of Amarillo, Texas. Two characters of mythological fame in the region are Lem Blanchard, the Paul Bunyan of Kansas, and Pecos Bill who was so swift with eye and arm that he could "rope a streak of lightning."

These figures have provided part of the drive on the Plains which sought to improve the lot of the Plains citizen. Often these leaders were misunderstood. William Allen White—"The Sage of Emporia"—admits that in his youthful years he had little understanding of the forces that motivated "Sockless Jerry" Simpson. The experience of additional years later made him look upon "Sockless Jerry" with greater understanding and more charity. But in the meantime, much rancor developed between the Kansans of the humid part of the state and those of the Plains.

CHAPTER 12

Civilization Tested by Drought, Dust, and Depopulation

The way of life of the Plains has been largely agricultural in character and is so even today, for though
urbanization and industrialization have made advances in recent
years, and though there are large cities bordering on the Great
Plains area, there are few large cities in the region itself. As an
essentially agricultural area, however, the Plains have faced
severe economic problems. For the nation and the Plains, too,
agriculture was in a disadvantageous position during the interim
between the two World Wars, and depression in agriculture
was a forerunner of depression in the industrial and urban economy. Many economists assume it to have been one of the direct
causes of the total economic depression of the thirties.

DEPRESSION IN THE AGRICULTURE
OF THE NATION

It is a well-established fact that agriculture, in America, is in a disadvantageous position for the reason that it is highly
competitive. The almost six million farm and ranch operators of
the nation, until the midthirties, sold their products in a competitive price market. Unable to control volume of production
or price, the only solution was one of still greater production
for the majority of farm and ranch operators. This condition depressed prices still more. Unable to shift readily into other lines
of production, for many reasons, this meant a self-generating
depression of income for the agriculturalists.

Coupled with this was the fact that farmers and ranchers

had to buy goods and services in a market that is more nearly non-competitive and had to pay the prices demanded of them. Thus they were caught between the upper and the lower mill-stone—ground to a depression status.

Industry and labor, on the other hand, have been moving into a more favorable position. Industrialists and businessmen tend to protect themselves by controlling volume or price or both, thus operating more nearly in a monopoly position much of the time. Labor unions have moved in the direction of collective bargaining and union organization, though this is far from being in a monopoly position compared to industry and business.

To overcome their disadvantageous position, agriculturalists have sought remedies in various directions, often with the help of government. One remedy has been the establishing of co-operatives, especially of the producer kind, as an attempt to assist in the control of price or volume and quality of production. Another remedy has been in the direction of obtaining more favorable credit terms, to help cut the interest costs, to lengthen the period of mortgage repayment, and to provide capital in order to change into other avenues of production. Here government has had to furnish public credit, for private investors consider agricultural loans to be high-risk ventures.

A third remedy has been in the direction of controlling, in various ways, the quantity of farm products put on the market. A first attempt came with the federal government's purchasing and withholding from the market various farm products, an activity exemplified by the purchases of the Federal Farm Board of the Hoover days. A more recent device has been the storage program with government price supports and the attempt at control of volume through acreage reduction, soil conservation payments, and other measures. The object has been to provide agriculturalists with an income that is more nearly on a basis of parity with other segments of the economy.

THE DEPRESSED STATE OF AGRICULTURE IN THE PLAINS

For the Plains, the depression before and during the thirties had more serious results than for agriculture elsewhere.

Farther removed from markets than much of the rest of agriculture, the longer freight haul, with farmers and ranchers paying the freight both ways, resulted in especially disproportionately small returns to the Plains agriculturalists. Without price-making forces in the region, the price of wheat, for example, was the Minneapolis price—minus freight; but the price of bread tended to be the Minneapolis price—plus freight. Being in a hinterland position, without the publicity media of newspapers and radios and without any large cities to experience the economic hardship and thereby call attention to these facts, the plainsman's economic position was not appreciated and understood, nor was it respected. The farm implement suppliers and the processors of feed and building materials continued to extract their respectable share of the consumer's dollar. Mortgage foreclosure and credit restrictions were used as whips to threaten the Plains farmer and rancher. So the relative poverty of the Plains agriculturalist was intensified.

A second ramification of agricultural depression in the Plains occurred on the institutional level. The credit system, the mortgage foreclosure procedure, the school and local government systems, the churches and lodges, the tax system, and certain other organizations were not adapted to conditions in the region. Restricted income resulted in greater hardship to support these institutional ways. The raising of standards and increasing demands on the part of these organizations put still greater pressure on the residents of the region. The results were tax delinquency, bankruptcy, mortgage foreclosure, and the exodus of population on a large scale.

DROUGHT IN THE TWENTIES
AND THE THIRTIES

Cultural patterns, imported from the humid area largely, were subjected to a severe test in the Plains during the decade of the thirties. The depression in the agriculture of the Plains during the twenties had sapped the economic strength of the people in the region. Taxes for public services were high; borrowing for public and private needs was high. Income was low. Reserves and equity that had been accumulated earlier had been exhausted. The spasmodic drought of the twenties had made certain the exhaustion of the income of almost everyone— assuming there had been opportunities to husband any in the face of all the other vicissitudes. Future income had already been mortgaged in the form of government-financed feed and seed loans to keep draft animals going and to insure another seeding. Then came the nationwide industrial and business depression which began in 1929. Next came the drought years of 1934 and 1935, and again those of 1936 and 1937. Then came a further business recession in 1937.

The story of the resulting poverty and relief in the Plains is told elsewhere. Reference need only be made to the emergency program of killing the starving cattle and pigs from the range and from the farm, and the plowing under of certain crops. Population exodus was extensive, but there was also an influx on the part of those coming back to the farm from industrial centers. Cash relief was extensive, but was soon considered immoral. So work relief became a substitute. But public works could not be undertaken on private property—that would be immoral for it would enhance private gain. The program failed to meet the needs of the Plains. Since village, town, and county governments were already financially embarrassed, the public works program had only very limited possibilities. The Works Progress Administration offered little opportunity in the Plains for there was little industry in the region—little industrial skill to maintain, rehabilitate, and retrain.

Then came the Rural Resettlement Administration and the purchase of certain lands in order to convert them into other more desirable uses. Also there emerged certain soil conservation measures and some irrigation development. These latter programs, including Rural Resettlement and Rehabilitation, were more nearly adapted to bringing about a constructive upbuilding of the region. During this period there emerged acreage controls, the ever-normal granary idea, crop insurance, and parity prices. These efforts were intended to raise the income of farmers and ranchers, and to assure them some measure of parity with labor and business. And during all this period, there were efforts at halting forced sales, the deferring of mortgage foreclosure, the re-evaluating and scaling down of farm and ranch debt, and the refinancing of credit.

All these efforts aided in the rehabilitation of the Plains in a measure. But the task was not completed, for then came World War II, and a favorable series of yield and price years during the decade of the forties. After that came Korea. So again the basic rehabilitation of the region was avoided.

Then came the fall of 1953. There had been extensive drought in the Southern Plains for several years, with threatened dust storms in prospect. This was the year of threatened drought in the Northern Plains, but a quick reversal due to late spring rains occurred, only to result in considerable rust damage. This, too, was the year of a resounding "aye" vote for wheat acreage control quotas and 90 per cent of parity prices, and a year in which a drastic drop in livestock prices promised to make a reality of the formerly despised Brannan Plan.

There is, indeed, evidence that all is not well in the agricultural life of the nation, and especially in the Plains. The test of the survival of civilization in the Plains has not yet run its final course.

DUST FROM THE GREAT PLAINS

The chief measure of the non-adaptability of the humid-area culture to Plains conditions is the movement of dust. Dust indicates an over-extension of farming into areas best used for other purposes. It also indicates an overemphasis upon intensity of farm operations and an ignoring of the fact that land should be idle, covered with trashy mulch, and allowed to store moisture by being cropped only in alternate years. Low prices and climatic adversities often force farmers to gamble that rain may come, with the hope of recouping former losses. Thus, for good measure, cropping is extended to undesirable areas, and alternate fallow rotations are rejected in favor of continuous cropping. Increased tenant operations give rise to exploitive farming practices. Finally, creeping drought, resulting in little plant growth, brings on dust blowing as the winds of a dry period mount in intensity.

Beginning with the thirties, the first real "dust blow" came in 1934. In the Southern Plains the first really destructive blow came in "April, 1934; followed by a second one in May, when

Southern Plains dust settled on the President's desk in the White House, and on the decks of ships in the Atlantic." But 1933 had also been a "dust blow" year. There were dust storms in 1935. The blowing became intense in all of the Plains. The federal government created the Soil Conservation Service and paid farmers to hold down the soil. But land kept on blowing.

In 1936 the nation studied the Great Plains and made a report to the President on "The Future of the Great Plains." Then came occasional rainy periods but the dust still blew. Dust blew even worse in the spring of 1937 than it had in 1935 or 1936.

Great Plains dust of 1937 settled on the farms in the Midwest, on the Great Lakes, and in the East. But progress was being made in the control of dust blowing. Special ways of cultivating and handling the fields began to pay off. And rain helped. It rained in 1937, even more than in the previous year. However, in the spring of 1938 experts warned that the largest area in history was in condition to blow. Of the Southern Plains Vance Johnson says, that "from 1935 through 1937, the Dust Bowl had been a great pear-shaped area, reaching down from the northwestern corner of Kansas to the Caprock in Texas. At its extremes, it was 500 miles long and 250 miles wide. But in the spring of 1938, the Dust Bowl became a fat circle about 300 miles in diameter. It withdrew nearly 200 miles in Texas, where slightly increased rainfall and better conservation provided a cover for the land. But it spread wider to east and west. Westward it reached about 125 miles into Colorado, eastward more than halfway across Kansas. In the center of the circle, dust blew as badly as it ever had."

But in the fall of 1938 there came rains. In 1939, only a fourth as much land was blowing as had blown the year before. Weather had become more favorable and farmers had improved their practices. Things began to look more favorable. Prices and the foreign market conditions—war demands—offered promise for those who had stayed on. But in February of 1941, the "dust blow" started again—in the Southern Plains almost as bad as the worst that had gone before. Fortunately, the rains came on time, the grain grew, and the land was once more anchored—with the help of good farming practices.

Then came the good years—price and yield—of 1942 and

after. Newcomers came into the area. The prosperity of 1944 was even better. The newcomers wanted more room to expand, and strived to change the soil conservation district legislation. In February of 1945, the old farmers in some Southern Plains counties voted against the proposed relaxation of conservation practices and won by a small margin only. So the promoters lobbied in the several state legislatures. In some cases absentee landowners received the right to vote on conservation measures. Meanwhile in Cheyenne County, Colorado, the newcomers had organized an improvement association, collared the absentee votes from Cape Cod to the Golden Gate, cast their votes for relaxing the soil conservation rules—and won. One newcomer walked from his seat to the ballot box 260 times. That was in 1945.

OPTIMISM IN THE PLAINS

But people of the Plains are optimistic. During these difficult years they had their pleasures, too. A fitting but ironic climax to the period of the hardships in the twenties may be illustrated by two events in Montana. One was the 1923 Jack Dempsey–Tommy Gibbons fight for the championship of the world held at Shelby, Montana, a Great Plains wheat town. Great Plains oil and wheat money tried to stage a comeback. While preparations were being made for the fight and during the ensuing boom the population of Shelby increased from 1,500 to 4,000. An arena, capable of seating 45,000, was built. But only 7,000 attended the fight and—it was a flop.

The other event was the importation, in the years 1925 to 1928, of professional ball players from the big leagues of the nation to play at Scobey, the wheat capital of eastern Montana, and at Plentywood (where there are few trees). The standing joke was to wonder whether the jack rabbits or the players could get around the diamond faster. Among the players were Charlie Risbery and Happy Felsch—for $800 a month and all found. Bets were made in $1,000 wads.

The earlier period had its optimism, too. Two Oklahoma towns—Lawton and Woodward—came into being practically overnight, both built on optimism almost entirely. The Kiowa–

Comanche Reservation in western Oklahoma was made available in 160-acre homesteads by lottery. In three days, between the first and third of August, 1901, Lawton had acquired four hundred temporary business places, mostly in tent headquarters, including a mobile bank and a newspaper. One year later, it celebrated its anniversary with a bullfight, the matador dressed in authentic Spanish costume, and with an Apache Indian dance, staged by the venerable old Geronimo who was then detained as a prisoner in nearby Fort Sill. Woodward, carved out of the Cherokee Outlet area, acquired five thousand residents between noon and sunset of September 16, 1893, as the result of the Cherokee Outlet Run. But the newcomers at Woodward were reluctant to settle the land after seeing it, and there were many homestead sites available again after several weeks. Woodward was later the home of Temple Houston, son of Sam Houston of Texas fame, and it is said that Temple Houston's exploits supplied Edna Ferber with the color for her principal character in *Cimarron,* her novel of Oklahoma. Let it be said of these two Oklahoma towns that they moved ahead in the ensuing half century to become populous places and important foci for the cultural development of their part of the Plains.

REVOLT IN THE NORTHERN PLAINS

But the optimism, which these ventures and incidents represent, was short-lived. The basic difficulties in the region could not be denied. So the Plains farmer eventually revolted. He did so with a special vengeance in the Northern Plains. The Non-Partisan League was organized, most fruitfully in North Dakota. The movement spilled over into Montana, South Dakota, and Minnesota. These Scandinavians weren't going to be done out of house and home without a fight—they knew something about co-operation and how it worked. Some had experience with co-operatives in their land of birth. A study by North Dakota State College professors showed that, in a single season, one Duluth elevator received 99,711 bushels of No. 1 Northern Spring Wheat, but shipped out 196,288 bushels. It received 141,-455 bushels of No. 2, but shipped out 467,764 bushels. On the other end of the scale, it received 201,267 bushels of No. 4, but shipped out none; and 116,021 bushels were received as "no grade," but none was shipped out. The farmers decided that there was "something rotten in Denmark."

So the Non-Partisan League was organized in 1915, and following the League program, North Dakota established its centralized banking system and a state-owned mill and elevator. Governor William Langer of North Dakota broke with the League in 1919 but raised the price of wheat with an embargo from 49 cents a bushel for No. 1 Dark Northern to 62 cents in five weeks during 1933. Langer declared a farm mortgage moratorium in 1933, and the governors of Minnesota, Montana, South Dakota, Iowa, Nebraska, and Kansas wired their congratulations. In 1937, the North Dakota wheat crop was infested by black stem rust. Much of the crop was 37-pound wheat. On the evening of July 22, 1937, the price for this wheat dropped 52 cents, from 89 to 37 cents. But the North Dakota State Mill and Elevator proved that, from a baking standpoint, the protein and gluten content was still just as good as for the better grade wheat. So Langer set the forces in motion which resulted in purchase of wheat by the State Mill and Elevator of North Dakota at 37 cents a bushel above the market price. A day later the Minneapolis market met this offer and, in instances, even exceeded it. A variation of this same situation occurred in 1938.

Thus, while dust covered up the price and drought situation in the Southern Plains, the farmers of North Dakota, and their governor, wrested some favorable prices during the drought years from the market manipulators—a benefit to all farmers in the Northern and Southern Plains in those years of drought.

This does not mean that Southern Plains farmers were less in the mood for revolt than those in the north. Actually, they were in revolt, too, but they were less successful. In the case of Texas, a one-party state, it is difficult to express displeasure as a Republican, not to say anything of the difficulty in expressing displeasure as an Independent. Revolt in Texas politics is in such forms as that of the Democratic "Regulars" who, representing financial interests, bolted in 1944 the Democratic party in protest against the Franklin D. Roosevelt administration. The Plains farmer and rancher in Texas can hardly revolt save when they are joined by such groups as the Regulars or by the Dixiecrats, who in 1948 represented the protest against and within the one-party system.

And Oklahoma had its revolt in the form of the Farmer-Labor Reconstruction League of the early twenties. Oklahoma farmers, the railroad brotherhoods, and the State Federation organized to rid themselves of some of their hardships. They were successful in electing their candidate, J. C. Walton, as governor in 1922, but he was impeached and suspended from office less than a year later. Likewise, the next elected governor, Henry S. Johnston, was impeached and convicted of general incompetence. Later came Alfalfa Bill Murray. Actually, drought, dust, and depression were so severe in the thirties that migration rather than political action became the avenue of escape for many Oklahomans. John Steinbeck depicted this situation in his novel *The Grapes of Wrath*. In Kansas, however, after the radicalism of the last decades of the nineteenth century, Kansas farmers, including those of the Plains area, were by and large apparently satisfied with the Puritanism that prevailed in that state. John Gunther described it as "the extreme particularity of Kansas."

During the thirties, through the Great Plains region in general, the enforced mortgage foreclosure sales led to another form of revolt—the Farm Holiday movement. One particular aspect of this was the "Penny Sales." When creditors pushed such a sale, farmers would band together and bid "one penny." They insisted on contract performance by the creditor. Thus the injured farmer often satisfied the remainder of his mortgage by the penny transaction. This form of threat did much to slow down mortgage foreclosure and bankruptcy proceedings.

THE RANCHER, TOO, HAD HIS TROUBLES

The farmer was not alone in experiencing the rise and fall of prosperity which accompanied the ups and downs of weather in the region. The rancher had like experiences. The winters of 1885–86 and 1886–87 were repeated in later years with lesser losses only because most ranchers had learned to shelter and feed their stock. The winters of 1948 and 1949 accounted for fewer losses because the army, with heavy tanks, snowplows, and planes, opened the roads and lanes to the cattle, and helped to get feed to them. In the thirties, the government had mobilized its services to get the starving livestock out of the region, or it had provided feed loans in large numbers and on liberal terms.

In addition to facing the problems brought about by severe winter weather, the rancher also faced the problems of overgrazing the range that accompanied drought and the need to raise more livestock in order to make ends meet in the face of price disadvantages. The Senate document *The Western Range* and *If and When it Rains* set forth the issue; the first represents the public agency view, and the second, the rancher view.

The public hearings on range conditions revealed that forage depletion averaged more than half on the entire range area in the thirties. Three-fourths of the entire range area declined in productivity during the thirty years prior to 1936, and only 16 per cent had improved. It was argued that excessive stocking was the outstanding cause of range depletion. Some 17.3 million animal units were grazed on range that could carry only 10.8 million units. The fact that four out of ten years had been drought years resulted in serious range depletion through overuse during the better years.

One of the financial handicaps of the rancher was the discrimination he suffered because of freight rates. The differential in rates could be only partially offset by cheap range feed. A multitude of public-land laws and policies were found to be an interference with the efficient use and upkeep of the range. The most spectacular misuse of the range was the result of poor grazing conditions on what was formerly crop land. It was estimated in public hearing that it would take more than one hundred years of good management to restore the range to its original grazing capacity of 22.5 million units, and fifty years to provide adequate grazing for the 17.3 million units now grazed.

The stockman was not at all convinced of this interpretation. Rather than attributing the depletion of the range to overgrazing, the rancher tended to argue lack of rainfall caused the difficulty, which would be corrected "if and when it rains." It was the stockman's view that the condition of the range resulted "from the worst period of drought in the memory of living man." To overcome the depletion, all that was needed was rain. The report, made in 1938, can be quoted as follows: "Dust storms come and dust storms go, and bureaucrats build up the need for big appropriations based thereon, while sensational writers harvest a big crop telling about it; but when the rains come, the grass grows and all is well on the range."

Again the stockman revived the argument that he had been done out of his heritage by the homesteader. This can be summarized best in these words: "It is ironical that the stockman who fought to prevent the breaking up of thousands of acres which he knew were best adapted for grazing, should be blamed for the dust storms which are the result of a mistaken government land policy. . . . It should be remembered that this area was marked on all early maps of the United States as the 'Great American Desert,' or 'Great Desert.' Had the lawmakers and homesteaders remembered this important fact, much grief would have been avoided."

Whatever the merits of the respective issues, the facts are that the stockman, when faced with drought, was having as hard a time to survive in the Plains area as the farmer was. The stockman, like the farmer, staked his hopes on "if and when it rains." He felt easier if he could pick a scapegoat—the homesteader. That was easier than facing the issue.

DEPOPULATION IN THE PLAINS

These difficulties in the Plains expressed themselves in loss of rural population. The Great Plains counties as a whole had their greatest rural population numbers about 1930. In that year there were 3,415,700 people living on the farms and ranches and the small towns (under 2,500) in the region proper. This was an increase of 410,400 since 1920 (see Table 5).

By 1940, rural population had dropped to 3,109,400. By 1950, it was even lower than in 1920, the number being about 2,783,-300. Yet there was an increase in urban population (towns 2,500 and over) in the Great Plains counties during this period so that there was a total population increase in these counties.

Montana appears to be leading the trend of rural-population decrease by about a decade. It is the only state of the ten that had a decrease in rural population during the decade 1920–30.

All the other states showed this same trend for the 1930–40 decade, except Texas, New Mexico, and Wyoming. All states except New Mexico showed this trend for the decade 1940–50.

TABLE 5. Rural population for the Plains portion of the Ten Great Plains states, 1920 through 1950.*

State	1920	1930	1940	1950
North Dakota	376.5	387.2	338.9	302.5
South Dakota	266.4	293.9	247.1	217.8
Nebraska	367.6	375.4	332.9	289.8
Kansas	284.2	302.5	258.4	235.0
Oklahoma	338.3	388.6	302.0	237.8
Texas	831.3	1118.5	1121.8	1018.1
New Mexico	54.6	62.7	67.9	69.8
Colorado	168.4	178.7	153.9	153.2
Wyoming	65.5	72.6	74.2	64.8
Montana	252.5	235.6	212.3	198.5
Total	3005.3	3415.7	3109.4	2787.3

* Taken from the U. S. Census for the Great Plains counties in each state.

Of course, there is no inherent merit in having an increasing population, nor is there necessarily an inherent disadvantage in a decreasing population. But, as will be shown later, the sparse rural population in the Plains always has been, and certainly is now, at that point where it is too small to support certain institutional patterns, unless there is far reaching change in the organization of those institutions and the manner and type of service rendered. In short, the sparse population and the trend towards increased sparsity is now a cost best defined as a social cost of space.

THE PLAINS IN TWO WARS

The prosperity in the Great Plains has been the result of two wars when prices and production were more than usually favorable for grain, livestock, and cotton. By the time of World War I much of the Plains was settled and mechanization was underway. Because of war prosperity, the agriculturalist and the stockman in the region had a windfall. Much of their unexpected income was dissipated to cover the losses from ex-

cessive credit during the war period and in the economic contraction of the early twenties. Nevertheless, many community
improvements were made at that time.

The second period of more than usual prosperity was during
World War II and in the years immediately following. Coupled
with still greater mechanization, the Plains agriculturalist and
stockman were able to honor their debts, make some improvements and expansions, and lay something aside. They also had
something for building new schools, hospitals, churches, and
homes. Not all, of course, have been as fortunate as some.

The region contributed much necessary food and fiber toward
helping win the two wars. Oil, coal, and water power were also
contributed from the region, especially in World War II. The
people of the region also contributed generously to the foreign
aid program following World War II. There was overexpansion
in production during both of these periods and an extension of
grain production into the more marginal areas. But these wars
could not have been fought so cheaply and so effectively without the production of the Plains.

The solution of the problem of Plains prosperity appears to
be one of flexibility—the ability to expand and contract when
necessary and to shift between cattle, sheep, wheat, sorghums,
cotton, or some combination of these—and the Plains people
themselves know that such production flexibility is a partial
answer to their economic difficulties. But they do not have the
newspapers, the radio, the television stations, and the communication media in general to effect the flexibility. The region
must have the support of the rest of the nation to implement
flexibility—capital for the necessary conversion, income while
the transition is underway, and the building of industrial opportunities in lieu of depending chiefly on agriculture.

In addition, a measure of flexibility must be introduced into
wheat and cotton growing and into the livestock production of
the more humid areas where there are more alternatives to shift
to when adjustment is necessary. Flexibility in production is
not the exclusive responsibility of the Great Plains agriculturalist. Some of the surpluses of wheat, cotton, sorghums, and
livestock are produced outside the Plains. With modern mechanization and larger operating units, the Plains wheat and cotton farmers can offer tough competition to those raising wheat

and cotton as by-products in the more humid region. Livestock, when fattened in the region with sorghums and cottonseed cake, can also make the profit margin too small for the Midwest feeder and livestock producer. Such price competition in agriculture, between regions, is not a solution to the situation for the Plains or for the agriculture of the rest of the nation. This is especially so when much of the rest of the economy operates under monopoly rules. That is the situation in agriculture today.

THE BASIC DIFFICULTIES IN THE PLAINS

The conditions of drought, insect invasion, and depression in the decade of the thirties demonstrated the unsuitable character of humid-area ways for the Plains. There are those who argue that these were the most serious conditions that might have been joined together at any one time and, therefore, were an exception rather than the rule. Adaptations, therefore, need not be so drastic.

But this is not a realistic interpretation.

Conditions such as prevailed in the thirties are not the most destructive possible for the region, and this is true for two reasons. First, drought and other hazards for the Plains during a period of prosperity and inflation for the rest of the nation would be even more of a blow to the Plains than that which the decade of the thirties delivered. Then, at least, the depressed dollar was able to buy goods and services in effective amounts—the relief dollar was able to reach around. An inflated dollar would cause added hardships.

Secondly, the Plains are now in a highly-commercial economic stage. Many costs of operation that were formerly variable and could, therefore, be postponed or avoided are now fixed costs. For example, weed spraying of wheat fields yields such a significant added product that a farmer must spray in times of good or poor moisture conditions and this becomes a fixed cost of operation. This is true of most of the operation and family living costs of the highly mechanized and specialized farms and ranches of today. This fact of high fixed-costs makes farming and ranching in the Plains more vulnerable to instability than ever before.

In the past, the humid-area civilization has been able to survive only because of certain ultimately undesirable trends in the farming and ranching of the region. Among these were overstocking of the range, expansion of farming into unstable areas, exploitation of water resources, excessive tenancy, uneconomic operation of farm and ranch units, drawing on windfall gains including inheritances, insecurity of income, and poverty.

The perpetuation of these undesirable trends has its roots in certain attitudes of mind which would destroy the Plains, its resources and people, in the long run. Among these attitudes are the following: that man can conquer nature; that natural resources are inexhaustible; that habitual practices are the best; that the owner may do with his property as he likes; that expanding markets will continue indefinitely; that free competition is an effective balancer, as between agriculture and industry; that property and land values will increase indefinitely; that the factory farm is generally desirable; and that the individual must make his own adjustment.

All this means that the humid-area civilization, imported into the Plains has been found wanting. Drought, dust, and depopulation are the measuring sticks of this non-adaptation of humid-area ways. The solution is to press for greater adaptations in all areas of institutional living in the Plains.

To make certain that those who are doubters can recognize clearly the need for adaptation, two tasks need still to be done. These include a description of unsuitable governmental institutions for the Plains and an analysis of unadapted land and financing procedures for the Plains.

CHAPTER 13

Unsuitable Governmental Institutions for the Plains

During the period since their settlement, the Plains have inherited, from the humid parts of the nation and the world, many institutions which frequently have proved themselves unsuited to the conditions of semiaridity. A major characteristic of any institution, of course, is that it has a solid core of social organization and values which remain uniform regardless of time and place. Institutions, by their very nature, have little plasticity and do not readily lend themselves, when transplanted from the site of their origin and development, to the change necessary to fit new situations.

It was, therefore, inevitable that inherited institutions from the humid area should be projected upon the semiarid Plains without modification. In order to have modifications, a strong counterforce in a region—a force of an institutional character— is necessary to point up the need for adaptation. There were no such counterforces emanating from the Plains. Not even the technological inventions and discoveries, which were taking place when settlement first reached the Plains, provided a force strong enough to influence imported institutions. And since there were no basic modifications made in these institutions when they were first brought to the Plains, it is now even more difficult to bring about the necessary changes in order to adapt them to Plains life.

Resistance to adaptation is a major source of difficulty in the Plains today. Technological adaptation in agriculture, and even in business, can not overcome the problems that arise from poor adaptation in the institutional sphere. Of what profit is it to a wheat farmer of the Plains if he fits his individual farm practices to conditions in the Plains and, thereby, makes ends meet, if, at the same time, local government is not suited to Plains conditions and, as a result, drives the farmer into bankruptcy? He is still bankrupt, and the institution is still incapable of functioning effectively. In place of local government, one might use the example of church organization, hospital financing, school financing, road building, or any number of other institutional services.

The purpose of this chapter is to emphasize the nature and importance of the unsuitable institutions for the Plains with examples from (a) constitution writing, (b) local government, and (c) school district organization.

HUMID-AREA ORIGIN OF CONSTITUTION WRITING

Humid-area thinking has left a deep impact on the constitutions of several Plains states from the early days of constitution writing down to the present. The projection of the slavery-freedom issue, through the vehicle of the Kansas–Nebraska Incident, was only one of the first of such impacts.

An omnibus bill admitted four states into the Union in 1889. They were North Dakota, South Dakota, Montana, and Washington. At the time, national thought was much concerned with the abuses of big business intersts and their control over government. People were demanding curbs on corporate powers and also constitutional protection against abuses by the legislative, executive, and judiciary branches of government. Correctives in constitutional organization were national objectives, promoted by people from the humid area of the nation. There was great anxiety and an urging that the new states provide these protections. Thus, local and regional needs were overlooked and overridden, or at least drastically de-emphasized.

The situation is clear from what happened in the Dakotas. The work of the North Dakota Constitutional Convention was only just getting underway when there was introduced a finished document, complete in detail. In view of recent abuses by vested interests, local newspapers and public opinion were much concerned about the origin of the document. Its authorship was ascribed to W. M. Evartz, a lawyer from New York, and there was a general belief that the Northern Pacific Railroad, in some way, was involved in the transaction.

At a later date the authorship of this finished document was established and justified as follows. Professor James Bradley Thayer of the Harvard Law School was purported to have been the author of this completed document, known as File 106. He was assisted in its preparation by Henry W. Hardon and Washington F. Pedrick. The explanation is that in 1889, when the Territory of Dakota was about to be admitted to the Union as two states, Henry Villard was chairman of the finance committee of the Northern Pacific Railway, the most important corporation operating in the territory. He consulted Charles C. Beaman, then one of the leaders of the New York bar, and was advised that, if he could get Professor Thayer to draft the constitutions for the new states, the benefits of all that expert knowledge and sound judgment could accomplish would accrue to these states. Professor Thayer undertook the task. His draft of the constitution was submitted to the conventions of both North and South Dakota and was, in large part, adopted by them.

The influence of humid-area historical thought in the writing of the constitutions for these states is thus very evident. Professor Thayer, an eminent scholar and teacher of constitutional law, trial by jury, and the origin of common law, was an urbanite and an Easterner, who was not acquainted with the semiarid Plains, the problems of distance, and the consequences resulting from sparsity of population. He had no appreciation of the need for financial reserves in government and the mobility of farm and ranch operations necessitated by the environmental conditions in the region. The constitutions of these states, therefore, failed to stress institutional adaptation to regional conditions.

Colonel Clement A. Lounsberry, in his *Early History of North Dakota,* was convinced that there were few indigenous provisions in the constitution adopted by North Dakota. He points out that the constitution of North Dakota culled many of its contents from the 1889 omnibus bill itself. From Illinois came the provision on county courts. From Minnesota was taken the provision relating to the role of public school lands, and the investment of moneys derived from their sale. From Pennsylvania came the provision relating to the Board of Pardons. From New

Hampshire came provisions as to amendments of the constitution. From the Thayer document, introduced by E. A. Williams of Bismarck, came the preamble and many of the legislative provisions. From California, some material for the taxing of railroads. The inscription of the Great Seal, "Liberty and Union now and forever, one and inseparable," came from a speech given by Daniel Webster in the Senate of the United States. From the United States Constitution came some provisions relating to the declaration of rights.

Even the once current belief that the Criminal Codes, of North Dakota territorial and later statehood days, grew out of a Western background, namely California, has been rejected. According to one Judge Shannon: "It is erroneous and gravely misleading to say that our (North Dakota) codes were taken bodily from California, as serious results might spring from such a notion. A few facts will overthrow it. The authors of the codes, comprising such eminent jurists as Fields, Sherman, Bradford, Graham, and Noyes, after years of labor, made their final report of the Civil Code to the New York Legislature in February, 1865, and within a year thereafter the legislature of Dakota (Territory) adopted it. Rejected there (in New York), it found a home and was welcomed here (in Dakota). California followed our lead six years later. . . . Our civil procedure of 1867 was not borrowed from California, but was extracted from the New York original of 1849, the parent of most of our modern codes on the subject."

That these "Omnibus" states, in writing their constitutions, were not actually aware of the need to fit the instrument of government to the conditions of the region is also clear. Major John W. Powell had made his famous report on institutional adaptations for the semiarid lands of the West two decades earlier. He was especially concerned with the advantage of larger land holdings, setting aside reservoir sites for future development, integrating the dry land with the potential irrigated areas, and forming organized communities for land control. He appeared before the Montana Constitutional Convention, and also that of North Dakota, to explain the problems and the needs as he saw them.

There is nothing in the Montana proceedings, or those of North Dakota, indicating that the constitution writers saw the problem as outlined by Major Powell. Though there was much debate in Montana about irrigation needs, the control of water, and the sparsity of population, the delegates lacked experience in dealing with the problems of a semiarid land. They failed to grasp the opportunity to forge a constitution that would encourage the development of suitable institutions.

The reason for this failure becomes evident from a brief study of the residence background of the constitution writers. Montana had seventy-five delegates to its constitutional convention. Nine were born in Europe, and two in eastern Canada. Thirty-two were born in New England or Eastern states, specifically ten in Maine and ten in New York. Twenty-one were born in Midwestern states east of the Mississippi, including eight from Kentucky and five from Indiana. Only eleven of the delegates were from the adjacent prairie states, six having been born in Missouri, three in Minnesota, one in Kansas and one in Iowa. Their birth and early rearing in the humid area of Europe, the East, and the Midwest, undoubtedly was a hindrance to the delegates in understanding the problems in a semiarid land. Only about half of the delegates had lived in the Montana Territory ten or more years prior to the year of the Convention. Fifteen of the seventy-five had lived in the territory five years or less.

For North Dakota the situation was not significantly different. Colonel Lounsberry has this comment: "It is an interesting and notable fact that forty-five of the seventy-five delegates were elected from the Red River Valley counties and counties immediately adjacent thereto, twenty-six (came from the area) between the Valley counties and east of the Missouri River, and nineteen (came) from the vast area west of the Missouri River." This shows that the convention membership was weighted in favor of the non-Plains area of the state.

Other Plains states had similar experiences in their constitution making. The constitution-making spirit of Oklahoma was dominated almost entirely by nationwide rather than Plains issues. The Enabling Act of 1906, resulting in a constitutional convention for Oklahoma, had as its object the bringing together of twin territories—the eastern part of Oklahoma dominated by the tradition of the Five Civilized Tribes, and the western part dominated by the "blanket Indian" reservation situation and by the conditions brought on by the several "runs" of settlement.

The most pressing issues, having nationwide appeal and there-fore forced upon the constitution writers of Oklahoma, included the initiative and referendum measures; the attempt to curb ex-ecutive authority by introducing clauses to keep the governor from succeeding himself; the attempt to curb business power by creating a corporation commission to regulate public service business; the attempt to control public carriers by limiting pas-senger fares to two cents per mile; the restriction of child labor and women's working hours; prohibition on the contracting of prison labor; the introduction of a mandatory primary system of nominations; and the prohibition of the sale of liquor. Even woman suffrage was an issue that consumed much debate. In addition, oil development had gotten underway in Oklahoma, prior to constitution making, and has exercised control over state politics ever since, in spite of attempts to control such abuses, and hence, little time was or has been spent on adapting the constitutional governmental procedures to semiarid conditions in that state.

It is evident then that the historical and the then current economic forces that played a role in the writing of the consti-tutions of these several Plains states, and the experience of the delegates, were such as to emphasize humid-area ideals typical of the experience of the nation at the time. And once certain constitutional and governmental ideas were established in any of the Great Plains states, those ideas—regardless of their suit-ability to the region—had a tendency to influence any subse-quent constitutional writing or drawing of legal codes in the Plains area. One example of this is that the North Dakota Cor-poration Code, formulated early in that state's existence, was later taken over almost without change by Oklahoma when it became a state. There have been few forces, in the Plains, intelli-gent enough to assure the invention of new institutional devices especially suited to conditions in a semiarid land. This becomes more apparent when considering some of the aspects of local government.

UNSUITABLE LOCAL GOVERNMENT
FOR THE PLAINS

Local government in the United States is of four types: county, township, school district, and incorporated municipality —whether village, town, or city. The evidence is clear that these forms of local government had firm acceptance in the humid-area tradition of the nation; so firm indeed, that they were carried into the Plains without the necessary modification for their efficient operation in a semiarid land. Especially was this true in the tier of Plains states bordering the humid Midwest; it was less true of the western tier.

In addition to the four basic types of local government found in the United States, two more types, resulting from combining forms of county and township governments, are identifiable. In the New England states, town government has always reigned supreme, without the aid of county government. In the South, however, influenced by the plantation system and English tradition, the county, without township subdivisions, became the smallest unit of government. This county form of local government moved westward through the southern part of the nation, reached California, and then moved eastward again into much of the arid and Rocky Mountain West. Conditions of aridity, sparsity of population, early mining influences, Spanish land settlement influences in the Southwest, and the impact of migration were factors in keeping township government from developing here.

But the remainder of the nation, west of New England and north of the deep South and west into the Plains, developed one of two types of local government that combined the county and the township. One, the county-supervisor-township system, encouraged the independence of the township from the county, and the township officials were elected separately from the county officials. This pattern moved westward from New York to Michigan, Wisconsin, and Illinois and was introduced into Nebraska and the Dakotas. The other type, the county-commissioner-township system, had a closer relationship between the township and the county since the chairman of the township board automatically became a member of the board of county commissioners. This type spread from Ohio into Indiana, Iowa, Minnesota, and Missouri, and from there into the Plains states of Kansas and Oklahoma. In the Dakotas an element of choice was introduced, allowing the local people to decide how many congressional townships might join to form a civil township, and allowing for unorganized townships to function.

It is apparent that the eastern tier of Great Plains states suffered from a humid-area push of ideas which assumed that both the township and the county were necessary to deal with the affairs of men. The western tier of Great Plains states, farther removed from the push of humid-area ideas, influenced by the arid West and mining conditions, and influenced from the South, by the early cattleman's culture, found it possible to survive without the aid of township government. An illustration of the strength of the humid-area push into the eastern Plains states is Article IX, Section 4, of the South Dakota Constitution which reads as follows: "The legislature shall provide by general law for organizing the counties into townships, having due regard for congressional township lines (six miles wide and six miles long) and natural boundaries, and whenever the population is sufficient and the natural boundaries will permit, the civil township shall be co-extensive with the congressional township."

In Montana, on the other hand, the word "township" was applied to the area smaller than a county for which voters might elect two constables or two justices of the peace. These areas could vary considerably in size. They were for the convenience of administering justice and law in the horse-and-buggy days. All other local governmental functions were administered on a county level. The use of the word "township" as above illustrates the carry-over of the humid-area ideas, even into a state like Montana, much farther removed from the humid-area influence than were the Dakotas.

Since local government is so important in supporting the settlement and institutional pattern on the land, it is necessary to emphasize the contrast between the push from the East and the West, by reference to the Dakotas and Montana, though the Dakota laws have undergone some change in this respect by now. The North Dakota Constitutional Convention was influenced by humid-area ideas from the East; that of Montana more by Western conditions. F. N. Thorpe ("Recent Constitution

Making in the United States") says of the four "Omnibus" states (North and South Dakota, Montana, and Washington): "In their constitutional provisions the states go in pairs; North and South Dakota, Montana and Washington—a result not strange when the geographical position, the natural resources, the economic interests, and the influence of the constitutions of neighboring states are considered. Thus the influence of the constitution of California (1879) is perceptible in the constitutions of Montana and Washington, and that constitution was repeatedly quoted in the conventions of those states. The Dakota conventions were influenced by the constitutions of Illinois, Wisconsin, Michigan, and Minnesota and, generally speaking, by the constitutions of those states with which the delegates, by previous residence, were familiar, or the Territory with which, by present economic interests, they were concerned."

Here we have a basic cleavage between the eastern and western portions of the Plains, a split of interest and function that has always made it difficult for the two series of states, in the same region, to function co-operatively for their mutual interest. This divided allegiance is traceable, in part, to the fact that the Montana pattern conforms more nearly to an institutional arrangement modified by arid and semiarid conditions, while the North Dakota institutional arrangement did not undergo such adaptation. And, of course, the stream of population migration exerted a decided influence—the immigrant population of Montana coming from the South and West, that of North Dakota coming from the humid East and Europe. The stream of migration into Montana, to a large extent and for a considerable time, originated in or traversed other arid and semiarid parts of the nation, and, as a result, certain governmental modifications had already been made by the time the immigrants reached Montana. Such, however, was not the case in the Dakotas. In general, the divided allegiance which these two states represent—allegiance in one direction on the part of Montana, in another direction on the part of North Dakota—is typical of all the Plains states. The eastern tier of states affiliate themselves with their eastern neighbors; the western tier with the West.

Had it not been such a small geographical unit, the civil township might have been adapted to serve the Great Plains. The tendency was to keep it identical with the congressional township of six square miles or some multiple—the system used to survey the land of the nation. At the North Dakota convention there was a strenuous fight because the committee on county and township organization wished to compel the adoption of the commissioner-township system. Each township was to be organized and was to elect three directors; the chairman was to be a member of the county board of commissioners. Such a rigid system meant insecurity of county governmental organization until the townships were first organized. The conflict was finally resolved by a suggestion that local people be given the option to vote on the size of the township and the number of congressional townships, or multiples thereof, to be included.

One of the chief drawbacks to mixed local government is the cost. The township in North Dakota has several officials whose functions include the assessing of real and personal property, the building of roads, and the administering of certain police and judicial functions. The township officials once even had the responsibility of overseeing the public poor relief program. School district limits often coincide with the organized civil township; especially has this been true in the past. Montana, which has no township government, does not have all this cost.

Admitting that township government permits participation of the people in their affairs at another level, there is some doubt concerning the wisdom of such participation when population is sparse and financial resources are limited and unpredictable because of hazardous climatic conditions, or excessive variation in ability to pay. Certainly township government adds to the burden of administrative costs, even though officials may perform some functions in place of their being performed by county officials.

The problem of burdensome financing of township government in sparsely populated areas is further complicated by excessive inequities in wealth and tax-paying ability. Some townships contain the right-of-way and taxable property of certain public utilities such as railroads, highways, railroad land grants, public power lines, and other public service utilities. Other townships, even those immediately adjacent, also support these services, but do not have access to the revenue their taxable properties provide. Those townships without public utilities do not have the tax advantages that others do, and the burden falls more heavily upon local private property alone. Only county-wide and state-wide levies and taxes can assist in evening out some of the consequent injustices. A unit of local government of larger size would distribute the advantages and benefits from such public utilities more equitably or, put in another way, would place the burden of taxation on all more nearly alike.

County government in Montana has avoided some of these inequities in tax sources, tax-paying ability, and unco-ordinated planning on the local level. The counties are larger than in North Dakota, thus giving the Montana counties a possibility to over-come some of these inequities. North Dakota has fifty-four counties, each averaging about 1,337 square miles. Montana has fifty-six counties, each averaging 2,609 square miles.

The smaller average size of the county in North Dakota is directly traceable to the importation of humid-area beliefs and ways, including township government. Without doubt the exist-ence of township government in North Dakota set the stage for smaller county units. These patterns were all predicated on humid-area ideas—a much denser population, more churches, schools, towns and cities than the area could afford. This is clear from the discussion of county and school district organization by Everett Dick in *Sod-House Frontier*.

Montana, in the days of its organization as a territory and its acquisition of statehood, was influenced by the mining and the larger cattle interests. This influence—from the West and the South—accounts for the existence of larger counties in Montana and a more adapted pattern of government than is found in North Dakota. But Montana did not escape the efforts of the "county busters" to bring humid-area ways into the Great Plains. The peer, in this respect, was Dan McKay. His most fertile field was in eastern and northern Montana, settled preponderantly by agriculturalists from the humid area, where, as the result of his efforts, the counties are smaller on the average than in the re-mainder of the state.

Contrasting Montana and North Dakota, then, the presence of the township form of government in North Dakota is clear evidence of the importation of institutions from the humid area. Its absence in the eastern Plains portion of Montana, which is much like that of western North Dakota, is the counterpart—the failure to import the township unit—and demonstrates that township government is not a basic requirement for living in the region.

Another local government service—and cost—is the local school district. In North Dakota, where the township government prevails, the school district is frequently even smaller than the township. This was especially true prior to recent school consolidations. But in Montana, the school district is the only unit of service smaller than the county—other than the incorporated municipality. An understanding of the forces at work demonstrates that the presence of the township and the small school district in North Dakota generally meant—or at least meant before consolidation—an extremely small school district. Such districts, in the case of Montana, though still small and confronted with the problem of reorganization and consolidation as in North Dakota, are larger by virtue of the absence of township government.

The problem of too many school districts and too small school enrollment can be demonstrated by conditions in Kansas. In 1942, the Kansas Legislative Council released a study entitled *Closed Schools in Kansas.* Based on data for the school years 1940–41 and 1941–42, the study revealed that Kansas ranked "third highest among the states in the total number of school units but third lowest in average enrollment per unit." For the period 1928–33, Kansas had an average of 8,588 organized elementary school districts, 7,297 of them one-teacher schools. In the year 1941–42, there were still 8,266 such districts, 7,271 being one-teacher units. For 1928–33, the average per cent of districts with closed schools in any one year was 3.1, a percentage which had increased to 19.4 by the school year 1941–42.

The Kansas report admits there are variations in school organization and school problems in certain areas in the state, and there is one tabulation which lists the state school districts geographically—those in the eastern, the central, and the western parts of the state. But nowhere in the report is there a basic contrast of the elementary school situation between the Great Plains and the humid-area portions of the state. The expressions

"Great Plains," "semiarid," or "dust bowl potential" are never used. Instead, it is assumed that the entire state has a reasonable degree of similarity. Variation in sparsity of population, variation in distance for school children transportation, and variations in social cost of space appear to have no meaning for the writers of the report, and, therefore, no basic contrasts are made between the situation in the humid area and the Plains parts of the state. Consolidation, no matter what the distance of travel or the social cost of space, is recommended for both parts of the state. There appears to be no recognition that consolidation may be a penalty to the child in the Plains region.

The Kansas evidence illustrates, strikingly, the need for school reorganization in the Plains part of the state, and the process appears already to be more generally underway there than in the humid part of the state. But the emerging pattern is not necessarily one adapted to Plains conditions. The report does not emphasize the migration of farm families to town for educational purposes, or the permanent town residence of farm operators. It does not mention the traveling teacher as a substitute for the traveling pupil, or the substitution of the radio for the schoolroom, as possible solutions to the elementary school problem in the Plains.

To demonstrate that the Kansans who wrote the report were not aware of the striking differences between school conditions and needs in the Plains and those in the humid part of the state, the following simple retabulation of data in the report is revealing. Reference is made, in the report, to counties having the highest and the lowest portion of closed schools, regardless of location, in or out of the Plains. Yet close inspection of these same data reveals that of the twenty-two counties having 30 per cent or more of their elementary school districts with closed schools for 1940–41, all twenty-two were in the Plains, west of the ninety-eighth meridian. The situation was similar for 1941–42. In that year twenty-nine counties (out of a total of 105) had 30 per cent or more of their elementary school districts with closed schools. All but three were Plains counties, the three being in the border area just east of the Plains.

This is a very striking relationship between school problems and location in the Plains. Increased state aid for transportation and consolidation is not the total answer, as will become clear when the humid-area part of the state—if there is extensive state aid—has to carry most of the cost of elementary education in the Plains part during an extended series of drought years. On the other hand, to permit the children of the Plains to be only partially educated during a protracted drought period because state aid is not available is not a solution to the problem either. The fact is that the elementary education program for the Plains must be quite different from that in eastern Kansas. It will require a program that will depend on some state aid, coupled with the development of financial reserves against such hazards, a greater mobility of teacher and school, and a greater flexibility in the program than is now the case. Those are the hard facts that Kansans need to learn about their school conditions and needs in the Plains.

Kansans need not feel rebuffed, however, for not facing up to this problem. The residents of other Plains states are in exactly the same predicament. The problem has not been faced anywhere, and help is not likely to come from teacher-training institutions. Until the differences in the educational needs of the Plains and non-Plains portions of these states are clearly understood and then incorporated into legislative and policy action, the school problems of these states will be only partially solved. The task of inventing a school pattern for areas that are thinly populated and threatened by severe fluctuations in public revenue is an immense one and has gone begging because leaders have not learned to think in semiarid terms.

CHAPTER 14

Unadapted Land and Finance
Policies for the Plains

For agriculturalists to live and survive they must have land and credit. Therefore, the patterns of ownership and control regarding land shape much of the remaining institutional patterns that prevail in a region. Also financial credit is necessary to control land and to acquire the livestock, equipment, and man power to handle the land; therefore, credit too is a basic force in shaping the institutional patterns in a region. And coupled to the need for land and credit is the need to provide security for old age. Yet there have been, perhaps, no poorer adaptations in the institutional life of the Plains than the current (a) unsuitable land policies, (b) unadapted credit arrangements, and (c) unstable security for old age.

UNADAPTED PUBLIC DOMAIN POLICY

Earlier, reference was made to the policy of alienating the public domain of the Plains as a result of the Homestead Act. The homestead policy not only destroyed the earlier, much more adapted land policy developed by the cattlemen of the pre-homestead era, but it forced the cattlemen into unethical and often illegal ways of maintaining a ranch unit. In addition, the homestead policy brought an unadapted settlement pattern into the region. The 160-acre homestead was totally inadequate for providing the income necessary to support a family and the institutions necessary on the land. The rectangular land-survey system, a counterpart of the 160-acre homestead and the township system of government, was equally ill-suited to the condi-

tions of the region. Together, these forces helped shape an unwise settlement and community pattern for the people of the
Plains.

But there is another aspect of the public-domain problem
that is a measurement of the push of humid-area ideas into the
Plains and the degree of non-adaptation to local conditions. As
already shown, the powers granted counties, the manner of
creating counties, the basis for their authority, and certain other
procedures in county and state government are indicative of
the governmental differences between Montana and North Dakota, the one showing a more Western and perhaps more adapted
influence, the other exhibiting more clearly the influence of the
humid East. Nowhere is this more clearly demonstrated than in
matters of handling the public domain.

Montana is known as one of the public-domain states, and
North Dakota is not. A total of 34,834,411 acres were in public-
domain categories in Montana in 1945. This is 37 per cent of the
total land area, and includes forest land, grazing and Indian
lands, general land-office land, parks, soil conservation land, and
that belonging to other federal agencies. North Dakota had only
2,165,188 acres in such public domain, merely 5 per cent of its
total land area. North Dakota had only 520 acres in forest land
compared with 16,333,259 acres for Montana. North Dakota had
no land in the public grazing service category while Montana
had 5,920,299 acres. North Dakota had 736,377 acres in Indian
service lands compared with 6,502,866 for Montana. Only 104,-
191 acres were still in the hands of the general land office for
North Dakota compared to 1,821,247 acres for Montana. The
only category of federal domain for North Dakota that was
comparable to that of Montana was soil conservation land. The
amount for North Dakota was 1,066,459 acres compared with
1,918,248 acres for Montana.

Clearly, the underlying machinery and philosophy of government are vastly different for the two states. Montana has a
proportionately larger amount of land controlled by the federal,
state, and county governments, and by local grazing districts
than has North Dakota. In short, Montanans have always used
public lands in conjunction with private lands. Leasing arrangements are a part of many farm and ranch operations. North
Dakota, however, has always followed the humid-area policy

of getting all the land into operators' hands; quickly getting tax-default lands off delinquent rolls by sales to private persons, even at the risk of getting them back into the delinquent category at a very early date because of poor soil and yields. North Dakota has not been interested in other than individual land control.

Montana, on the other hand, has had experience with group methods of land control. It was the first state to organize grazing districts—a step which contributed to the eventual passage of the federal Taylor Grazing Act. In the case of co-operative grazing districts, such group control may involve private ownership by individuals, by corporations, or by lease from public agencies. In any case the operator is not forced to own all the land in his operating unit.

In North Dakota, with respect to the disposal of public lands for the common schools, certain individuals strongly favored a long-time retention of public lands, administered on a lease basis. There were lengthy arguments in favor of such a policy, but the arguments for immediate disposal by sale were urged more strongly. A compromise was reached that favored a policy of setting up effective protection for a public-land fund and the administration of a land-sale program. The sale meant getting the land into private hands, but the fund meant that the proceeds could accomplish the objective intended in the original school grant. The sales were to be deferred for a time and to be on an installment basis, thus avoiding the need for much reinvestment of money in competition with private lenders. Unfortunately, a ten dollar per acre minimum price was placed on school land in North Dakota, a legislated price often far beyond the true value of the land. One third of the purchase price was due during the first five years; the second third during the first ten years; and the final third during the first fifteen years. The humid-area idea of getting public land into private hands was modified in North Dakota, but not warded off as effectively as in the public-domain states.

The difference in public-domain policy, like that in governmental organization, divides the Great Plains States—excepting Texas which has its own public land policy—into two groups. The eastern tier of Plains states—North and South Dakota, Nebraska, Kansas, and Oklahoma—experienced the push from the humid-area East and none of them is a public-domain state. The western tier—New Mexico, Colorado, Wyoming, and Montana—are all public-domain states. Why these four western states contain the larger acreage of federally-administered lands remaining in the public domain is perhaps explicable for two reasons. One reason may be that the four western Great Plains states possess in their western regions large areas of mountains and forests which, before it was too late, the federal government realized were worth retaining in the public interest—more worth retaining, in the opinion of some, than the semiarid Plains. A second reason, however, may well be that greater pressure was brought against the government, in the second half of the nineteenth century and as the era of settlement reached its height, to dispose of what seemed to be the arable Plains, with much less pressure being brought to bear in favor of disposing of the nonarable mountains and forests. Probably the national land policy in effect at the time the Great Plains states emerged was the result of both: a national desire to preserve forest and recreational lands, and the Eastern settlement push demanding the disposal of the Plains. At least, as federal land policy was practiced, the eastern tier of Plains states no longer contains significant amounts of public domain, while the western tier yet possesses large federally-controlled tracts.

The insistence upon the alienation of all public lands into individual operator hands has a humid-area background. America was settled, especially the northern part, by Europeans—with small farm or small business backgrounds—in search of land of their own. Many had come from countries where land holdings were too small to give the family a living; many had never owned land. The reaction against such landlessness resulted in a heavy emphasis upon ownership, preferably of small holdings. The New England town organization was an immediate outgrowth of this reaction. The existence of free land, to the west but also in the humid part of the country, assured the extension of this policy of alienating land into the hands of operators by the Harrison Land Act of 1800, the Land Act of 1820, the Pre-emption Act of 1841, and, finally, by the Homestead Act of 1862.

But in the semiarid Plains and the arid West, such a policy broke down. Farm and ranch operations, of necessity, had to be in larger tracts. At prevailing high prices, many of them speculative, ownership by an operator of all the land in his operating unit was an impossibility. Certain adjustments had to be made. First, legal adjustments were made in size of homestead, allowing for larger units, but these adjustments generally came too late or were still inadequate. Second, families continued to live in poverty on small pieces of land and then created still greater poverty for themselves by buying additional land from tax delinquent rolls or, at high competitive prices, from a neighbor who was losing his land through mortgage foreclosure. Most of those who survived this adjustment did so only through windfalls from inheritances, relatives, marriage, and previous earnings from outside the region, or unexpected income from unforeseen price rises.[1]

A third possible adjustment—not yet made—is in the form of developing a long-term lease arrangement. Such leases could be from private individuals, from private land holding agencies such as insurance companies, banks, railroads, and land companies, or from public agencies such as the school districts, the counties, the state, and the various departments of the federal government.

By developing a long-time lease program or perfecting its counterpart, namely the grazing allotment; by having such public lands make guaranteed payments for public services in lieu of taxes and by developing a method for participation of the land user in the decisions concerning the conservation and use of such public and private lease lands, it would be possible to work out an adapted land-control and land-use pattern for the individual operator in the region. The fact that the eastern tier of Plains states have so little public domain is evidence that the humid-area ideology of land control still has the upper hand in much of the region. The fact that even in the public-domain states there is an occasional uprising against the administration of public lands, as there was from 1945 to 1948, is evidence that

---

[1]This statement will hold in the long run, even including the present relatively prosperous period. Land once worth $2 to $5 per acre is now exchanging for $50 and $75 per acre or more, on the assumption that the total payment can be made out of two or three crop incomes. But tax payments on such high assessment values, in years of drought will be very burdensome, unless it is anticipated that the assessments will be considerably lower. Also, the next generation of purchasers may not have such favorable price and production years. If the seller does not expect to get his return upon resale, this is evidence of a windfall gamble.

residents in the area also suffer from a humid-area land-control pattern of thinking on occasion.

The difficulty here is that the nation has not yet faced the realities of shaping an adequate land policy for itself. This is true even for the humid areas of the nation, but doubly so for the semiarid and arid regions. How does a young man start to farm or ranch for himself, without accumulating an unwarrantably large debt in the form of land, equipment, and livestock purchases? How is land to be transmitted from generation to generation under conditions of large capital investments? In the Great Plains this is an especially urgent problem because of the unpredictable nature of the farm and ranch income—an unpredictability that arises from the normally unpredictable character of the climate.

The source of the difficulty arises from the original humid-area concept that there must be private operator ownership of all the land in an operating unit—a type of ownership that is seldom practiced in the business and manufacturing part of our economy. This has been considered the only suitable way of controlling land or allocating it for use. Yet private ownership by the operator is but one way of doing these necessary things, as has been well shown by industry. Not all the land, at least, need be owned by the operator himself. Certainly the leasing of other privately-owned land is another possibility. Private ownership would still be involved, but not necessarily ownership by the operator. Long-time leases, with proper protection of both owner and tenant interests, can assure wise use and proper allocation. Perhaps it is even desirable that private individuals, other than the operator, should own some of the nation's land. Finally, certain lands, which for economic and social reasons are best suited to public ownership, can be similarly utilized in a wise manner through a long-time lease program.

The western tier of Plains states, along with the remainder of the public-domain states, are experimenting in these matters of long-term lease. By means of such arrangements, private as well as public lands can be placed into the hands of the farmer or rancher—the true operator of the land—who cannot always afford to own, in his own right, all the land in his operating unit. But the humid-area concept of outright private ownership, by the operator himself, of all the land in an operating unit represents a barrier against the acceptance of a land policy that is adapted to the needs in the Plains. The absence of public-domain lands in the eastern tier of Plains states is evidence of the prevalence of an unadapted land-control pattern. The great concern with what is called excessive rates of tenancy among farmers and ranchers is another sign of an unadapted land-control pattern for the Plains. A program to decrease tenancy is concerned with making all operators outright and full owners of their land. But this may be impossible and even undesirable for many of the farm and ranch operators of the Plains. At least it may be impossible for them to own all the land they require in an operating unit.

UNADAPTED CREDIT POLICY

A good investor is one who does not "put all his eggs in one basket." He diversifies his risk by investing his savings in different enterprises. The tragic thing about the farmer in general, and particularly the Plains farmer and rancher whose risks are especially high, is that the peculiar concept of owner-operator status emphasized by the humid-area East has meant just the reverse of a wise investment policy. By means of this peculiar Eastern concept, the farmer or rancher of the Plains has had to "put all his eggs in one basket." In an area of high risk in the first place, the Plains farmer and rancher have had to carry most of the risk all by themselves, especially in the more difficult years. The credit that came into the region sought protection by means of mortgage foreclosure. Neither party—creditor or debtor—was benefited by this foreclosure procedure, as a rule. And because of lack of faith on the part of private loaning agencies in the thirties, it was the backing of Uncle Sam, largely, that furnished the credit for Plains farmers and ranchers to reorganize their credit structure and continue their operations. All these difficulties are evidence of an unadapted credit policy for the Plains. But what is credit anyway?

Credit is a complex business transaction that serves in place of actual money. Modern society could not function without it. In its simpler sense, credit is a contract to pay under certain conditions; a more formal definition is that credit is the ability to command the goods or the services of others in return for a promise to pay at some future specified time. Behind the credit system are the savings of many people who do not consume all their current earnings, and allow others to use them for an interest return. Some forms of credit are even based on savings to be accumulated in the future. Credit is readily made available when there is a high certainty of repayment or contract fulfillment by the parties involved. When the certainty of repayment is endangered, the basis for credit—the savings of others and the negotiability of future credit contracts—is partially or totally withdrawn.

The nation's money and credit structure and philosophy have a European origin as well as a peculiarly American flavor. Since credit is the product of transactions in the market place, it is readily understandable that it had an urban origin, especially in the United States. Credit, in its origins, was more closely related to business, trade, and industrial activity than to agriculture. Not until the Federal Farm Loan Act came into being, creating the Federal Land Banks (1916), and the Federal Intermediate Credits Act of 1923, were credit procedures more nearly tailored to the requirements of agriculture.

Also the nation's money and credit policy was originally built in and for a humid area where there is high predictability in rainfall, yield, and repayment ability. Under such conditions, if a loan contract is made intelligently, taking into consideration price fluctuations and other normal variables such as the usual hazards in agriculture, the chances of loan repayment are good. The only truly unpredictable factor is the character of the person who borrows the money—the debtor. For protection against this unforeseen aspect of "weak character," the person or agency making the loan has the aid of the mortgage foreclosure clause. That is the only legitimate and morally sound reason for using the mortgage foreclosure clause—recovery in the event of an unwise character loan.

There is currently much talk of risk and uncertainty concerning agriculture. Stripped of its academic complications, there are two basic ideas involved. The first is that such risks and uncertainties in agriculture arise from price fluctuations and from those minor agricultural hazards found in humid areas—insect

186

and disease hazards, damage from storms and variations from normal weather.

In the Plains there is a second type of risk and uncertainty: the more violent fluctuations—above the normal hazards—with their resulting unpredictability in yield and income. In the Plains the mortgage foreclosure clause has been, too often, used to recover the creditor's equity in the event of inability to pay arising from such natural unpredictability. For this reason, the humid-area credit policy was and is not adapted to Plains conditions.

A truly adapted credit policy for the Plains would be one that would take into account this second type of unpredictability of loan repayment resulting from the fact of semiaridity. It would clearly recognize and state that repayment, for reason of lack of income due to unpredictable crop and livestock yield, could be postponed. Flexibility in repayment demands would have to be included in the credit arrangements. The mortgage foreclosure proceedings would not apply, except, as in the humid area, in case of character deficiency. In other words, a credit policy, adapted to the Plains, would need to have its origin in a semiarid, not a humid, region.

As it is, the institutional push from the humid area has saddled the Plains with an unadapted credit policy, one whose unsuitability is not clearly understood even today. The absence of flexible repayment measures, except in the case of the Farm Credit Administration, is evidence of the non-agricultural and humid-area origin of credit.

And the fact of unadaptability in credit policy for the Plains has contributed to much suffering and exploitation. It has encouraged unethical practices on the part of both lender and borrower. It has opened the door to the indiscriminate use of the foreclosure clause on the slightest pretext.

In the end, the mortgage holder also lost, since he found himself the eventual owner of land and equipment which he could not resell, except to the unsuspecting. Continued ownership on the part of the mortgage forecloser, usually not an operator, subjected him to the same hazard the former owner had faced—tax delinquency or borrowing money under the same conditions. In the meantime, the Plains acquired and have kept the reputation of being an undesirable credit risk—not because of the weak moral character of the inhabitants but because of the unsuitable credit policy so unwisely imposed on the region.

The solution to this problem would be a credit policy adapted to the conditions of the Plains, coupled with the idea of diversification of risk. The unadapted credit policy of the past is a factor in accounting for the undesirable aspect of the land-control policy—full private ownership of all the land by the operator—which was also imported into the region. To get credit, it was necessary to encourage ownership in full by the operator. The reverse was also true—to have ownership it was necessary to obtain credit through an unadapted credit policy which practically guaranteed that the borrower would not repay and, therefore, could not become the owner, unless he had special windfall gains.

Upon unadapted and weak credit and land policies, the settlers attempted to build communities and a social system. The wonder is that they were able to build at all. In reality, the building of a community structure was accomplished only through the suffering of the inhabitants and the early death of many.

UNADAPTED SECURITY MEASURES

In addition to the fact that ownership of the land gives the operator one kind of control of its use, and serves as collateral for credit, such ownership is also a social-security measure. The ownership equity serves as a fund for old-age security, and presumably an owner-operator is never unemployed. Therefore, he needs no unemployment compensation. Since 1935, the majority of urban residents, including the businessman, have acquired financial protection for old age and assurance against unemployment through the unemployment compensation program or make-work schemes of the full-employment acts. This has meant greater protection through increased diversification of risk for the urban people. They are compelled to place some of their own savings into an additional basket, over and beyond private insurance, private savings, and home-ownership investments. Such increased diversification of savings is the basic principle behind the social security program.

But farm and ranch operators, by virtue of national policy, were excluded from the social security program until 1955. The lack of diversification in the agriculturalist's savings program, by restricting the program to land ownership, was further compounded by making the agriculturalist, in his own individual capital enterprise, also carry the load for old-age security. In few enterprises, other than agriculture, has there been such a lack of diversification and such an emphasis upon concentrating all the "eggs in one basket."

In the Plains, the absence of real old-age security, by virtue of putting all eggs in one high-risk basket, is especially acute. It has been shown how the goal of land control through ownership is an especially hazardous undertaking for the residents of the region. It has also been shown how the unadapted credit policy has limited the possibilities of achieving such ownership, and how the mortgage-foreclosure technique may strip the owner of his hard-won equity following a series of unpredictable low rainfall years. From this it is apparent that the remainder of such equity for old age is indeed small, unless there have been windfalls.

That old age security, through the ownership channel, has failed to accomplish its goal is demonstrated by the high proportion of aged who are receiving old-age assistance in the Plains states. In Montana, for example, the number of old-age assistance cases was equal to 165 per thousand population age sixty-five and over, as of June, 1954. For Wyoming the rate was 199 and for Colorado, 376. For New Mexico it was 318, for Texas 374, and for Oklahoma 440. For Kansas the rate was 165, for Nebraska it was 130, for South Dakota it was 182, and for North Dakota it was 157. For the nation it was 184, including the South which has a very heavy load. Six of the ten Plains states had a higher rate than the nation and four had a lower rate. This contrasts with the following low rates for some of the industrial states: New Jersey, 46; Delaware, 57; Maryland, 59; Virginia, 71; and New York, 75.

Since the problem of security for the aged is so urgent, a further analysis is important. It becomes apparent, upon study, that reliance upon the Old-Age Assistance program, because it depends upon the tax base for support, represents a special hazard for the aged people in the Plains, and the taxpayers of the

Plains too. It is an unadapted form of old-age protection. The Old Age and Survivors Insurance program is a much more adapted arrangement for the Plains, since it has the financial resources of the entire nation behind it. It represents a risk diversification program in that the residents of all areas, no matter what the financial and business status of the area, have equal security under the program.

The Old-Age Assistance program is supported by a grant from the federal treasury, equal to somewhat more than half of the cost of the program. To that extent, the resources of the entire nation also support the program. But from that point on the situation is entirely reversed. For Montana, for example, the remaining half of the cost is paid out of taxes, equally divided between the state and the county. When the Plains counties are hit by an unpredictable series of dry years, the taxpayers of the state and the counties are expected to continue to meet their obligations for such Old-Age Assistance grants. In short, just when the taxpayer is least able to pay, he must continue to meet his obligation. He has only his own resources to fall back upon for his share. For the Old Age and Survivors Insurance program this account is already paid for by the prior deductions from the beneficiary himself and from the employer. The program is also supported by the resources of the entire nation.

For the Great Plains states, this financing arrangement is especially significant. The population of this region is largely agricultural, not industrial, as in the humid-area states. Consequently, the aged likely to be in financial need have been supported largely, until very recently, through the Old-Age Assistance program, while in the humid-area states a significant portion of this support comes out of the Old Age and Survivors Insurance program. Here we have had the ironical national policy of having nationwide resource support and risk diversification for the humid-area population, who do not experience the unpredictable fluctuations typical of the Plains, but denying that nationwide resource support and risk diversification for the residents of a semiarid region which has such unpredictable fluctuations. In short, the poor of the Plains region, by virtue of national legislation, were in the past, forced to band themselves together in their relative poverty, while those who could afford to support themselves more readily were banded together amidst their relative plenty—plus the resources of the entire nation at their command.

Such an old-age security program for the Plains people hardly spelled parity with the program for the rest of the nation. Such a program could hardly be described as suited to the needs of the people of the Plains. It was, in fact, one of the most unadapted practices that might be imagined in an age when old-age security is a matter of special pride. The answer was, of course, to place agriculture in the Old Age and Survivors Insurance program so that the residents of the Plains might have old-age security equivalent to that of the residents elsewhere, plus the support of the resources of the entire nation. Such a practice is more truly adapted for the Plains and the peculiar risk facing its residents.

To cite the evidence in this respect the following figures are pertinent. Montana and New Hampshire have about the same total population, the same proportion of gainfully employed, and the same number of persons receiving benefits from the combined programs, namely the Old-Age Assistance and the Old Age and Survivors Insurance programs. The difference is that Montana is largely agricultural and is a typical semiarid state. New Hampshire has a significant segment of its gainfully employed engaged in industry and is a humid-area state. More of its population, in need when aged, is supported through the Old Age and Survivors Insurance program.

In June, 1954, Montana had 165 out of every thousand people aged sixty-five and over receiving Old-Age Assistance, compared with 108 for New Hampshire—a state of approximately the same population size. In the case of Old Age and Survivors Insurance the situation was reversed: Montana had 20,900 recipients; New Hampshire had 31,600. The Old-Age Assistance cost per inhabitant for the fiscal year 1953–54 was approximately $12.15 for the residents of Montana and only $8.79 for residents of New Hampshire. The per capita state and local cost was $5.49 for residents of Montana and only $3.97 for residents of New Hampshire.

Therefore the Montanan paid a cost that was higher than need be, and he did this through both years of drought and years of plenty. The New Hampshire resident paid a smaller share and could afford such payments more easily, year in and year out, because he is not faced with such climatic fluctuations and consequent variation in income as is the resident of Montana. Until the 1955 extension of the social security program changed the picture somewhat, a far greater share of the old-age bill in New Hampshire than of the old-age bill in Montana was paid for out of the prepaid contributions of beneficiaries and was guaranteed by a program supported by the resources of the entire nation.

The identical analysis may be made for the remaining Great Plains states with similar results. It is apparent, then, that the social security program until very recently has not been adequately adapted to the needs of the residents of the Plains. The idea of security has had its roots in humid-area philosophy.

The lack of awareness for so long of the insecurity of a social security program for the Plains was the product of another Plains fact, namely, the minority status of the population. The residents of the region, lacking facilities for communication, have not known the facts and their meaning about many of their own problems. They have followed the leadership of the agricultural residents of the Midwest, especially of the Corn Belt—those agriculturalists who, surrounded by humid-area climatic conditions, are deeply steeped in those peculiar land-ownership, land-control, farm-credit, and old-age security benefits that have harmed the residents of the Plains. The Farm Bureau way has been the humid-area way; its programs have been tailored to humid-area conditions. The Farm Bureau programs have not been tailored to fit the needs of the semiarid and arid agriculture of the Plains and the West. Yet many Plains farmers continue to dance to the tune of the Farm Bureau.

Here, then, we have evidence that, unlike certain technological discoveries and developments which were particularly adapted to the area, the social and economic institutions have not, on the whole, undergone adaptations to the basic conditions in the Plains. What few adaptations there have been have come largely by the way of the South and the arid West. The humid-area push westward into the Plains, in the northern part of the nation especially, was coupled with the extension of small-farm agriculture and the growth of industrialization in the North.

The western tier of Plains states have experienced more

adaptation than the eastern tier. This is especially true of matters pertaining to local government, public-domain alienation, and credit facilities for agriculture.

There is, however, throughout the entire Plains area, emerging a whole host of new group services for people. Among them are expanded education, security programs for the aged, public health and hospital facilities, and medical-care programs. These services have their roots, not in agriculture, but in urban and industrial practices largely. Unfortunately, this means they have their roots in conditions of humidity. It is especially apparent that these new institutional devices, not having their roots in agriculture, are least likely to be based upon an awareness of the problems facing the people of the Plains. Here is the source of a new push of living patterns onto the Plains, patterns that are not aware of the need for adaptation to regional conditions. Of course, some progress is being made—such as the revision, effective 1955, of the social security laws concerning agriculture. But much more progress needs to take place.

And to be suited to the Plains, all programs and the institutions that support them must have certain characteristics. These characteristics have to do with reserves, mobility, and flexibility —the keys to adapted living in the Plains.

CHAPTER 15

Sutland and Yonland Communities[1]

The institutional pattern which any particular area may have is greatly determined by the manner in which the area was originally settled and by the area's environment. But in the United States, certain historical and cultural forces have operated in such a way as to alter or prevent the natural growth of institutions in certain areas and have fostered not organic institutions appropriate to the scene but have encouraged the appropriation and transplanting of institutions already established in other and different areas into an area where they are out of place. One of the main cultural forces in the United States—perhaps one of the strongest—which has contributed to this growth of inappropriate institutions in many parts of the country, particularly in the Great Plains, has been that expectation or assumption that what is true of one part of the nation must necessarily be true of another. The tendency to universalize out of particular situations has resulted, in the United States, in the assumption that population density is similar everywhere, that the nature and size of local government units should be the same everywhere and perform similar services, that towns will be of similar character—with like patterns of interdependence and specialization—throughout the country, and that the structure of society will be similar in every region. As a result of this assumption, the same economic and social institutions have been established in all parts of the nation without anyone's questioning the assumption in the first place or without

[1] The major part of this chapter originally appeared in *Rural Sociology* (December, 1953), and is here reproduced with minor changes only. Recognition of the original publication is herewith accorded to *Rural Sociology*.

anyone's actively recognizing the environmental differences that exist between one area and another in a land so vast as ours.

That these false assumptions continue to exist, even flourish, is evident in national advertising which proceeds on the belief that there is one economy, one social pattern, one set of values, one level of taste common to the United States. The assumption is that what is good for the East Coast must necessarily be good for the Plains and the West—that what the businessman in Yonkers, New York, likes surely the merchant in Garden City, Kansas, will, or should, like also. The media of mass communication, the assembly-line manufacturing companies, the transcontinental chain-store retailers—all operate on this assumption of common tastes and needs and have geared their entire business structures to take advantage of such a falsely-conceived but nevertheless widely-accepted observation about our country.

In spite, however, of the propagation of the myth that a single national pattern of social organization can serve the entire country, a change in social organization has been occurring in the Great Plains—a change away from the accepted national pattern and away from those institutional patterns for so long assumed to be the only patterns available. Certain basic situations in the Plains such as the variation in population density, the availability of some services and the unavailability of others, the great distances necessary to travel to reach many of those services which are available, the diversity of local resources and the variation of those resources from one locale to another—all these situations operate in the Plains to force social organization away from any artificial national pattern and to adjust to the needs at hand. More specifically, these situations are bringing about an increasing division in local social organization on the Plains—a division that must be understood and taken into consideration if a realistic evaluation of institutional and social life and functions in the Plains is to be made.

YONLAND AND SUTLAND SETTING

There are two types of setting in which people live and in which communities function in the Plains—the "sutland" and the "yonland." These terms are not in general use, but their

meaning nevertheless is real. In place of these terms the plainsman uses locality names for each such specific area, or he uses
a wave of the arm. But this does not tell the newcomer or the
inquirer anything about the areas. The terms "yonland" and
"sutland" have the advantage of giving immediate meaning to
the social and community life in any part of the region.

The sutland, the Plains over, is the more densely settled, often
stringlike, area of habitation along the major avenues of transportation. Generally, this area includes the railroads, which are
frequently paralleled by the major highways, bus routes, and
by the public utilities such as telephone and telegraph lines, gas
lines, and power distribution facilities. Here, also, are found the
larger towns and cities and all that they imply—specialized and
enlarged wholesaling and retailing; banking; shipping and processing for livestock and grain; storage; and specialization in
hospital and medical-care facilities. Here, also, are located the
advanced high school facilities, the larger church centers, and
the occasional colleges and universities. In addition, the governmental agencies, state and federal especially, tend to be located
in this area. Sometimes, though not always, the sutland includes
the irrigated area.

In short, the sutland is the location of the main arteries for
the wholesaling, business, industrial, educational, health, governmental, and social functions in the region, plus being the site
of concentration for certain types of agricultural specialties. It
is the home of the "sutler," who historically was the supply agent
at the army post before the day when the army maintained its
own supply services. Such areas are, therefore, appropriately
called the "sutland."

Away from the sutland are the "in-between" areas, generally
without the major transportation avenues and the public services and utilities found in the sutland. The towns are smaller, as
a rule, with more limited services and facilities. Sometimes they
are simple service centers only, inland in character. Community facilities are less specialized and often less developed, for
there is a real problem in getting adequate finances and sufficient people to support the services.

This area is the "yonland" of the Plains—the area "out yon-
der," out from the sutland; the area without adequate services.
It is not the hinterland, for the Plains are all a hinterland. It is

not the inland, for the Plains are all inland. The outback, as used for the Australian inland, comes nearest to the meaning of yonland. But the outback refers to a single large land mass. This is not the case in the Plains. Here the yonland represents smaller areas that are dispersed among the sutland areas. Furthermore, the outback is an arid land. The situation in the Plains is a semiarid one, where there is considerable population distributed throughout the entire land.

Viewed in panoramic manner, the conditions characterizing the sutland and the yonland undoubtedly have a decided impact upon community and social organization, making a sort of constellation for each respective type. And there is a great measure of interdependence between the yonland and the sutland, with the promise of more such interdependence in the future. The relations between the two are dynamic rather than static.

No attempt is here made to identify a set of final and infallible criteria for distinguishing between the sutland and the yonland, but an example will serve to make the contrast clear. A special tabulation of data for an area in southeastern Montana was undertaken and the results are shown in Figure 14. For the sutland, all minor civil divisions with a third or more of the land area in irrigation, and some adjacent strategic dry-land area, was separated from the land area having irrigation of less than a third of the acreage per minor civil division or none at all as of 1940. A second step was to include sufficient irrigated area to encompass about thirty thousand rural people. For the yonland, the tabulation included as much adjacent dry land (minor civil divisions with less than a third of the acreage in irrigation or none at all) as was necessary until about thirty thousand rural population was encompassed. A third criterion for the sutland, not basic but incidental, was the expectation to achieve a population, in total, of about seventy thousand, both rural and urban, on the assumption that this number would represent a minimum approximation necessary to support certain essential services such as a full-time public health unit, an adequate public library, and a 300-bed hospital.[2]

The results of this procedure are shown in Table 6. In 1940,

[2] For example, to be efficient and adequately serviced, it is estimated that a full-time public health unit should serve at least 60,000 persons; that a public library program should serve a like number; that an efficient 300-bed hospital is capable of serving an area of about 60,000 people.

the sutland area had a rural population of 29,083. It also included an urban population of 37,974. The total population was 67,057, just short of the 70,000 goal. To get this number of people, it was necessary to include the more densely populated portions of seven counties, covering an area of 2,227 square miles, twice the size of Rhode Island. The average population density per square mile was 30.1, compared with 44.2 for the nation as a whole, and 674.0 for Rhode Island. Since the 67,057 people resided in seven counties (and represented the largest proportion in six of the counties) it is apparent that their proportionate share of money spent for county government, schools, and all the public services and private businesses, when pooled together, could support one set of institutional services much more efficiently and effectively than is now the case. In short, these data imply that even in the sutland area, the residents are paying a high cost for their services. Even in the sutland, space represents a high social cost.

For the yonland, involving a very large part of all of south-

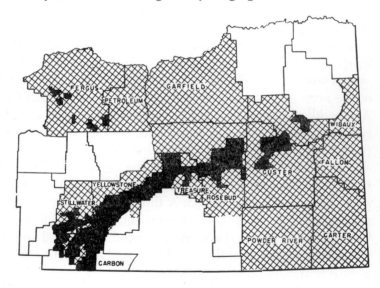

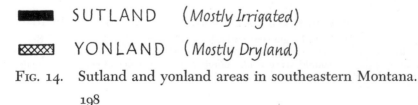

FIG. 14.   Sutland and yonland areas in southeastern Montana.

198

eastern Montana, the tabulation included a land area sufficient to encompass 29,834 rural people, a reasonable approximation of the 30,000 goal. But this entire area included only 7,178 urban people or a total of only 37,012 persons, about half the minimum total number (70,000) wanted. To get even this many people, it was necessary to include an area of 32,077 square miles. This is almost twenty-seven times the land area of Rhode Island, or the equivalent of Connecticut, Massachusetts, Vermont, and New Hampshire combined. The density was only 1.2 persons per square mile, a density slightly less than that of much of the Plains. Only about 20 per cent of this population was urban; the remainder was farm population, and the population in towns and villages having less than 2,500 people. All of six counties and large portions of seven additional counties had to be included.

The tabulation shows certain changes between 1930 and 1940. There was an increase in the total population during this

TABLE 6. Area and population characteristics of a sample sutland and yonland part of Montana, 1930 and 1940.*

Characteristics	Sutland		Yonland	
	1930	1940	1930	1940
Area, in square miles	2,227†	2,227†	32,077‡	32,077‡
Rural population	24,215	29,083	42,582	29,834
Man–land ratio (density)	10.9	13.1	1.3	0.9
Urban population	30,730	37,974	6,570	7,178
Man–land ratio (density)	13.8	17.0	0.2	0.2
Total population	54,945	67,057	49,152	37,012
Man–land ratio (density)	24.7	30.1	1.5	1.2
Per cent urban	55.9	53.9	13.4	19.7

* Taken from the U. S. Census of Population for minor civil divisions. Data for 1950 were not used because the minor civil divisions (school districts) for which population counts are recorded for Montana underwent so considerable a change in boundaries between 1940 and 1950 that comparisons were impossible. This was not so severe a problem for 1930 to 1940.

† This area is twice the size of the state of Rhode Island, and included the more densely populated portions of seven counties.

‡ This area is thirty-one times the size of the state of Rhode Island, almost the equivalent of Connecticut, Massachusetts, Vermont, and New Hampshire combined.

decade, in the sutland, accounted for by an increase in both the rural and the urban. For the yonland there was a striking decrease (25 per cent) in population for the total. Since the urban had an increase, this decrease was all in the rural. The population change for the decade 1940 to 1950 was not determined.

From this comparison it is clear that the social, community, economic, and service organizations in the yonland are likely to be very different in type and extent from those in the sutland. Space represents a much higher cost in the yonland than in the sutland, though it is high there, too. It is apparent that the yonland is dependent upon the sutland for many services. In turn, the sutland is dependent upon the yonland.

It is the independence of the two—because of space—as well as their direct interdependence that makes it necessary to distinguish between the sutland and the yonland. This necessity can be illustrated by reference to the school-tax situation. Until very recently in Montana, elementary schools were supported by local school-district and county funds, and only a minimum of state subsidy. Legislation has now gone into effect to have the state collect and contribute a much larger proportion for elementary education, and for very good reason. The sutland has a much more lucrative local tax base than the yonland, and the sutland tax base is also a more stable one. For example, the sutland generally contains the railroads and the public utilities in its property taxable for elementary and high school purposes. But these public utilities are dependent on business from the yonland also. The products of the yonland are hauled to the sutland for final shipment, handling, and storage. The fact that the sutland is the receiving area for the yonland products means that it has a windfall of storage, processing, and other business facilities that enter into the tax base there. By this very fact they are not available for tax purposes to the yonland. The yonland is largely dependent, for its tax base, upon personal, real estate, land, and livestock property.

Here, then, is an illustration of the economic interdependence of the yonland and the sutland, two areas that are differentiated, one from the other, for no other reason than historical precedent and space alone. It is only fair that the yonlanders have access to a portion of the tax revenue that is now monopolized and jealously guarded by the sutland. Only through the device of tax assessment and collection on a state-wide basis can the yonland realize its fair share of tax revenue from the economic activity cycle that originates there. But the residents of the sutland will not be happy in sharing their more favorable tax base with the yonland, for they claim a vested interest.

However, a simple shift from a local to a state-wide tax base for certain public services is not enough to bring about the necessary adjustment in public revenue between the yonland and the sutland. Since personal, real estate, land, and livestock property are the major sources out of which public revenue is extracted for the yonland, the assessment values are likely to be inflated and higher than is the case in the sutland. Resort to a state levy on this source would only result in a still greater burden for the yonland residents. Because of the assessment inequity, it causes a further flow of tax revenue to the sutland, rather than the reverse. Before such a state levy is effective in getting revenue from the sutland to the yonland, it will be necessary to have state-wide uniformity in property evaluation, assessment, and tax levy. Thus the interdependence between the sutland and the yonland becomes even more apparent.

In the face of the differentiation between the two, this interdependence between the yonland and the sutland is far more complex than implied by any simple illustration. It involves the relation of dry land to irrigated land in matters of farm and ranch unit organization, the relation of livestock grazing to a feed base, the extension of public health activities and medical care and hospital services from the sutland clinics and hospitals to the yonland residents, and the relations of the sutland church to the small congregations in the yonland. These are only several additional illustrations to point up the need for social organization to bridge the gap between the yonland and the sutland communities of the future. It is a problem that attends the high social cost of space in the Plains.

SPACE AS A SOCIAL COST

The relatively sparse population in both the yonland and the sutland of the Plains has numerous implications for the institutional pattern and the social organization in the region.

Space itself is a social cost. This has been well emphasized by A. H. Anderson ("Space as a Social Cost"), who worked out the relationship between cities of certain size and the size of the trade areas attached to these cities in the Plains states. For cities of similar size, the trade area was found to be considerably larger in the Plains proper than in the humid area to the east of them. Also, there were many fewer cities in the Plains. His conclusion is that "communities spread over the larger areas are extremely tenuous, and their problems of organization obviously differ from those of the more compact communities."

Anderson found that many of the Plains communities had a radius of as much as forty-four miles or more, while a radius of seven miles placed most people in contact with cities in the more humid part of the eastern tier of Plains states. He concluded that these facts of population sparsity in the Plains must mean higher expenditures, so that space itself has become an overhead cost of living. This, in his opinion, can be minimized by two types of adjustment, already partially underway, namely, "adaptation of services to sparse areas, and reorganization of the residence patterns." Unfortunately Anderson did not distinguish between sutland and yonland communities in this respect. The contrast in geographic size of community for the yonland and for the sutland might be expected to be as significant as those between the Plains and the non-Plains.

It is not easy to measure the extent of the social cost of space. Nor have the areas of social life in which they might occur been identified. Many occur in the form of subsidies from local, state, and federal governments. Some appear as deferred (public welfare) costs that arise from inadequate (rehabilitation) services of an earlier period. The higher capital outlay and operating expense for rural electrification are such costs, as are also portions of the costs for R.F.D. mail service and for road construction. The cost of maintaining a two-dwelling household for school purposes, one on the ranch and one in town, represents a higher cost of living, including a social cost for space at a time when family expense is already increased. A substitute for the two-dwelling arrangement is costly school transportation expenditures, or an allowance for room and board equivalent, also a social cost of space. The lower-quality service aspect, often eventuating in greater costs, is a social cost and can be seen in the inadequate institutional facilities for religion and for hospital care in many areas of the region, as well as in the inadequate facilities for the aged, the mentally ill and retarded, prisoners, and juvenile offenders. A contrast of this social cost of space in the yonland, as compared with the sutland, would also be revealing information about community and social organization in the Plains.

Because of the numerous factors of quality of service that bear on social costs, and the unavailability of dependable data to test the hypothesis, the measurement of social cost of space is only in the beginning stages. An elementary analysis in the area of school costs would seem to justify the statement that perhaps as much as 16 per cent of the variation in elementary and high school costs can be attributed to distance alone—just simple mileage.[3] Should this hold for buying and selling, for recreation, and for the numerous other items in the standard of living, the living expenditures for residents of the Plains would appear to be weighted down considerably by space cost alone, especially so in the yonland. In a drought year, or series of years, this cost, if inflexible, might curtail severely the remaining items of family living for residents in the Plains.

It would appear that a form of protection against such bankruptcy in levels of living (and purchasing power) for Plains residents can be accomplished by the proper co-ordination and integration of services between the sutland and the yonland areas of the region. Such integration appears to be necessary, not alone with respect to resource management and the public-service tax base, but also with respect to the actual co-ordination in the rendering of the services. The affiliation of a small yonland hospital with a sutland base hospital—and the medical, clinic, diagnostic, and nurse specialty advantages that can be obtained thereby—is a case in point. Illustrations of such yonland–sutland integration are not unusual for individuals and their personal affairs, as for example in the case of the rancher on the range who has a feed base in an irrigated area, even at considerable distance from the ranch headquarters. It is on the

[3] The simple correlations involved were statistically significant, as were also some multiple correlations. Secondary data tend to be too crude for the refined measurements required, and a final test of this hypothesis will depend on obtaining primary data. This elementary analysis was made by the author on a county basis for thirty-seven Plains counties of Montana.

group or social organization and institutional level that the integration needs to be developed.

POPULATION LOSS AS A FACTOR
IN COST OF SPACE

One aspect of the social cost of space in the Plains is the increase in these costs because of the threatened decrease in population, especially in the yonland. This is apparent from the earlier tabulation (Table 6) which showed a decrease from 49,152 to 37,012 persons for the yonland sample area between 1930 and 1940. Since there was an increase in urban population in this period, the decrease was entirely in the rural population. The central concern becomes one of how far population decrease in the yonland can be tolerated, at the expense of increased social cost, before the social costs become so high that a far-reaching change in population and social organization should be deliberately induced. It appears that the Plains, especially in the case of the yonland, are now or will soon be facing the following test of population-resource balance: When does the population decrease and the resulting higher per capita cost for services turn into a disadvantage because the social cost of space becomes so high that per capita income is less of a measure of welfare than is total income for the area? In short, more people productively employed at a somewhat lower per capita income may produce a larger total area income than fewer people employed at higher per capita incomes. The social cost may be considerably higher in the last instance.

What proportion of the Plains area finds itself at this crossroads point has not been determined. That some areas are at this crossroad is apparent to any observer. That this is most typical of the yonland is also apparent. That a proper integration of the yonland and the sutland can postpone the arrival at this crossroad, or can be the means for the social rehabilitation of an area that has arrived at this point, is also clear. For such situations, the need now is one of public education, grass-roots invention of techniques, and finally initiation of an action program.

To point up the likely population trends for the Plains region, a special tabulation was undertaken for Montana. The object was to determine the trend of true population growth for a sample area of the region and to determine the resulting change in population composition.

It was assumed that the census for 1920 offered a reasonable starting point from which to project population estimates for Montana. The area of study was to be regarded as a self-contained unit, unaffected by migration. By applying the current death and fertility rates to the base population of 1920, it was possible to determine the survivors of, and the new births to this population for 1930, 1940, and 1950. The estimated population could then be compared with the actual census population. The comparison made revealed a difference in number, age, sex composition, and rural-urban distribution between the hypothetical and real populations. Since current fertility and death rates were used, there was only one other factor that could account for the difference in number and composition of the population. This was population mobility in its direct and indirect impacts.

Conclusions from the study are as follows: Montana's total population, based on the expansion of the 1920 base, could easily have been 50 per cent higher in 1950 than the census enumeration shows it to be had there been no in and out migration. For the Plains part of the state, and especially for the yonland, this increase would have been nearer 80 per cent, most of it in the rural areas. The difference is due to out-migration of former residents. This mobility factor had an impact upon all age groups, but especially on the number of older people and on children. The youth population had been less affected than commonly expected. The impact was also more severe on women than on men, and on the rural than on the urban. In fact, the urban population in the sutland and in the yonland gained from such migration. These impacts were different for the Plains part of the state than for the mountain part, being frequently less intense and in the reverse order for the mountain area. To test the validity of the Montana case, parts of the tabulation were extended to include the Dakotas, Nebraska, Colorado, Idaho, and Wyoming. The situation for the Plains part of Montana was found to be generally typical of what was true for these other states, the major difference being that Montana showed a lead in these trends by about a decade.

In summary, the probabilities are that the Plains, especially in the yonland and the rural areas generally, will experience difficulty in maintaining future population numbers. This will intensify the problem of social organization for the yonland of the Plains and also for the sutland. It will fall upon the people in the sutland to extend more of their services into the yonland if the people there are to have the basic services essential to health and good education. If it appears desirable to maintain present population numbers in the Plains, or to increase numbers, it will be necessary to provide economic opportunities so that youth can remain in the region. These opportunities will most likely be in industrial and service jobs in towns and cities of the sutland.

COMMUNITY ORGANIZATION
IN THE PLAINS

Some observations are necessary on the relationship of community life and organization to this pattern of population sparsity in the Plains, especially in the yonland. The data for this analysis come from a study of community organization in a range-livestock county of Montana.

Though this area of study—Sweet Grass County, Montana—is in the sutland, it is sparsely populated, having only 3,621 people, with a density of two persons per square mile, and it is tributary to a much more densely populated part of the sutland, namely Billings and vicinity. When moving out from the center sutland part of the county one quickly finds himself in a yonland situation. Therefore, some of the conditions in Sweet Grass apply also to the yonland. From this study it is apparent that group life and social organization are vitally affected by sparsity of population, extensive geographic distances, high mobility of the population, low participation because of distance, and the weakness of neighborhood and community functions.

It was found that traditional community life was so indefinite and weak that the expression "locality grouping" appeared preferable to the traditional expression "community." Many of the services to people were supplied by agencies and associations of the governmental and special-interest group type and depended upon the formal functionary for group action. The "community," in the voluntary and non-legal sense, could seldom command the resources and manpower to perform the necessary tasks. The area of service for the major activities was generally county-wide, even for informal organizations; and a number of important "community" functions were performed by the county. The evidence appeared to suggest that the county, as a political and service unit, may come closer to being the "community" than any other area or grouping of people within its boundaries.

A more generalized observation is that the sutland areas of the region, with the help of past traditions, nationality, topographical, and historical influences, at one time had strong neighborhood and community characteristics, in spite of recency of settlement. There are still such areas. Among the historical influences were heavy concentration of population, generally in the sutland, in the expectation that the region could support nearly as dense a population as the more humid parts of the nation. With the help of the adjacent smaller towns and villages, some of these more compactly settled parts, generally in the sutland, still have considerable traditional social organization of the neighborhood and community type.

In between these is the yonland, the marginal social organization area where community organization is more tenuous and in transition and where there is considerable dependence upon sutland centers for services. It is here that many people lead relatively isolated lives, at best dominated only by locality group organization. Occasionally there are strong traditional communities in the yonland, especially if the centers happen to be county seats.

In spite of the prevalence of the formal agency type of social organization in Sweet Grass County, and the large territorial scope of coverage, it appears that personal face-to-face contacts form the basis for much association, even in formal groups. But the functionary, especially the county agent and his helpers, have to stand ready to keep social organization active.

Figure 15 is a schematic approximation of social organization in the Great Plains at present. The factual basis of this analysis rests chiefly on observation and on some detailed research. The chief characteristics of social organization in the Great Plains

Open country

Nigh-dwellers
The rural school
The family
The farm organization locals

THE YONLAND

The village as a service station

*The disappearing
neighborhood and
community, and
emergence of
areas of local
association.*

The co-operatives for farmers and other
    local business enterprises such as:
        (a) Grain elevators
        (b) Oil stations
        (c) Stores
        (d) Creameries and others
The bars, pool and gaming halls
The movies
The church
The elementary schools (and sometimes
    high schools also)

The town
(generally the county seat)

THE SUTLAND

*The formalized
group level
of service
administration
on a service
area basis.
This is not
now a com-
munity in
most instances.*

Elementary school, including farm
    families who move to town
More specialized buying and trading
    services
The high school
The church
The hospital and health services
Co-operative group services such as:
        Irrigation districts
        Soil conservation districts
        Weed control districts
Marketing organizations for wool,
    livestock, and feed
Formal county functions
Formal farm organizations

The city

Highly specialized services
Grazing district headquarters
Livestock marketing centers

FIG. 15. The trend of social organization in the Great Plains.
The trend of social organization in the Great Plains involves the tendency (a) of rural population to decrease as urban population
increases; (b) of service areas, both rural and urban, to increase in
size; and (c) of all organizations to move toward increased formality

include the following: (a) A striking change, occasioned by mechanization and use of modern transportation. This change is in (b) the direction of a striking increase in size and area of service and association, even for informal group activity. In a sparsely populated area, effective social organization, to function, faces the problem of having insufficient people to participate, to support, and to serve the activity. For rural areas, this change is also (c) from open-country and hamlet-centered to town- and city-centered social organization, with the hamlet or village as only a minor and accidental link, unless it is a county seat. This is true for both the sutland and the yonland. These smaller places tend to remain as locality centers for association on the informal level, and only infrequently can they promote a "community" project.

Finally, in a sparsely populated area, increased size of area alone is not enough to make it possible to have effective social organization. This is especially true when town and country interests, and space itself, begin to introduce a greater variety and heterogeneity of interest. Therefore, social organization in the Great Plains tends (d) to take on a formal and legal emphasis. Under these conditions, county boundaries are soon reached and, therefore, the question of having formalized and legal county services in place of informal group services becomes a real fact in the choice to be made by the inhabitants. The decision to perform the function ultimately, then, falls into legal and public channels, such as the legally-constituted school districts, the irrigation districts, the weed-control and soil-conservation districts, or the county itself.

Many traditionally organized counties, patterned after ideas from the humid area, are too small in size, population numbers, and taxpaying ability to provide some of the necessary services by themselves. Therefore, multi-county services, or county and school district services with state support, are immediately in prospect. This creates tensions and problems in social organization, in town-country relations, and in intertown co-operation.

The rural school, in the open country, and the locals of farm

---

and to emphasize legal status. Social pressure is such that, in all activity and organization, progress is considered always in terms of *away from* the yonland, *toward* the sutland.

organizations are in a critical situation in the Plains region. Supported only by family life and by associations between nigh-dwellers (not neighbors) in many areas, their survival cannot be anticipated unless there is a militant effort directed at community and social reorganization. Farm and ranch people themselves contribute to the breakdown of these locality services in the open country. Many move to towns and cities for the education of their youngsters in both elementary and high school. An increasing number move there for year-round residence, and commute to their farm and ranch quarters. These people often vote for inadequate support for schools and other public services in their own locality. They find it inconvenient to attend the farm local meetings in the open country. Mechanization and the premium on timely farm operations minimizes the role of neighborliness. Thus, the open-country social life is characterized increasingly by nigh-dwelling rather than by neighborliness.

The small village, once the center for community life, has often become merely a service station. In it may be located the co-operative enterprises of the farmers—such enterprises as elevators, oil stations, creameries, cotton gins, and other services. Here, too, are found a limited number of other private business services, perhaps the consolidated elementary school, and, sometimes, a small high school. Here, also, may be the pastorless church. But chief of all, here are the bars and the pool and gaming halls. These are the loitering places in which are found the nearest substitute for neighborliness among the nigh-dwellers of the open-country. Here farm workers, migrant laborers, livestock and grain truckers, custom contractors, and farm operators gather to transact business and to meet people.

But the formal organizations, the group activities once performed by the community, are centered in the larger town—usually the county seat. Here certainly is the high school, the hospital, the formal county services, the formal farm-marketing headquarters for wool, livestock, and feed commodities. Here, also, are the county agent, the production credit association, the bank, and the Production and Marketing Administration headquarters. Here can be found the officers and the technical services for irrigation, weed control, and soil conservation districts. In addition, the specialty services and shopping requirements can be satisfied here.

Whether these towns—usually county seats—are the community centers of the future, and the entire county the area of the community, is still to be tested by time. It appears that many voluntary services, once performed by the community, have been delegated to formalized and legally-constituted agencies. Perhaps that is the result of sparsity of population, great distances, and the fact of minority-group living in the region.

This trend in the weakening and the reshaping of traditional social organization in the Plains is not unrelated to the existence of the yonland as contrasted with the sutland, and the absence of social organization to bridge the gap that now exists between the two.

Sparsity of population, with a trend towards further population decrease in the rural areas, has undermined the traditional humid-area beliefs of "community" in the Plains. There is emerging, in the Plains, something new in social organization. There appears to be an emphasis upon formal and legal organization in order to encompass the larger areas that are necessary to command resources and population adequate enough to provide certain services. The functionary (paid official) appears to be essential to the functioning of a program if the organization is to survive and perform a task. The situation is strikingly more critical for the yonland than for the sutland. There appears to be no way of abolishing the separation of the sutland area from the yonland, if for no other reason than that distance itself prevents bringing the two together. But there is also a need for integrating the sutland to the yonland, or vice versa, and to have a proper division of labor for many services. Certain services must be made to reach out from the sutland to the yonland in a mutually accommodating form. For other services, there must be an adapted counterpart in the yonland that is properly integrated with sutland headquarters. Undergirding all these interdependent sutland–yonland services must be an equitable way of financing the programs.

CHAPTER 16

The Hinterland Role of the Great Plains

The Great Plains are a hinterland, an area set apart.

Plains people look to other areas of the nation for their markets and for the refined and processed goods and services they consume, while they furnish others with raw materials. It is a well-established economic fact that the suppliers of raw materials are in a less advantageous bargaining position and receive less income for their efforts than do the refiners and processors of raw materials. Because of this hinterland position and the ensuing economic disadvantages, the residents on the eastern edge of the Plains have their attention drawn to the Midwest, while those on the western edge look toward the Pacific Coast. The Plains people are, therefore, unable to act in a united fashion.

HINTERLAND ASPECTS
FROM A POPULATION STANDPOINT

The relative sparsity of population in the region accounts, in part, for the hinterland status of the Plains. The ten Plains states, in their entirety, had somewhat more than 17,000,-000 people in 1950, an increase of 9.3 per cent over the 1940 population (see Table 7). The 1950 figure is about 10 per cent of the nation's population. All states but North Dakota and Oklahoma had an increase during the 1940–50 decade.

The entire Great Plains proper had a population of 5,500,000 in 1950 compared with almost 12,000,000 who lived in the Plains states but outside the region proper. This meant an average density of 9.4 persons per square mile in the Plains proper compared with a density of 22.6 for the non-Plains portions of these states. Between 1940 and 1950, the increase for the Plains was greater, namely 14.9 per cent, than for the non-Plains portion (9.3 per cent).

The significant thing here is that the Plains proper are a hinterland to the rest of these states, as well as to the nation, because of the small weight that Plains population can exercise in state and national affairs. This is more typical of the western tier of Plains states than is the case for the eastern tier.

In 1950 about half of the population in the Plains proper was urban, while for the non-Plains portion of these states more than half the population was urban. In both instances, the heavy proportion of urban population, for an otherwise agricultural area, means a strong leaning in the direction of urban influences outside the region for the reason that the urban influences in these states are not oriented towards but away from the Plains. This becomes more apparent when it is realized that there has been a striking increase in urbanization, and a heavy loss of rural population, in the Plains proper and also for the non-Plains parts of these states.

Were the urban population of the Plains concentrating its efforts on playing an effective role in adaptation to Plains environmental conditions, the preponderance of urbanization would be helpful to the region. But in actual fact, the urban population is the vehicle by which the remainder of the Plains is attached as a hinterland to the urban and industrial economy of the nation. This arises from the function of urban areas in the Plains. They are the depots for exporting the Plains raw materials and for unloading the marked-up consumer goods that are sold to the Plains people. It is at this very point of rural-urban contact in the Plains that there is much enmity and conflict between the agriculturalists and the urbanites in the region. The reason is that it is at this point the hinterland status of the region becomes most apparent—the economic life of the region and the individual pocketbook are involved.

THE AREA TORN APART

The fact that the Plains are a region encompassing only portions of ten states, with the remainder of each state fac-

TABLE 7. Population in thousands for Great Plains states classified by Plains and non-Plains and rural–urban residence for 1940 and 1950*

State	Grand Total	1940					
		Total	Plains Urban	Rural	Total	Non-plains Urban	Rural
North Dakota	641.9	398.1	59.2	338.9	243.8	72.7	171.1
South Dakota	643.0	314.8	67.7	247.1	328.2	90.4	237.8
Nebraska	1,315.8	440.2	107.3	332.9	875.6	406.8	468.8
Kansas	1,801.0	317.7	59.3	258.4	1,483.3	694.6	788.7
Oklahoma	2,336.4	387.4	85.4	302.0	1,949.0	794.3	1,154.7
Texas	6,414.8	2,205.3	1,083.5	1,121.8	4,209.5	1,825.5	2,384.0
New Mexico	531.8	127.7	59.8	67.9	404.1	116.6	287.5
Colorado	1,123.3	200.4	46.5	153.9	922.9	544.3	378.6
Wyoming	250.7	107.2	33.0	74.2	143.5	60.6	82.9
Montana	559.5	309.8	97.5	212.3	249.7	114.0	135.7
Ten States	15,618.2	4,808.6	1,699.2	3,109.4	10,809.6	4,719.8	6,089.8

* Taken from the Population Census for 1940 and 1950.

ing in another direction away from the Plains, gives the region a torn-apart character. This is so significant that it requires a concrete illustration.

From the standpoint of climate and topography, western North Dakota and eastern Montana are identical. One would expect them to act as neighbors. Yet, in reality, there is little communication between the two. North Dakota is within the sphere of the metropolitan influence of the Twin Cities of Minnesota and also of Chicago. Montana, on the other hand, is largely within the sphere of the metropolitan influences of the West Coast cities. It is difficult, therefore, for the Plains portions of North Dakota and Montana, as neighbors, to have a basis for common reference. There are no effective urban forces, no outstanding newspapers, and no effective instruments of communication to tie them together and to attract the interests of these people.

The situation is further intensified by the fact that North Dakota also has the most influential segment of its population living in the humid Red River Valley, with its peculiar agriculture. Montana, on the other hand, has had its most vocal and influential segment of population living in the mountain region. It is a far cry from the Red River Valley of the Flickertail State to the Shining Mountains of the Treasure State. But more than

Grand Total	Total	Plains Urban	Rural	1950 Total	Non-plains Urban	Rural	State
619.6	378.9	76.4	302.5	240.7	88.4	152.3	North Dakota
652.7	319.6	101.8	217.8	333.1	114.9	218.2	South Dakota
1,325.5	430.0	140.2	289.8	895.5	481.7	413.8	Nebraska
1,905.3	333.5	98.5	235.0	1,571.8	894.8	677.0	Kansas
2,233.4	357.8	120.0	237.8	1,875.6	1,019.5	856.1	Oklahoma
7,711.2	2,874.8	1,856.7	1,018.1	4,836.4	2,981.4	1,855.0	Texas
681.2	176.1	106.3	69.8	505.1	235.6	269.5	New Mexico
1,325.1	208.3	55.1	153.2	1,116.8	776.3	340.5	Colorado
290.5	120.1	55.3	64.8	170.4	89.3	81.1	Wyoming
591.0	325.1	126.6	198.5	265.9	131.4	134.5	Montana
17,335.5	5,524.2	2,736.9	2,787.3	11,811.3	6,813.3	4,998.0	Ten States

the physical space of the Great Plains separates the two. The Red River Valley is as different from the mountains as either of them is different from the Great Plains.

Added to these differences are striking diversities of interests in the urban population of both states. Butte, Montana, has been depicted as one of the most urbanized small cities of the nation. It is the stamping ground of the Anaconda Copper Mining Company and the Montana Power Company—the Montana twins. Its Miners' Union Local Number One is one of the oldest in the nation and stands as a testimonial of the city's chief interest—mining. Fargo, North Dakota, is different. There the urban population is largely dependent upon the processing of farm products, merchandising, and the small trade typical of a humid-area agricultural economy. Financially, it is tied to the economic power-complex that reaches out from the Twin Cities of Minnesota.

Thus, on the physical, social, economic, psychological, and political levels, the Plains residents of Montana and North Dakota are pulled in opposite directions. They stand in a more distinct contrast to the remainder of the residents of these same states than is generally supposed. And the same situation applies to the remaining Plains states. Under such conditions it is difficult to achieve unity of purpose, direction, and ingenuity in solving Plains problems.

Still another force contributing to the hinterland role of the Plains is the tearing apart influence exerted by metropolitan centers from outside the region. A glance at Figures 16 and 17 discloses many stringlike attachments pulling the Plains in various directions, never consistently in one direction for the entire area. And the underlying forces responsible for such a tendency are business, trade, manufacturing, transportation, communication, and governmental services.

For instance, Figure 16 shows eighty-eight different federal governmental functions pulling Montana in a variety of directions, as indicated by headquarters location: three agencies pull Montana to Spokane, eleven pipe it to Denver, one pulls it to Lincoln, five attract it to Minneapolis, four direct its attention to Salt Lake City, five siphon it to Portland, twenty-one attract it to San Francisco, one draws it to Kansas City, three pull it to Chicago, thirteen siphon it to Seattle, two pull it in the direction of Omaha, one attracts it to Sacramento, one filters it down to St. Louis, and only seventeen have their headquarters in Montana itself.

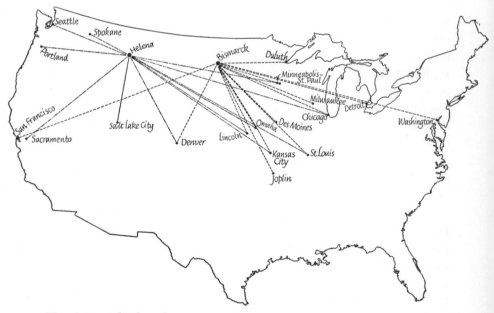

FIG. 16.   The headquarters of federal regional agencies, outside the Great Plains, to which Montana and North Dakota report.

The situation is not dissimilar for North Dakota except that it is drawn more clearly to the eastern cities. The same eighty-eight federal governmental functions dissect North Dakota as follows: twenty-six agencies pull it to the Twin Cities, three to Washington, D. C., and four to Montana. One attracts it to San Francisco, two to Denver, and three to St. Louis. One siphons it to Des Moines, four to Omaha, and twenty-five to Chicago. Two attract it to Kansas City, two to Lincoln, and four to Milwaukee. One pulls it to Joplin, Missouri, one attracts it to Duluth, and one pulls it to Detroit. Only eight of these federal governmental services have headquarters in some city in North Dakota.

Governmental agencies, even when operating on a regional basis, contribute to the dilemma of the region. Located in scattered cities outside the region, the agencies tear the Plains apart. The Plains cannot operate as a unit.

Also symptomatic of the tremendous "pull" exerted by both the East and the West is the situation of higher education as illustrated by the location of colleges and universities in the Plains area. A fact not always realized (see Figure 17) is that, excluding a few schools in Texas, there are no land-grant colleges or state and privately-supported universities in the Plains proper. There are, of course, schools in the area—a few state-supported colleges of education and colleges of technology, a few small denominational colleges, and a number of municipally-supported junior colleges—but the universities themselves and the larger land-grant and private colleges are located on the fringes of the Plains, in the humid part of the states along the eastern border and in the mountain area for the states on the western border.

A further hindrance is created by virtue of the fact that the few seats of higher learning that are located in the Plains have been staffed by men and women who received their education outside the region. The dearth of adequately trained professional people is related to a lack of graduate school facilities in the institutions located in the Plains states. A large share of the professional and non-agricultural opportunities for the undergraduate students from the Plains have been outside the region, not within it. Institutions of higher learning in the Plains, therefore, are required to shape their programs to non-Plains needs—not only for the sake of their graduate personnel, but for their undergraduate students as well. And this will continue until there is a greater demand from within the region for the talent of the youth of the Plains. Of necessity, then, these institutions are silent partners of the forces that keep the region set apart.

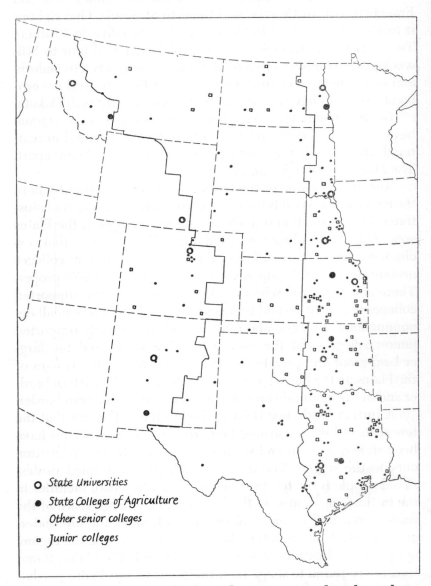

○ State Universities
● State Colleges of Agriculture
· Other senior colleges
▫ Junior colleges

FIG. 17. Institutions of higher education in, and within a hundred miles of, the Great Plains.

LACK OF NORTH–SOUTH COMMUNICATION

Another force that prevents the region from functioning as a unit is the lack of adequate facilities for communication
in a north–south direction. The major railroad and highway
facilities run primarily east and west, cross continent connec-
tions, not north and south. Airplane travel, trucking, and bus
service are the basic transportation means for north and south
communications, and even these are comparatively recent—since
World War II—and still need to demonstrate that they can get
a "pay load."

A few examples will serve to illustrate the point. To travel
via rail from Helena, the capital of Montana, to Cheyenne, the
capital of the neighboring state of Wyoming, there is a choice of
two routes. One involves a distance of 703 miles and 32½ hours
of total travel time—averaging about 25 miles per hour, and two
changes of railroads. The other involves a distance of 886 miles
and 28 hours of travel time—averaging 32 miles per hour, and
three changes in railroads. And this route is not the only one that
is unique for its inconvenience. There are many others. For instance, to get to Billings, Montana, from Denver, Colorado, a
distance of 600 miles as the crow flies, it takes 23 hours, and the
train mileage is 712, without any transfer of trains. An alternate
route takes 22 hours and a distance of 670 miles. The average
rate of travel is 30.9 miles per hour, on the first route, 30.5 miles
on the second.

If the reader believes that the two routes are slow and indirect, he should take a journey from Billings, Montana, to San
Antonio, Texas. The cross-country distance is about 1,250 miles.
It is possible to commute between these two points by way of
three alternate rail routes involving numerous stopovers and
changes. One is from Billings to Omaha, to Kansas City, then to
Dallas, and on to San Antonio—a rail distance of about 1,892
miles. A second way is from Billings to Denver, Pueblo, Albuquerque, El Paso, and then to San Antonio—a distance of 2,009
miles. The third is by way of Denver, Amarillo, Fort Worth,
Waco, and then to San Antonio—a distance of 1,737 miles. A
trip on any of these routes is first hand evidence of the inadequacy of north and south communication in the region.

THE COLONIAL ROLE

OF THE GREAT PLAINS

The colonial-like role played by the Great Plains region in economic matters is a well-established fact. According to John Gunther (*Inside U. S. A.*), even Texans, with reluctance and sometimes anger, will admit that Texas is an exploited and colonial possession and perhaps "the richest colony on earth, India excepted." Ironically enough, this colonial status—which is disliked, even bitterly resisted, by the Plains people—is regarded as divinely decreed and beyond power of control. This is the case in the face of the fact that the average American thinks of himself as having unlimited ability to invent a "know how" to change things if he does not like them.

Certain limited action has been taken to raise the Plains out of their hinterland status, but this is only a halting step. And Plains residents, living as minorities, have in their midst those who are most opposed to destroying their colonial role. For example, gigantic efforts are underway to tame the floods of the Missouri, to develop irrigation, to utilize some of the natural stream flow for power purposes, and to aid in developing some of the resources in the region. Yet many residents of the region are opposed to such development. The struggle that has been going on relative to this project resolves itself, in large measure, around the issue of economic power—authority, if you will—to keep the people of the Missouri Basin in a hinterland status versus the power of self-determination on the part of the residents themselves. Yet many residents do not see this as the central issue.

A colonial status implies several things. One is that the area involved has its economic activity restricted to that of producing the raw materials for others to refine. Probably more than any other, the Plains region is in such a raw material stage of development. The chief export items are wheat, livestock, corn, cotton, natural gas, oil, some coal and some ores. Very aptly, the region has been described as an area of "men without factories."

The price for these products is determined by outside forces and unfortunately, to the disadvantage of the Plains producer.

For instance, there is the Plains wheatgrower. The price he receives is the Grain Trade Exchange—Buffalo, Chicago, Minneapolis—price, minus the freight and hauling charge from his farmstead. But the price he pays for his bread tends to be a price of the flour in the bread determined at the same outside markets, plus transportation charges into the Great Plains. The livestock grower, the cotton grower, and the corn grower are in the same boat. They have to pay transportation costs on items they sell and on items they buy. This includes high transportation costs of farm and ranch equipment, and transportation (Tulsa plus) for the gasoline and tractor fuel processed in the region itself. Omaha, Kansas City, Tulsa, and Oklahoma City, as well as Dallas and Fort Worth, all just to the east of the Plains proper, often pretend to speak for the Plains, and in times of prosperity they glory in the fact that they service the region. In reality they are at the spigot ready to tap the riches that flow from the Plains in the form of wheat, cotton, wool, livestock, oil, natural gas, and other raw material or semi-raw material wealth.

Exploitation exists also in the realm of natural resources. Natural gas and oil have been piped out of the Great Plains states to industrial centers outside the region. In order to derive some benefits, the states concerned have tried to levy an extraction tax, or its equivalent, but have been unsuccessful. As soon as gas is piped into another state, legal talent has rallied to the support of the corporate interests and, in the name of the interstate commerce clause, such tax levies have been declared unconstitutional. The metals, ores, and talcs of Montana, South Dakota, and Wyoming have been only partially refined locally and have then been shipped out for further processing. Electric power, much needed for local development, has been transmitted out of the region even at the expense of interfering with the water requirement for irrigation. Pulpwood is being shipped out of Montana to satisfy the paper and pulp mills of Wisconsin.

Grafting the freight rate charges onto the price at the headquarters point, no matter where procured, is known as the basing-point-plus principle and is applied to articles coming into the region as well as on those processed and used in the region. This applies, for example, to oil processing. The price of gasoline, without state taxes at Billings, Montana, where there are several refineries, was 24.5 cents per gallon on June 12, 1953. In Illinois (at Palatine) where no oil is produced, the cost of the same regular grade gasoline was 21.9 cents per gallon. Tulsa is the reputed basing point for such gasoline prices. It is this price-making mechanism for resources processed and used in the region which is a decided factor in the colonial-like status of the Great Plains.

Still another reason, already implied, is high transportation costs for the region. This is clearly set forth in Wendell Berge's analysis of the problem (*Economic Freedom for the West*). Figure 18 is a reproduction of Berge's map showing various freight rate territories in the nation as they presently exist. Berge writes that fundamentally "the transportation problem in the West is the problem of the railroads. For the foreseeable future, rail transport will largely determine the conditions under which western industry as a whole operates." In his opinion it is futile to build plants or to seek capital in the West if the handicap of transportation cannot be overcome. He writes further: "To both regions (the South and the West) continuous disadvantage in transport cost has meant not only the loss of local industry and the inability of new industry to rise. It has meant a perpetual reduction in purchasing power, a gradual drift of population to the more favored regions and, in some sections, it has meant the closing of schools and the loss of homes and farms. Bitter experience has taught the people of these regions a basic lesson—that it will avail them little to build factories, to develop power projects, to seek new industries and new capital, unless the slow poison of transport handicaps can be eliminated."

This is not the place to exhaust the numerous and complex reasons, arguments, and facts concerning the discrimination in freight rates for the Plains. It is sufficient to know that they exist and that they exert a destructive influence on the economics and social health of the region. The passage of the Bulwinkle Bill in the Eightieth Congress, giving railroads the opportunity to compound their discrimination, is evidence of the insidious discriminatory hold possessed by the vested interests concerned, and the efforts directed toward perpetuation of such discrimination.

The net effect of the colonial policy on the Plains people is increased costs and substandard earnings. For a more detailed picture the reader is referred to the work of others. Walter P. Webb, for example, has clearly stated the case, as a historian, for the South and the West in his book *Divided We Stand*. A. G.

Mezerik has described the same situation, as a journalist, in *The Revolt of the South and the West*. As a lawyer and former public servant, Wendell Berge has made his contribution through his book *Economic Freedom for the West*. And the economist Morris Garnsey ("The Future of the Mountain States") has also added ably to the clarification of the facts and the issues in this respect.

The process of lifting the Plains from their lowly position as a "colony" to the respectable status of a region will be long and probably quite difficult. What the Plains desperately need is industry. Presently, the Dakotas, Wyoming, Nebraska, Colorado, and Montana together have a value of manufacturing activity that is less than that of Missouri alone. The major dependence is now on agriculture. Therefore, in times of drought, the income is low and often in the red. With industry there could be a stabilization of income to the advantage of private business enterprise, and public tax supported services as well.

Accompanying any efforts towards industrialization, people of the Plains will have to speak up for themselves and insist on rigid enforcement of antitrust laws and pertinent Supreme Court decisions. Unless they do so, the "cry" raised by interested pres-

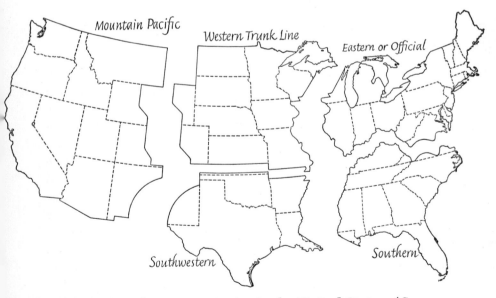

FIG. 18.   Freight rate territories in the United States. (*Source:* Wendell Berge.)

sure groups will keep the region in a colonial status. For example, in 1949 the United States Supreme Court declared the basing-point principle as practised by the Portland Cement Company to be illegal. There rose a great cry of anguish and it will be remembered that Congress passed legislation in 1950 setting this decision aside. But the Plains people did not know of the issue, could not act for their best interest, and did not have the avenues to express themselves vociferously.

In spite of the difficulties, there can be no doubt that the hinterland status of the Plains will be corrected eventually. To do this it will be necessary for the public to appreciate two things. First, no nation can survive as a democracy so long as some of its less fortunate regions are held down by those more fortunate. The well-known expression to the effect that the "chain is only as strong as its weakest link" is applicable here, too. Secondly, the moral support of the entire nation will be needed to overcome the tenacious financial hold that some groups have over the Plains. Like the South and the West, the Great Plains alone cannot correct the situation, for they do not have the means at their disposal. Action must be endorsed by all.

AGRICULTURE AS A
REGIONALIZING FORCE

There is, in the Plains, one man-made force that holds the region together. That is agriculture, despite the fact that it is plagued by division. The types of agriculture in the region, whether livestock, cotton, or grain operations have certain fundamental characteristics in common.

Outside of irrigation farming, the agriculture of the region is of the "extensive enterprise" type—large dry-land farm and livestock units associated with sparsity of settlement, great distances, and limited economic, social, and public services. There is, in all these types of agriculture, the critical issue of timeliness in operation and degree of flexibility which gives them a unity. This unity has been enhanced by increased dependence upon mechanization. For all these characteristics in common make the agriculture of the Plains region quite different from that of the adjacent areas to the east and the west.

The Plains types of agriculture, compared with those to the West and the East, are unique and have much in common because they are marginal operations. They are the types of agriculture that prevail after other types have been eliminated. The corn belt, dairy, and cotton types of agriculture have as their cornerstone the idea that there is a sufficiency of moisture. Diversification is possible and always approximated if not fully accomplished. But Great Plains conditions limit the possibilities of diversification in favor of specialization and the single-enterprise kind of operations. Thus dry-land wheat or cotton farming become a substitute for the diversified farming of the Midwest, and may be interchangeable with each other, within limits, or with livestock ranching, depending largely upon the income-cost relationships in each. Generally, livestock ranching is a more "extensive enterprise" operation even than dry-land cotton or wheat.

The Plains type of agriculture has undergone much adaptation to conditions in the region. These adaptations, too, make for a degree of uniformity among the different types because the adaptations are intended to cope with the vagaries of the semiarid climate, especially that of limited rainfall. Moisture reserve building, flexibility of operation, speed of operation, especially adapted plant and animal varieties—all these make for a common awareness among the agriculturists and give the region a unity that is now the major force holding the people of the region together. And the strongest element in this force, making for unity in agriculture, is the activity that follows after the production phase—marketing, financing, pricing, transportation, and distribution. It is these aspects of agriculture which also have made for a splintering of the economic groups in the Plains, and which have given the Plains a hinterland status. When the Plains gain control of these matters the colonial status of the region will be removed.

Here, then, we have a region about the size of the original thirteen colonies with a population of 5,500,000. It is a region very different from the humid East and the Far West in terms of climate, natural vegetation, soils, and native animal life. But it is also a region that has been set apart, exploited, and laid prostrate by the areas outside. Manifestations of this are to be found (1) in the form of the institutionalized ways of doing things brought in from the outside, (2) in the role of cities and population-centers immediately outside the region, (3) in the lack of north-south transportation and communication, and (4) in the shape of market, price, and transportation rate discrimination. All these economic, political, sociological, and psychological forces combine to make a hinterland of the Plains. The primary-producer phase of agriculture is now the only major force, besides the geographical peculiarity of the Plains, that gives unity to the region.

But there is a striving for solution of the many Plains problems—a striving that is likely to give the Plains a greater unity than they have ever had before.

CHAPTER 17

The Minority Status of the People

Many of the economical and political events that have occurred in the Plains since the days of the cattleman and the sheepman have served to bring about the disparity between that which is actually possible in the region and the things which are expected of it. This does not mean that the possibilities for the Plains, north and south, are greatly limited. Rather, it means, that they are on a different scale from the standards thrust upon the region by the humid-area industrial and urban civilization which has projected itself into the region.

The result of these unadapted institutional ways has been severe suffering, in periods of drought especially. Often this has culminated in dust and depopulation. There has been difficulty in supporting community life and the institutions which are intended to serve the people. There has been subjugation of the region to a hinterland status.

MINORITY STATUS OF
PEOPLE IN THE PLAINS

All these things have led to frustration of the residents of the Plains. This frustration has come to express itself in minority-group conduct. On a smaller scale, this is well illustrated by the "no man's land" complex that prevails in the Panhandle of Oklahoma. The Panhandle has always been, and is today, a true no man's land. Included in the Spanish domain, by the treaty of 1821, it passed into the control of Mexico and, then later, into the control of Texas. But it was separated from Texas by the Compromise of 1850 because it lay north of the slavery line established in 1820. Being south of the Kansas–Colorado border, no one wanted it. So orders were that it be included in the territory of Oklahoma by virtue of the Organic Act for that territory. The residents were so frustrated by this shoving around that in 1887 the homesteaders and ranchers met at Beaver City in an unsuccessful attempt to create a Territory of the Cimarron. The residents in all parts of the Plains, on occasion, have had like frustrations and like yearnings.

This minority status of the residents of the Plains is a tragedy of great proportions in a democracy such as the United States. First, it means that the Plains residents are on the prod. They fight at the drop of the hat—among themselves and with people outside the region. And this conduct has a tendency to be self-perpetuating. Secondly, minority status means that the residents of the region cannot now unite to protect themselves against exploitation by others. The schisms between groups are too great. Thirdly, minority status means that the residents cannot express themselves objectively and clearly so that others, less predatory in spirit, can readily join with them to correct the basic difficulties in the region. Emotions are too deeply rooted for rational action. Fourthly, minority conduct in the Plains has become so deep-seated that it will take much patience to correct the situation. And, finally, the correction of the situation will necessarily require the help of a thoroughly democratic approach, perhaps best accomplished by the institution of true regionalism.

EVIDENCE OF MINORITY BEHAVIOR
IN THE PLAINS

The residents of the Plains live as minorities for many reasons. They live in island-like communities separated from each other in many ways and for many reasons. The Plains communities are fragmented, attached to this city or that outside the region, attracted to this interest or that outside the region. They are not complete communities. Special-interest affiliations with the power groups and centers outside the region serve only to make the plainsmen pleaders of special interest. This fact often sets plainsman against plainsman, resulting in conflict among fellow citizens, and aids in widening the schisms among them.

This situation in the communities, along with the great distances involved, makes the plainsman an individualist, one not highly social and not prone to act through groups. The people have fragmented personalities. There is a kind of anarchy of individualism. Faced with the prospect of no group solution to difficulties within the region, people attach their loyalty to special interests outside the region and destroy their own chances for solidarity among themselves. They develop personality traits which exhibit withdrawal behavior or extreme aggressiveness.

All this interferes with the basic economic development of the region. Sons and daughters leave home and go outside the region to find employment and economic opportunities. Parents often become discouraged and distrustful. They, too, think of exploiting the opportunities at hand and then leaving for other places. So they sell their farm or ranch or their business, often for more than it is really worth. This heaps a burden on the new generation, which will only repeat the traumatic experiences of former generations.

Then there is the fact that the Plains cannot develop political action to solve its problems. Each state in the region is pulled Plainsward, and also away from the region. Usually the majority of the voters of the state live outside the region proper and have the aid of cities to support the non-Plains point of view. These towns and cities are in the shadow of metropolitan centers which are oriented away from the Plains but thrive on their raw materials.

Finally, the severely limited number of large cities and large, influential newspapers in the region has resulted in a lack of region-wide self-expression. Events are not portrayed in their impact upon the region and its people. There is no ready way to bring basic knowledge before enough people so that a basic remedy may be applied to the situation.

The result of all this is a feeling of insecurity and frustration. This in turn, leads to action that is based on emotion rather than fact. People often pick fights, carry "chips on their shoulder," resort to name calling, or withdraw into an "ivory tower." Not only individuals but entire groups act in this manner in the Plains.

The situation was clearly evident in the conditions that prevailed in 1953. The Plains wheat grower voted a resounding "aye" in favor of wheat acreage control and of prices at 90 per cent parity. Of course many buisnessmen and cattlemen were not happy about such a vote on the part of the wheatgrower.

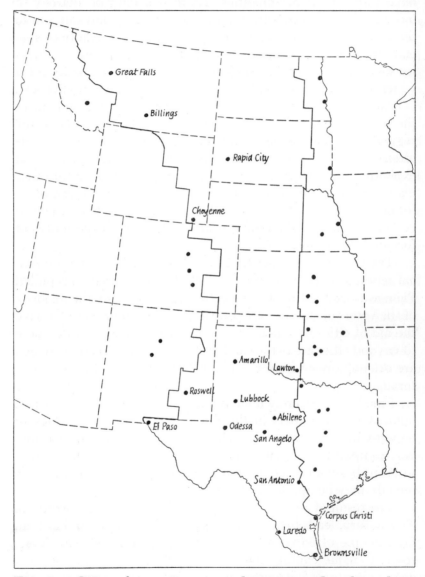

FIG. 19.   Cities of over 25,000 population in, and within a hundred miles of, the Great Plains.

Yet, when the Plains cattleman marketed his livestock that fall, the drastic drop in cattle prices brought him face-to-face with the same problem—how to get enough for production to meet costs and make a living. The spread between the price of cattle and the consumer price of meat became the focal point of complaint rather than the basic fact of lack of control over marketing channels for meat products. The same cattleman was formerly, in 1951, the bosom pal and spokesman for the feeder, the packer, and the middleman who, in 1953, were accused of husbanding the price spread.

So the cattleman finds himself "behind the eight ball." He does not like this. He becomes frustrated and angry. And so it is with the Plains wheatgrower and cotton grower. Surplus wheat and cotton in the nation's economy means curtailment of wheat and cotton, not in the Midwest and in the Old South, but in the Plains where there are no alternatives except livestock. For the livestock men there are no alternatives but wheat, or cotton, or sorghums.

The plainsmen, then, have been involved in a basic struggle for economic survival in a commercial economy over which they have no control. A substitute for the ruinous competition in the demand-supply market place (unlike the controlled market for the industrialist and the businessman) has been the co-operative, which has been considered an invasion of the prerogative of the businessman inside and outside the region and has called forth vociferous condemnation. Another alternative has been increased efficiency in farm and ranch operations. But resort to such widespread efficiency has brought only temporary gain to individuals. Efficiency has not been a basic solution for the Plains as a whole, in the rivalry of agriculture with the rest of the economy, as shown by the price spread between beef on the hoof and beef on the consumers' table. Another possible substitute for the difficulty is government-support prices or incomes for farmers and ranchers. This, too, would call forth vociferous condemnation.

So the frustrations of the plainsman have not been allayed. Minority conduct has increased rather than decreased under these conditions.

SPECIAL MEANING OF
MINORITY IN THE PLAINS

It remains to explain why the minority situation in the Plains is unique and peculiar. When governing themselves democratically, men necessarily differ in their convictions and beliefs. In a democracy, many of these convictions and beliefs are attached to the most vital issues that affect living. This means that action must follow, sooner or later. Otherwise frustrations will occur. But democracy must have the vehicles and the machinery for resolving the diverse goals and beliefs so that action can take place.

What is included in the terms vehicles and machinery for resolving issues? Included are cities, for it is here that people come together, pool ideas, invent new ways, and disseminate them. It is here that the vehicles for communication are concentrated—the radio, the newspaper, the magazines, the speakers, and the libraries. It is in the cities that formal government is located. Representatives of the people can congregate and vote on this issue and that. It is in the cities that laborers, employers, businessmen, farmers and ranchers, medical people, real estate brokers, financiers—and the lobbies for all these interests—congregate to influence their representatives. All these things are the vehicles and the machinery by which people in a democracy decide on an action program.

The Plains do not have cities that function in this capacity, nor do they have region-centered radio, newspapers, magazines, news analysts, and speakers to aid in performing this democratic function. The segmented population of the respective states cannot now be politically united. Great distances and the cost of space make these things difficult to have under present conditions.

It is inevitable that there are minorities in a democracy—groups whose objectives are temporarily not realizable. The majority does not administer the program of the minorities, but is prepared to protect their rights. Sometimes, on certain issues, the majority makes limited concessions; and, occasionally, the majority is merely a coalition of minorities. Nor is a majority vote on one issue a guarantee that all the same people will vote with the majority on another issue. People are not always on the same side of the general issues. Consequently, the majority leadership must use strategy in determining the timeliness of an issue. Leadership must resort to like strategy when it comes to considering the evidence that should go hand in hand in debating an issue. When a minority has gained the strength of additional members to outvote all the other groups, its program can be put into operation. Thus the former majority, in turn, may become a minority.

The significant thing is that the Plains residents do not see an opportunity to have their situation clearly recognized, ever. There is not now the hope or the probability that the minority status of the people in the region can ever be resolved, or that the residents can align themselves with an outside group that will assist them with their basic problems. Therefore, the most treasured values of democracy for the Plains people are incapable of achievement under present states' rights rule or present extreme centralization in federal rule.

Being denied these hopes, the Plains residents are necessarily frustrated, and their conduct is necessarily pathological. And therefore, they have resorted as the usual thing, to extremes in minority behavior. To solve their minority status, the Plains people must be permitted to enter the political arena in a democratic way. This, as will be seen later, can be accomplished through the avenue of regionalism.

CHARACTERISTICS ASSOCIATED
WITH MINORITY CONDUCT

When people are frustrated they exhibit conduct characterized by aggression or by withdrawal. Under each of these there are clearly recognized patterns of behavior. It is not the object here to arrange these behavior patterns in some order of importance. It will be sufficient to recognize the existence and the prevalence of these patterns of behavior.

These patterns of minority behavior on the part of Plains residents are not always clearly recognizable because they have not acquired the clear definition which one might expect. This results from the sparsity of population that prevails, and the need for social contact, even among people who have deep animosities for each other. "Bumping" is a well defined custom by means of which the minority pushes the majority. But this can be done best only when people congregate in large groups. In the Plains, where population is sparse such "bumping" is of little avail. There is an apparent mixing of all people. There is intermarriage between rancher and wheatfarmer families or cotton-farm families, and between rural families and families living on Main Street. Such associations give the illusion of unity among the Plains residents. But "scratch his back, and you have a Tartar!" This is what one finds under the skin in Plains society. This observation can be best tested in the bars and in the numerous drinking places in the Plains. There, satire and irony are not customary; a brawl after a drink is the more direct method of resolving animosities.

Because of the lack of well-regulated behavior, such as "bumping," the minority behavior in the region is less subtle. It takes the form of highly personalized conduct, accompanied by deep animosities or intense loyalties. Often there is a spirit of gambling, even in the face of known odds of overwhelming proportions. Much of the behavior can be classified as a resort to "name calling" and "chip on the shoulder" conduct, often in the form of "leading with the chin." There is a tendency to settle difficulties on the spot, in informal and extralegal fashion, including resort to vigilantism and contempt for authority. This was typical conduct in the early days of the cowman–sheepman wars, the homesteader–cattleman raids, and the fence-cutting wars.

Other minority behavior can best be described by the use of face-saving substitutes which themselves then become the basis for action. This is what the rancher of today does when he blames his present difficulties on "the sod buster who ruined the range." Also, there is that conduct which takes on the character of a purgative catharsis. Often it takes on the form of fanaticism in religious behavior. Frequently, conduct is of the Dr. Jekyll–Mr. Hyde type, like that of some congressmen from the Plains, when, being ordinary small cowmen while at home, they ride high, wide, and handsome—in spurred boots—in the nation's capital. Then again, aggression is apparent in the organization of vested-interest groups which function for their own welfare exclusively and "carry water" for others to the disadvantage of their fellow plainsmen.

There are still other organized patterns of minority behavior typical of plainsman conduct. Among these are involvement in deliberately created conflict in order to create loyalty among the group when dealing with certain issues; attack on vested-interest groups as a technique of dealing with issues; deliberate creation of a feeling of insecurity to arouse attention; building up a defense mechanism in the face of barriers to action; and the fostering of a spirit of sectionalism. These tend to be more in the nature of deliberately planned techniques, used by leaders, to create group solidarity, though they often are unconsciously-formed behavior patterns used by minority peoples.

Much of the literature dealing with minorities rests on presumed racial differences among people. This is not the only condition, however, giving rise to the problem in the Plains. Presumed racial differences have entered into some local situations —for example, the Plains Indians have undergone hardships because of race in certain parts of the region, and the Spanish Americans, often also called the Mexican Americans, have been racially discriminated against in parts of the Plains area, particularly in southern Texas. And, of course, Jim Crowism as well as the Ku Klux Klan activity were rampant in Oklahoma and Texas for a time, even in the Plains portions of those states.

Nationality differences are frequently the basis for creating and perpetuating minorities, but this is only an incidental condition in the Plains and is fast disappearing. Sometimes differences in religious beliefs are the basic factor in accounting for a minority situation, but this again is not the only or major basis for defining the problem in the Plains. There are, however, some local areas where religious beliefs assist in creating cultural islands—for example, Mormon, Roman Catholic, and Mennonite settlements, as distinguished from Lutheran, Methodist, and other Protestant religious communities, are somewhat culturally isolated.

The factors of race, nationality, and religion account for some of the minority groups in the region, but only a small part. The more urgent aspect of the minority situation in the Plains comes from the fact that the condition pervades all the agricultural life of the region, and life on Main Street as well. This is such a significant aspect of life in the Plains that the next several chapters will be devoted to identification of these minority groups.

A condition that frequently accompanies minority status is that the group in power is seldom aware of the important albeit minute differences among the minority groups. This has been true of the relation of the people of the nation towards the residents of the Plains. Because of the one-way flow of information, namely into the Plains, the people of the nation have not been aware of the differences in interests among the many groups in the region. To the average Easterner or Midwesterner the residents are all either "cattle barons," or "wheat kings." They are all "poverty ridden homesteaders," or "irrigation farmers," or all are "cow punchers." To get a hearing, it has been necessary for Plains people to act out the role assigned them. This has called for originality and ingenuity; it also has made for confusion and has created the conditions that can give rise to schizophrenia.

Under such conditions it is easy for a leader to become an actor, rather than a true representative of his constituents. Such "acting" has contributed to the practice of selling oneself and one's fellow citizens "down the river" simply for the purpose of ego satisfaction. It has aroused the suspicions of the respective groups and leaders towards one another. It has fostered the continued existence of minority groups in the Plains.

CONSTRUCTIVE ROLES OF MINORITIES

Minority behavior has not always been destructive of political, social, and cultural unity. History has demonstrated that minorities have contributed greatly to the progress of nations and civilization. The settlement of America was the result of forces that expelled a minority of religious and political dissenters from Europe. Out of this grew a great nation. The Constitution of the United States is a compromise document—the product of several minority points of view on the mechanics of government, if not its major principle of strong central government. These are examples of minority causes which eventually came to full fruition and were successful because they had access

236

to the vehicles for expression and consolidation of effort. They were successful movements.

The Plains region, too, has its constructive minority groups. Such minorities, in doing things for themselves, have been unselfish and have promoted the welfare of all in the region and, also, that of the entire nation. The difficulty has been that such minorities have not had a majority in the region against which they might exert their constructive role and thus bring to fruition a constructive program. There has been an absence of vehicles—television, newspapers, radio, and communication generally—to bring about constructive action in the region. Occasionally, under great stress, a minority may have appeared to take on the shape of a majority. But that very shape subjected it to intensified attack by other minorities. All this minority confusion is quicksand on which to build a long-time constructive program. Additional vehicles for the proper working out and functioning of democracy must become available, finally, to solve the problem of minority behavior in the Plains.

Though there are constructive minority groups in the Great Plains, the significant thing, then, is that all the groups actually function as minorities. The absence of large cities and adequate communication facilities, coupled with the fact that much of the existing communication is exploitive and destructive, means that there can be, at present, no effective consolidation of people into a majority group.

The Great Plains—the land of minorities—is a prostrate land now; a part of the national economy, but a part that does not yet possess the techniques necessary to control its own affairs. The task ahead is to build a way of life that will give the inhabitants of the Plains a hand in the control of their destiny.

CHAPTER 18

Traditional Minorities in the Plains

There are, in the Plains, certain traditional minorities. They are the result of race, nationality, and religious situations not necessarily peculiar to the Plains. Their island-like concentrations are more apparent only because of the greater physical isolation in the region—the greater distances, the absence of much region-centered communication, and the agricultural nature of earning a living. There are not the socializing influences of the labor unions, the industrial payroll system, the educational services, and the unemployment and the old-age pension phases of the social security program to assist in the absorption of these minority peoples into the Plains way of life.

THE GREAT PLAINS INDIAN

The North American Indian, though a citizen of the United States, represents a minority wherever he lives—with perhaps the descendants of the Five Civilized Tribes in Oklahoma as exception. He has been made a minority figure by definition. On the reservation he is considered a "ward" of the federal government—a minor who cannot make certain legal decisions. Generally, he has a certain way of life provided for him by the guardian Indian Service, because it was once believed that the Indian could not learn to live the American way of life, and the American people have tried to discharge their moral obligation to the Indian by the device of keeping him a minor.

The Plains were one of the last frontiers for the American Indian. The Plains were the region most difficult for the whites to conquer; therefore, they were set aside as Indian Territory as early as 1825. When the westward move of empire could no longer be kept out of the Plains, the Indian had first to be subjugated and it was inevitable that reservation sites should be established on the Plains.

By the 1950 federal census count, about half (160,261) of the Indians reside in the ten Great Plains states. They are present in largest numbers in Oklahoma, New Mexico, South Dakota, Montana, and North Dakota. With the exception of New Mexico, they are also concentrated, in significant numbers, in the Great Plains portions of these states. They constitute about one per cent of Great Plains population—a substantial minority from the standpoint of the distribution and the utilization of resources, and the solution of the Indian problem. Especially is this true when the region has inadequate means of communication to aid in the formation of an Indian policy.

The way of life of the North American Indian varies from reservation to reservation, depending upon the cultural origin of the respective tribes and the influence of changing Indian policy. It is not possible here to describe the way of life of the many Plains Indian tribes, except to point out that it contains the traits of minority behavior—strong "we group" feeling, elaborate defense mechanisms, disorganization, personality segmentation, and frustration.

The vicinity of almost any Indian reservation is the scene of intense poverty and human greed. The root of much of the difficulty is the wardship status of the Indian. Under certain conditions, the ward Indian cannot sell his land holdings. Through inheritance he has title to many small tracts of land, often as small as 1/22,400 parts or .008 per cent of an acre, in what was even originally a small holding. The Indian cannot farm these small dispersed tracts advantageously. Since money is easily divided, the Indian, or the agency in his behalf, leases the lands to a few white operators, for cash. Even then, certain tracts have been so small that it has taken ten years to accumulate one Indian-head penny's worth of cash rent.

Because of this pattern of land inheritance and use, the Indian has been unable to farm. There being no other jobs available, he is unemployed most of the time. He sees that his lease to the white man has become the object of speculation, exploitation, and fortune hunting. The minority role of the dispossessed Indian, and the dominating role of the exploiter, are readily apparent.

The Indian's reservation site is different from other cultural islands in the Great Plains. Whereas many of the Plains residents live as isolated occupational groups—the stockman in a grazing area, the dry-land wheat farmer in a spring wheat or in a winter wheat area, the cotton grower in a cotton area, and the irrigationist on a project area dictated by topography and climate— this is not generally true of the Indian reservation. Here the tendency is for the minority groups, the Indians and the whites, to live in the same community though somewhat segregated. Thus the reservation sites are an island of conglomeration, an area characterized by an admixture akin to the contents of a melting pot. The reservations are a place where Indian, wheatgrower, rancher, businessman, and many other people come to seek their fortunes. The resulting social disorganization in such areas promises that the contacts and associations are usually not of the constructive kind.

To bring the description of the problem up-to-date, reference needs to be made to the fact that the Indian reservation sites are often endowed with oil and other precious ore resources, with large power dam and irrigation reservoir locations, and with potentially irrigable lands. Several of the proposed Missouri Basin reservoir projects for flood control, irrigation, and power use are located on Indian reservations or nearby. In one instance, the proposed irrigated area, namely, the Yellowtail Reservoir Project on the Crow Reservation in south central Montana, is almost entirely confined to the Indian reservation. It is one of the most promising areas in the entire Missouri Basin, and activity on the reservation is at a feverish pitch. Will the Indians on this reservation, as the result of the scramble for economic opportunity, finally be able to rid themselves of their minority bonds, or will they become a truly landless minority?

The Reorganization Act of 1934 was intended to free the Indian from the effects of the former policy which practically destroyed the tribal organization and furthered the seizure of the lands by non-Indians. The new act was intended to aid the Indians in achieving control over their lands and to administer their affairs democratically as a public corporation. Actually, it placed great power of discrimination into the hands of the Indian Bureau officials. It is likely to result in keeping the Indian of the Plains in his wardship status upon the reservation for a long time.

Certain Indians on the reservations have become leaders because they have learned to act their minority role for selfish gain. Their interest has become focused and centered on the Indian Agency Administration and on the centralized Indian bureaucracy in the nation's Capitol and in the Congress. At the same time, these Indian leaders get out of touch with the members of their own tribe and their wishes.

This situation has created the setting for "role playing," political machinations, internal dissension and strife, and personality frustrations typical of minorities. Unable to resolve the problems locally, and the people of the region unaware of the problems and unable to act, the resulting problems and tensions are transmitted to the Great White Father. All possible beneficiaries—Indians and whites—have their eyes on Washington in the hope that windfalls may come their way. No one does anything for himself.

Recently, there has been talk of giving all Indians full citizenship status, with the privilege of attending the same schools, hospitals, and public service agencies, and receiving the same services as all the other population. This is known as the Indian Service Withdrawal proposal. Those Indians who do not already have full citizenship—many of course do, certainly those in Oklahoma—appear to be in a quandary as to whether they should elect the road to withdrawal or remain under the protection of the reservation and the Indian Service.

Such a withdrawal program would mean the liquidation of Indian trust funds and inheritances, the cancellation of treaty obligations of long standing, and possible loss of potential income from power sites, oil, and other resources that are only now becoming a reality. The Indian minority has no reason to believe that this is not another way of exploiting them. Many Indians would spend their trust and inheritance windfalls in a short time and then would be on relief the remainder of their lives. Meanwhile these public welfare bills would need to be financed by the remaining residents of these states—states into which the Indians were pushed in order to make room for the whites elsewhere. In reality, this involves national, not state's rights, obligations. Many old Indians would be twice dispossessed, once when placed on the reservation and once when withdrawn from it.

Here, then, is a major problem in the Plains that arises from the fact that the Indian has been treated as a minority for a long time. How will democracy provide the necessary social organization for the Indian to live as an adult anywhere he chooses?

THE SPANISH AND LATIN AMERICAN

While the Indian was the first known resident in the Plains area, the Spanish and Latin Americans represent the descendants of the first whites in the region. Their forebears settled in Mexico, made excursions into the Plains, and established settlements along the southern edge at a date as early as those of the first white settlements along the eastern coastlands of America.

The Southern Plains have a substantial number of Spanish-speaking people. They are held together by common forces, such as language, Catholicism, poverty, a resentment of racial discrimination, organizations such as the League of United Latin-American Citizens, and a knowledge of a cultural contribution they have made to the entire Southwest. The Plains region, and the non-Plains remainder of the Southwest, have inherited a rich cultural background from this source.

Among the inheritances from the Spanish and Latin American culture are influences on western land laws and policy, especially in the case of Texas; certain patterns that have to do with the Western open range system of livestock handling; and some basic patterns for irrigation and Western water use. From the same source come such Western words and expressions as *corral, lariat, coyote, arroyo, chaps, rodeo, rio, adios, portales, siesta,* and *patio.* In fact, the early cattle industry of the Great Plains, and its many intricate techniques in handling cattle and range, came from Old Mexico by way of Texas. Many Spaniards and Mexicans were among the first cowboys.

In addition, much of the architecture of the Southern Plains and of the entire Southwest has its origin from this same source. Many church and religious customs, community festival activities, and certain ceremonies have a similar background. Santa Fé and San Antonio have added rich traditions and customs to the lives of the people in the Southern Plains.

But the Spanish and Latin Americans are a distinct minority in the Plains. In 1940 there were about 1,861,400 Spanish-speaking people in the United States, with 85 per cent of them living west of the Mississippi River. Two-thirds of this percentage lived in the Great Plains states, and somewhat less than half lived in the Great Plains proper, largely in New Mexico, Texas, and Colorado.

There is a striking stratification between the Spanish-Americans and the Latin Americans. The former represent the descendants of the original conquistadores, those who trace their ancestry to lordly estates and nobility, and also the peons who trace their ancestry to the workers on those estates. They also include some more recent migrants from Spain. The latter group is composed largely of Mexican immigrants and their children. Quincy Guy Burris, in the book *One America*, points out that the "contact of older generations of Spanish speaking residents with the few immigrants who came to these states (Texas, California, and Arizona) was charged with mutual dislike and bore fruit in a distinction. Those who claimed descent from the conquistadores called themselves Spanish Americans and looked with scorn upon the newcomers. Actually, many of the Spanish Americans are of Spanish and Indian blood. So are the Mexicans, with perhaps a little admixture of darker blood somewhere in their chemistry. However trivial this demarcation may appear to be, it is a persistent one."

Actually then, this group of Spanish-speaking peoples represents two distinct sub-minorities. Rivalry and conflict between the two is deep. Occupational differentiation within the community is a basis for the rivalry. Both groups are generally engaged in agriculture, usually in ranching, sheepherding, cotton growing, sugar beet raising, pecan shelling, gardening, cooking, and day labor generally. Some few work on the railroad gangs, in mines, and as clerks. The Mexican Americans are more generally employed in the piece-rate and the day-wage jobs, and at menial occupations.

Many of both groups are migrant laborers. The Latin Americans (Mexicans) move far into the Northern Plains for work in the sugar beet fields. As migrants they live an exploited economic life, away from schools and homes much of the time. Their ready assimilation is thus impossible, and their minority status is likely to continue. This is also true of the Spanish Americans. Both groups constitute cultural islands in limited areas of the Plains region, areas of relatively permanent settlement from which the seasonal laborers migrate throughout the region.

The basic attitudes and customs that differentiate these two groups are steeped in the rivalries between minorities which really have much in common. The common traditions that surround both groups have become such basic values that they are likely to intensify rather than temper the minority status of both groups.

Collectively, these groups represent a minority that has continued associations with Mexico. Their religious, social, and language customs have a historical significance which makes their fusion with the rest of the Plains people an impossibility at present. Only through the medium of region-centered communication and social organization can they be absorbed into the social web of the land in which they find their seasonal and regular work.

The importation of seasonal workers from Mexico during World War II and following, and the infiltration of "wetbacks," has served to intensify the minority status of these peoples. This intensification is borne out by the signs in eating places, bars, and hotels which read: "The management reserves the right to serve." Yet, at least one governor of a Plains state became so irate at Mexico when she refused to send migratory laborers to the United States that he proposed severance of diplomatic relations with Mexico during World War II.

THE NEGRO IN THE SOUTHERN PLAINS

The extension of cotton growing into the Plains, and the importation of the cotton economy, along with the migrant worker, resulted in the introduction of the Negroes as a minority group into the region. For example, George Washington Carver, famous Negro educator and scientist, is reported to have home-steaded fifteen miles west of Ness City, Kansas, from 1888 until 1891. Engaged in geological activity as a side line, he predicted the discovery of oil under the rock strata of Ness County.

The 1950 census figures show that about 1,248,612 Negroes lived within the boundaries of the ten Great Plains States. This was 8.2 per cent of the total Negro population. While the Negro population constituted 9.9 per cent of the national total, they made up 7.2 per cent of the total population in the ten Great Plains states. In the Great Plains proper Negroes (about 90,680 persons) made up only 2 per cent of the total 1940 population. By far the major portion of these Negroes lived in the Southern Plains—in Texas, and in western Oklahoma and Kansas. Their economic activity is not confined to cotton growing, however. Some are engaged in general farming, and in vegetable and fruit raising; others live in cities and small towns, engaged in the usual minority occupations available to Negroes.

The Negroes of the Southern Plains form an association of people characterized by behavior typical of a minority. The minority status tends to push the Negro of the Plains into the towns and cities. There is less of a place for them in the agriculture of the region, except as migrant workers, than in the agriculture of the rest of the South. The minority concentration of Negroes in towns and cities is one explanation for the greater urbanization and the existence of more towns and cities in the Southern compared with the Northern Plains. The minority concentration contributes to difficulties attending seasonal and migratory agricultural work in these southern villages and towns, where poverty is more stark and is especially high among the Negroes.

It is inevitable that the Negroes of the Plains have a close cultural tie with those of the humid-area Delta and the South generally. This results from the race ties and also from the common cause of discrimination against the entire Negro race on a national scale. The race tie is a vehicle for the direct flow of unadapted ways into the semiarid Southern Plains—minority group ways which come into the Plains and are especially ill-adapted for living in the region. Because of the high cost of space, it is especially difficult to support a dual set of institutions, be they schools, churches, lodges, hospitals, or other activities. Therefore, the Southern Plains people, including the Negroes, have an added task—that of fitting their Negro–white relations to conditions in the Plains.

This illustration, showing the push of unadapted ways into the Plains, even to the point of pushing the nation's Negro–white race problems into the Plains and tying the region to the race relations situations outside it, is dramatic. But it is also typical of what has happened in other areas of social organization.

NATIONALITY AND
CULTURAL MINORITIES

Nationality origin of the early settlers has been a factor in the creation of cultural islands in rural America. The Great Plains is no exception. Much of the late nineteenth and early twentieth century settlement on the Plains was by nationality groups, many from southeastern Europe, often sponsored by religious agencies. Imported methods of farming, reverence for church leadership, dependence upon parochial school, and the perpetuation of the mother tongue were factors in the building of cultural islands, and have been factors in their perpetuation. The members of some of these nationality groups brought with them adapted seed-grain varieties and suitable methods of farming for the Plains. This was especially true of the sectarian groups who came from the Russian Plains—the Mennonites and other settlers from the Volga, many of whom settled in the Plains of Kansas. It was among these that Mark Carleton found the adapted wheat varieties which led to his experimentation with adaptation of plants to Plains conditions. The tragedy was that cultural isolation did not make these adapted ways readily available to others in the region.

For the nation as a whole, the foreign-born constituted 6.7 per cent of the total population in 1950. For the ten Great Plains states, they constituted only 3.4 per cent of the total population. For the Great Plains proper this figure was 6.1 per cent. The foreign-born are, therefore, a larger minority in the Great Plains region than in the ten Great Plains states, but smaller than in the nation as a whole. This supports the conclusion that, by the time of settlement of the Plains, the pull of foreign population to urban and industrial opportunities in America was already well underway.

However, certain nationality groups that established themselves in agriculture are prevalent in the Plains states and in the Great Plains region proper. For the entire Plains states the seven top-ranking nationality groups include the Germans with 19.3 per cent of the foreign-born, followed by the Russians with 7.5 per cent, the Norwegians with 4.5 per cent, the Swedes with 4 per cent, the Czechoslovakians with 3.1 per cent, the Italians with 3.2 per cent, and the English with 4.2 per cent. The Germans are numerically more prevalent in Nebraska, Texas, and Kansas; the Russians in North Dakota, Colorado, Nebraska, South Dakota, and Kansas. The Norwegians went preponderantly to North Dakota, South Dakota, and Montana, while the Swedes settled largely in Nebraska, the Dakotas, Colorado, Kansas, and Montana. The Czechs settled largely in Nebraska and Texas; the Italians in Colorado, Texas, Nebraska, and Montana. The English settled in all the states of the region. The cultural characteristics of the nationality settlements are adequately described in *One America,* by J. S. Roucek and F. J. Brown.

These nationality groups have, in the past especially, represented distinct cultural islands in all of the Great Plains region. They have exhibited forms of conduct typical of a minority, among which are a strong "we group" feeling, rivalry and conflict, suspicion of others, limited contact with others, and slow assimilation into the American way of life.

Often the second generation has become Americanized to the point of rejecting parents and the foreign customs that might have represented a rich cultural heritage. In their place the second generation has substituted behavior patterns from New York or Chicago which are equally foreign to the Plains. These conditions make it difficult for the people of the Plains to join hands in the solution of their problems and in developing suitable institutions and farming practices. These conditions have made possible the continued infiltration of unadapted ideas from outside the region, and have been a factor in the inability to establish adequate means of communication within the region to assist in developing an adapted way of living.

Finally, the long continued existence of nationality cultural islands has provided a source of cheap labor, very easy for the more powerful and selfish interests outside and inside the region to exploit. This exploitation has drained the area of resources, manpower and wealth which might otherwise have been employed constructively in building a reasonably prosperous regional economy. Rivalry among these minorities makes for a duplication in institutional services in the communities of the region that robs the people of the strength to fit their way of living to the prevailing conditions. A visit to a Hutterite community in the Plains, even today, brings forth the full meaning of minority status in the Plains.

Many of these nationality minorities are undergoing gradual, though often only artificial, assimilation. Except for certain groups, like the Hutterites, they will represent less of a barrier to building a way of living for the future. The prospect is, however, that the second and third generation descendants of emigrants will become identified with other minority groups, and will merely add numerical support to the remaining minorities, without modifying the problem in the region.

For the plainsman, north and south, it is a shock to realize that he is surrounded by such a variety of traditional minority groups. He is shocked because he is not acquainted with his own region, and is living in a cultural island of his own, separated by distance and by the absence of communication. He travels the highways and the railways east and west. Little long-distance travel takes place in a north-south direction. So he is not acquainted with the population diversity in the region. In addition, the communication that does lead into the region has the force of separating the different parts from each other. It does not unite the Northern, the Central, and the Southern Plains.

To fully appreciate the absence of communication between the Northern and the Southern Plains, it is only necessary to recall that the immigrants, who moved into the region, congregated in the Union Depot at Chicago and there broke their home ties with their fellow travelers. Those who wished to go to the Northern Plains traveled via the Northern Pacific or the Great Northern railroads. Those who wished to go to the Southern Plains boarded the Rock Island which eventually put them on the Santa Fé, the Southern Pacific, or the Kansas Pacific. To go to the Central Plains it was necessary to travel on the Burlington or the Union Pacific. In any case, these roads fanned out, then as now, as from a hub, and the emigrants who parted by these ways seldom again met.

The Indian remains on or near his reservation. The Negro of the Southern Plains seldom travels north and south. The Spanish American lives in the Southern and Central Plains and makes only periodic excursions into the rest of the region along well defined routes and for specific kinds of jobs. The Hutterites and Mennonites remain in their communities. Those belonging to other nationality minorities have escaped from the region completely, or, remaining there, have enlarged their area of contact only slightly.

Until recently plainsmen met each other in their travels accidentally in Chicago or in Los Angeles. Sometimes they met in New York, St. Louis, Omaha, Seattle, or San Francisco. Seldom did they meet in Denver. They rarely ever met on the Plains. More recently oil discoveries in the Williston Basin in the Northern Plains have attracted Texans and Oklahomans in large numbers. Traveling combines in the wheat harvest season now bring Southern plainsmen into the north and Northern plainsmen into the south. The National Farmers Union, with headquarters in Denver, is now assisting in welding together the plainsmen of the north and those of the south. Outside of agriculture and oil, there appears to be no other force that is making for a feeling of regional awareness at this time.

CHAPTER 19

Minorities in the Rural Areas

In addition to the traditional minority groups there are other minorities in the Plains. Several important minorities are to be found among the agriculturalists of the region. The inclusion of these groups as minorities will irk many plainsmen, but this very anger is an indication of minority status. It is this fact—that most of the residents of the Plains are identified with one minority group or another—which gives the region its most pressing problems.

THE STOCKMAN
ON THE GREAT PLAINS

The stockmen are a distinct minority group in the Plains in comparison with the total number of agriculturalists; they are also a minority group from the standpoint of their lack of control of the economic affairs which surround them. The minority role of the stockmen is verified by their attitudes, their conduct, and their associations.

To understand the minority role of the stockmen it is necessary to review certain facts about the ranching industry and its historical development. Ranching usually requires large-scale capital investment. Lending agencies including banks, loan companies, individual investors, government credit agencies, and the railroads, with headquarters in the East and in urban centers, have always had a strong hand in the affairs of the livestock industry. History is replete with illustrations showing that when the Plains and Western livestock industry had to be saved from economic depression, drought, and other weather catastrophies, it was saved with the aid and frequently for the benefit of these capital sources, not for the benefit of the individual ranchers.

Secondly, livestock is a perishable commodity, and grades and quality standards cannot be applied readily. It is an industry in which consumer choice can range all the way from high quality beef to lower qualities; to pork, lamb, and mutton; and even on to other substitutes such as fish, poultry, and dairy products. These facts have meant that the commission buyers, the slaughterers, and the packing companies have always sought to extend their control over the consumer and the producer as much as possible. Therefore, effective methods of control have been worked out to influence the ranchers—methods including propaganda, subsidy for the grower organizations, and common political aims.

In the third place, the livestock industry of the Plains has been largely on the primary-producer level—beef, except for breeding stock, is "put on the hoof" and grown to only partial maturity. From that point on the beef goes to the feeders of the Midwest. This is still largely true today, except that some now goes to packers as choice grass-fat slaughter beef and some goes to irrigated feeding areas in the Plains, in the Rockies, and in the Far West. The terminal markets and the feeders, and the financial interests going with the Midwest feeding phase, represent a third control-element on the welfare of the Plains stock grower, and again the controls come from outside the region and direct the attention of stockmen away from the Great Plains.

These three phases of the livestock industry help explain the minority status of the stockmen in the region. Why the interests of the stockmen are centered, first of all, on activities outside the region, and only secondarily within the region is readily apparent. This interest outside the region has resulted in the isolation of the stockmen from other economic groups within the region, and has given rise to a lack of co-operation all round.

Recently stockmen have achieved some measure of control over the financial aspects of their operations. The local Production Credit Associations, co-operative organizations originally subsidized by the federal government and now largely owned and controlled by the members, make available to the stockmen a form of operating credit which gives them a measure of independence. Similarly, a real estate loan from the Federal Land Bank offers another measure of independence compared with the earlier financing of the industry. But there are other factors which continue to shackle the stockmen to a minority status.

To fully appreciate the minority role of the stockmen, it must be understood that the basis for much of their behavior has a historical origin. The stockmen—men on horseback—still consider themselves the proud bearers of many traditions of the Plains. Historically, men on horseback, in comparison with men on foot, have always symbolized leisure, authority, poise, and power. The early cattlemen were no exception, in their own minds, nor were they in the minds of the squatters, the settlers, and the sheepherders. These attitudes still carry over into today when the truck and auto are generally used as substitutes for the horse.

The stockmen, even now, claim to be the rightful users of the Plains grasslands. It is their conviction that they were "done out of their heritage by the dry-land farmers." The dry-land farmers are looked down upon even now, as squatters and interlopers, as the settlers who ruined the range. A native of the Plains is careful never to identify the stockmen as dry-land farmers, unless prepared to receive deep reproach.

These are some of the reasons for considering the ranchers and stockmen as a minority distinct from the farmer minority in the Plains. These facts are evidence of a strong sense of "we group" feeling, generally associated with minority conduct and the related behavior best described as a "defense mechanism."

The rancher-stockmen often live in a settlement pattern approximating that of a cultural island. Many such areas are clearly characterized as grazing land. Environmental conditions, such as nature of the soil and topography, nature of the native vegetation, sparsity of precipitation below the point of grain growing capacity, proximity to public lands or privately held cooperative grazing districts contribute to the segregation of ranching areas from other types of farming areas. However, there are many situations where this segregation is not clear and in which ranchers and farmers grow both grain and livestock and live as nigh-dwellers.

Segregated areas tend to have a way of life that is unique and that is clearly identified by such forces as school and town relations, county administrative policy, and federal agricultural program policy. The county agent in a range county acts differently from the agent in a dry-land farming area because of the difference in customs, philosophy, and type of extension service required. Federal agency personnel in a range area acts differently from that in a dry-land area for like reasons. The stockmen's associations, either a cattlemen's or sheepmen's organization or both, tend to replace the Farm Bureau, the Grange, or the Farmers' Union which are likely to be strictly defined as "farm organizations." Representatives of the railroads, the packers, and the wool industry—all looking for customers—are welcome visitors in the ranch community, especially at the time of the local organization's annual meetings. These visitors often entertain the stockmen with dinners and with liquor. On such occasions, everybody has a good time and the educational program is usually incidental.

In the opinion of the dry-land farmers, it should not be surprising, then, that the ranchers tend to ship their cattle to old-line packers and commission companies. The dry-land farmers expect the cattlemen and sheepmen to speak the words of the "monopoly" interests of Eastern investors and packers. After all, so the dry-landers say, it is one group of gentlemen to another group of gentlemen, for the purpose of holding the line against the dry-land farmer invaders—especially when the latter are associated with such radical ventures as co-operatives, a federal program of price parity subsidy, and ever-normal granary activities.

But the situation is more complex than indicated. The rancher-stockmen of the region do not represent a consolidated minority among themselves. In fact, the cattle rancher does not see eye to eye with the sheepman at all. Each represents a distinct minority of his own. Historical facts, range-use conditions, economic influences from outside the region, and national economic policy play upon and accentuate these differences.

The market and feeder differences, the financial backing differences, and differences in market outlets—Boston wool buyers for sheepmen and Midwest packers for cattlemen—all these represent a multiplicity and diversity of outside contacts, which keep the sheepmen looking in a different direction from the cattlemen. From the standpoint of international relations, the sheepmen are interested in tariffs on wool, regardless of the effect of lambs and mutton on the price of beef and hogs. Cattlemen are interested in tariff, not as it affects the price of beef, but as related to hoof-and-mouth disease and as it affects the political line-up in matters of governmental policy.

Again, on many things, not all cattlemen see eye to eye. The ranch operators who depend entirely upon private holdings for their grazing land and feed supply consider themselves at a distinct disadvantage compared with the operators who graze a significant portion of their livestock on public lands. By nature of the location and distribution of such lease lands, ranchers in entire communities may be solely without them or else may be significantly dependent upon them.

The nature and history of land policy has a bearing on this schism between stockmen. The states along the western side of the Plains are known as public-land states; those on the eastern side are not. This difference involves such fundamental matters —ranch management costs and the value of land—that ranchers from these two segments of the Plains do not find a common ground for action. Livestock people split on this point, often by communities, and it is a significant factor in creating sub-minority groups among the livestock people themselves.

Here then among the stockmen, and between the stockmen and the dry-land farmers of the Plains, is a basic divisiveness which makes it difficult to have joint and common action on regional problems and situations. Each group, subject to eternal pressure, has been forced to play a role which has made for disunity within the region. The dependence of the stockman on forces and special-interest groups outside the region has attracted and retained his attention in that direction. The absence of adequate communication devices within the region has made it impossible for stockmen to resolve their own differences into a common cause among themselves, not to say anything of the inability to resolve their differences with the dry-land farmers.

THE DRY-LAND FARMERS
OF THE GREAT PLAINS

Dry farming or *dry-land farmers* are expressions that are unique and typical of the Great Plains and the West. These expressions become common, not on the boundary between the Great Plains and the humid-area east of it, at the ninety-eighth meridian, but far inland in the Plains. This fact demonstrates that in the push westward, many settlers who came to the Plains still insisted on being humid-area "farmers" even after crossing over into the semiarid region.

That area between the middle of the Great Plains and the eastern border of the Great Plains which does not use the expression dry farming or dry-land farmers is the area most likely to be ill-adapted to Plains climatic conditions. It represents the area that is akin to a "stone around the neck" of the Plains. It defies the development of solutions to Plains problems. Here is the origin of a cleavage among residents of the Plains which is even more destructive of regional unity than is the conflict between dry-land farmers and stockmen. It is an important explanation of the minority group feeling in the Plains area.

The dry-land farmers, as distinct from the ranchers and stockmen, represent a second large minority in the region. They are the largest group and the most forceful one, politically, in the region. Economically, the dry-land farmers have more control over their needs than any of the other minority groups, and economically, therefore, they have earned the distrust of other minorities in the Plains.

Throughout all the Plains the traditional distinction between stockmen and dry-land farmers is still a significant fact in causing the latter to feel self-conscious. Therefore, the dry-land farmers show an aggressive form of behavior. In most instances this has led to a strong "we group" feeling on the part of dry-land farmers. The dry-land farmers often play the role of the dominant group towards the stockmen and other groups. They also play an important role in national politics and governmental affairs. It is not entirely an accident that programs concerned with price parity, the ever-normal granary, and crop insurance are conscientiously and considerately applied to the wheat farmers.

In all fairness, it should be pointed out that the nation is confronted with a real problem of getting fair prices and a fair income to the wheat farmers. The price-support program of the mid-fifties has been experimental in nature and is justifiable until the nation finds a better solution to the problem. For the

Plains economy this is especially important because wheat-growing is a major enterprise. Yet this very "bottle feeding by government," in the opinion of ranchers, segregates the dry-land farmers of the Plains for censoring not alone by the stockmen of the Plains but by the citizens of much of the rest of the nation.

There was a time, not so long ago, when the dry-land farmers of the Plains were completely at the mercy of economic and political forces outside the region. History shows that many farm settlers had brought savings with them from other areas in the nation and lost or wasted them by engaging in unadapted farming methods. Also, many dry-land farmers were financially depleted as the result of the various climatic hazards that beset them, year after year, and which made crop success an impossibility regardless how much the farmer may have tried to adapt himself to the Plains region. By the time the depression of the thirties struck, many dry-land farmers were already on the verge of economic exhaustion. The failure of the national economy, the farmer's own poor financial state, and the series of drought years in the Plains all contributed to bringing the dry-land farmer to economic despair. As the depression continued, many of those farmers who were at all able left the region. Many others, stayed and scratched out of the land a minimum sort of existence. For either group, some sort of economic assistance became increasingly necessary. As early as 1929–30, the federal Farm Board had attempted to sustain agricultural prices by keeping farm surpluses off the market but the attempt had been unsuccessful. During the New Deal administration a few years later, farmers became eligible for federal relief benefits administered by such organizations as the Federal Emergency Relief and Public Works Administration—the farmer was eligible to receive government relief employment, farm equipment, grain for planting, and even cash. But these forms of assistance could not actually eradicate the problem which the dry-land farmer faced in the Plains; at best, economic assistance from outside the Plains region could only temporarily and partially alleviate the condition in which the dry-land farmer found himself. By 1935, the situation had grown so severe that the federal government sponsored a plan of resettlement and rehabilitation for the farmer, but this too was unsatisfactory—a certain inherent pride and courage prevented the Plains farmer from surrendering so completely to defeat and he resisted being removed from his own land. But somehow, dependent as he was on outside economic aid and as subservient as he was, in spite of himself, to economic and political forces over which he had little control, the dry-land farmer survived, little by little recovered, and eventually began to devise means for an independent control of his own affairs.

More recently and as late as the fifties, in their relations with the economic system outside the region, the dry-land farmers feel that they have made a beginning toward a reasonable degree of control over their affairs and that much of their progress toward economic independence has been the result of their own efforts—namely by way of the co-operatives. The experience of the thirties, the prosperity of the forties—both contributed toward educating the Plains farmers in the techniques of co-operation. And the dry-land farmers feel grieved because their fellow plainsmen, the stockmen, have not exercised a similar initiative in their own behalf. The dry-land farmers are aggrieved that the stockmen have not co-operated with the wheatgrowers though willing, at the same time, to gain from the benefits of the farmer's activity—for example, it is reputed that the oil and gas co-operatives initiated by the dry-land farmers, have put money into the pockets of many ranchers. The dry-land farmers would like to see the ranchers co-operate in these efforts which mean a better life for all.

The facts substantiate the belief that the dry-land farmers have gained some reasonable control over their economic affairs. The Farmers' Alliance, and Populism activity of an earlier period, in Texas, Oklahoma, and Kansas especially, brought financial and marketing gains to the wheat and cotton growers of the Southern Plains particularly. Later the Non-Partisan League program of the Northwest, the North Dakota State Mill and Elevator program, the North Dakota State Banking program, and the efforts of Governor Langer of North Dakota are among the major steps in this process. The activities of the National Farmers' Educational and Co-operative Union and the Grange placed greater control of production, marketing, and consumer affairs into the hands of the Plains wheatgrowers. The influence of the Farmers' Union Grain Terminal Association was an effective instrument in opening the Grain Exchange to free and open market activity. The Farm Holiday activities during the thirties were another phase of this attempt on the part of dry-land farmers to rid themselves of external controls.

The federal government, in its acreage control and parity price program for wheat, through the aims of the ever-normal storage and crop insurance programs, and by other means, has assisted the dry-land farmers in freeing themselves from these same external controls. The role of agriculture in the 1948 elections was another demonstration of the political consciousness of farmers, including those of the Plains.

To accomplish these ends, the wheat farmers of the Plains have resorted to building a strong "we group" feeling among themselves. Since ranchers of the Plains have not participated in these activities readily, they have become identified as the "out group" to the dry-land farmers; the "coat-tail" riders; and even as "enemies," in the opinion of the dry landers.

But the dry-land farmer group has significant subgroups within its own rank, for there is not yet established a common cause among all the dry-land farmers of the region. There is reason to believe that the subgroups among them represent minority groups themselves, with all the characteristics of minority-group behavior. Reference has already been made to the dry-land farmers and the humid-area "farmers" along the eastern edge of the Plains. Included in the group of dry-land farmers is a significant proportion who do not diversify, but specialize in single crop production on an exclusively commercial scale. They have their own peculiar interests and problems, and, to an extent, their own way of living. They are least tied down to the land for year-round residence, and many now reside in cities and towns and operate their lands from these homes.

Compared with the specialty or one-crop dry-land farmers, many Plains farmers practice considerable diversification in their enterprise. This diversification rests on a philosophy so sufficiently different from one-crop farming that a common purpose and aim among all Plains farmers has not yet been reached. The economic aspects of such diversified farming enterprises are set forth in a special Bureau of Agricultural Economics study. For the Plains, diversified types include the areas in which there is a combination of (1) spring wheat and small grain, (2) spring wheat and corn, and (3) cash grain. Other areas have a combination of (4) spring wheat and roughage, and (5) winter wheat and grain sorghum (see Figure 20). These farm type areas are in addition to those preponderantly of the cotton, the spring wheat or winter wheat specialty, and the livestock types.

The above description of the characteristics of the several dry-land farmer groups makes it clear that they represent a

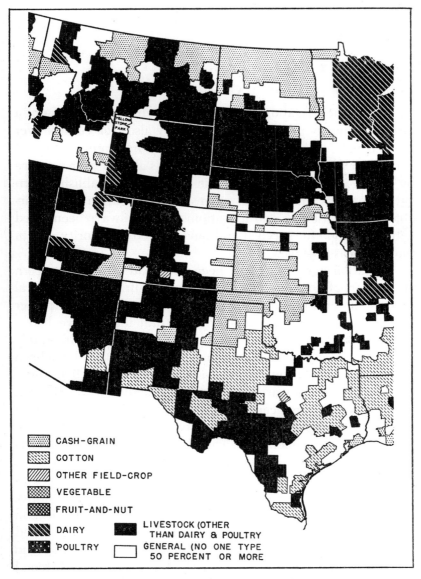

CASH-GRAIN
COTTON
OTHER FIELD-CROP
VEGETABLE
FRUIT-AND-NUT
DAIRY
POULTRY
LIVESTOCK (OTHER THAN DAIRY & POULTRY
GENERAL (NO ONE TYPE 50 PERCENT OR MORE

FIG. 20.   Generalized types of farming in the Great Plains.

259

minority, in contrast to the stockmen and other groups, and that they, in turn, constitute a number of sub-minority groups. Strong elements in the dry-land farmer group continue as a "we group," with all the behavior typical of aggression that is necessary in order to maintain group solidarity and to hold past gains and expand upon them. This results in conflict with others of the dry-land farmer group who are less aggressive.

THE IRRIGATION FARMER
OF THE GREAT PLAINS

The irrigation farmers of the Plains, too, represent a distinct minority group in number. They also lack control over their economic affairs, and they have only a minimum of contact with other groups in the region. There has always been concern by humid-area farmers and those on already established irrigation projects that further expansion of irrigation is undesirable. Reclamationists and irrigationists have always been faced with a struggle for survival and have played a minority role in the nation as a whole.

Irrigation agriculture has been the focal point of concern on the part of non-agricultural interests. Railroads, agricultural processors, farm equipment manufacturers, speculators, power interests, and many other non-agricultural forces have had a hand in its destiny. Irrigationists have sometimes deliberately aligned themselves with such groups; more often they have been purposefully joined by such non-irrigation interests. The sugar interests of the nation are such a group concerned with irrigation development. More recently, reclamation construction has been of the multiple purpose type, seeking to provide flood control and power development also. Therefore, private power interests have had a prejudicial eye on irrigation.

Thus irrigation interests, primarily concerned with agriculture and farming matters in the Plains, are a distinct minority within a larger network of minorities having nationwide and even international interests at stake. Michael W. Straus, United States Commissioner of Reclamation, put it as follows at the 1949 National Reclamation Association Meetings: "We have listened to a lot of speeches by a lot of personages who have appeared before the National Reclamation Association, in the parade of passing years. And, listening, I, like any of you, have always pondered the motives, the angles, the influences and the interests behind the various views that these orators have voiced." These entangling alliances of the water users and irrigation farmers have created such a compromise that irrigation spokesmen have called for limiting the membership in reclamation and irrigation associations to the irrigationists and water users themselves. The Nebraska Reclamation Association adopted such a resolution and has tried to modify its program accordingly.

The irrigation farmers live in communities approximating cultural islands. Some of the irrigation development in the Plains is of the individual type, undertaken by single farm operators or small groups. The nature of the topography and the amount of available water for irrigation has afforded only a very limited development. Such irrigationists often live and act as if they were part of the larger community and often have a significant proportion of dry land attached to the operating unit.

A large majority of the irrigation development, however, is in the nature of "projects," requiring extensive development and capital expenditure which can be undertaken only in a collective manner and involving the long-time amortization of costs. The nature of irrigation farming, the location of irrigated areas, and the administrative character of project activities have resulted in the island-like segregation of the population residing in such irrigated areas. Certain other factors such as high turnover of operators, speculation in land, specialty forms of agriculture, dependence upon processors of specialty crops, and the influence of Main Street promotion, business and livelihood interest in the agriculture—all these have further emphasized the insular nature of the irrigation projects.

Thus the irrigation way of life differs, in striking fashion, from that of the surrounding dry-land area. There is a greater interdependence between town and country, the presence of considerable migratory labor and resulting problems, and peculiar weed and erosion control problems. Farm organizations—such as a local irrigation association, or specialty crop associations like a local beet growers association—assist in this segregation.

Irrigation farming has meant concentration on intensive

types of agriculture. In addition to dairying and intensive hay production, the development has been in the direction of crop specialties where the demand is quickly filled. Consequently, competition has been severe, and commodity specialization has been general. Irrigated areas devoted to bean and pea growing, sugar beets, fruit, and vegetable specialization and similar crops have been typical. These developments along commodity lines have resulted in a close affiliation with specialty marketing channels and organizations. This has contributed to the segregation of irrigation farmers into many subgroups, most of which again play a minority group role in their contacts with markets outside the region.

A brief description of the sugar-beet growers as a minority, distinguished from other irrigationists, will suffice to illustrate the point. In addition to the pro and con issues of the tariff, and the proportion of the domestically consumed sugar that should come from domestic sugar-beet sources as contrasted with domestic and off-shore cane-sugar sources, the role of subsidizing the price of sugar is a factor that causes constant anxiety to sugar-beet growers. Aside from the economic and political issues as to whether sugar beets should or should not be grown, there is also a purely agronomic problem. For much of the higher Plains, sugar-beet culture is the only practical large-scale soil conditioning and weed-control crop. This aspect may be a much more important reason for growing sugar beets than is the economic aspect relating to the tariff when considering the greater welfare of Plains agriculture.

The need for seasonal labor, in varying and sporadic but large quantities, has been a further complicating factor. The almost absolute monopoly control exercised by the sugar processors concerning who should grow sugar beets, by what farming methods, under what price conditions, for what share of the by-product returns from beets, and the presence of an entire host of related factory-grower situations, represent a source of intense irritation, enforced co-operation, and segmentation of interests.

From this brief description it is apparent that the status of the sugar-beet growers in an irrigated area is distinctly that of a minority group. Their preoccupation with their own problems is so intense that co-operation with other irrigation farmers is limited, and their contacts with nonirrigation farmers and with stockmen are almost non-existent. The situation for other groups of irrigation farmers who specialize in other crops (potatoes, dairying, peas, beans, etc.) are not significantly dissimilar from those of the beet growers.

THE DRY-LAND COTTON GROWER

Western Oklahoma and Texas are often classified as belonging to the Southwestern states and as distinct from the Plains. This is clear evidence of the importation of humid-area thought patterns and ways from the cotton South. The chief reason for attaching the Southern Plains area to the Southwestern states is that cotton is grown in this part of the Plains. But this part of the Plains also grows wheat, livestock, and sorghums —enterprises typical of semiarid climatic conditions.

The projection of the humid-area cotton farming thought pattern into the Plains is a contradiction of the fact that the cotton South once before, in the Civil War days, was stopped on the ninety-eighth meridian. It is clear evidence that the dry-land cotton grower of the semiarid Plains is the "caboose" of the cotton South as the latter plays its drama in the humid-area arena of one-crop farming against a background of international free trade, cotton crop parity, and cotton production control. It is evidence of the separation of the dry-land cotton grower from the remainder of the minorities in the Plains.

The fact of this isolation of the dry-land cotton grower and his reduction to minority status in the Southern Plains becomes striking when it is recalled that this part of the Plains is the birth place of the early cattleman's culture which spread northward into the rest of the Plains. When it is further realized that livestock raising, winter wheatgrowing, sorghum production, and cotton growing, are direct competitors for the same land, capital, and management in this part of the Plains, the segmented character of these residents on commodity lines readily identifies the nature of the minority situation in the region.

Cotton is grown in nearly all parts of the Southwestern states. In only thirteen of the sixty-six types of farming areas is cotton not grown as a major crop. One of the new cotton growing areas, showing much promise, is the dry-land cotton development in the Southern Plains. Here a combination of factors, including adapted varieties, irrigation, mechanization, and labor conditions combine to make cotton production an important competitor of cotton grown under humid-area conditions.

In spite of the similar economic role of the cotton, livestock, and wheat farmers in the Plains, the cotton growers represent a distinct minority group in the region. This is true for several reasons. First, they are members of a larger minority—the cotton growers of the South. This directs the attention of the Southern Plains cotton growers, not to their own Plains problems, but to cotton, to the entire South, to the nation's capital, and to the international situation. It is apparent from this that the Plains cotton growers have much of their attention focused away from the Plains and the other groups in the region.

For a second reason, the Plains cotton growers function as a minority. Almost the entire institutional mechanism associated with Southern Plains cotton growing has been bodily carried over from the humid South, except for modifications that are related to greater mechanization. Among these institutional carry-overs from the humid-area South are the factors associated with tenure—problems associated with being an owner, part-owner, tenant, sharecropper, cash rent cropper, white tenant, Negro tenant, plantation-farm manager, modified plantation operator; with other problems associated with credit policy, leasing arrangements, cotton gin and storage facilities; and a host of other traditional and institutional arrangements.

Even the thought patterns in research matters suffer from this institutionalized tie-up between the humid-area cotton South and the dry-land cotton of the High Plains region. The very fact that a monumental research work on land tenure in the Southwest dealt largely with the tenure arrangements in an east-west manner is indicative of the magnitude of the pull on the Southern Plains, and the Southern Plains cotton grower, into a humid-area cotton South rather than into a great Plains orbit of institutional life. Although the authors of the study recognized dry-land cotton farming as separate from humid-area cotton growing, the real significance of dry-land cotton growing was not demonstrated; and the fact of poor institutional adaptation to Plains conditions was not emphasized.

264

THE ROLE OF SORGHUMS

AS A UNIFIER OF PLAINS MINORITIES

Sorghums are especially well adapted to semiarid climatic conditions, though not as well known in the Northern as in the Southern Plains. Some varieties have been developed for fodder, and others for cash crop production, the latter having increased tremendously in recent years. Sorghum yields outrank corn yields in the Plains. Its livestock-feed values are the equivalent of corn, especially so when mixed with cottonseed byproducts. In addition, it ranks with corn or wheat for alcohol manufacturing purposes. From the standpoint of its adapted farm-management use, sorghums are a replacement crop for both cotton and wheat and for feed, in drought periods, and will mature after late seeding under dry conditions.

Sorghums, though so well-adapted to Plains climatic conditions, have been slow to be accepted in the Northern Plains states. This is evidence of the limited character of north-south communications in the region, and is also evidence that the agriculturalist of the South now has little in common with the agriculturalist of the North. The lines of contact for both are presently largely along east-west avenues, with little opportunity for presenting a united front from the standpoint of Plains problems.

When a livestock feed is processed out of a mixture of sorghums, low-grade wheat, and cottonseed by-products, and becomes a universal livestock feed for ranchers in the entire Plains, both north and south, then a basic step towards regionalism for the Plains will have been accomplished. The present emphasis upon organization for agriculturalists along commodity lines makes for a segmentation in the American agricultural economy that keeps the growers apart and helps fragment them into subgroups. In the Plains, where economic survival is elemental, this contributes to making minorities of these commodity groups. Their status as raw-material producers means that their dependence upon markets and processors outside the region further fragments the agricultural populations of the Plains and keeps most of these people in a minority status.

The task ahead for a proper solution of the problems of Plains agriculture is first to recognize it as agriculture in a semiarid region—one that is at present pulled hither and yon by non-Plains forces and by indigenous climatic vagaries. Secondly, it must be recognized that Plains agriculture is not a unity, but characterized by basic schisms into fragmented parts, dominated by minority behavior patterns. These minority behavior patterns force themselves upon the Plains agriculturist to the extent that he merely plays a role—a role not conducive to building the area as a region offering constructive opportunities for the youth who are to follow.

CHAPTER 20

Minorities in the Towns

Urban inhabitants of the Plains exhibit minority behavior as surely as do the residents of the rural areas.
Cities of the Plains do not now offer the necessary leadership
and direction for dynamic development of the region, and there
is not now, within the towns and cities, the psychological unity
that is necessary in order for the people of the region to think
for themselves, to build for themselves, and to do things for
themselves. The situation is all the more tragic because the
minority behavior demonstrated by the urban population of the
region does not now develop and attract the leadership that is
necessary for regional self-expression.

There are few large cities in the Great Plains—none over
70,000 population, save Amarillo, Lubbock, San Antonio, El
Paso and Corpus Christi—which truly function as regional centers. Urban life and social organization in the Plains is dominated by the larger urban centers beyond the borders of the
region—Denver, Spokane, the Twin Cities, Chicago, Omaha,
Oklahoma City, Wichita, Kansas City, St. Louis, Dallas, and
Fort Worth. The towns and cities in the Plains proper are little
more than satellites of the larger cities on the periphery. They
are spokesmen for the metropolitan centers outside the region.

Who, then, are the minority groups that predominate in the
towns and the cities of the Plains?

THE MANAGERIAL MINORITY

The Plains are not completely without industrial activity. There is a minimum of transportation development that

must be administered. There are numerous small industries that function sporadically—industries devoted to cement and gypsum extraction and processing, coal and clay extraction, talc and ore extraction, and power production and distribution. There is small scale machinery manufacturing and repairing. In addition, there is extraction of oil and its refinement, extraction of natural gas and its distribution, and the processing of certain agricultural products such as sugar beets, flour, grains, feeds, and cotton.

Capital and management for the development of the resources of the Plains has generally been imported from outside the region. There are exceptions, of course, and sometimes resident capital, managed by resident personnel, has sought to process some of the region's resources. But local processing of resources, subject to control from outside the region, has given rise to island-like industrial areas, managed by personnel who have not been readily integrated into the social structure of the region. As the result of being promoted into and out of the region as circumstances and home office policy have demanded, this personnel represents a minority population—one that has made little constructive contribution to the building of the region.

Often this minority has been critical of the region and its economic and social opportunities. Frequently these managers have meddled in politics and legislation far beyond their fair stake, and on occasion they have even been a party to keeping the locality impoverished, since their principal function has been to keep down operating costs, especially in the form of taxes. On occasion, others in the local community have identified themselves intimately with these migrant managers and have copied their attitudes of exploitation—of "grab and run." This has subjected the manager group and the coattail riders to severe censorship and has made of them a minority group looked upon with distrust and condemnation.

A few examples will demonstrate the nature and the extent of this situation. Gold, in the Black Hills, has been exploited with only temporary material benefit to the locality and the region. The exploitation has been supervised by a managerial minority who have not intended to live in the region for long, and special dispensation has been necessary to keep the industry going.

The processing of sugar beets has long been controlled by one of the most centralized and wealthy financial circles in the nation. The function of the management personnel has been to do those things that benefit the industry, not those things necessarily good for the community. The factory operations themselves have been highly seasonal, requiring much seasonal labor. The solutions for the accompanying problems of relief, unemployment, and migration of workers generally have been left to the local community.

The railroad business throughout the region is managed by people from outside and the details are tended to by personnel who are promoted into and out of the region. Railroad rates are considered discriminatory by the residents, and railroads have always been a focal point for anger. Colorful characters have promoted railroad activities not necessarily for the benefit of the region, while resident people have often been moved about like pawns in an industrial chess game.

Also, there are, in the Plains, many gentlemen landowners—some of them even nonresident. They have contributed to special problems, including high farm tenancy, undesirable land-use practices, stumbling blocks to taxation-adjustment programs, migratory farm labor conditions, and unnecessarily high land values because of speculative buying. The sporadic attempts by legislatures to pass laws against corporate ownership of land and to institute graduated land-tax measures or homestead tax exemption measures are evidence of the dislike and animosity towards the gentleman landowners on the part of the remaining agriculturalists of the region. To be a gentleman landowner in the Plains is to invite suspicion and distrust.

Another example of resource exploitation, by a managerial minority, which invites bitter antagonism is in the field of natural gas distribution. Rate-making devices are designed to profit the non-resident stockholder and the management. Frequently the transmission facilities of these services cross state lines. Extraction taxes, by states, have been declared unconstitutional on the grounds that they represent interferences with interstate commerce. In the meantime, the managing personnel often "play" at running the community, and some represent "listening posts" to feret out political trends and hopes for public improvements by local residents that may mean more taxes for these concerns.

There has not been sufficient political courage in these states to marshall local public opinion in favor of an interstate compact device as a way to obtain public revenue from the resource use and extraction activities of these industries. One of the purposes of the Port of New York Authority, for example, is to accomplish joint action among several states in assessing, taxing, and distributing tax receipts from such a multi-state business enterprise. In the Plains such united action appears to be impossible; therefore, exploitation is inevitable. And the Plains residents know this. It makes them angry, but they remain helpless.

A final example to demonstrate the existence of a managerial minority and the role played by them is in the field of oil extraction and production in the Plains. A significant share of the nation's oil resources and production are found in the Great Plains portion of Montana, Wyoming, Oklahoma, Texas, Kansas, and more recently in the Williston Basin of Montana and North Dakota. Such oil developments are controlled by national and international capital from outside the region largely, with a resultant invasion by administrative and managerial personnel that is not small in numbers. Much of this personnel belongs to the managerial minority of the Plains.

It is the belief of many residents of the Plains that the settlement of the tidelands oil issue spells foreboding things for the Plains. Oil resources extend from the high Plains of Texas into the Gulf of Mexico. The same companies that process oil in the Plains of Montana, Wyoming, Oklahoma, Kansas, and Texas have an interest in tideland oil. People feel that the attempt to get oil lands into the hands of the states is a device to exploit tideland and on-shore oil under the less rigid controls exercised by the states rather than under the eagle eye of Uncle Sam. The managerial minority, in the opinion of many Plains people, will again function as exploiters rather than as builders of the region. A. G. Mezerik has some pertinent things to say about this in his book *The Pursuit of Plenty*.

From the above examples it is evident that the Plains, as raw material producers, are especially subject to exploitation by a managerial minority. The task of this group of itinerants is to transfer the benefit of Plains resources to the owners outside the region, and to accomplish this they have a peculiar philosophy— one not designed to build the region in its own right. It is apparent, therefore, why this group has become a special target for the feeling of distrust displayed by the rest of the minority groups in the region. To be one of the managerial minority is not an enviable status to possess. And to be a local resident who is also a rider on the coattails of this minority is most unpardonable. These are conditions that make for the segregation of a minority in the Plains—the managerial group—whose conduct contributes to divisiveness and jealousies, to ill will and distrust, to political enmity, to destruction of resources and a way of life that will result in eventual prostration of the region.

THE LABORERS OF THE GREAT PLAINS REGION

Labor, as a minority in the Plains population, consists of two groups. One is the highly organized group including the railroad workers, the miners, the communications workers, the bartenders, the printers, the truckers and teamsters, and the oil workers. Because they are affected by interstate travel and business, these groups tend also to be affiliated with national unions. The very crux of organization and existence of this segment of labor in the Plains is dependent upon outside aid and advice, since dependence upon their own numbers would mean little organized labor. Their scattered distribution and small numbers in the Plains would make it impossible even to organize, much less to function as a union.

The very fact of this dependence upon the outside for aid and advice creates some specific problems for this group. Actually, they have relatively little contact with the community and with the rest of labor in the Plains area. Labor policy and tactics, shaped in the highly urbanized and industrialized East, are standardized and tend toward industry-wide agreements. Such policies are not adapted to the economic and social conditions—created by the Plains environment—of sparsity of population and the lack of urbanization. Therefore, there is now a more serious conflict and basic misunderstanding between labor and management, and between labor and the public, in this region than need be the case. The conflict is recognized in the fact that the imported organizer is considered an "enemy" by the public, and sometimes by the other laborers in the community.

Since the communication that takes place is between the organized labor group in the Plains and national headquarters, there is an almost complete absence of communication between the organized group and the remainder of the minority groups in the region. The problem of minority group segregation is, therefore, intensified rather than mitigated. Certain Plains agricultural groups have attempted to include the welfare objectives of labor in their policy, farm price, and farm program considerations. Most of this effort for such co-operation comes from the agriculturalists in the Plains, not from labor itself.

The second element of organized labor in the Plains consists of the usual craft groups—the carpenters, bricklayers, plumbers, tinsmiths, mechanics, common laborers, hod carriers, and others. In most Plains communities these craft unions are necessarily small in membership and weak in influence. Only when they affiliate into a local trade and labor council can these unions begin to exercise their legal rights. Because these groups are less highly affiliated with strong national organizations, they obtain little aid and advice from national headquarters. Nor do these unions have a channel on a regional level whereby they may seek an affiliation concerning regional problems. The absence of adequate communication within the region makes these laborers a distinctly ineffective and nonvocal minority in each community. Antilabor legislation in the Plains states, such as that which has flourished in the form of little Taft-Hartley laws, is, therefore, to be expected. The great wonder is that the laws have not been more drastic.

The Plains have regional labor problems that need study and adequate legislation. These have to do with unemployment insurance and adequate reserves for it, workman's compensation, especially in industries closely allied with agriculture, workers' disability insurance, minimum-wage legislation, especially as related to migratory and transient laborers including those in agriculture, legislation dealing with fair employment, collective bargaining procedures and techniques, and labor standards. Present legislation of this nature is outdated because laws have not been revised.

In the past, the region has had much migratory labor for industrial, urban, and agricultural needs—the sheepherder, the cowboy, the sugar-beet worker, the harvest hand, and the miner among them. Their position in the economic life of the region has generally been akin to the pay received and the working conditions that prevailed—very low and very poor. The cowhand who received thirty dollars and keep per month was not an important buyer of producer goods; therefore, he did not contribute to prosperity and full employment in the business economy. Often he was not a citizen of the community, not a consumer, not a taxpayer. His habits, including his work activity, frequently were sporadic, intermittent, and unpredictable.

There is much to do in the way of an intelligent labor policy and employment program if the region is to have employment opportunities consistent with present day standards of living and if the residents are to have the mechanics and repairmen to keep in repair the gadgets on ranch and farm homes now powered by rural electrification. Many of the Plains states, however, have received a poor reputation among working people as the result of past unfortunate labor conditions. These states, especially in the northern part, are at the end of the migratory labor route. If the weather is favorable and the employment opportunities elsewhere are limited, the migrant workers come to the Northern Plains; if not, the area is short of labor.

The Missouri River Basin development program is importing much labor from outside the region. The youth of the region are becoming acquainted with the accepted ways and working conditions of organized labor. The continued dependence upon seasonal labor in agriculture, even with increased mechanization, and the need for constantly training a new labor supply present a problem needing solution. All these conditions will require legislation of the type that will make for favorable working conditions and wages. To have and to hold an adequate labor force in the region, the minority status of the workers will need to be removed. The initiative for this will lie with the other minority groups—the farmers, ranchers, and businessmen and not with the laborers alone. The laborers have been so effectively ground into a minority status that they are not now able to furnish much leadership from within their own ranks.

THE PROFESSIONAL GROUP

IN THE GREAT PLAINS

The professions include the doctors and dentists, the nurses, the teachers and the school administrators, the lawyers, the ministers, the librarians, the welfare workers, and others. That these represent minority occupations and special interest groups in almost any situation is granted. Many among them have even been guilty of using the "cloak of professionalism" to separate themselves from the rest of the population. This has not always been the fault of the doctors and lawyers and ministers, however, since professionalization is partially inherent in the degree of specialization and training required of them. But the members of these professions have done relatively little to purposely identify themselves with the welfare of all in the community.

On the other hand, the remaining population has done relatively little to absorb the professionals into the fabric of community activities. In the Plains, where communication within the region and among the minority groups is inadequate and limited, the resulting isolation of the professional groups has been severe.

There are numerous reasons for the isolation of these professional minority groups. First, many professional persons come from outside the region and, therefore, do not know its peculiar problems and needs. Not understanding, they have difficulty identifying themselves with the problems and needs of the region. Also, professional training institutions are almost exclusively outside the region. The relatively few training facilities and the in-service training schools in the region are staffed and unduly influenced by personnel who have acquired experience and reputations outside the region and not within it. Therefore, there has not been developed the necessary spirit for adapting practices and services to the conditions found in the area.

Secondly, these professional groups tend to be affiliated extensively with nationwide professional organizations which emphasize the "special interest" phase of the occupation involved and not the "community" phase in which the professional person works. For example, the school teacher organizations emphasize salary, tenure, and curricular matters. Desirable as this is, there is the larger task of developing an adapted school organization and financing program for the region—a semiarid land with great distance, sparse population, and low enrollment figures. The doctor, the lawyer, the minister, and the other professional persons show a similar lack of imagination and enthusiasm for adapting their professional practices to the community needs in the Plains.

Finally, a large segment of the professional group is relatively transient. The individuals enter the area for experience; then seek opportunities elsewhere. Therefore, they generally have an eye on their professional standing in relation to their fellow colleagues outside the region. This is done in the spirit of getting a "boost up the professional ladder." Generally, such professionals are of little value to the community and the region for they do not stand hitched, nor do they fight for necessary changes. This is true, not alone for the teacher, but for the minister, the social worker, the lawyer, and the doctor.

An example of failure to face the risks in the region on the part of the medical men has been their sponsorship of the Blue Shield programs on a state basis. In order to cope with the threat of national health insurance, Blue Shield medical programs have developed in most states. But population is sparse in the Plains states, and the risk of financial insecurity in insurance matters is higher than in the humid states because of the special hazards in income producing ability in the region. Blue Shield programs on a state basis are, therefore, poor risk programs with high chances of failure in extended drought periods, with consequent loss to the participants. They are unwise insurance programs because only people from higher risk areas are included.

Uninformed about these risk problems, the medical promoters in the region have followed the national propaganda line which is not shaped to the conditions in the Plains. This is demonstrated by the twenty-one year long controversy in Oklahoma that raged between the Elk City Cooperative Community Hospital and the Beckham County Medical Society supported by the nationwide American Medical Association. The controversy began in 1929 when the Farmers Union Hospital Association established a co-operative hospital in Elk City under the direction of Dr. Michael A. Shadid. The Beckham County Medical Society for the next twenty-one years attacked vigorously the co-operative hospital and its medical plan, and not until 1952, as the result of a lawsuit brought by the co-operative medical group against the Society, were staff doctors of the community hospital allowed to join the Society, the Oklahoma Medical Association, and the American Medical Association.

In nearly every professional field, the minority status of professional groups is not now a truly constructive force in inventing better adapted programs for Plains conditions. Plains people know these things and are deeply resentful. In order to bring about a true integration of these professional persons with the community life and needs of the region, the impetus will need to come largely from non-professional people themselves, and only incidentally from those in the respective professions, whether in medicine, health, welfare, hospital care, the ministry, or in education. But as long as the remainder of the population also functions in a minority-group fashion, the task will be difficult.

To say that these institutional adaptations cannot be accomplished is fatalistic and destructive. The interest and loyalty of the young people in the region can be maintained only if the professions in which they may enter, or which they consider a significant part of the standard of living, are available to them within the region. Without young people the region cannot survive, except in an exploited status. Too many young people now receive higher education, become acquainted with the standards of a good life, and will not stand idly by and accept second-rate standards. The past exodus of young people with education is evidence of this fact.

THE BUSINESS PEOPLE

OF THE GREAT PLAINS REGION

The Main Street people of the Plains represent a distinct minority in numbers and in the fact that they are controlled largely by interests from outside the region. The absence of large cities in the region serves to emphasize the minority situation of the Main Street residents. If there were such cities, cities that were truly indigenous and really represented the welfare of the region in a basic way, the Main Street minority might perhaps more nearly reflect the needs of the region than is now the case. The fact that Main Street is merely the outlet for industry, commerce, trade, finance, and business of the large urban and industrial forces from outside the region is strong evidence that the loyalties and attachments of the Plains businessmen are to their "bread and butter" sources.

Rufus Terral, in his book *The Missouri Valley*, presents clearly this picture of the factoryless Plains in a chapter entitled "Men without Factories." He points out that population follows the smokestack and that the absence of industry in the Plains states means that the security of all is impaired. Population is lost to the Plains and the services of public institutions are retarded for want of tax revenues which industry could supply. Some wants of people go largely unsupplied and some resources are unused because there is only limited industrial development in the region.

To show the dilemma the people of the region find themselves in, it may be pointed out that as of recent date, the paper and pulp mills of Wisconsin now cut stumpage and pulpwood in Montana and ship it to the Wisconsin mills. It has been thus with flour milling, meat processing, cotton processing and wool processing for a long time. The Plains have been drained of their resources at a profit to others outside the region who do the processing, with the result measured as a lowered standard of living in the Plains.

Morris E. Garnsey (*America's New Frontier—The Mountain West*) has demonstrated the difficulties associated with the absence of industry in the Plains and mountain states. He points out that an area in which the economy rests on raw material production alone, and not on processing, will remain relatively poor. His figures demonstrate that such is the case for the mountain and Plains states. Senator James E. Murray of Montana ("The Force of Social Organizations in Regional Development") has set forth a striking comparison of business volume decline and continued low recovery in the Missouri Basin states compared with the Tennessee Valley region and the rest of the nation.

Industry appears to be more prevalent in the Southern Plains (especially Texas, Oklahoma, and Kansas) than in the northern part. This is largely more apparent than factual, since much industry tends to be in the humid eastern rather than in the Plains portions of these states. Oil exploitation and refining, and to an extent cotton ginning, have created employment and payrolls, even in the Plains area of these states. In addition, the favorable climatic conditions have brought to these Southern Plains states, including the Plains proper, some air base and army service camps and some production activity that have increased the urban population. These tend, however, all to be temporary developments, even in the case of oil and natural gas, and in the long run bring problems of economic instability and fluctuation that compound rather than minimize the problem of risk.

The lack of business and industrial activity in the Plains is deeply resented by many of the residents. Because of its absence youth is leaving, local consumer markets are limited, and public revenue sources are limited. Businessmen are thought of as lacking courage to build the region. Many, it is felt, are satisfied with the job of being the outpost representatives of non-resident business and industry. For these reasons businessmen suffer few kindnesses from the agriculturalists of the Plains.

In the face of such attitudes, it is expecting too much of the businessman to ask him to communicate good will between Main Street and the remainder of the minority groups in the region and to serve as a leader in developing the region. Such a leadership role has been accomplished by some businessmen, on occasion, by playing one minority against another, and by waiting for anger to cool, and then by becoming acceptable again. But this playing one group against another has been remembered, and businessmen are twice suspected by the other residents. To depend on leadership from Main Street businessmen to build the foundations of an adapted way of living in the Plains, is like walking on quicksand.

Main Street has sometimes been active in promoting agricultural ventures. One of these ventures is irrigation. Some of the Main Street spokesmen have been sincere in urging it, seeking to increase the welfare of themselves, their community, and their region. Others have sought selfish ends exclusively—windfalls which they might liquidate before leaving the community. Still others have been spokesmen for vested interests and have subverted efforts at developing industrial and processing activities in the region.

Therefore, farmers, and ranchers too, have turned to the co-operatives to assist them in getting better services and also a larger share of the nation's income. These co-operatives are necessarily located on Main Street. They have included oil stations, elevators, cotton gins, implement shops, hardware services, grocery stores, supply houses, storage and sorting facilities, insurance businesses, shipping associations, breeding rings, creameries, weed and soil erosion control districts, rural electrification centers, and others.

These co-operative ventures are considered an invasion of the area of business belonging to Main Street. A basic conflict has, therefore, developed on Main Street. On the one hand are the farm co-operatives. On the other hand are the retail outlets for the most urbanized and industrialized businesses of the nation—Ford Motors, General Motors, General Mills, and International Harvester, to name only a few. The local dealers for these large concerns have specifically defined trade areas and marketing quotas. Thus these urban and industrial power complexes are at the core of defining rural life values and community organizations for farm and small town people. The Main Street businessman finds himself in the very center of this power-complex thrust in rural areas.

For this reason the fight against the co-operatives on Main Street is elemental and of the death struggle type. In the Plains, where towns are few and sometimes the only town in the county is the county seat, the conflict reaches out to touch everyone. Main Street is a "closed shop," closed to farmer-rancher co-operatives, but Main Streeters consider it smart business to own and operate a farm. It is these conditions that single out the businessman as a minority group. For a farmer or a rancher to sit with businessmen at the Rotarian luncheon table is akin to cutting his throat, in the eyes of most plainsmen.

What makes the fight on Main Street so tragic is that the businessman slavishly follows and swallows the line of certain propaganda agencies such as the National Tax Equality League, purely a propaganda organization, with high paid officials and with headquarters in Chicago. Its dedicated aim is to fight the farm co-operatives, and to provide lucrative employment for officers. To do so, it collects contributions from Main Street businessmen and then feeds its propaganda into the rural communities. The critical character of this agricultural-businessman struggle can be measured by the recurrent hearings on the subject in Congress, and the introduction of the subject into the political campaigns of 1946 and 1948.

In North Dakota, for instance the eastern business interests attempted a trial balloon in the state legislature in 1946. Certain legislation was to be proposed to cut the farmer away from some of his hard-won victories in that state. A majority of the legislators, mostly Main Street businessmen, lawyers, and some farmers, had been "favorably lined up" by the non-resident interests. Glen Talbot, president of the North Dakota Farmers' Union, heard about this "line-up" and went to the capitol accompanied by some of his supporters. He was ushered from the State House and it was proposed that he be threatened with arrest for disturbance of the peace. He immediately issued a further call to the Farmers' Union of that state and this time a large membership made their appearance. The legislators were "buttonholed" and the "line-up" was broken.

But this was not the end of the efforts to oppose agricultural interests in North Dakota. Farmers' Union had begun to sell its own insurance to the farmers of North Dakota. For several years the state insurance commissioner had employed delaying tactics in issuing the annual license for the sale of insurance by the Farmers' Union Insurance Company. In 1947, after much delay, the issue came to a head in the form of a statement from Talbot that certain political changes would be made. The farmers of North Dakota organized the North Dakota Farmers' Union Progressive Alliance, and entered into the political affairs of the state "to stay," and also won the right to sell their insurance.

These affairs in North Dakota postdate, by about a decade, the attempt on the part of the central grain trade to capitalize on the assumed weaknesses of the dry-land wheat farmers on the Northern Plains. Both in 1937 and again in 1938, the grain trade offered to buy low protein-content and No. 3 grade wheat at unusually low prices. This grain, in two successive years of climatic hazard, was available in large quantities. William Langer, then governor of North Dakota, used the facilities of the State Mill and Elevator and those of the State Bank of North Dakota to inflate the price to a reasonable level and the price was soon met and maintained by the central grain trade.

It is struggles such as these that make the Main Street businessman of the Plains, north and south, a minority group. It is conditions such as these that make for disunity and disharmony in the region. The lines are sharply drawn. Many businessmen imported as newcomers into the region, are drawn into this struggle without understanding the basic issues. Recent newcomers, coming in times of prosperity, lead sheltered lives on Main Street for a time. Drought, hail, grasshoppers, and other hazards have little meaning for them and they are not prepared for these adversities when they strike. So business is restricted and often closed down entirely when these hazards appear and are of long duration; services to farm and ranch people are cut off, and this adds fuel to the fire. It was the curtailment of these services in the decade of the twenties and again in the thirties that gave impetus to the growth of farm co-operatives.

The businessmen of the region have little communication with the remainder of the population. Their minority status can be resolved only when there is adequate communication among all groups. The Main Street businessmen must learn of the problems faced by farmers and ranchers of the region and the progress these Plainsmen have made by way of suitable adaptations. Businessmen must learn to apply similar adaptations to their businesses. They must furnish some of the leadership to build a way of life for the region. This means a basic program of adult education for the Main Streeters.

J. H. Kolb and E. de S. Brunner (*A Study of Rural Society*) have put it as follows: "The issue is squarely before rural people today, farmers, and villagers alike, as to whether they will organize a community of sufficient size and solidarity to give them the social utilities and institutions which they feel they need, and at the same time develop a point of view which will be recognized in larger political, educational, and religious spheres. National and state politics, as well as urban education, and religious interests, have used disorganized rural society too long as a pawn in issues in which local rural interests are little concerned, if at all."

This statement is applicable to rural–urban relations throughout the nation. But it is particularly applicable to the Plains, where the urban forces come from outside the region largely. In addition to demonstrating that he will co-operate with his fellow citizens of the Plains to help them build communities suited to conditions in the region, the businessman is obligated to prove that he will not be a subversive force in this undertaking.

It is clear that the Plains are a land of minorities. This is, in part, the result of the insecurity found in the region. In part it is the result of the set-apart character of the region. In another sense, it is the result of unadapted institutions and cultural patterns in the Plains.

If the Plains region remains a land of minorities it will eventually destroy its resources and its people. It will become a poverty area of the nation. The nation will suffer as a consequence.

This cannot be. The minority status of the residents must be resolved. The Plainsman must live as a full partner in democracy, must make his fullest contribution and carry his fullest responsibility.

This the plainsman can do. In agriculture, especially, there have been certain basic adaptations to conditions in the region. These are models that can be copied and improved upon by others in the region. To accomplish this it will be necessary to have region-wide organization in the Plains. The solution for this is to be found in regionalism itself.

CHAPTER 21

The Need to Adapt or Get Out

The need, in the Plains, is for people to make certain adjustments and adaptations to the fact of semiaridity. Otherwise the majority of people must leave the region, and the few who remain will have one of two choices—to live a feast-and-famine type of existence or to have, year in and year out, a standard of living considerably lower than most other parts of the nation. Certainly the few people who remain will be affected so drastically by the high social cost of space that subsidies will no longer serve to give parity of living.

In the case of those who remain, the feast-and-famine type of existence or the lowering of the standard of living will bring about a form of adaptation too. Either of these conditions will require certain basic adjustments away from the parity concept now prevalent in national policy and implied in the standardization that has become so typical of the American way of life.

The difference between this alternative of eventual adaptation and that of making a basic and planned adjustment to start with will be that the former would be an irrational and trial-and-error type of existence, while the latter would be a rational, controlled, and co-ordinated type of adaptation. Immediate planned adjustment would be a humane and intelligent process and would itself be an experiment having far-reaching benefits.

THE BENEFITS FROM ADAPTATION

And it is not the Plains alone that would be affected by this process of adaptation to Plains conditions or by the alternative of getting out of the region. The Plains are now a hinterland. This means that the rest of the nation derives a windfall gain from the exploitation of the region. A planned and co-ordinated type of adaptation to Plains conditions would necessarily require the co-operation of all in the nation. The current windfall gains to those outside the region would necessarily need to be given up. Industrial and business development would need to be shared with the Plains residents. Investment and employment opportunities would need to be made available to the Plains.

In return, the Plains would provide a plentiful supply of food and other raw materials for a higher national standard of living. Because of the resulting greater economic independence and security, the Plains would require less subsidy than now and be less of a problem area in all respects. Finally, such adaptation on a regional basis would result in an experiment in regionalism to test its prospects and possibilities. Since all the nation is in need of regionalism as a device to solve current difficulties, this experimentation in Plains regionalism would return benefits to all other parts of the nation. These benefits would outweigh the temporary windfall gains that now accrue to a few individuals who are able to keep the region in a hinterland position.

Failure on the part of the rest of the nation to co-operate with the Plains in this constructive effort will detract from the welfare of all. While there will be continued windfall gains for some for a time, these temporary gains will decline with the gradual decline of productivity in the Plains. The nation will have less food and fiber for its people and also less of certain other basic resources. In addition, the nation will have a poverty area on its hands, with a demand for repeated welfare programs and services. In the end, it will be necessary to rebuild the region anyway, but at a more costly rate.

CULTURAL AND GEOGRAPHIC

DETERMINISM

Because of what has been said about the need of adaptation to conditions of semiaridity in the Plains, there are those who would describe this need as an outgrowth of geographic determinism. This particular deterministic point of view holds that social life, in all its aspects, is the product of environmental conditions such as climate, soils, water, plants, and other geographic forces. There have been many champions of this interpretation of social life and institutions, and there has been much information marshalled in its support.

The contrasting point of view is best described as cultural determinism, though there are variations of it known as economic, historical, or religious determinism. This position holds that culture itself, the values and devices it has, determines, finally, the course it will take. What nature does not provide, man will seek to make and provide on his own. He will eventually grow food artificially and make rain, for example. This point of view, too, has many proponents, and there is much evidence to support the position.

It is perhaps fair to say that the facts, in the last analysis, support neither of these extreme points of view, but a middle ground position. Undoubtedly geographic and environmental conditions establish certain limits beyond which culture can not go. With these limits, culture has considerable room for producing variations that result from culture itself. For a semiarid climate and a preponderantly agricultural way of life, these limits are probably more critical than for a humid-area social system. If culture drives institutions and social organization beyond these limits, difficulties develop, resulting in suffering to man. If the culture for a semiarid land has its roots in a humid-area situation, and there is a continuous push from this direction, it is entirely probable that the people of a semiarid land will have special difficulties.

BASIC SUMMARY
OF THE PLAINS PROBLEM

To make the problem clear in connection with the Great Plains the following summary is in order. First, it should be apparent, from what has been said in earlier chapters, that the Great Plains are a unique geographic and environmental area in that they are semiarid in contrast with other parts of the nation. They have proportionately fewer resources to start with than have the East and the Midwest.

Secondly, it must be recognized that the greater resources in the humid-area civilization, which is also highly industrialized and urbanized, are augmented and made still greater by the virtual appropriation of a large part of the resources of the Plains. The Plains are chiefly a raw material producing area, but the raw materials are exploited by and shipped to the East and Midwest for processing.

Thirdly, the humid-area civilization has additional resources. Because it is the center of financing and marketing, it exercises certain controls that give it other benefits and advantages. Among them are control over prices and price-making forces and demand-supply relationships. The Plains are without these advantages, except for very minor controls exercised by a limited development of co-operatives, and by current price-support and production-control policies, abetted by governmental policy, regarding certain commodities.

Fourthly, upon the limited and exploited resource base of the Plains is built a complex civilization now shaped to humid-area conditions, high industrialization, and intense urbanization. This civilization has projected itself upon the Plains in an unheeding and forceful manner. But the Plains region is now incapable of supporting this projected humid-area way of life.

Humid-area civilization necessarily rests upon the resource base, and there are special ties and props between the resources and the institutional aspects that shape the civilization. This brings into focus the fifth aspect of the comparison between the humid-area industrial East and Midwest, on the one hand, and the Great Plains on the other. These special ties or props have three major characteristics. They are (1) certainty and stability of income; (2) certainty and stability of contract performance; and (3) certainty and predictability of future income-cost relationships.

A little study shows that these characteristics represent the heart of the economic system in American urban and industrial society, and also in the agriculture of today. The plentiful resources, used in conformity with these three conditions, make it possible to support the total civilization in the humid area. These three traits color the values and the institutional structure of the

American economy. They are a significant part of the cultural pattern of this country.

These three props are also projected into the Plains region. But the facts of semiaridity in the Plains do not permit these three conditions to occur. There cannot be certainty and stability of income in the Plains, nor can there be certainty and stability of contract performance. There cannot be certainty and pre-dictability of future income-cost relationships. The hazards typical of a semiarid land do not permit these things to occur, unless there are certain additional provisions not typical for or needed in the humid area.

This introduces the sixth aspect of the problem in the Plains. There must be adaptation to Plains conditions. The ties or props previously referred to must be reinforced. They cannot be dis-carded, but they must have additional supports. The fact that the humid-area way of life does not have these additional sup-ports and does not project them into the region, though it pro-jects itself into the region in many other ways, means that it is difficult to establish them for the Plains. It is for this reason that the culture of the Plains is ill-adapted to the conditions of semiaridity. It is not the fact of semiaridity that causes the difficulties in the Plains, but the fact of an unadapted culture that does so. This places the emphasis on making certain adap-tations in the institutional structure and social organization of the region, not in the geographic and environmental conditions alone. This is a most significant fact in seeking solutions for the difficulties in the Plains.

These aids or supports for the props, previously mentioned, are in the form of specially created reserves, increased mobility, and enhanced flexibility—all necessary in order to assure cer-tainty and stability of income, certainty and stability of contract performance, certainty and predictability of future income-cost relationships. The absence of these aids makes the Plains a high risk area; the inclusion of these aids would help in putting the Plains on a par with the humid area. This is on the condition that the exploitation of the region will be halted, and on the expecta-tion that there will be some processing in the Plains, consider-ably more than there is now. An additional condition is that the Plains will have a measure of control over their financial affairs and the marketing of their products.

Failing to make these adaptations, the Plains will continue to be a high-risk area; its people will continue to live as minorities; the region will degenerate to a level of poverty; and many people will move out of the area.

THE TASKS AHEAD

The tasks ahead for adaptation will not be easy, yet they can be accomplished. Many models have been developed in the Plains for economic and cultural action that will result in the creation of reserves, flexibility, and mobility. Many of these models are successful but need to be disseminated among all the people. The nature of these models for adaptation will be discussed in later chapters.

The task of speeding up the process of adaptation and dissemination is an important one. It will be necessary to create a spirit of co-operation and tolerance for these things on the part of the rest of the nation. It will be incumbent upon the Plains people to transmit these adapted ways to future generations. These ways, therefore, must be firmly imbedded in a cultural pattern, made to appear inevitable and customary, until they at last acquire the sanction of tradition.

To do all these things, the region will need additional resources. It will be necessary to carry on more study and research. There must be region-centered communication, and this means that the region must have cities and economic opportunities of an industrial nature.

Finally, to have all these things, the Plains must develop and use the instruments of true regionalism. Regionalism is an emerging fact in America and the world over. There are initial models that must be perfected and put to the test. These aspects will be treated in the concluding chapters.

In conclusion, then, the road to the solution of the problems in the Plains, including the problem of minorities, is in the direction of adapting institutions and a pattern of culture to the conditions of semiaridity. The results will be a benefit to the residents of the Plains, to those of the nation, and to the peoples of all the world.

CHAPTER 22

New Ways for Water, Land, and Plow

There is a common belief that it took only the coming
of the railroads, the invention of barbed wire and the
windmill, the acceptance of the sod house, and the invention of
farm machinery to subdue the Plains. As already pointed out,
these were necessary before settlement could get well underway; following the influx of settlers, however, additional inno-
vations, adaptations, and inventions were necessary.

INVENTIONS IN WATER CONTROL

AND IRRIGATION

One such additional innovation had to do with surface
water control and irrigation. The purpose here is not to make an
exhaustive analysis of the origin of the Western water doctrine
and of irrigation, but to show that humid-area water rights did
not and do not fit the semiarid needs. Certain adaptations had
to be made.

Americans in the East, the South, and the Midwest live by
the riparian water doctrine which was imported from France and
England, both humid lands. The riparian doctrine holds that
the owner of land contiguous to a stream has certain rights in
the flow of the water beyond the right of the owners away from
the stream; water in a stream cannot be diverted away from the
stream itself; the right is one of using the water, not one of appropriating its ownership. In other words, all the landowners on
the stream have equal rights to the use of the water in the stream.
Least of all, is it possible to divert water out of streams by means

of ditches to lands not immediately abutting onto the streams. Therefore, irrigation is an impossibility under the doctrine.

An example showing the inadequacies of the humid-area doctrine and the need for the invention of a suitable system is provided by the history of irrigation development in Colorado. According to a study by historian Robert Dunbar (*Colorado and Its People*), the first settlement on the Cache La Poudre River was at Greeley, Colorado. Two irrigation canals, leading out of the river, were constructed by colonists in 1871. There was no downstream demand for water, hence the diversion was possible.

A second settlement was established at Fort Collins, twenty-five miles up river, and two canals were constructed there in 1872 and 1873. The dry year of 1874 resulted in a water shortage at Greeley because of the extensive irrigation at Fort Collins. This created a conflict and the issue of priority was raised, i.e., should water be appropriated since it was scarce and should there be a system of giving first priority to some and not to others? More pressing, was the issue concerning what basis was to be used to decide priority. The Colorado Constitutional Convention of 1875 decided that the priority of appropriation and use was to be the governing factor in such disputes.

In the interim another issue was raised. In 1874, a proposal was made to construct a large canal out of the same river above both Greeley and Fort Collins. The canal was to be seventy miles long and was to take water at a considerable distance away from the river. This raised the question of how far water could be transported away from its natural course.

These and other issues in Colorado precipitated legislation in 1879 and 1881, which, along with later amendments, created Colorado's present water laws for irrigation. The result was a set of institutions new to Anglo-American experience, institutions that had not been necessary east of the ninety-eighth meridian. The Colorado law became the model for Wyoming, Montana, and Nebraska. These new institutions for water became known as the doctrine of appropriation as distinguished from the riparian doctrine.

This doctrine of appropriation, in its application to the West, is summarized as follows by Webb: (1) Its origin was west of the one hundredth meridian and was unknown in the humid portion of the country. (2) It permitted the use of water for beneficial or useful purposes as distinguished from the reasonable use of the modified common law. (3) It permitted diversion of water from the stream regardless of diminution of the stream. (4) It made possible the use of water on either riparian or non-riparian lands. According to the common law, all the land not immediately adjacent to the stream would have been left high and dry, but under the arid-region doctrine, the reclamation of this land became possible. (5) The arid-region doctrine denied the equality among users that was so steadfastly maintained by the common law of riparian rights. The arid doctrine granted the first appropriator an exclusive right and the later appropriators rights conditioned upon the prior rights of those who had gone before. (6) Under the common law, a riparian owner's rights, though not inalienable, remained his without any specific act of commission or omission on his part by virtue of ownership of the land. He did not forfeit the right if he did not use it. Under the arid-region doctrine, on the contrary, the continuation of the privilege or right depended not so much on reasonable use as upon beneficial use. Not to use the water, for example, was to forfeit it.

The Colorado illustration, showing the transition from the riparian doctrine to that of appropriation, was not without precedent, for the Colorado legislature had a model to copy. The origin of the doctrine of appropriation stemmed from mining developments and requirements in California in the late forties. Since the land at that time belonged to the public domain, appropriation of mining claim sites was the only means by which each prospector could pursue his activities. To pan the gold, it was often necessary to bring water to the miners' claims by means of ditches, diversions, tunnels, and flumes. It was only natural that the miners' courts in the mining communities should apply to water the same priority principle that had been applied to the staking out of gold claims on the public domain.

In a comparatively short span of time, these customs were translated into California law, and moved from California to Colorado. It took the federal government fifteen years to come to the same conclusion that California had accepted in one year. The federal law sanctioning the arid-region doctrine of appropriation and beneficial use was passed by a special act in 1870.

Subsequently, various government agencies undertook to

study the arid lands of the Great Plains and the West. One of the most famous reports of this period, dated 1879, was prepared by Major J. W. Powell. It stressed the need for new land and water use policies, an adapted land-settlement pattern, and an adapted institutional organization and way of living that was intimately suited to the conditions of the arid and semiarid lands. Major Powell prepared two bills for Congress to bring about these aims, but these were never passed. Eventually in 1888, 1890, and 1891, Congress passed acts for irrigation surveys and the withholding of public lands for prospective reservoir sites.

The year 1890 was a drought year. William E. Smythe, an editorial writer for the *Omaha Bee,* resigned and devoted his efforts to the publication of *Irrigation Age,* which he founded as the first periodical of its kind. He took up the crusade for irrigation. His activity resulted in a series of local conventions held in western Nebraska and a state convention at Lincoln where arrangements were made for the first National Irrigation Congress, to be held at Salt Lake City in 1892. Other congresses of a similar nature followed at Los Angeles in 1893, at Denver in 1894, and in succeeding years at Albuquerque, Phoenix, Lincoln, Cheyenne, Missoula, and Chicago. The work of these congresses was supplemented by the efforts of the National Irrigation Association, formed in 1897 at Wichita, Kansas.

In the meantime, the Carey Act was passed in 1894. Its purpose was to cede specified amounts of the public domain to the states for reclamation purposes, urging the states to develop irrigation on these lands. But by 1900, the National Irrigation Congress had given up the idea of ceding lands to the states and urged instead (1) the reform and unification of state water laws, (2) the repeal of the desert land law, (3) increased appropriations for investigation of water resources, and (4) the creation of a national commission to devise national plans for the reclamation of arid lands.

In 1897 Captain Hiram M. Chittenden, United States Army Corps of Engineers, made a study of proposed reservoir locations which contained the first official statement that the federal government should participate in the development of irrigation projects. By 1900, the platforms of both major political parties favored national aid for irrigation. In 1901, Frances G. Newlands of Nevada introduced a bill in Congress which, when revised and amended, became law in 1902—the first National Reclamation Act.

Thus, irrigation policy, thought, and action had gone through five successive stages. It started with (1) irrigation efforts by and for individuals and proceeded to (2) corporate undertakings for associations of farmers similar to stock companies. This was forced upon the interested parties as water became more scarce. The next stage (3) was the district proposal as advocated by Major J. W. Powell. This was followed by (4) the state programs as provided for in the Carey Act. All these stages were inadequate because of the need for extensive capital and because of the basic scarcity of water, coupled with the problem arising out of the character of the land policy and the need for over-all planning. Thus emerged the final stage, namely, (5) the national approach as expressed in the Reclamation Act of 1902.

For the purposes of clarification, it should be emphasized that development and implementation of the appropriation doctrine was accepted in total only in Colorado, Montana, Wyoming, and New Mexico following the pattern of the Colorado system. The other Plains states—Texas, Oklahoma, Kansas, Nebraska, South and North Dakota—modified the riparian common law only slightly. Their modification might be described as the Western-American doctrine of riparian rights.

One group of states, North Dakota to Texas, inclusive, bordering on the humid region, only partially modified the humid-area ideas, as though they were afraid to make a complete transition. The remaining four Great Plains states, Montana to New Mexico, completely rejected the riparian doctrine and substituted in its place the new doctrine of appropriation.

To this point the discussion of water law has been for surface water only, however. In the future, underground water for irrigation will be at a premium, and use and control practices will need to be developed for this resource. This is especially urgent for the Southern Plains where surface water has been less predictable and plentiful than farther north. A major source of irrigation in the Plains of New Mexico, Texas, Oklahoma, and Kansas, even today, is from the extensive underground beds deposited thousands of years ago in the reservoirs underlying those states. But because of the lack of adequate controls, thriving communities built up on such irrigation have suffered decline and almost complete annihilation. Inadequate controls of the underground water has resulted in the fall in the water pressure and water table because of excessive use or the tapping of the water level at more strategic locations, perhaps a hundred miles distant. New Mexico, not without difficulty and frustration, is a pioneer in the use and control of underground waters. Texas is in urgent need of solving the problem. Interstate aspects are involved, as are the contradictory and conflicting interests of farmers, ranchers, recreationists, urban water users, industrialists, and suppliers of pipe, well, and pump equipment. A forthright attack on the problem of use and control of underground water modeled after the fashion of the appropriation doctrine for surface water is inevitable and overdue for the Plains, north as well as south.

It is necessary to point out that irrigation is not a panacea for all the ills of the Plains. Most of the Plains proper cannot be irrigated. But irrigation can be more extensive than it is in the central and the eastern parts of the region, and also in the southern parts. Within the Missouri River Basin area, including the mountain valleys east of the divide and excluding the area south of the headwaters of the Kansas and Osage rivers in the Great Plains, there was a total of 5,027,100 irrigated acres in 1940, mostly in the larger river valleys and foothills area. This is only 1.3 per cent of the land area involved.

The Missouri River Basin Development Program, also called the Pick–Sloan Plan, calls for the irrigation of an additional 4,760,400 acres in this area, plus supplementary water on 547,304 acres already irrigated. A large proportion of this newly-irrigated area is proposed for the Northern Plains proper. How a large portion of the unirrigated areas can be stabilized and made more secure by being in some way attached to the irrigated base is still largely to be worked out, though certain patterns of utilization have been emerging.

In the Southern Plains, surface water irrigation has been important along the Río Grande, the Pecos, the Colorado, and the Brazos rivers in Texas; the Red, bordering Texas and Oklahoma; the Canadian in Texas and Oklahoma; and the Arkansas River in Kansas. Only the first and the last of these, along with the Canadian, have a reasonably stable water potential, as rivers go in the Southern Plains. This is because their far reaches extend into the Rockies, and because they traverse a number of states, thus bringing the finances of Uncle Sam to the rescue in the fuller development of this scarce resource. In contrast with the multi-state aspect of the Missouri and the Columbia, or even the Colorado of the West, it is clear why multi-purpose and basin-wide development in the Southern Plains is still in its infancy. But that this irrigation development for the Southern Plains will come to full fruition is also clear.

There were other inventions related to irrigation which had to be originated and perfected before irrigation practices could work efficiently. Among these were the subdivisions of the project areas into ditch districts and administrative organizations; a system of tending the ditches and providing "ditch riders"; a system of measuring water in the streams, the main canals, and the main and lateral ditches; methods of placing water on the land itself; methods of handling the soil under irrigation conditions; types of management of crops best adapted to irrigation; and the drainage and reclamation of land in irrigated areas so as to avoid its destruction by drowning. A discussion of the complexity of these institutionalized patterns cannot be included here. But they are important segments of the total pattern of irrigation and represent indigenous developments in the mountain and Plains region without help from the humid area.

AN ADAPTED
LAND SETTLEMENT PROPOSAL

In 1862, the Homestead Act was passed, allowing 160 acres to qualified citizens over twenty-one years of age. Although a democratic measure, granting the opportunity to any citizen regardless of his status in society to be a property owner in his own right, it was not especially applicable to the Plains. Subsequent events demonstrated that a much larger acreage was necessary to sustain a family.

In recognition of the inadequacy of homestead legislation, the Timber Culture Act was passed in 1873. It was based on the belief that the Great Plains should have timber and forests which, according to some, would serve as rain makers! The act allowed the homesteader an additional 160 acres, provided trees were

295

planted and nurtured on 40 acres. But legislation could not alter nature's destiny that the Great Plains be treeless. The Act was repealed in 1891.

The first major modification of the Homestead Act was the Desert Land Act passed in 1877. It allowed 640 acres, not free, but for $1.25 per acre with the requirement that it be irrigated within three years. Specifically it applied to the lands in New Mexico, Colorado, Wyoming, Montana, and the Dakotas, but not to Nebraska, Kansas, and Oklahoma.

From the viewpoint of the plainsman, the law was an absurdity. There was not enough water to irrigate this much land per farm, nor could a single farmer incorporate this much intensive land use into his operations. Many abuses resulted. In central Montana the local practice was to plow a furrow a few inches deep and about fifty feet long, through which water was allowed to flow whenever it was available. Some settlers did not even take this much trouble. In the presence of a witness who later testified for the claimholder, a barrel of water was poured into a ditch and the irrigation system was established.

Another feature which did not make sense to the plainsman was the price charged for this land. Desert land, supposed unfit for habitation unless irrigated, was to be sold at $1.25 per acre while good agricultural land had been given away free in the amount of 160 acres. In certain areas, the price was a distinct overcharge. This land cost, in addition to the cost for the irrigation system on 640 acres, resulted in excessive borrowing or in closed opportunities when capital was not available. The costs involved in reservoir construction, main channel and ditch construction, and the land leveling were too great for the lending system then in practice, even if a project were undertaken collectively by a number of farmers.

The shortcomings of these acts emphasized the failure of the nation's land policy for the Plains. The policy in Texas had shown a new road. Powell's proposal had shown a new way. There was, therefore, no reason why the nation should have continued its unadapted policy for the Plains. But the nation would not learn. The humid-area push upon the semiarid Plains could not be arrested. This is well-illustrated by the rejection of the Powell proposals.

Major Powell made his famous *Report on the Land of the*

Arid Region of the United States to the Secretary of Interior, Carl Schurz. It was referred to the House of Representatives with recommendations for Congressional action which would have established an adapted land settlement pattern for the region.

The recommendations included two proposed bills. One was intended to authorize "the organization of pasturage districts by homestead settlements on the public lands which were of value for pasturage purposes only." The other was intended to authorize "the organization of irrigation districts by homestead settlements upon the public lands requiring irrigation for agricultural purposes." According to the letter of transmittal by Secretary Schurz, these bills were "intended to carry into effect a newer system for the disposal of the public lands of the arid region and to promote the settlement and development of that portion of the country." The Commissioner of the General Land Office concurred in these matters.

The content of the Powell proposals included the recommendation that the lands of the arid region first be classified into three groups: (1) the irrigable lands, lying along the benches and banks of the rivers; (2) the forest lands, lying high up on the mountain sides and tops; and (3) the pasture lands, lying between the irrigable valleys and the forested mountains.

A summary of Powell's proposal for the settlement of the arid region of the United States included the following statements on irrigable lands: "Within the arid region, agriculture is dependent upon irrigation. The amount of irrigable land is but a small percentage of the whole area. The chief development of irrigation depends upon the use of the large streams. For the use of large streams, co-operative labor or capital is necessary. The small streams should not be made to serve lands so as to interfere with the use of the large streams. Sites for reservoirs should be set apart, in order that no hindrance may be placed upon the increase of irrigation by the storage of water."

Powell's report also contained the following statements about pasturage lands: "The grasses of the pasturage lands are scant, and the lands are of value only in large quantities. The farm unit should not be less than 2,560 acres. Pasturage farms need small tracts of irrigable land; hence, the small streams of the general drainage system and the lone springs and streams should be reserved for such pasturage farms. The divisions of the lands should be controlled by topographic features in such a manner as to give the greatest number of water fronts to pasturage farms. Residences of the pasturage farms should be grouped in order to secure the benefits of local social organization and co-operation in public improvements. The pasturage lands will not usually be fenced, and hence herds must roam in common. As the pasturage lands should have water fronts and irrigable tracts and as the residences should be grouped and as the lands cannot be economically fenced and must be kept in common, local communal regulations or co-operation is necessary."

For the region west of the one hundredth meridian, Powell felt it desirable to have adapted institutions. For irrigation his proposal was that:

1. Nine or more persons can qualify to form an irrigation district and acquire homesteads in such a district.

2. This organization is required to make the necessary rules and regulations for the use of water and the parceling of the land as best suited to member benefits.

3. That all lands amounting to at least 320 acres can be classified as irrigable lands, but that each person is not to have more than eighty acres of such irrigable land.

4. That the right to water shall inhere in the land and that such rights shall be conveyed with the title to the land; but that non-use of water for a period of five years shall be cause for the lapse to the right of water.

For the pasturage land proposal, Powell suggested the following:

1. Nine or more persons may organize a pasture district and acquire homestead sites therein.

2. That such an organization have the necessary by-laws, rules, and regulations concerning the smaller irrigated parcels and the administration of the conjoint or severally-owned and operated lands in the district.

3. The amount of land in one ownership is not to exceed 2,560 acres, and its contiguous distribution is to be handled in accordance with the rules promulgated by the group. Any irrigated lands held conjointly with the pasturage land by one operator shall not represent a monopoly of water use.

4. That any rights to water inhere in the right to the land

and not separately therefrom, except that five years of non-usage shall constitute a lapse to the water right.

Powell suggested the abandonment of the rectangular system of survey. Along with the proposal that the residences be grouped for purposes of economy and convenience in rendering public services, these proposals represented suitable adaptations for land settlement for the Plains. In size of pasturage land operations, the Powell proposal was half that of the size of units allowed under Texas land laws.

The bills proposed by Powell were not passed, though he continued to urge such legislation until his death. The rejection of these bills and the unfortunate steps taken by Congress in the direction of the limited and conditional enlarging of homestead units for the semiarid and arid regions are evidence of the inability of men, with their ideas from humid and forested areas, to comprehend the problems of arid regions.

The nation continued with its unadapted land policy for the West. In 1890 the allowable homestead entries were reduced from 640 to 320 acres in size under the Desert Land Act. In 1904 the Kinkaid Act was passed, applying only to Nebraska. Its object was to dispose of the rejected lands in the western part of that state, permitting the acquisition of 640 acres as a homestead. In 1909 a similar homesteading principle was extended to nine additional Western states and in 1912, to three more states. The 1909 act was called the Enlarged Homestead Act, which allowed an entry for 320 acres but with the requirement that the homesteader cultivate half the acreage.

The 1912 Homestead Act reduced the residence requirement from five to three years. The homesteader could also absent himself for five months out of each year. Webb concludes his evaluation of this act as follows: "This act seemed to grow out of the realization that on the remaining land the average family could not hold out for five years. The point of starvation was reached short of that, and, consequently, it would be humane to shorten the required time of residence to three years. The homesteader was furthermore permitted to absent himself five months out of each year, presumably with a view to making something to live on while enjoying his free homestead."

The needs of the cattlemen and the sheep growers were not recognized by Congress until 1916. Beginning then, they were permitted to homestead 640 acres of land fit for grazing only, and the improvements were to serve in place of cultivation. The water holes were reserved to the public, as were the trails leading to the water. With all its shortcomings, Webb describes this act as the only one ever designed to dispose of land to stockmen. "The effect of the law was to lure into the region people who were ignorant of conditions and sure to fail. It is said that the chief of the Bureau of Forestry declared it a crime to open the land under the Act of 1916."

The failure to legislate an adapted land policy for the Plains had unfortunate repercussions for agriculturists and townsmen alike and for the institutional patterns arrayed upon the land. Stockmen resorted to the principle of the customary range and the idea of priority use enforced through their associations. Extralegal methods of settling land-control issues came into vogue —cattle and sheep growers' wars, burning of nestor shacks, killings over land occupancy, cutting of fences, starving out of the trespassers, and resorting to using the tax-delinquency route in order to repurchase land for taxes only. These are typical of extralegal devices used by minority peoples when they do not have a hand in the control of their destiny.

FARM TECHNOLOGY

Those believing the Great Plains to be a land of milk and honey, ideally suited to the plow, soon found themselves disappointed. Little did they realize, until subjected to the hard school of experience, that the land of the Plains required a different handling. To break it and to prepare it as a seedbed, even in the humid-area manner, required all sorts of machinery which was being invented just at the time when the major settlement of the Plains was getting underway. But many of these inventions were for the humid prairie conditions, not for the semiarid Plains, and most of the inventions, could not be purchased by the Plains settler for lack of money.

As noted earlier, the steel walking plow was quickly converted into the gang plow, making it possible to cover a larger area more easily. By the eighties, the large red-wheeled, four-furrowed gangs were in general use. Hand in hand with these came the disk, the lister, the drill, the corn planter, the reaper, the binder, and the thresher-separator, the mower, the hay rake, and the harrow. Migratory farm hands were already traveling the prairie and Plains to help in the harvest fields.

But all this equipment was expensive and reached the humid regions first. In 1879 the Dakota bonanza farm of George W. Cass, president of the Northern Pacific, included about 17,240 acres and was managed by Oliver Dalrymple. That year, the double gang plow, drawn by four horses, was in use. There were brigades of seven to twenty teams in a field, a brigade of twenty gangs being able to plow a section per week. For harvest there were several brigades of binders in the fields, usually consisting of a dozen machines in a brigade. That year there were twenty-one threshing machines in use on this farm. A total of four hundred men were employed for harvest and threshing. In 1880 there were 82 such bonanza farms with more than a thousand acres each in the Red River Valley; by 1890 there were 232.

These large farms were the exception, and they had capital to work with. Most settlers had no more than the 160-acre homestead, or a 320-acre farm at most, and only a part of this was under plow. Nor did they have much of this equipment.

Most of these machines were not appropriately designed for the peculiar requirements of the region. It must be remembered that most precipitation in the Plains occurs in April, May, and June. A successful crop is one that can be in the ground early, can grow and mature quickly, and is ready for harvest before drought conditions take effect. Timeliness of operation is, therefore, very important. And the drier the preceding year, the more urgent this timeliness.

In other words, successful crop farming in the Plains called for speed and flexibility. It had to be based on drought-resisting crops—those having a short and early maturing date. An alternate fallow system of farming, one that would store the limited moisture of one season and add it to the rainfall of the second year, assisted in avoiding crop failure.

The horse was too slow to provide the necessary timeliness and flexibility. The large traction engine—the steamer and the oil pull—was also slow, in addition to being cumbersome. It could not be used for a multitude of farm operations and, therefore, was not sufficiently flexible. Large traction engines were an advantage only because they pitted power against a dry soil in the case of fall plowing. This was often only a plowing operation with little opportunity to prepare the seedbed to conserve the moisture, thus increasing the risk in agriculture.

However, timeliness and speed of harvesting the grain are as important in the Plains as is timeliness and speed in seedbed preparation and seeding itself. Otherwise, hail, windstorms, and grasshoppers might destroy what a desirable amount and timely rainfall, as well as timeliness of planting operations, had brought to the stage of ripening. Harvesting with the binder was slow and contributed to farmers' thinking in terms of humid-area harvesting—binding, shocking, stacking, and eventually, threshing. Much of the precious grain was lost, with estimates running as high as 10 and 12 per cent. Some years the grain was too short for the binder; other years it was irregular and spotty in height in the field, making the loss in harvesting excessive.

The header, as a substitute for the binder, came into use in the seventies. Many farmers who had used the binder did not take to it quickly. But the true Plains farmers quickly accepted the header. The cut grain was lifted from the cutting platform by an elevator into a header barge. Usually there were several such barges per header, one unloading at the stack while the other was being filled at the machine. The cutting bar and platform on the header could be quickly raised or lowered to do a better job at harvesting than was true of the binder. Thus, more of the grain, tall or short, could be saved. The header also had a wider cutting swath than the binder, aiding in speedier operation. The dry climate on the plains insured a more uniform ripening of grain in the field, so that loss from spoilage was low. The grain went from the field into the stack immediately rather than remaining on the field in shocks. This, too, cut down on the hazards.

From the header to the combine was only a short step. This was a combination harvester and thresher, first invented in the eighties. It came into wide use only after 1920, after the small tractor came into general use. For a time the combine was not readily accepted because farmers from the humid area thought that grain must "sweat" or "heat" in the stack or in the shock before it was ready for threshing. Only when it was recognized that this heating process might take place in the granary or ele-

302

vator without harm, and when it was realized that climatic conditions in the Plains did not actually warrant this heating process —only then did combining make headway. Speed and timeliness in harvesting had been accomplished.

During the evolution of this pattern of farming, until 1930, the end results of these inventions were not always a blessing to the farmers. Often the availability of only partially perfected machines led to overextension of credit, with bankruptcy and mortgage foreclosure as the end result. Reliance on short-term credit, resort to unsympathetic mortgage foreclosure procedure, exploitive and speculative land and credit practices, and failure to anticipate drought, grasshoppers, dust blowing, hail and blizzards increased the chances of failure. In the face of all these conditions the machines often were the final blow—the precipitating factor that brought disaster because the social system was not adequately fitted to the environment.

But farming on the Plains up to this stage of description, dating into the thirties, was still largely humid-area farming. In practice, even today, there is still a considerable amount of humid-area farming only partially adapted. That this is so is proved by the prevalence of the expression "to plow." Truly adapted dry-land farming today, on the Plains, is a "plowless" type of agriculture. Truly adapted dry-land farming has a new way for the plow. There is no word for this plowless operation other than the word "tillage."

What is this new way of the plow? What instruments are used? In place of the plow, the dry-land farmer uses the one-way, which is a disklike operation. The soil is not turned over as in plowing, but is simply disturbed. A substitute for the one-way are the lister, the gold-digger, or the duckfoot. These, too, do not turn the soil, but permit the stubble to remain on top of the soil in the form of trash—a protection against soil blowing, and an aid in moisture penetration.

More recently, in some areas, there have emerged still more refined forms to carry on tillage practices of the kind that are replacing the plow. One such implement is the Noble blade, invented in Canada. It is a simple straight blade, or a two-shovel instrument, some ten to twelve feet in over-all width, with a strong frame and requiring much power. The single blade, or the two shovels, travels underground. It lifts and shakes the top

303

soil and allows it to fall back in place. The object is merely to loosen the soil and to break the roots of the weeds. The implement allows the stubble to remain in the form of trash. Another instrument, similar in principle, is the Graham Hoeme, originated in Amarillo, Texas. It differs from the Noble blade, in that it has several shovels—as many as eight to twelve–in place of a blade. It, too, covers a swath of ten to 12 feet at a cut and consists of a strong frame with spring-like teeth to which the shovels, spikes, or tongues are attached. These can be set to penetrate to a depth of eight, twelve, fourteen, or sixteen inches. They tear the subsurface soil and disturb the top soil as little as possible.

The interesting thing about these machines is that they are identified by their trade names. As yet, there is no word to describe the operation they perform. They are not a plow, and they are used for repeated operations to kill the weeds and keep the soil loose in the fallow stage of farming. They substitute for the plow, the disk, the harrow, and the packer—all the operations prior to seeding. Covering a wide swath, the acreage handled per day is tenfold the number handled with the plow.

Some Plains farmers use a rod weeder in place of the gold-digger, the Noble blade or the Graham Hoeme for later tillage operations. The rod weeder is a solid rod, two inches in thickness and fifteen or twenty feet in length, mounted on wheels and so constructed that the rod operates at the same depth as the usual tillage operations. The rod is pulled along under the surface while rotating on its axis. Thus it disturbs the roots of the growing weeds and kills them. Plans are now afoot to use a hollow rod with a system of chains traveling through the hollow part to carry the seeds. Thus the rod weeder may, in time, be converted into a seeder also, drastically different from the press or conventional drill now in use.

These new substitutes for the plow in the Plains have one common characteristic. They require tremendous power. Their use is dependent upon the modern tractor or caterpillar for efficient operation. These power units must be large enough to pull sufficient equipment at a speed that will enable the operator to perform his duties in a timely manner. In addition, the equipment for the several operations must be of such size and capable of combinations in such arrangements that the tractor can be used efficiently at all times—for seeding and combining, especially. The cost of the equipment, especially the power unit, is so high that maximum utilization spells the difference between profit and loss.

This new way of the plow is not yet used by many dry-land farmers in the Plains, especially not among those on the eastern edge of the region. On the eastern edge the small tractor and the small size of farm—the humid ways of agriculture with emphasis upon continuous cropping—are still deeply rooted in the minds of the farmers.

ADAPTED FARM OPERATIONS IN WHEAT

Dry-land agriculture in the Plains now calls for a proper balance between mechanization, speed, adapted crops, suitable tillage and management practices, storage, and the maintenance of reserves and insurance. Especially is this true of wheat and cotton farming. The major difficulty is now one of getting adequate financing—credit and personal savings—for the necessary investment and operating costs.

A wheat farm of the type that is now generally established in the Great Plains is operated as follows. It is not measured in terms of acres, but in terms of the number of tractors in use. A one-tractor (45 H.P. drawbar) wheat farm generally has about 1,220 acres of crop land. Half of this is in fallow and half in crop and is generally handled on an alternate stripping and perhaps even contouring basis. If it is a winter wheat operation, planning might start with summer fallow. Since the tractor travels at an effective speed of 4.5 miles per hour, it takes about twelve to fourteen days of fourteen hours each to do the summer fallowing on 610 acres. During the remainder of the summer, generally two or sometimes three weeding operations are performed with the rod weeder or with the Graham Hoeme or the Noble blade. At ninety acres per day, this consumes fourteen to twenty-one days. By mid-summer, the crop seeded during the previous fall in the alternate fields is ready for harvest. The combine operation, at fifty-five acres per day, takes about twelve to fifteen days for the 610 acres. At the same time, the wheat has been hauled.

Immediately following the combining, the alternate fallow land is ready to be seeded for next year. When the moisture conditions are right, perhaps augmented by the prospect of local rains, this fallowed land is seeded. At 61 acres per twelve-hour day, it takes about ten to twelve days to complete this operation.

If spring wheat is the basis of the operation, the work schedule differs somewhat and the timing is more critical. The farm still consists of 1,220 crop acres, with 610 in fallow and 610 in crop. The fallow operations on the unplanted area occur in the summer, perhaps somewhat later than in the case of winter wheat operations. This, too, is followed by weeding operations. Then comes the harvesting of the crop area. In this case the seeding operations on the fallow land are delayed to the spring. Spring seeding of wheat is a critical operation since spring is also the rainfall season, and timeliness at this point is highly essential. Usually the seeding is preceded by a final fallow operation to loosen the soil or the two operations are performed simultaneously by one power unit.

Except for machinery repair, hauling some farm-stored wheat, preparing seed for next year, and mending a few fences, all the work on the dry-land farm is completed with these operations. All together, the dry-land wheat farmer cannot find more than one hundred days of work on the farm, unless he has livestock also and other cash crops. But these operations do not often mix efficiently with the wheat unit in the Plains.

By timely seeding and summer fallowing, the average yield of winter wheat from this acreage during good and bad years will be about 17.5 bushels per acre—a total of 10,431 per farm. For spring wheat, the average yield will be about 12.8 bushels per acre—a total of 7,808 per farm.

The yield must provide the income for the farmer's family living expenditures and for all operation costs. Should he have more than the usual number of good years in a series, he makes good money. This is also the case if prices are more than normally favorable. If yields and moisture are normal, fluctuating between dry, wet, and average years, he makes a reasonable income at peacetime prices. He must learn to handle his finances wisely for family living and for farm operation costs, in order to carry over from a good year through a poor yield year. He must expect a series of poor yield years, one after the other, and in anticipation of these he must have additional reserves. He can do this with the ever-normal granary and crop insurance programs, if he is not too extravagant with his income during good years and not too stingy in building up operating reserves.

CHAPTER 23

Specially Suitable Institutions

Individuals and research agencies, among them the agricultural experiment stations and the United States Department of Agriculture, have invented some techniques of adaptation for the Plains. The task of invention has been so gigantic and time consuming that much remains to be done, but the results thus far accomplished have borne much fruit. Income for agriculturalists and towns people has been made more certain than formerly, and the feeling for the necessity of adaptations has become more prevalent.

Unfortunately these inventions have occurred in crop and livestock production and technology chiefly. The spirit of seeking for adaptations has not been extended with the same degree of urgency and enthusiasm into fields of social organization and institutional services. But progress is now getting underway in these areas too.

When the small adaptations in the production and the technological aspects are put together in a meaningful way, they take on institutional and idea significance. The details, put together, take on the characteristic of a pattern which becomes a model or example for adaptation in purely social areas. This has been true of dry-land agriculture, for example.

BRIEF HISTORY OF DRY-LAND FARMING

Dry-land farming or agriculture is a system of land use, crop management, farm management, agronomic practices, and timing of operations developed to meet the requirements of climate and precipitation in a semiarid land. Indigenous to the Plains, it is an agricultural method which took years to develop and to refine. Actually dry-land agriculture had its origin in four separate sections of the West. These were (a) the Great Plains, (b) the Great Basin of Utah, (c) the Columbia River in Washington, and (d) California. Experimentation was started in the 1860's, and the beginning practices became reasonably well-known in the Plains by the late 1880's.

One of the early exponents of dry-land agriculture was H. W. Campbell who came from Vermont to settle in northern South Dakota in 1879. A complete wheat crop failure in 1883, when only the year before was a bumper crop, alerted him to the fact that the Plains was a semiarid land. Of a scientific turn of mind, he began to study the problem and wrote two books about dry-land farming—*Soil Culture and Farm Journal* and *Soil Culture Manual*.

Campbell's ideas were based on the belief that storage of moisture in the soil was imperative—a must. To bring this about, he developed and recommended the dust-mulch system of farming, including the alternate fallow practice. The details proved to be erroneous and very unwise in many respects. Either the mulch formed into a crust through which moisture could not penetrate readily, or, in times of wind and drought, the mulch exposed the fields to excessive dust blowing. Campbell, however, was proceeding on a correct premise—the moisture in the soil had to be preserved. He was experimenting.

The ideals of Campbell received general recognition and the Experiment Stations took on the task of defining the problem, isolating the various parts, and then subjecting these to tests and experimentation. Thoughtful leadership for research was necessary. One of the leaders was F. B. Linfield, a Canadian by birth, who experimented and conducted agricultural research from 1893 to 1937, first in Utah and then in Montana. First a professor of agriculture, later director of the Montana Agricultural Experiment Station, he encouraged and guided many research workers who contributed to the final development of a successful dry-land farming system.

Another leader was J. E. Payne whose work on dry-land farming in Colorado was published in a bulletin in 1900. Simultaneously, much work was done at the Utah College of Agriculture.

From there the interest spread to New Mexico, Wyoming, Nebraska, the Dakotas, Kansas, and Texas.

At this time the United States Department of Agriculture also assisted in the solution of dry-land problems. In 1905, E. C. Chilcott was put in charge of dry-land farming investigations. In 1910, he published his well-known studies on cultivation methods and crop rotations for the Plains. At this time, also, the work of the Dry Farming Congress got under way, meeting for several years in cities in and about the Plains and the West.

These and other researches were concerned with one problem, that of how to preserve the moisture in the soil of the semi-arid land. On the basis of these findings, the dry-land farming system developed practices that were unheard of in the humid East. There are four major parts to the tillage and cropping parts of the system.

First, the tillage practices in dry-land farming are those that only loosen the soil somewhat and assist in weed destruction. Deep plowing is no longer recommended for the Plains. Instead, as shown earlier, there came into use the one-way and the gold-digger, and, finally, the Noble blade or its counterpart, the Graham Hoeme. These machines do not have a moldboard and do not turn over the soil. Cultivation is for the purpose of encouraging moisture penetration and weed control. Stubble is not turned under but is allowed to stand.

The second adapted tillage practice for the Plains is summer fallow. Its major purpose is to accumulate two or more years of moisture in the soil, to aid the penetration of moisture as it falls, and to remove the weeds which otherwise would deplete the limited moisture by evaporation.

The third practice is the maintenance of trashy and stubble cover on the soil. This is known as trashy fallow, an aid in snow stabilization, moisture penetration, and resistance to soil blowing. In combination with stripping (the alternate location of narrow strips of fallow and crop land at right angles to prevailing winds) the soil is readily held in place, even under severe wind conditions. A last resort against severe wind erosion is the practice of listing, namely the intermittent ridging of the soil to form wind brakes. This is done with a lister, an adapted machine.

The fourth practice consists of the utilization of drought resistant crops, among them winter wheat and sorghums, which will be discussed later.

TILLAGE PRACTICES FOR

DRY FARMING

Rather than deep furrow plowing and continuous cropping, it has been proved that shallow tillage and fallow, letting the land remain idle in alternate years, is the most effective method of managing soil and maintaining moisture under conditions such as prevail in the Plains. The underlying theory is that with proper practices, moisture from the current year can be stored for the succeeding crop year.

The discovery of summer fallow was largely accidental. One reputable account of its origin is as follows. In 1885–86 Angus MacKay of Canada was unable to plow and seed all his farm land in the spring. He had to help fight the Plains Indians. Upon his return in the early summer, he plowed the remaining land and kept it clear of weeds. The next spring he seeded this, along with the land cropped the previous year. The fall harvest showed a strikingly higher yield on the fallow land. This set MacKay to experimenting. The result was the origin of summer fallow. But this was a difficult practice to sell to farmers from the humid area. To permit the land to lie idle every other year was considered the height of folly.

True summer fallow means that land is tilled during the late spring or early summer. The later weed-control practices are simply a continuation of the initial tillage operations with the same implements, unless a rod weeder is used. The idea of summer fallow could not make much progress until farmers of the Plains became acquainted with the alternate cropping system, and until farms were large enough, and land cheap enough, so that half the farm land might lie idle in one year out of two. This called for less farm population than originally settled in much of the region.

It should be made clear that the true summer fallow idea for the Plains is not a soil fertility building measure. Moisture is generally insufficient to encourage the bacteria and chemical action that is necessary to enhance the natural fertility of the soil. Rather, it is a moisture conserving measure only.

The acceptance of the true summer fallow or alternate cropping practice received a boost in popularity when winter wheat varieties came into use, and when the speedy tractor was able to add timeliness to the operations. Successful wheat raising was thus accomplished for the Plains—successful if supported by certain other adapted practices.

PLANT ASPECTS OF DRY FARMING

Tillage practices are only one part of a well-rounded dry-land farming system. Adapted crops are as necessary as adapted tillage practices. It took a long time to find adapted crops for dry-land farming.

Plains settlers who have migrated from Russia, particularly the Mennonites, had higher yielding wheat and grain varieties than the settlers from the humid land. The same was true of the Russian settlers in Canada. Upon study, it was learned that these Europeans had imported their homeland varieties, perhaps better adapted to semiarid Plains conditions than the native wheats and small grains.

This fact, along with other information, encouraged the United States Department of Agriculture to establish the Foreign Agricultural Explorer program. Crop and horticultural specialists were sent throughout the world to collect plants better adapted to semiarid conditions than the native varieties. One of the first explorers was Niels E. Hansen of South Dakota. As head of the horticultural department at South Dakota State College for many years and director of the Experiment Station (1905–37), he did much to promote better living in the Plains through plant adaptation. He made eight tours as plant explorer, seven of them to Russia and Siberia, and side trips to China, Turkestan, and North Africa. His first trip was in 1897–98 and his last in the mid-thirties, when he was identified with the horticultural and agricultural research programs for Siberia.

Hansen's chief plant introductions from other semiarid lands included the Hansen bush cherry; hybrid plum cherries; apricots; pears; alfalfa; red clover; sweet clover; wheats of the Kubanka, Arnautka, Krasnoturka, Belloturka, and Chernokolska varieties from Russia, Turkestan, and China; perennial wheat from Siberia; crested wheat grass; brome grass; and certain vegetables. Crested wheat grass came from east of the Volga, brought here in 1897. He brought all the brome grass he could find—twelve tons—on the same trip from the Volga. In four of the six trips to Siberia, alfalfa was the leading plant work. In 1906 he introduced the yellow flower alfalfa from Russia. He also brought a natural hybrid called Cossack. He was able to find only a half teaspoonful of seed of this variety. In 1897–98 he found the Turkestan alfalfa in the Samarcand country—a bacterial wilt resistant variety. He brought nine tons to the United States, the first of its kind to come to this country.

Another explorer, following immediately upon Hansen, was Mark Alfred Carleton. A Kansas farm boy, he grew up amid drought hazards typical of the region and experimented with plants in his college days and as a rural school teacher. Finally, as a cerealist with the United States Department of Agriculture, Carleton became a plant explorer to the steppe areas of Russia, Turkey, Siberia, and China. Acquainted with the Mennonites of Kansas and the adapted varieties of grain they had brought with them, it was his goal to go to the source of these plants. It was he who was chiefly responsible for finding and importing the Kubanka (durum) and Kharkov (hard winter) wheats to the Great Plains and who helped select more suitable offspring.

The Canadians also explored and imported wheat varieties and selected strains that added to the success of dry-land farming. Their major contribution was the perfection of marquis wheat, tested at the Indian Head Experiment Station under the watchful eye of Angus MacKay. Marquis was the product of a cross-breeding program between Red Fife and Hard Calcutta from the Himalayas of Asia.

These are among the more dramatic personalities who brought adapted plants to the Plains, but there were numerous other researchers too. The work of improvement in the experiment stations and the farm field plots was as arduous and time consuming as that of the explorers.

From all the studies made the following appear to be basic characteristics for adapted plant life: (a) early maturation of the plant; (b) a flexibility in growth and plant structure which assures the ability to take advantage of changes in the length of the precipitation season; (c) a strong stem to insure resistance to wind and hail; (d) a flexible root system which makes it possible to get to the moisture, whether near the surface or at greater depths; (e) the ability to enter a rest stage, taking advantage of early spring and late fall rains and thus provide green feed early and late; (f) high yield in seed or roughage or both; and (g) other drought resisting characteristics such as low evaporation through plant growth, and continued life through prolonged periods of dormancy.

Any single plant variety can not, perhaps, acquire all these characteristics. The task is to breed a variety that can inherit the largest number of these characteristics and transmit them successfully to later generations.

MECHANIZATION ASPECTS
OF DRY FARMING

Modern dry-land farming would be a failure without the present speed and time-saving aspects of the tractor and without the power that it offers. It is the tractor that makes for mobility of operations. The ability to hitch the power unit to different pieces of equipment is also significant.

Adapted varieties of grain and adapted farm practices still would mean failure in dry-land farming if the power unit were the horse. A basic problem in the pre-tractor days was the slowness of operations. Plowing was a long drawn-out process and so was the seeding. Early maturing varieties were of little advantage when planting was late. Early maturation was only a partial advantage when harvesting operations were necessarily slow. Only quantity of equipment and manpower could then increase timeliness, and these were far too expensive for most dry-land farmers.

The large steamer or oil-pull engine, while slow moving though powerful, was a timesaver in one way. The time spent in caring for, hitching up, and lining out a span of horses several times a day could be used in actual field work—if the engine would start readily. But such an engine had decided limits. It could not be readily substituted as a power unit for a variety of tasks. Horses were still necessary for many operations. Repairs were difficult to make and time consuming. This stage was still short of ideal mechanization.

Then came the modern tractor. It was speedy and had ready maneuverability. It was efficient in both fuel and time use. It could be purchased in various sizes to fit the scale of the ranch and farm operations. Not cumbersome in its mobility, it also had great flexibility. It could be hitched to many types of equipment for a variety of tasks. The attachments (equipment) were fitted to the power output of the various size tractors.

Here, then, finally, emerged a power unit (and equipment) that had the characteristics necessary for survival in the region —reserves, mobility, and flexibility. Here were the traits of the native animal life of the region—the power of the bison, the speed of the antelope, the mobility of the jackrabbit, and the adaptability of the coyote. These characteristics, coupled with efficient management, meant that the farm operations could be timely and flexible. They could take full advantage of the adapted characteristics of the plants that were suited to the climatic requirements of the region.

OTHER ASPECTS OF DRY FARMING

But dry-land farming, to produce successfully a family living, has to be geared into still other patterns. And here, too, progress has been made. For example, such farming requires considerable capital outlay for the purchase or leasing of land, for tax payments, and for other operations such as fuel, repairs, and hired help.

For the capital outlay for land, the Federal Land Bank has developed a flexible repayment plan. By arrangement with the Farm Credit Administration, the farmer can make two types of payment on his loan. One applies on the regular interest and principal account. The other, called a future payment fund, is paid into a separate account, a reserve which takes care of the payments due in years of no income. The skill required is to keep the payments into the reserve fund large enough to take care of the necessary repayments during the longest stretch of no-income years. This is a flexible loan repayment program that avoids the necessity of mortgage foreclosure and is especially adapted for the long-time capital investment type of credit needed for the Plains farm and ranch operators.

The more difficult task is to arrange for a source of income to cover short-term credit needs for operating costs for a year, or series of years, when there has been no income. Dry-land operators have learned to husband seed grain to carry over a few years. But what of the direct operating costs such as taxes, fuel, repairs, and hired help? And what of the family living costs during such periods of no income?

The crop insurance program is designed to cover some of these costs. The major issue is whether such insurance should cover direct operating costs only or living costs as well. If both of these costs cannot be covered, what other adjustments can be made by the local community? What about the present rigidity in school costs, in the public health and road building costs, in prepaid hospital and medical care costs, in church membership costs and other institutional expenditures? Can the organizations and institutions that render the services develop similar adapted techniques so that the dry-land farmer of the Plains can make an easier adjustment to meet his operating and family living costs during extended periods of no income? Must these remaining segments of the society fit themselves as neatly and precisely to the demands of the Plains conditions as has the dry-land farmer? Do the adapted techniques developed in dry-land farming offer a key to the nature and character of such adaptations for other than the dry-land farmer?

IRRIGATION AGRICULTURE

IN THE GREAT PLAINS

It was pointed out earlier that irrigation and the Western water appropriation doctrine were developments native to the arid West, the Rocky Mountain area, and the Great Plains. As future irrigation is extended eastward into the eastern part of the Plains, and even beyond into the Midwest, these adapted practices will move east. It will be one of the few cultural developments that have moved from west to east in the United States.

But when irrigation and the doctrine of appropriation are considered in detail, it is evident that they are only two parts of a much larger pattern. This larger pattern of irrigation agriculture in the semiarid Plains is different from irrigation in the arid region, and certain aspects of the pattern are still in the process of invention. The development of the river basins, with irrigation as one of the major objectives, is a basic influence that is forcing the inhabitants of the region into new patterns of thought. The people of the Plains region are looking about for new ways and new techniques to fit irrigation agriculture into the total economy.

This can be made clear by pointing out that irrigation agriculture is of two types, each with a distinct pattern of its own. One might be described as the "oasis-like irrigation project," typical of the arid West and transplanted bodily into the Plains. The other might be described as the "irrigation agricultural economy," which is really an integration of the irrigated base with the dry-land area and promises to be a form of integration of the sutland with the yonland. The first, the oasis-like irrigation, consists of an irrigated area that is largely self-sufficient and independent of the surrounding dry-land area or the yonland. This is especially true of the organizational aspects of irrigation. The project is a separate unit with its own financing, project administration, and community services.

In the case of such projects, which were typical of irrigation development until recently, most activities were confined to the project area and the people on the project. Institutional organization was such that only the people on the project were considered to be the beneficiaries of the development, and they had to carry the total reimbursable costs. Such organization gave rise to the island-like characteristics of irrigation—the oasis type of settlement in the midst of an arid desert, in a fertile valley surrounded by mountains, or along the bed of some Plains river. It supplies one of the chief sources of income for the sutland.

In the case of the arid West, such an oasis-like development of irrigation was inevitable. Since there is little or no settlement away from the irrigated areas, all the population is served by irrigation in one way or another. But in the semiarid Plains there is population in the non-irrigated areas. Therefore, the basic idea behind such oasis-like irrigation projects in the semiarid

317

Plains is something alien to the Plains. People are separated into two groups: those with irrigation and those without it. This alien aspect is the hope that the irrigated area could be made humid-like by substituting irrigation for rainfall and leaving the remainder of the population to their disadvantageous position. It is expected that, through irrigation, the project area will become fortunate in being able to support and adopt the humid-area culture, imported from the Midwest and the East.

What happens is that the humid-area culture and the unadapted ways acquire an "operational base" from which to extend the unadapted influences into the heart of the Plains. The result is that irrigation farmers, and the business and professional people in the small towns and cities on or adjacent to the project, do not see the necessity for making basic adaptations to the Plains conditions. They continue to give their allegiance to humid-area cultural values rather than helping build values and institutions adapted to semiarid conditions. The project population is at odds with the population not on such projects. The existence of such irrigation projects is a basic factor in creating the minority behavior typical of the Plains.

The issue before the people of the Plains is whether the river basin-development programs—whether it be the Río Grande, the Canadian, or the Missouri—should be of the type that will further impress a humid-area culture upon the region, or whether it will assist in the development of true regionalism for the Plains. It is clear that if the proposed development follows the older concept inherent in the oasis-like irrigation project, there will be a further extension of irrigation projects along the rivers on the Plains, which will serve as an added "operational base" for the invasion of unadapted humid-area ideas.

Irrigationists will be kept separate from dry-land farmers and ranchers. Main Street businessmen and professional people will remain segregated from the irrigation farmer, the dry-land wheat farmer, the rancher, and the cotton farmer. The businessman from an irrigated area will be at odds with the businessman from the neighboring dry-land trade center. The spirit of minority behavior now typical of the Plains will continue and become more intense because the "operational base" for the humid-area culture will have come that much closer to more people.

However, the irrigation development under the river basin

programs can be of the second—a new—type. It can take on the form of a true "irrigation agriculture economy" rather than that of an irrigated oasis-like island development. Irrigation agriculture, rather than serving as an "operational base" for an imported humid-area culture, can be the foundation for a semiarid agricultural economy in the Plains. By proper integration between dry-land agriculture and ranching on the one hand, and irrigation on the other hand, it is possible to bring together the sutland and the yonland of the region and on this build a regional economy that will benefit all in the Plains—dry-land farmers, ranchers, irrigation farmers, laborers, businessmen and professional people.

The cost of irrigation can be distributed to all in the region alike. The benefits therefrom can flow to all in the region alike. The irrigated areas, coupled with power development and the introduction of adapted industry, can assist in the growth of economic opportunity and population—the basis for the development of a truly adapted way of living for the Plains.

To accomplish this it will be necessary to have social organization and institutions that will break away from the oasis-like project idea and serve the people of larger areas and the entire region. Irrigation can become an integral part of dry-land agriculture and ranching, rather than a competing or an unrelated segment.

That progress is being made along this new thought channel is already apparent. The Missouri River Basin, in its entirety, is now known as a project. The single development areas, once called projects, are now called units, implying that they are a part of a larger whole. Part of this progress arises from the overall bookkeeping and financial procedure inherent in a multipurpose development program. To justify the high development costs of some units which could not stand alone, it has been necessary to defray some of the costs by benefit charge-offs from power or other economically more feasible developments on other units. Such an over-all bookkeeping device is, in itself, an institutional procedure that can point the way for other institutional devices that will serve the entire basin and the entire region, rather than one single unit.

But there is other evidence to indicate that the integration of dry-land farming and ranching with irrigation is a probability

319

and also a reality. Officials of the Reclamation Service are on record with public statements to that effect, including policy statements emphasizing the need for power and industrial development within the region as a partner of irrigation agriculture. Though it has been difficult to put these policy statements into operation, certain proposals for development have actually incorporated this integration of interest and land use into formally written agreements of operation. Research has pointed up the practical values that have followed from such integration on older established projects which have moved from their former oasis-like project bounds to a wider base of operation.

The significant thing here is that the Missouri River Basin program is underway with the force of Congressional approval and financial commitments involving billions of dollars. Since it is a multi-purpose type of development, the program is inventing institutionalized procedures and activities that no longer are oasis-like and project-bound in character, but area- and region-like in scope.

Before the development program is completed there will be involved, not alone irrigation, but power, recreation, wild life, flood control, navigation, conservation, and industrial activity as well. In addition, not alone the economic but the social organization and institutional phases of Plains life—including hospitals, libraries, schools, local and state government, law and court procedures—will be involved.

Under such conditions, it is possible that dry-land agriculture and ranching, found largely in the yonland areas, can be more readily integrated into the irrigation or sutland part of the economy. The business and the professional segments of the economy can contribute their fair share to the development of the region, rather than anticipate "windfall gains" alone.

AREA DIVERSIFICATION

These newly emerging and adapted practices in dry-land agriculture and in irrigation for the Plains, coupled with the probable institutional adaptations that will finally come about, can be summarized by the expression "area diversification." This is a new Plains concept—one that is indigenous to the region and only recently coming into its full meaning. The term has been invented to describe the economic aspects of the newly emerging integration of the sutland and the yonland, though the last two terms are of even newer origin. Area diversification carries with it more than farm and business management implications. It includes community building and social organization.

In the humid Midwest, diversification applies to the individual farm or business enterprise—a diversification of activity on the farm so as to round out the year's employment, to insure crop rotation, and to avoid the risk of failure by spreading income production among several sub-enterprises. In the Plains this type of diversification has only limited possibilities. In its place is emerging a group-like type of diversification, for an entire area; not on an individual farm basis.

Area diversification means the integration of two or more specialized production areas into a diversified whole. It means specialization in wheat or cotton in those parts best adapted for them, but integrated with an irrigated or a ranching area or both. It means specialization in ranching in those parts best adapted to ranching, but integrated with an irrigated feed base. It means the co-ordinated flow of production and consumption, not between the different operations on a single farm, but between the different parts of an entire area—the different parts used in accordance with the principles of comparative advantage and best land use. From a social-organization, marketing, distribution, and service-area standpoint, area diversification means the interdependence of the sutland and the yonland parts of the region.

At the hub of this practice of area diversification stand the community facilities used by the entire area. Area diversification may mean a reorganization of the settlement pattern by having population concentrated in fewer but more strategic parts of the region. It may mean more emphasis upon the village or town centered year-round residence of the farm and ranch operators, especially their families. It may mean the emergence of a modified form of village-centered farm community in contrast with the isolated farmstead or dispersed type of rural community so typical of much of rural America. The seeds for such an emerging community may be found in the town residence of many farm and ranch families of the region today.

There is also an economic basis for this new community in the Plains. In the horse and buggy days it was inevitable that the farm buildings be located near the center of the farm or ranch. The slow and frequent trips from farmstead into the fields made this economically desirable. The infrequent trips to town, the absence of RFD and REA, and the limited use of the high school meant costs that were relatively low in comparison with the cost of trips from the farmstead to the fields. Today, with ranching and farming highly mechanized, the frequency of trips between farmstead and fields is cut to a minimum, compared with the increased cost of services at the other end of the scale—frequent shopping and recreation trips to town, RFD, REA, transportation to town for elementary and high school education, and related costs. Many of these costs are now borne in the form of expensive subsidies by the general taxpayer.

There is, therefore, a decided shift in these costs, comparing then and now, and they are the economic reasons behind the shift to the community centers as the hub of area diversification in the Plains. This is but one aspect of the social cost of space in the region.

Here, then, are a series of methodologies and institutions which appear to be adapted to conditions in the Plains. Chief among them is dry-land farming consisting of several parts, including the field practices, the adapted plant varieties, and the mechanization of equipment. But it has additional aspects, including the management of economic and business activities and, therefore, reaches into all parts of the economy.

Each of these parts consists of smaller traits. Their adaptation and perfection has been a long process. Their co-ordination, so that individual farmers can employ them under all conditions, is still not complete. A major task is to get dry-land farming so geared into the values of the total culture that these adapted usages become like second nature to man.

A further obligation is to gear still other phases of living—the more institutionalized part of society—into this pattern of dry-land farming. This has already been accomplished by the flexible credit arrangement in the case of the Federal Land Bank loans. It is rapidly emerging in the form of crop insurance to apply to operating costs. But the principle needs to be extended.

Adaptations need to be extended to all levels of public and private service institutions—schools, hospitals, medical care programs, libraries, churches, co-operative business enterprises, banking, and all types of Main Street business. Agriculture can not carry the burden for adaptation all by itself.

In a larger sense, these adapted institutional forms await the development of an adapted type of irrigation agriculture. This involves the use of land in an integrated manner, probably taking the form of area diversification. In its most complete sense, area diversification means the integration of the yonland and the sutland. In such a development the reorganized village community—some modification of the clustered or string village type—will perhaps become important in the Plains. But such a development is not a panacea. Variations of these patterns need to be evaluated and tried in an experimental way.

The greater task is to create an intellectual and fact-finding atmosphere within the Plains to encourage the indigenous invention of suitable institutional forms on all levels of activity in the region.

CHAPTER 24

Keys for Survival

For civilization to survive and thrive in the Plains three basic traits are necessary—reserves, flexibility, and mobility. These traits need to become ingrained in all forms of activity, especially in the more vital and costly institutional patterns of the region. The institutional forms imported from the humid region must acquire one or several of these traits in order to function effectively in the Plains situation and to give the region the stability that is sought by people everywhere.

The addition of these survival traits to the imported institutions makes it possible for those institutions to contribute to the culture progress of the plainsmen who naturally have the same goals and purposes in the Plains as men do elsewhere. However, the purposeful addition of survival traits to institutions adds complexity to the social life, and it is necessary that a high value be placed by the plainsman on these traits of survival in order to guarantee and insure their perpetuation beyond a single generation. For it is these very highly valuable traits which lend uniqueness to the cultural pattern of the Plains and make it different from cultural patterns in other parts of the nation.

As seen from the facts given earlier about climate, the Plains are peculiar because of the unpredictable fluctuations in the amount of moisture that falls in the region. All growing things in the Plains must adapt to this variable condition; certainly native plants and animals of the region, and also many imported crops in the region, make and have made this adjustment.

But man lives not alone with the aid of adapted plant and animal life but with the aid of a complex social system. Adapted crops and stock cannot alone fill the gap between the unpredictable fluctuations in weather, the plainsman's constant hazard, and the cultural stability which the plainsman constantly seeks to achieve. The rich values of an appropriate social system and many of the institutions which a stable social system employs and makes possible can be acquired only if certain things are done—the creation of necessary reserves, the introduction of flexibility into certain social operations, and the acquisition of mobility in still other aspects of the social order. These are the characteristics necessary for a social system if it is to survive in the Plains.

RESERVES AS A BASIC TRAIT

Reserves, in any situation but particularly in the Plains economy, are of two general types—individual and corporate. By definition, of course, reserves are that quantity of chattel— without particular regard to kind—set aside in prosperous times for later use when resources may be less available and a reserve supply, of whatever kind of chattel is in question, will make the transition from ample supply to a dearth of supply less jolting and difficult. Reserves are most usually thought of in terms of money—cash in the bank, convertible assets, and so forth—but in a large definition of the term reserves must include any form of wealth or resources or commodity which at a future date may not be available. Individual reserves are, as the name indicates, those reserves built up by the individual for his own protection, while corporate reserves are those reserves built up by institutions, businesses, even social groups for their own or, in some instances, for public use. In general, of course, individual reserves are more difficult to establish than are the corporate.

Individuals cannot easily build and husband reserves when faced with the constant need to spend their earnings in order to compete financially with others. Certainly the object of all American advertising is to detract the individual from the saving of his money, and that the individual needs help to accumulate a reserve is exemplified by the compulsory aspects of income deductions for old age and survivors pensions, for income tax payments, and for unemployment compensation. Perhaps private insurance is the form of reserve in which Americans invest the greatest amount of money, but even this investment is not made unless constantly encouraged by the insurance salesman and by the organized and institutional propaganda efforts of the insurance companies themselves.

Residents of the Plains, like those of the rest of the nation, save as the result of the legal compulsion and the organized propaganda, but this is not enough in the Plains since special savings must be laid aside for the extra weather hazards typical of the region. Ranchers and farmers have made some progress in this respect. It is not uncommon to see "blacktop" haystacks in the hayfields of ranchers. These are stacks of old hay carried over from years of plenty. The nutritional content of such feed may be low, and insect and rodent damage may be high, but even so the feed is preferable to no feed at all and the subsequent ruination of a ranch organization built by years of hard effort and large capital outlay. Farmers also have learned to carry reserves of seed grain, and many farmers and ranchers have laid aside financial reserves in the bank to tide them over during years of low income. However, the increased costs of operation are no longer as flexible as formerly. For example, weed spraying is now a general practice on many farms, even during years of drought, and thus certain costs of operation are now necessary, year in and year out, whether there is a crop yield or not. The need for reserves is, therefore, more pressing now than ever before.

The tragedy is that businessmen, professional people, laborers, and institutions on Main Street too frequently do not have reserves of their own for the inevitable drought periods and their only recourse is to continue to charge fees and prices at a high level, even in the drought periods, until their customers, employers, or clientele are no longer able to pay them. Therefore, the individual reserves developed by farmers and ranchers do no more than postpone the day of reckoning and bankruptcy since isolated individual reserves are eventually depleted in an economy where many others have failed to save. Those farmers and ranchers who are most conscientious and consistent in developing individual reserves are the ones most severely penalized in the end.

It becomes clear, then, that the practice of setting aside individual reserves on the part of farmers and ranchers has, as far as being an advantage, decided limitations. In addition, such individual reserves of wheat, cotton, livestock and livestock products result in a penalty, for they tend to lower the price in the market place. The experience of the Federal Farm Board, during the Hoover Administration, in storing wheat and cotton in reserve illustrates the severe price-depressing effect of such reserves. It is necessary, therefore, that there be a corporate rather than an individual approach to the solution of the problem. The idea of reserves needs to be institutionalized and ingrained in the cultural pattern of the region.

An example of the institutionalized way of building reserves is contained in the loan-repayment procedure of the Federal Land Bank especially as developed by the administration of the Spokane branch for experimentation in the north and western parts of the Plains. This government agency devised a system of loan retirement that involves two payments, each into a separate fund. One is the usual contractual payment, maturing at regular intervals, on interest and principal. A second payment can be made into a reserve fund which draws interest and automatically replaces the regular interest and principal payments when these cannot be met from current income. The only problem is to guess correctly the amount necessary in the reserve fund to carry over during the longest possible period of income curtailment. The arrangement rejects the necessity of mortgage foreclosure or debt adjustment procedures. Also, the note is negotiable as a long-time credit instrument. However, the payment of money into the second fund is a voluntary matter and a relatively new thing. Elected as an option in loan-repayment arrangements by some farmers and ranchers, it yet lacks the sanction of custom and institutional force that would make it a real answer to a basic need.

The principle of reserves has been advocated and, in a measure, has received practical application in the field of farm cropping and agronomic practices. Here again, though, it is primarily an individual matter. Quick maturing varieties of grain, coupled with summer fallow practices, have become increasingly more popular as a part of farming, and the use of such grains and of fallow practices is a way of building and using moisture reserves effectively. Studies have shown that yields of spring wheat, grown under a continuous cropping system, are less productive, yielding from 49 to 70 per cent of the summer fallow yield. For winter wheat, continuous cropping shows a yield of 38 to 55 per cent of the fallow yield.

Ranchers, too, have resorted to certain practices for moisture conservation, among them grassland contouring to slow the run-off; the building of properly distributed water holes to avoid the concentration of stock and trampling of the range in certain areas only; and deferred and rotation grazing to give grass a chance to grow, become established and reseeded, and thus use moisture more efficiently. Overgrazing is often the result of not allowing the plant to reach a certain stage of maturity before grazing. Reseeding, sometimes with better adapted grasses, assists in developing reserves. But, again, these are individual practices not yet supported by institutionalized efforts.

There are many other vital phases of the total cultural pattern in the Plains to which the principle of reserves must be extended on the group and institutional level. The principle should apply, for example, to school and county financing, to the maintenance of state governmental services of all types, to the operation and maintenance of churches and hospitals, to prepaid medical care programs, and to farm co-operatives. These are considered to be essential group services. They must be continued in operation during drought periods and should, therefore, have the principle of reserves incorporated into their very core of organization. The individual farm and ranch family living-cost reserves and the reserves built up to provide for the farm or the ranch operational costs in years of no income—all these may come to naught if the school districts, the county, and the state government extract a heavy tax toll just at the time when income is curtailed by the coming of normal drought periods.

The point perhaps needs elaboration. In many parts of the Plains, farm property taxes have been especially burdensome in dry years. A state-wide income-tax system would appear to be a much more just system of taxation and, therefore, it has been proposed as a substitute for the property-tax system. The major difficulty is that in years of no income, because of drought, the income tax would produce little public revenue. Therefore, major reliance upon an income tax has always been rejected by the people of the Plains. A property tax, with the threat of

328

tax delinquency and tax foreclosure sale, has generally been considered a more certain even though more tortuous way of extracting the tax dollar.

But these burdensome land- and property-tax levies and inequities in years of no income can be avoided by creating tax reserves during years of plenty. There is no reason why the principle of reserves should not be applied to school, county, and state financing as readily as to individual farm and ranch operations. Such funds could be adequately protected by constitutional and legal devices, by auditing procedures, and by public statements.

Apparently all the Great Plains states are in need of rewriting their constitutions so as to include the idea of establishing well-protected financial reserves for public services. That this cannot be done is not true. Insurance concerns of the nation have specialized in this field and already have well-developed techniques.

But greater dependence upon the income tax, in preference to the property tax, is only desirable for the Plains provided that reserves are developed. Present income-tax procedures are actually ill-adapted to conditions found in the Plains because they do not allow for the accumulation of necessary reserves. A national law, the federal income-tax paying procedure is made to apply equally to the arid West, the semiarid Plains, and the rest of the humid portions of the nation and it is a typical example of the manner in which the humid-area way has been projected onto the farmers and ranchers of the Plains without necessary adaptations. Drastic inequities have resulted. To eliminate these inequities, revision is necessary.

The problem is this. Farmers and ranchers of the Plains may have a good income one year or for a series of years. During the succeeding year, or series of years, they may have no income because of drought. The ranchers may be forced to sell most of their livestock, including their costly breeding herds. Everything has been called income, and taxable, even though two or three years later the ranch must be restocked. Many of these ranchers and farmers may be without family living income even though they have provided for farm or ranch operating reserves. Having accumulated no such operating reserves, they are in a still worse financial position; they cannot even dip into the accumulated operating reserves to buy the family living. How will they pay for food, clothing, and other immediate living needs? What the Plains farmers and ranchers need is the ability to accumulate a reserve for operating costs and for living costs before paying income taxes.

There is no reason why Plains farmers and ranchers should not be allowed to calculate their income and expenditures on a five-year moving average base. Each succeeding year might be added to the base and the fifth year past dropped from the calculation. To make the principle work, each farmer and rancher might be allowed to buy tax-free government bonds in an amount equal to the necessary reserves for operations and family living costs. Perhaps the farmer and rancher could be permitted to collect tax-exempt certificates in the amount of such necessary reserves and once they had accumulated their necessary reserves, they would pay on all income like everyone else. But always these payments would be made with the protection of having the untaxable reserves as a protection against the years of no income brought about by the special hazards of the region.

There is a reason why all farmers and ranchers, whether in the Plains or in the humid areas, should have an opportunity for income-tax revision. Agriculture everywhere is faced with certain hazards. But for the Plains rancher and farmer, a revision is especially necessary since it is possible to predict with almost absolute accuracy that the special hazards of the Plains will apply. Only the time of their occurrence is unpredictable.

Some income-tax experts might argue that farmers and ranchers can report their income and outgo on an accrual or cash basis and use the carry-forward-carry-backward provision. Under this arrangement operating losses, costs, and income can be carried back one year and forward five years. Thus it is possible to claim refunds on a tax paid for one year earlier, or to reduce the taxes paid in the five years following the loss. However, this does not provide for the longer drought periods and discourages the flexibility that is necessary to survive in the Plains. Furthermore, the procedure is purely an escape device and a subterfuge. It imposes unnecessary moral obligations upon the individual farmer or rancher. It places the burden of proof always upon the individual. The problem of setting aside reserves in the Plains before income tax payments are made is so critical that it requires a forthright and honest solution—not a subterfuge. In addition, were this principle of reserves recognized in the income-tax law, it would impose upon government officials and lawyers the responsibility of recognizing reserves as a fundamental principle in the way of living for the Plains.

It is necessary to discuss the principle of reserves from another angle, as it applies to certain current agricultural programs and policies, especially the ideas of crop insurance, the ever-normal granary, and production control through the medium of acreage restriction. Wheat will be taken as an example because it is a crop found in the Plains generally.

The crop-insurance program is clearly designed to build reserves. It is intended to even out income variations of the intense kind found in the Plains. Still in an experimental stage, the program has been an evolving one and has differed in detail by areas. In some areas the program is designed for individual farm operators; in others, for a group of operators on a community or county basis. In the case of the latter, there is an element of subsidy present in that those operators with a consistently higher yield help carry the burden for those with a consistently lower yield.

The risk of a crop failure is determined for a number of years and is converted into an average-bushel principal payment by the farmer. For example, for any particular wheatgrowing county in any of the Great Plains States it has been determined that a two-bushel annual premium will pay for the risk of such failures. In short, the wheat farmers pay for their own protection in the form of setting aside a portion of their favorable yield toward a reserve, which becomes income during less favorable years. Usually this is sufficient for operating costs only and does not apply to family living costs. Whatever the respective merits of the several experimental efforts, the crop insurance program for wheat is a basic approach to the fluctuating income caused by the natural hazards of the Plains. It is a basic reserve building technique that must be made increasingly more perfect.

However, such a crop insurance program cannot stand alone. If the remaining institutional structures—including local government, schools, and road building—are not supported by reserves of their own, the cost of their unsuitability is simply transferred to the taxpayer. The wheat farmers, who have developed a reserve program for their own operating cost needs, are forced to divert their reserve for the support of that segment of the economy which has not made similar adjustments. Failure of these other institutional structures to build reserves of their own results in a subsidy to them, a subsidy squeezed out of the farmers who have been trying to fit themselves to the needs of the region.

A second government activity for wheatgrowers, containing the element of reserves, is the storage or ever-normal granary program. A storage program is necessary for two reasons: to provide a constant flow of wheat to the consumer and to protect the farmers against unusual price variations and, therefore, unwise income fluctuations that arise from yield variations. An ever-normal granary program is a basic necessity for the Plains production effort and for the benefit of the total economy of the nation.

The only question that arises is whether such storage is the business of the farmers as individuals or whether it requires a group program, either through farmer-owned co-operatives or through the channels of government itself. Complete reliance upon individual storage is a failure because such uncontrolled storage of grains creates an unpredictable supply that is a constant threat to the market price. Storage must, therefore, be a group effort, with adequate guarantees to the current price-making forces in the market that such stored grain will not be dumped unexpectedly and inopportunely.

Again, regardless of the merits of the details of operation, the basic purpose of the ever-normal granary program—that of maintaining a non-price destroying reserve—is fundamental to the success of wheat raising in the Plains and also to the prosperity of the national economy. Ways can be worked out to store the grain on the farm or in public storehouses, or both. For the Plains, it may be desirable to allow the wheat farmers to have annual saleable quotas and to allow them to raise two or three years of crop in one year and to store it. By means of the annual saleable quotas, they could sell, in one year, only the amount of their quota.

The third governmental program for wheat farmers is concerned with price guarantee through some kind of production control, be it acreage, yield, or sales quota restrictions for the individual operator. This program is not now designed primarily to build reserves. Its intent is to control the price of wheat. This production control program is more nearly related to the problem of flexibility, and will, therefore, be discussed under that section. The significant aspect is that production control activities for wheat relate back to the question of reserves—the crop insurance and ever-normal granary programs—and their value. Production curtailment of wheat volume is now essential; otherwise the benefits of the reserves will be dissipated by low prices —prices far below parity. The reserves in the crop insurance and in the ever-normal granary programs would become merely starvation income for a peasant population.

The discussion, thus far, has been in terms of the wheat farmer only—and wheat is a relatively storable commodity. Plains cotton production is faced with similar difficulties and so is Plains livestock production. Certainly the ranchers have similar problems of accumulating reserves for family living and operating costs for which programs have not yet been developed, and for the ranchers to develop reserves will be more difficult than for wheat farmers. The wheat programs to build reserves have been in the nature of an experiment thus far, a possible model to be copied by others.

In any case, the matter of building reserves for the wheatgrowers is a reality to the extent that usable techniques are being rapidly invented and perfected. The same spirit of seeking for adapted techniques must be extended to the livestock operators and the cotton growers if they are to keep pace with the security of the wheatgrowers. Agricultural policy is now largely concerned with the detailed form such techniques will employ. Once the need for this principle of reserves in the Plains is fully recognized, its application will be simple. The result will be greater stability and security for Plains people.

It will not be easy, however, to incorporate the idea of reserves into the nonagricultural structure of the Plains culture. The greatest stumbling blocks are the Main Street businessmen and professional men, especially lawyers with an insensitive legal mind—too often steeped in the tradition of humid-area law. Virtually having a monopoly in holding legislative and executive positions of government, these lawyers are frequently made less sensitive to the need for reserves by their own economic security derived from corporate retainers. The tragedy

333

is that, coupled with other Main Street associations, the blindness by Main Streeters to the need for reserves may yet destroy adapted farming and ranching in the region.

Main Street residents, including the legal profession and the corporation managers, must provide for reserves of their own to tide over the operation of business activities in the cities, towns, and hamlets of the region during years of drought, hail, and other hazards. As more industry develops in the region, some of it will be close to the raw-material producing stage, the first step in processing. Any unusual variation in yield and production will affect these industries as it does agriculture itself. For example, the threatening drought during the summer of 1948 in the Northern Plains increased the volume of lower quality livestock shipped to the small packing plants in the region, and immediately, the profit margins of the packers were adversely affected. Local flour milling, cotton ginning, and feed processing are similarly affected by drought conditions. Tractor and truck fuel dispensers, equipment repairmen, and farm equipment dealers experience similar profit margin contractions when agriculture is in difficulty. These then are only a few of the reasons why local industry and Main Street business will be called upon to have reserves to survive these periods of climatic variations in the Plains.

FLEXIBILITY AS A BASIC TRAIT

One of the basic truths about social life is that institutions quickly become immutable and inflexible in their operations. And a stable climatic environment aids in establishing this institutional rigidity. But in the Plains, the very fact of semiaridity makes for instability, and there is, in fact, a need for flexibility in all phases of institutional and social life—a flexibility that must be constantly encouraged.

Since agriculture on the Plains is marginal in character, flexibility is always implied. The shift from wheat or cotton to livestock or from livestock to wheat or cotton is always going on. There is also a constant shift from sheep to cattle and back again within livestock operations. In the past, the operator was forced to absorb all the losses incurred in such shifts, and this

334

will be generally true in the future. But that is no reason why the social structure, simply because the imported humid-area culture insists on remaining rigid, should also extract an additional toll from the price paid—in energy and effort if nothing else—by the individual for such shifts. Without doubt flexibility in the social system, by being adapted to conditions, can lighten the burden placed upon the individual when such adjustments are called for.

The struggle between the need for flexibility and the drive toward inflexibility is well illustrated by the production-control program for wheat in the Plains. The high price level and the high demand during World War I, and immediately thereafter, resulted in a major shift from livestock to wheat and cotton. There was also a shift from sheep to cattle. The lack of agricultural opportunities following World War I kept much of the land in wheat during the twenties and thirties, even while many of the farm and ranch operators were "liquidated" by bankruptcy.

The conditions of this period, 1920–30, operated as a resistance to the necessary contraction of wheat and cotton acreage. The consequent high production resulted in severely depressed prices. During the thirties, agricultural programs were instituted to achieve parity income for wheat and cotton growers. To accomplish this, certain subsidies had to be given to farmers. They were intended to help the individual grower defray some of the costs in changing to other lines of production. Some were for much needed and desirable conservation practices. Others were a payment for the difference between the market price and the price farmers should have in order to receive income comparable to that of the non-agricultural population. But, generally speaking, the market demands during the thirties were so limited for any type of commodity that new production lines were not easily found. The chief exception was the great expansion of sorghums in the Southern Plains.

The issue, in the thirties, was largely one involving the idea of flexibility—the need for flexibility in farm prices to accompany flexibility in non-agricultural prices and income; the need for flexibility in the total amount produced to stimulate an upward price trend; the need for flexibility in farm management and production to influence the amount produced; and, finally, the need for flexibility in individual farm operations to shift from one kind of production to another.

The detailed procedures to accomplish this objective of flexibility were numerous. Again, in the case of Plains wheat production, the issue was one as to whether production controls should be on an acreage basis or on a farm yield basis. Acreage controls were selected and technology and management efficiency increased, but no real solution to the problem resulted. Again debate raged whether the acreage limitation should apply to large farmers only, or to all alike, large and small. The decision was to apply the rules equally, "across the board" to all, and again the results were less than desirable. Some plainsmen debated also whether the "good managers," those who had been following soil conservation practices of their own, were to be discriminated against, compared with the "poor managers" who had not followed such practices and were now paid to do what the former had already been doing. Again, the rules were inflexible. Still others felt that marginal areas should receive all the acreage cut, and operators in the established areas should not have curtailed acreages. But again, the rule of inflexibility prevailed. And the question remained, was it possible to get the marginal producer out of wheat and into something else?

Then came the World War II years and the problem of how to make the rules flexible was avoided for a time. Following the war, came the postwar period when flexibility became the keynote for agricultural policy—flexibility in the form of the sliding scale for farm commodity support prices in the shape of the Hope-Aiken law. A counter proposal was the Brannan plan which preferred the flexible prices of the market place, supplemented with a variable bonus payment out of the federal treasury to accomplish stability of prices and income for farmers and ranchers.

Then came Korea and the real issue was again avoided. Following the peace in Korea, the issue facing farmers once again was that of accomplishing necessary flexibility so that production could be shifted from commodities likely to be in surplus to others less likely to be in surplus.

This brief summary of agricultural policy, especially as it affects the Plains wheat farmer, is presented here to show that the need for flexibility in Plains agriculture is a continuing and current need. The successful application of flexibility in many areas of agriculture is still to be tested, for, in the Plains, flexibility in prices in order to get a parity income for agriculture is still only a partial solution. What of the flexibility necessary to shift from one production line to another and to get out of some of the marginal production lines and areas entirely? Who is to stand the cost in such instances? The industrial world has the aid of an income tax charge-off for a quick and full depreciation of the new plant built during emergency and war periods as an inducement for shifting to emergency and war goods lines of production when the national welfare hangs in the balance. For Plains agriculture there is no such a taxpayer-borne charge-off.

The significant thing is that flexibility for wheat, cotton, and other production has been the subject of scientific experimentation and is on the threshold of practicality. The task is to experiment with it on a regional basis to meet the peculiar needs of the Plains. The application of flexibility practices will have a significant impact upon the institutional and community phase of Plains society, for in the social area flexibility is resisted as much as in matters of farm and ranch management and land use. For example, cropland has generally been more heavily taxed than has range land. Shifts in land use from crop agriculture to livestock, in such areas, would mean lower tax revenue for public services. Therefore, resistance is strong to land reclassification for tax purposes, a reclassification which might aid in the shift from surplus wheat to deficit livestock. Public land agencies—for example the administration of school land—are not eager to shift the use from wheat to livestock because of the lowered lease revenue for school purposes. If such lands are leased to the livestock grower, without classification into a lower tax-rate category, the livestock operator's taxes will be higher and will contribute eventually to higher costs.

Here then is illustration that the introduction of flexibility in one phase of the Plains cultural pattern is necessarily accompanied by the need for similar flexibility in another phase—the more institutionalized aspect of the social order, land use, assessment and taxation for schools and for state and local government, arrangements for hospital and public health care, support for churches and libraries. The tax device can be used to

337

encourage flexibility by these agencies of public service, or it can be used to forestall flexibility. Flexibility of income for these services can mean the death of these institutions, unless other adaptations are made.

That there is need for flexibility on the institutional level is demonstrated by the existence of flexibility in the native plant life of the region. Such flexibility is found in the ability of plants to mature earlier or later depending upon the season. Another example is in the amount of and variation in the curling of the leaves, which avoids excessive plant respiration. Flexibility is also found in the ability to change the amount of protective coating on the leaves, the extent of pore openings in the leaves, the size of the leaves, the proportion of leaf size to the stem, and the intensity of the green in the plant. These are all characteristics of flexibility, by means of which the native plant adjusts itself to the environment.

In the field of adapted crops, man has made much progress in seeking out flexibility. He has learned to recognize flexibility in his observation of native plants. By plant breeding he has even stepped up the process of flexibility in native crops. The best adapted farm crops are those which can mature early and quickly, if need be, but can also continue longer as a growing crop if the climatic conditions permit. Crested wheat grass is such a crop, and so are the various sorghums. Flexibility is being sought in wheat also, one aspect being the breeding of perennial seed wheat in order to vary growth and maturity with the conditions of the season.

Progress has also been made toward greater flexibility in farm technology. Farm implements are acquiring greater flexibility, as illustrated by the all-purpose uses of the Noble blade and the Graham Hoeme. The smaller tractor is one of the keys to increased flexibility in farm operations, compared with the earlier, slower moving and cumbersome machines. Farm management itself is acquiring greater flexibility. Strip cropping, along with alternate fallow, are an illustration of increased flexibility, for they aid in the rotation program of the one-crop system. Distances covered and size of operations require more flexibility under such conditions.

However, there are limits to flexibility of operations. Flexibility must be supplemented by the idea of reserves. A wheat farmer with alternate crop-fallow must halt his operations two years in succession, if he is to halt them one year because of an assured drought. Otherwise he will upset his farm operations. If, however, he has reserves for seed and operation costs, he can gamble on some operations even though they may result in failure. His flexibility is increased and in that case he can continue his operations, in spite of a predicted failure, and still cover his costs.

Cattle ranching in the Plains has moved away from flexibility and has, as a result, suffered much difficulty. Perhaps it should return to some modified form of its earlier greater flexibility. Its inflexibility has come about because of the greater emphasis upon baby-beef. The contrast between baby-beef operations of today and the three–four-year-old beef system of an earlier period will make the illustration clear.

To receive a certain amount of ranch and family income the rancher can do one of two things. Either he must raise greater numbers of baby-beef, or he must mature a smaller number of head to a greater weight. In the first case, he needs a larger cow herd to give him the necessary total saleable weight than is true of the second type of operation. The cow herd is a costly item, for it is the factory in which the rancher has invested his money.

In a drought of two or three years duration or longer, should it be necessary to curtail the herd, the only alternative for the baby-beef operator is to sell a portion of the costly foundation herd. He would be selling his baby-beef anyway; so contraction means the disposal of the cow herd. It will take considerable capital and time to rebuild the herd later. The wet part of the climatic cycle may already be nearing its end before his ranch is again fully stocked.

But the rancher who ordinarily markets three- and four-year-olds has the opportunity of cutting back on his herd immediately by disposing of his younger stock along with the older marketable cattle. He need not resort to the selling of his foundation herd.

And the point here is that this operation is more adapted to conditions in the Plains than that of the baby-beef rancher because of the greater flexibility.

Some ranchers insist on stocking their ranches with both yearlings and other animals up to three and four years of age.

This is done to achieve greater flexibility than is found in the baby-beef system. Some ranchers introduce flexibility by having a smaller herd, one that can be supported in the drier years, and supplementing this with cattle purchased as feeders when pastures are long. This type of operation runs the risk of having to pay unwarrantedly high prices for feeder stock.

Flexibility, on the whole, is less apparent in the social organization and institutional structure in the Plains than it is in dryland farming and ranching aspects. But there are several illustrations of institutional patterns the further extension of which would quickly lead to enhanced flexibility. One has to do with getting hospital and medical care to people in a sparsely populated area.

Until recently, and even now, large areas of the Plains have been without doctors and hospital facilities. The personnel and services are located in the occasional larger town, often many miles away from the yonland population. When people of the region have adequate income, as they have had in the fifties, they immediately undertake to build hospitals and advertise for doctors. But old, established, and traditional ideas are used to get this service—a structure of concrete and stone, and tying a doctor down with a contract and an investment. Non-flexibility is at the core of the promotion.

But another plan, that of having an entire area organized into a health-hospital-medical care program, has taken root in the region, and this means a larger area is organized into a hospital service area. Hospitals of various sizes and types are strategically located throughout the area. Small communities may have health centers only, a maternity home only, or a small rural hospital. Larger communities have larger facilities. An attempt is made to locate general practitioners in the smaller communities, along with public health personnel. The larger communities have specialists along with general practitioners and also have specialized facilities along with general facilities. By means of mobile clinics and ambulances, it is hoped to get specialized services to people in the smaller communities or to get the patient to the specialized facility. It is expected that doctors throughout the area will have conferences and a flow of patients in such a manner as to get better medical care to the entire area.

Such a plan is only now emerging in the Plains. Many communities have a modified form of this pattern, emphasizing one phase or another. However, such a plan has possibilities of materializing into a more fully developed program. The entire program puts the emphasis upon flexibility and also mobility, not on stability or rigidity as has been the custom. Until a fully matured plan of this type is in general use in the region, medical and health services will be inadequate and limited.

Another area of service in which there is the beginning of flexibility, but where the need for it requires considerable expansion, is in elementary and high school education. The traditional "little red school house" came out of a period of stability and a humid-area background. The sentimental attachments are symbolic of the inflexible ideas built around it. Yet flexibility, largely forced upon Plains people by necessity, is developing in this pattern also. Some Plains communities have school session during the summer months and vacation from December through February. Many farm and ranch families now move to town for the school year, introducing flexibility into the family and the home, if not into the residence and school system. Certainly the role of husband and wife in family matters becomes flexible in this instance. Consolidation has reached its limits in terms of space and time travel, hence flexibility of program is now a necessity.

Montana is experimenting with an enlarged school district for administrative purposes, yet retaining the smaller community-centered teaching program for the pupils under the supervision of the larger administrative area. This means flexibility in school financing and taxation procedure. The mobile teacher, in place of the mobile student, is another possibility of achieving flexibility in education. The teacher-administrator relationship would need to be more flexible in such a program. Class hours, curriculum, subject rotation, school board procedure, supervision, salary payments and budgeting—all of which formerly contributed to non-flexibility—would need to become more flexible under such conditions.

MOBILITY AS A TRAIT

Mobility is a basic trait for survival in the Plains. To have it in the greatest possible degree means that it must operate in conjunction with reserves and flexibility. An adapted cultural pattern for the region will require the perfection of techniques to achieve greater mobility. These techniques must penetrate into and become a basic part of all the institutionalized patterns and forms of social organization of the region, if suffering is to be less severe in the future and the social system more secure than formerly.

Mobility, as we have seen, is a basic characteristic of much of the native animal and plant life of the region. Native plants, to survive, have especially exaggerated characteristics of mobility. And the Plains Indian was mobile, with few exceptions. His techniques to accomplish mobility were numerous and hallowed by much ritual and tradition. Certain areas, such as the valley of the Yellowstone and the Gallatin rivers in Montana, were the neutral hunting grounds for all Indian tribes—an international zone to obtain food in peaceful ways.

And the old cattleman and his way of life thrived on mobility. He shifted his herds. He controlled the far range to the divide by virtue of controlling the water holes and the banks of rivers. His cattle outfit was mobile. The system of range management was built on the idea of mobility. And the sheepman's operations were similarly mobile.

But mobility was not prized by the agriculturalists who came into the Plains. They brought instead a humid-area culture with basic values just the reverse of mobility. Immobility itself was prized—the sentimental attachment to the home place; the longing for the old homestead; the reverence for the plot of earth that could be felt with the hands and treasured; the awe for the soil that had become hallowed because it was built by the toil, sweat, tears and even blood of the predecessor. Because of all these attitudes the home place was built and held at a high price in suffering and heartbreak. But this has not been the choice of many plainsmen in recent decades. They have moved out of the region in large numbers.

According to humid-area ideology, it was first necessary, in order to own and control land, to locate the claim, to record it, and then to fence it in. Unfortunately, in the Plains, the fence boundary marking this claim to immobility often stopped just short of the running creek. Therefore, the family—father, mother and children—spent much time priming the pump and extracting the water from great depths for livestock and garden patch use. Eventually, by hard work, accumulated savings and strategy, the family outbid their neighbors for a three-year lease on the adjacent 160 acres of public school land which had a running creek. This competitive overbidding for the school land occurred a number of times, perhaps, the land with the creek being passed around among several families before finally being put up for permanent sale. The land inconvenienced several families as it passed into or out of the hands of each and the competitive bidding for the purchase of the land resulted in an unwarrantedly high price. The coming of drought, ending in tax delinquency, resulted in the resale of the land to another family. To move the home from the homestead claim to the land with the creek and to allow the former to pass through bankruptcy was unthinkable. Such was the price of immobility.

But mobility is again returning to the Plains. It promises to become far-reaching, not alone for farm and ranch management, but for the institutional structure and social organization in the region.

The following illustration emphasizes the point. Farmer A had been living on the homestead site for many years and recently he had occasion to electrify his farm and home buildings. However, it would cost him $2,500 to extend the power line to his property. Economy-wise and used to mobility, he studied the situation and found that, by spending only $800, he was able to move the entire homestead site—farm and home buildings— to the main power line. So he did. Only a plainsman, finally aware of the meaning of mobility, would be able to break with tradition in this manner.

Again, the rancher in the public domain area frequently depends upon public grazing lands many miles away. He moves his livestock between rotating pastures, from summer to winter range and back again. Often money is pooled to hire common herders or range riders who stay on the range.

On the wheat farms, modern technological improvements and speed permit the operator to farm noncontiguous pieces of land—many miles apart. Equipment, on wheels, can travel rapidly or can be transported by trucks and special hauling vehicles when longer distances are involved. "Sidewalk" or "suitcase" farming has been used in the past as a term of derision to describe such farming, but usually this criticism was based on values best described as "immobile." An increasingly large number of farmers and ranchers use the expression in a constructive sense now. Mobility in the region may mean that "sidewalk" farmers and ranchers are truly adapted plainsmen.

The school situation serves to emphasize the need for mobility in the region. Sparsity of population makes it difficult to have good quality educational programs on the elementary level in many areas of the Plains. Therefore, it has become increasingly customary for the mother and the school children to move to town for the school term. Sometimes, father remains on the farm to "batch," sometimes he moves to town and commutes to the farm. Under these conditions the family has become flexible and mobile.

Ranching and diversified farming are less adapted to such practices. But even ranching shows the trend towards town residence of the family. Some ranchers feed and salt their stock by airplane, for it is easy to locate the stock from the air and there is less shoveling of snow. From the airport near town a quick survey of the ranch can be made in a matter of moments.

Without doubt the growing idea of mobility will mean a new community. Perhaps it will be a small community, but it will be an organized one. There are numerous reasons why the residents in dry-land wheat farming and ranching areas should be concentrated and in greater proximity to each other, thus furnishing the nucleus for a small rural community—the string village along a stream or highway or the more concentrated village type of settlement. The forces making for economy will eventually bring about this development. So will the demand for better education for children on the part of rural parents. Coupled with wise land use on an area basis—area diversification—the now dispersed residents of the region may find it possible to unite their interests and efforts in such a way that they can control more of their own destiny through community action.

The task ahead will be to extend the concept of mobility to other institutions and to social organization generally. Suggestions include the mobile specialist-teacher for rural schools, the mobile health worker and professional medical clinician, the mobile librarian, the mobile preacher and adult education worker.

At this point, reference should be made to the Flying Doctor

Service in the outback of Australia, and the Air Ambulance Service in Saskatchewan, Canada. These services are epitomes of mobility. After years of experimentation, the Australian Inland Mission, with the help of the government and the vision of great leaders, developed the Flying Doctor Service, and two-way radios are now located in almost every ranch home in the outback. The central stations, for example the one at Alice Springs, have a regular schedule for contacting all the ranches. If medical care is needed at one of the ranches, the doctor speaks to the family involved, asks for symptoms, diagnoses the case, and prescribes from a medicine cabinet in each home. He then keeps in touch with the family regularly. If his personal services are required, he flies out by air-ambulance. If the patient requires hospitalization, he is brought in by air-ambulance, often under the supervision of a flying nurse.

This service has brought so much happiness to ranch families in the outback of Australia that the principle has been extended to two-way communication between communicant and priest in religious matters, and school is taught through this device, involving teacher-pupil conversations and recitations. Specific curricula and lesson assignments have been designed. Work exchange arrangements are made between neighbors via this two-way system through the central station.

Saskatchewan based its Air Ambulance Service on the Australian pattern, with only slight modification; the Saskatchewan idea was imported directly from the Australian outback. Both experiments illustrate the idea of mobility in institutional matters, and demonstrate that such invention is possible in matters of social organization.

It is apparent, then that the essentials of an adapted way of living for the Plains includes patterns of behavior which encourage the building of reserves, which foster the conditions of flexibility, and which give rise to mobility.

Reserves, flexibility, and mobility can be acquired by individuals for their own benefit, of course. However, these means for survival on the Plains are so important that they must be extended to all individuals with the help of group and institutional devices. In addition, all group and institutional services must themselves acquire these traits.

The task then is to elevate these cultural traits, which mean survival, to such a level that they become the most important values in the cultural pattern of the region. They must be defined as indispensable and inevitable. Neglect in these things must be defined as socially sinful, for these survival traits must be integrated, even by compulsion, into the Plains way of life and receive full sanction throughout the area.

All this means that the people of the Plains must first understand their needs. Then they must do those things that meet these needs. To accomplish this they must have the vehicles with which to act—the services provided by cities, the communication media of newspaper, radio, and television, and regional organizations of government by the people of the region, for the people of the region.

CHAPTER 25

Growth of Regionalism in America

The Great Plains must have a regional consciousness and region-centered organization. Only with the help of region-centered organization can the Plains residents give expression to their consciousness and only in this way can they gird themselves for region-wide development and control of their resources. In many respects the problems of the Plains are also those of other segments of the nation—differing only in content and detail. Plains problems are found also in the South, the Rocky Mountain area, the intermountain West, the Pacific Northwest, and the New England states. Many of these areas, along with the Plains, are the victims of a colonial policy geared to the advantage of the Midwest and the East. What happens in the Plains, in the way of regional development, may serve as a model to be copied by other areas of the nation.

There has been, in the United States, a gradual evolution from sectionalism to regionalism. There is a striking difference between the two and the evolution has been of such significance that it is worth tracing at this point. The evolving regionalism needs only to be perfected and refined into a final and demonstrably practical form, and conditions in the Plains are such that experimental regionalism may well be tried and tested there before it becomes a reality elsewhere.

DIFFERENCE BETWEEN SECTIONALISM
AND REGIONALISM

Regionalism is different from sectionalism for several reasons. There is something undesirable about sectionalism in that sectionalism is an attempt on the part of an area to set itself up as independent and self-sufficient in respect to economic, political, and social matters. Sectionalism implies lack of co-operation with other areas and results in a narrow-minded stubbornness and self-pride. Regionalism, on the other hand, means an adjustment of a nationwide program or activity to the peculiarities of an area, and also the reverse, namely, fitting the possibilities of an area into the needs of the nation. The object of regionalism is always to accomplish the greatest possible degree of co-operation between an area and other parts of the nation and the world.

Sectionalism proceeds on the basis that the area will handle its own affairs however it sees fit, while regionalism takes for granted that a very definite co-ordination is necessary between the region and the nation. Sectionalism exhibits the spirit of dictatorship and often takes the form of one area exploiting another. Regionalism is typical of the spirit of democratic procedure and co-operation with other areas. Sectionalism places a premium on the uncontrolled individualism or anarchy of a group and of a state or a group of states, while regionalism implies controlled individualism.

It is also necessary to make a distinction between region and regionalism. A region is simply an areal or spatial thing, static in nature. Regionalism, on the other hand, is the dynamic social interaction that takes place within a region, emphasizing the participation of the people through their institutions and their group life. Therefore, regionalism represents the cultural and institutional as well as individual self-expression of the particular region. The simple delineation of an area as a region, separate from other regions, is not enough, for this omits the dynamics of life. The multiplicity of local governments has already overburdened the people with static and ineffective institutions that accomplish little. City-planning regions, interstate compact regions, metropolitan colonial regions, and governmental service regions have all suffered from this static situation. Regionalism differs from these in that it emphasizes the dynamic self-expression of the people in control of their own affairs. Hence, to be effective, regions must have channels of invention and communication and have techniques for action.

A DEFINITION OF REGION

A region is here defined as a large area having a high degree of homogeneity in several factors. Such a region should be large enough so that the inhabitants, in concerted effort, can support the economic, political, and social institutions and services essential to modern living.

There is an unfortunate tendency to define regions in terms of only one or two factors, such as geography or history, river basins or the area of metropolitan influence, traditional trade areas or past artificial political and governmental units. These identifications of a region are but starting points, however, and perhaps one of the several basic criteria for definition should be the future goals and purposes to be accomplished by the region. In this connection, it is necessary to emphasize that the region should consist of the natural fabric of community interests and relationships by which the people live. Political and economic factors must be included so that regionalism can control the forces that now make for extreme centralization, monopoly power, vested-interest group control and pressure-group tactics. Since regionalism is designed to give greater reality to local participation and democratic procedure, it must be based on the prospective cultural and social forces that may grow within and flow out from an area.

The region must encourage a new alignment of political, economic, and social relationships on an areal basis not too large to destroy personal contact or too small to fail to afford variety and adequate resources. The regional area must include all classes of people and all levels of occupation.

At this stage it should be pointed out that the United States is a nation of geographic and historical diversities. In some parts it is a land of cities and metropolitan forces largely; in others it is a land of rural and agricultural interests. Therefore, regions may need to be defined in terms of metropolitan city-planning interests in some parts of the nation and in terms of geographic, climatic, and topographic influences in other parts. In parts, regionalism may need to be based on the hope of having urban and industrial decentralization, while in others the emphasis

349

may need to be on building cities and urban centers of the type that will assist the new region to grow and express itself.

THE EMERGING FACT OF REGIONALISM

Regionalism has been gradually evolving in America out of the sectionalism and the localism of an earlier period. It has emerged for several specific reasons. Chief among these is that regionalism is an attempt to bring about the necessary rural–urban balance that a society requires in order to survive long. Regionalism is also an attempt to overcome the forces of extreme centralization of business, industry, and government, and to make possible the continued existence of smaller industries, part-time industrial employment, and decentralization of population.

Another reason for the emergence of regionalism has been the need for implementing the philosophy of self-help and self-development so essential to democracy. It has been pointed out that in an economy of abundance to which our technological age has aspired, regionalism is a primary necessity. It is an inevitable stage in the social growth peculiar to America's economic and social development—the opposite of localism, of sectionalism, and of provincialism with their restricted production efforts, tariff barriers, and suspicion of others.

The forces that have been driving the national culture toward centralization, selfish monopoly, special interest seeking, and pressure group domination have been an interference with democracy and private initiative. And the trend is not characteristic alone of the government of the nation. It is found in all walks of life be it labor, business, religion, service organizations and clubs, public utilities, literary writing, politics, youth organizations, social welfare agencies, recreation services, medicine, art, advertising, or government agencies such as the Corps of Army Engineers, for example. All these interests within our society have two things in common: (a) cornering the market, and (b) manipulating events to the advantage of the limited membership.

It is because of all these pressure group and centralizing forces that regionalism has emerged. Regionalism is an attempt

350

to preserve economic, political, and social democracy within the framework of America's constitutional democracy. This development of regionalism is so basic that it is necessary to trace its course briefly.

THE FORERUNNERS OF
THE FUNCTIONING REGION

A study of sociological literature reveals that there have been many stages through which the process of change from sectionalism to regionalism has progressed. All these stages have been steps on the road toward true regionalism—imperfections that were evolved to meet the temporary demands of society whose way of life permits only gradual change. Many of the less perfect forms of an earlier period still survive as remnants and as hindrances. But other forms in this evolving pattern are specific signposts of a permanent kind of development. The following diagram shows the stages through which this emerging regionalism has evolved.

THE CHRONOLOGICAL GROWTH
OF REGIONALISM

I. Static Concepts
A. Provincialism
  (1) Sectionalism in American life
  (2) Provincialism in literature
  (3) The region as a unit for scientific study
B. The functional region, short of regionalism
  (4) Metropolitan regions
  (5) Interstate compact regions
  (6) Service regions, especially for administrative purposes
C. The region as a tool in planning
  (7) City and resource planning regions
  (8) Experimental regions in the form of valley authorities

II. True Regionalism
A. The region as a governmental unit
B. The group-of-states administrative regionalism concept

351

PROVINCIALISM IN THE NATION

Other than the formation of the states and the federal union of the states, the earliest forms of areal organization that involved considerable land area in the United States were static. The emphasis was on self-sufficiency and on separatism, influenced by a hands-off and let-alone policy. The sections of the country of that period were not unities or dynamic entities that would perform a service for the area involved. The early colonists were separatists and nonconformists. They had broken away from their native governments to establish a way of life of their own. The new conditions of life were so rigorous that it was necessary to insist on a high degree of conformity of those within the colony, and interferences from outside were rejected. Some colonies were mere extensions into the New World, sponsored and supported by the mother countries. Contact was maintained with the homeland, but relations with other colonists were avoided. This was fertile ground for the growth of provincialism.

And indeed the spirit of sectionalism pervaded the colonies. The spirit of separateness was the barrier that had to be overcome by General George Washington in molding a Revolutionary Army, and it was the condition that had to be overcome in shaping the original colonies into a constitutional government. Sectionalism continued as one of the chief characteristics of the entire American frontier history, in the opinion of Frederick Jackson Turner. In its more intense forms, sectionalism gave rise to the Civil War and other notable historical events bordering on insurrection.

Sectionalism is still at the root of the recurrent states rights issue. It came to the fore with a vengeance in the presidential elections of 1948, when the National Democratic Party was deserted in a number of Southern states by political sectionalism known as the Dixiecrats. It appeared, also, as an east-west struggle for political and economic equality for the West in the period after World War II. It reared its head again in the defederalization of the offshore oil deposits in the early fifties.

Provincialism and its more pernicious aspect, namely sectionalism, are a cancerous growth on the body politic. In modern society, it is a destructive force, a hindrance to the full utilization of the technological and productive skill that the nation possesses. It is a bar to full employment and the abundance that can be enjoyed by all in the nation.

A second form of provincialism is known as literary regionalism—the recording of local history and facts concerning art, literature, and folklore. It represents a romanticizing of local heroes and events, lending color and creativeness to them for the local people. Such romanticism of the local area is truly great only when the localism has been fitted into a larger whole and when it is projected into a national, international, or universal setting. Such writers as Willa Cather, William Allen White, Stanley Vestal, John Joseph Mathews, and J. Frank Dobie have in their various ways written about areas within the Great Plains from a viewpoint not limited by local or sectional interest. Also, a sound literary regionalism has been fostered in the Great Plains by the University of Oklahoma Press at Norman—a press whose national and international outlook has contributed for over a quarter of a century to a heightened understanding of the region both by its residents and by outsiders.

That local literature which fails to meet the test of a broad outlook, however, is a sectionalizing influence and has often been little more than a degraded form of propagandistic profit making and mercantilism. Strangely enough, some of the literary works most narrow in their consideration of a region are written by men and women from outside the region altogether and who see it only as a provincial or sectional area. Even that literature which is most provincial, however, is sometimes so great in quantity that it can be used as a means of understanding what people think about their region and what their attitude towards it is, and when local literature is able to make this contribution it serves as a part of the raw material upon which a functioning cultural regionalism can build.

The term region has been used in the study and description of those things that make for similarity in an area, such as wheat production, cotton production, desert conditions, religious unity, political unity, or climatic similarity. The tools of science have been used to define and describe regions, contrasting one with the other.

Often these studies were undertaken to challenge sectional-

353

ism and to show the interdependence between different areas. Frequently they were used to justify the exploitation of one region by another. For example, many economic studies of this nature have been used to justify freight rate discrimination, the centralization of marketing forces, and the centralization of financial interests. From this has emerged a type of pseudo-regionalism, bordering on sectionalism, that has been used to justify the existence of conditions as they are. The classical economic arguments for the discriminatory freight rates, favoring lower rates for the long haul and higher rates for the short haul, are an example of the distorted use to which this kind of regional study has been put. Sectionalism rather than regionalism have flowed from this kind of rationalization.

Not all the studies emerging from this type of regional emphasis were used in such exploitive fashion. Some, especially the later ones, will prove to have been a step in the direction of true regionalism.

THE FUNCTIONAL REGION

In the chronology of regional growth, the functioning region next appears. This phase, initiated by metropolitan centers, is still short of true regionalism, and the idea of regions at this stage was still characterized by provincialism.

A type of region that has emerged and is still very dominant is the metropolitan center that has reached out to encompass the adjacent hinterland. This type of region has been well described by R. D. McKenzie (*The Metropolitan Community*). There are no formal administrative channels or any legal claims by the city to its area of subservience. The business, trade, communication, and transportation channels have simply laid claim to the territory as the city's metropolitan area—its region of appropriation and source of tribute.

The metropolitan cities of the United States have been classified into those of first rank and those of second rank. In the first are included Atlanta, Baltimore, Boston, Buffalo, Cincinnati, Cleveland, Detroit, Los Angeles, New York, Philadelphia, Pittsburgh, Seattle, Chicago, Dallas, Fort Worth, Denver, Kansas City, Minneapolis, St. Paul, and St. Louis. The last seven play

354

a major role in Great Plains affairs. Metropolitan cities of the second rank are Birmingham, Jacksonville, Richmond, Memphis, Portland, Salt Lake City, Louisville, Milwaukee, New Orleans, Spokane, Omaha, and Houston. Of these, the last three play a significant role in the Plains.

Many studies show how these metropolitan centers reach out and lay claim to the surrounding area through the vehicles of wholesale trade, newspaper circulation, agricultural marketing, and metropolitan retail influences. It is readily apparent from such studies that most of the Great Plains region is drawn into the sphere of influence of the humid Midwest. There are few opportunities for the people of the Plains to "talk back" to these metropolitan centers.

It has been proposed that cities become the center for a system of regional governments in the United States. That there are basic problems in government organization relative to cities and the surrounding area is a well-known fact.

Howard W. Odum and H. E. Moore (*American Regionalism*) do not think of these metropolitan areas as true regionalism because the metropolitan centers seek their own ends, regardless of the welfare of the people in the area, especially those at some distance from the center, and regardless of relationships to other great centers. In agreement with this view, Lewis Mumford (*The Culture of Cities*) points out that metropolitanism is nothing more than false cosmopolitanism.

A fifth type of region, the interstate compact area, involves a formally and legally defined type of co-operation between several states for the purpose of performing a specific but limited service. Here the need for administrative co-ordination has been specifically recognized and defined. Examples are the Colorado River Compact and the Port of New York Authority. The former involves an agreement among seven states to control the use of the waters on the Colorado River. The latter was established for the purpose of dealing with harbor construction, control, and policing, involving the states of New York and New Jersey. The federal Congress is on record as giving any of the states the privilege of forming mutual compacts for the control of crime; to avoid litigation over the taxation of common resources; to regulate interstate commerce and certain interstate utilities; to establish interstate labor commissions and attendant regulations and standards; to establish interstate water management; and to promote joint efforts in the conservation of natural resources such as oil.

The interstate compact has decided limits. In addition to having a very specific sphere of operation for each compact agreement, there are also difficulties in the enforcement of the agreement. In reality, the authority of the compact rests on no more than voluntary co-operation. This is hardly sufficient to master the job of administering the critical affairs of a metropolitan center, for example.

In the absence of a true administrative form of regionalism, there have emerged several other versions of the interstate compact. These include indirect control through subsidies from the federal government, delegation of power to the federal government by default, and unofficial co-operation between states. Examples are the Inter-agency Committee for the Missouri River Basin, the Colorado (Texas) River Authority, the Río Grande Federal Irrigation Project, the several phases of the social security program, the Hospital Construction Act, and the Interstate Oil Compact.

A sixth type of region is based on the principle of conveniently carving up the nation for purposes of offering services and public administration in the field of government as well as business. These service areas are supervised from some large city. Frequently a given area is not always served from the same center for all activities. Therefore, the area is torn apart and allegiance is attracted to different centers. This was demonstrated earlier by examples for North Dakota and Montana and is a situation typical of the Great Plains.

This type of region is different from that of metropolitanism in one sense only. In the case of metropolitanism, exploitation of the purchasing power and resources for the gain of the metropolitan center is the primary goal. In the case of the service areas, a measure of service is actually rendered to the region, but there is a tearing-apart process. The unfortunate part of this is that there is no specific identification of an area with a given center for a large number of services. Unity of action is impossible.

The region for planning purposes has been a specific stage in the growth of regionalism. There are two major types of this phase: (a) the city-planning or resource-planning region, and

(b) experimental regions in the form of valley authorities. These two forms are not yet regionalism in the true sense. They are in the stage immediately preceding true regionalism. They represent the highest perfection in terms of tools and administrative devices yet developed in the attempt to seek a solution to the complex administrative problems of the present.

City planning is an old technique. It was highly developed in Europe by the nineteenth century and was imported directly to America from several European countries. It has developed in America because of the rapid growth of cities. The resource-planning regions, such as the Pacific Northwest or the New England regions, are simply an extension of this European idea of city planning.

The need for regional planning for the city has arisen for two reasons. On the one hand, the existing units of government are so arbitrary and nonfunctional and so incapable of effective and businesslike co-operation in dealing with mutual problems, that another more capable level of administration is necessary. This is especially true of cities that have grown up on the borders of several counties or states, or cities, once separated, having now become joined by bridges and superhighways.

On the other hand, the variety and volume of imported food stuffs and other resources for living, production, and for survival of a city are drawn from such a large area that co-ordination of the channels for the flow of goods and services is absolutely necessary. These two forces, in their inevitable and relentless pressure, have precipitated the need for some type of regionalism.

City-planning regions, the seventh type of region, are an attempt to bring about co-ordination among the diverse local units of government in the large metropolitan areas. The resulting co-operation is of a purely voluntary type and, in the absence of formal legal compulsion, has generally failed. Only by extending the incorporated boundaries of the city, as a unit of government, has it been possible for the city to function reasonably well. Frequently an incorporated borough or village has insisted on standing in the way of such expansion. In some of the geographically smaller states, the cities, as governmental units separate from county and state, have budgets and population numbers that approximate those of the state.

357

It has become apparent that Greater New York, with its myriad units of boroughs, suburbs, adjacent rural areas, industrial sites, foreign trade and embarkation services, and metropolitan hinterland diversities cannot function unless there is effective co-ordination. Sanitary and water supply needs, open space requirements for recreation, policing procedures for inter-city traffic demands, milk shed services, warehouse and whole-saling facilities, the commuting of masses of people between home and job, and the "hot spots" on the fringe make it mandatory that the entire area function as an integrated unit. The task of achieving some co-ordination in tax matters is illustrated by the Real Estate Inventory of New York City taken in 1934. The urgency to settle the chaotic conditions related to city management in New York gave rise to the creation of a voluntary commission known as the Regional Survey of New York and Environs.

Other cities have been faced with similar problems and needs. The Chicago Regional Planning Association sponsored the survey of Greater Chicago, and St. Louis has a similar plan. The Philadelphia Tri-State District has been created for a like purpose and so has the Los Angeles Regional Planning Commission. Boston has a Massachusetts Division of Metropolitan Planning, and Milwaukee, a Milwaukee County Regional Planning Department. There is a regional plan for the Washington-Baltimore-Annapolis area and an Allegheny County Planning Commission for Pittsburgh.

Such city and national resource planning, including the related zoning ordinances, are "gentlemen's agreements" between the administrators of these various units of government. It is an attempt to formalize voluntary efforts that have no basis in law and governmental authority, or, at best, have severe limitations.

A final type of region, peculiarly American in character but still short of true regionalism, is the experimental region exemplified by the Tennessee Valley Authority development. It represents a constructive building up of an area from within. The TVA, a public corporation, with the aid of law, taxpayer's money, long-time loans, some nonreimbursable moneys, many resources, and a wide variety of services has been able to work co-operatively with the established private and public agencies

358

to assist in developing an entire region. The TVA involves co-operation with the existing agencies of seven states.

This experiment is based on the idea of co-ordinating certain activities in an entire river basin. These activities include flood control, power development, navigation, resource conservation and utilization, and industrial expansion. In the process of this development, private business has acquired new incentive and so have the public services of the small units of government—town, county, school districts—and the co-operating states and their agencies. Public and private power facilities, soil conservation, library service, elementary education, recreation, and use of leisure time have been extended to a greater segment of the population simply by means of co-ordinating the previously limited services into an integrated unit. The TVA has become a model for other regions and other parts of the world.

The Tennessee Valley experiment has numerous advantages and also some disadvantages. As a valley basin development, it is confronted by the difficulties of partial planning in that it excludes those areas in the states not in the basin proper. Its boundaries are as artificial as those of any other political unit. It fails to meet the qualifications of true regionalism because of the limits on participation by the people of the area.

As a stage in the development toward true regionalism, TVA is the best and most workable example thus far invented. In this respect, a quotation from Odum and Moore is in order. They say that "the great significance of the TVA is not primarily in its techniques for developing a valley of great resources as a unit. Important as this is, it is not the major function of government. The chief significance must be found in the TVA as a great experiment in the twin motivations of developing and utilizing both the physical and human resources and as a type of sub-region."

THE SHORTCOMINGS OF

EMERGING REGIONS

Experimental regionalism in the form of TVA has brought us to the threshold of true regionalism. One practical type of true regionalism beyond TVA, is regional government on an intermediary level between the federal and state governments. The second type is in the form of the group-of-states region as an administrative device. Both of these types will be discussed in the next chapter. It is necessary here to summarize briefly the shortcomings of the several stages of regional activity that have appeared in this chronological development towards regionalism in the United States.

None of the eight types of regions described above is sufficiently basic and practical to accomplish the needs of a modern democratic society. Actually, none of these forms can bring about the necessary co-ordination that is required among the existing multiplicity of present-day governments. When it comes to standing behind the execution of a co-ordinated plan, there is no authority of enforcement in any of these types. The voluntary co-operation that can be elicited by the bait of money and subsidy is like quicksand when it comes to practical administration.

With the exception of TVA to a limited extent, none of these forms of regional activity is capable of limiting the trend toward centralization and monopoly. In fact, several have contributed directly to their growth. Especially has this been true of metropolitan regions and the service regions found in business, trade, and government.

None of the eight types of regional activity thus far described has been able to implement the democratic participation of the people involved. TVA alone has moved in this direction, but in a paternalistic fashion, not in a legal and constitutional way. Pressure-group tactics and the special-interest group domination cannot be curbed by any of these forms of regionwide organization.

Thus every one of the eight types of regions here enumerated is but a step in the direction of the end product—full-fledged regionalism. They have merit only in that they are a recognition of the need of regionalism.

CHAPTER 26

A Practical Test of Regionalism in the Plains

True regionalism can be accomplished in one of two ways. The first is by regional government on a level higher than that of state government; the second is by administrative regionalism, calling for no important constitutional changes but able to perform the regional tasks required.

REGIONAL GOVERNMENT

The constitution makers of the United States were concerned with only two levels of government, namely federal and state, for at the time the Constitution was written there was no awareness that the industrial and technological activities of the nation might one day create, in large urban areas, power situations stronger than state government and competitors even of federal government. Neither were the constitution makers acquainted with the location and distribution of the resources that would one day cause difficulty in the administration of state governments. When the states were carved into shape, the power and resource factors that were eventually to become so important did not exist or were at the time unknown and were, therefore, not considered. To cope with the difficulties that have resulted from the constitutional distribution of state governmental authority, regardless of regional considerations, the federal government has had to appropriate powers to the point where it is now a gigantic authority.

Recommendations for the establishment of regional government have been proposed to overcome some of the difficulties which the localism of government in states represents on one hand and which the concentration of authority in the federal government represents on the other. These proposals fall into two major types, namely (1) those which provide for the retention of state governments but favor the establishment of regional governments at a third level and (2) those which provide for strong regional governments to replace state government.

Among the proposals that would institute a third level of government is one by William B. Munro ("Regional Government for Regional Problems") which would retain the existing state divisions. The regional governments would have executive and legislative organs and the legislature would be unicameral and elected on the basis of proportional representation. The executive branch could be chosen by the legislature. The regional governments would receive certain powers now in the hands of the federal government, and others still the prerogative of the states—particularly those having to do with commerce, agriculture, industry, labor, social security, parks, public lands, resource development, and reclamation.

A plan offered by Lewis G. Burdette ("Regionalism, A Plan for Uniting the States More Efficiently") specifies that the state lines be retained, but that the nation be divided into six regions. He suggests there be regional councils consisting of representatives from corporations, the professions, skilled workers, agriculture, and research. By means of interstate compact, the council would have authority in areas of banking and corporations; over public works, such as water supply and sanitation; police functions; in matters pertaining to crime, torts, and contracts; and in matters pertaining to wages, hours, and conditions of labor. The major task of the council would be to act as a consulting agency concerning the need for co-ordination on a legislative basis level.

Burdette's plan also provides for a regional circuit court of appeals and for a national Council of State made up of the members of the current Cabinet, and living former Presidents, the Vice-President, the chairmen of the six regional councils, the chief of the Budget Bureau, and the director of the Smithsonian Institute. This National Council would consider regional and interregional matters. In addition, there would be a third house in the Congress consisting of members of certain federal boards and bureaus, members of certain occupational groups, and members of the regional governments. Their legislative function would be advisory in relationship to the existing House and Senate, and to executive bodies in the federal government.

Both of these proposals are examples of how regional governments might be organized. They would require only a minimum of reorganization of existing procedures and authority, and some of this reorganization might be done by means of the interstate compact, as Burdette suggests. Only a few constitutional amendments—either federal or state—would be necessary.

And of course certain tax revenues would be necessary to carry out these plans. At present the major barrier to co-operation between states is the inability to finance, with state funds, certain transactions and public functions on a regional basis.

To overcome the present inadequacies of state governments and the higher cost arising from the organization of a third level of government, some proposals have suggested abandonment of state governments altogether, instituting in their place a system of regional governments. Such plans would require drastic changes in the federal constitution as well as consent of the states.

One such proposal by Arthur Pound ("The U. S. Redrawn") provides that the nation be districted into twelve regions, each with a regional government; that there be the total elimination of state governments and boundaries; and that there be a drastic limitation of federal governmental authority. The curtailment of federal authority, in view of the many acquired powers by appropriation, would be accomplished by decentralization, by reorganization of the legislative and executive branches, by cutting down the amount and variety of governmental machinery, and by moving it inland. Pound suggests that most governmental functions should be placed in the hands of the regional governments, limiting federal power to those originally delegated it by the constitution.

A second proposal in this sphere, by W. Y. Elliott (*The Need for Constitutional Reform*), is almost the opposite of that by Pound. Elliott believes that there should be a strong central government with granted powers. His proposal is, therefore, in the direction of a strong federation, not a union of sovereign states or even regions. He proposes that there be several regional governments, to replace the states, which would continue only as historical relics and as minor boundary units for purposes of administration. The regions would have unicameral legislatures and executive branches and would have representation, according to population, in a national House of Representatives. The functions of the regional commonwealths would be largely those of executing the federal laws.

The significance of Elliott's proposal is that the suggested regional governments are only one phase of genuine constitutional reform for the nation—reform in the direction of true federalism. Donald Davidson ("Political Regionalism and Administrative Regionalism") suspects that this rather than the need for regional governments is the true reason for Elliott's proposal.

In a third level of government, unless there is elimination of the states, critics foresee an unwarranted duplication in function, payroll, and employment. They also foresee a maze of tangled authority and judicial unscrambling of powers and rights. The proponents believe that a third level of government would bring about decentralization, definite placement of responsibility, and greater efficiency. They try to prove this by showing that certain federal functions have already, on occasion, been decentralized and placed in the regions. But the proposal for regional government, as a substitute for state government, requires such fundamental constitutional changes that its adoption appears unlikely at this time.

Granted the advantages of the proposals mentioned above, they contain some real difficulties. First are those difficulties concerned with the definition of the respective regions—what territory should be included in any particular region. A second disadvantage, and a very basic one, is that none of these proposals provides machinery for co-operation between regions. Co-operation is the essence of regionalism. In the proposals already mentioned there is no guarantee that the regions will act co-operatively any more than the states are able to do so at present. Under these proposals a single region may function as an independent power-complex unit, resulting in a piling up of power in all spheres of activity—power in the private corporate and monopoly fields of industry, business, and production; power in government itself; power in political and social organization; power in all spheres of life. One region, by virtue of its power concentration, would exploit another region. The federal government would be so busy arbitrating the evils of the enlarged interregional power struggle that little direction and common cause on the interregional level would result.

Here reference is necessary to the forces of imperialism within a nation. The Northeast has always been "the imperial capital region," says Davidson, "and the other regions, including even the West, have been the colonial dependencies from which it bought cheap and to which it sold dear." This has been accomplished in spite of the authority of the several states. That is the major reason for the hinterland role of the Plains region. It is also the major reason for the historical sectionalism of the South. Even TVA apparently can not cope with this historical situation, for it has been shown that transportation, in the TVA area, works to the advantage of getting goods out of the South but not into the South. The West generally has suffered from a similar colonial policy by the East. It is just this kind of exploitation that regionalism is intended to overcome; but the proposals thus far reviewed do not have the machinery to cope with this type of exploitation any more than the states are able to do.

The need for interregional governmental procedure can be illustrated by several examples from the present. The proposal to take water and power energy out of the Columbia River Basin and shift them to California would involve relations between two potential regions. The Big Thompson Diversion Tunnel in Colorado, for the diversion of waters out of the Colorado now flowing into the Pacific so as to make more irrigation water available in the Plains to the east of the Rockies, is symbolic of interregional relations. The fact that the Missouri River flows through three strikingly different geographic areas indicates that the proposed development of that basin would involve affairs in three different potential government regions. The St. Lawrence Waterway Project involves relations between several prospective regional government areas and particularly two countries, as is also the case for the Río Grande in the Southern Plains. Thus it is clear that there is a need for one region to co-operate with another, something now difficult for states to accomplish. Regional government would be faced with the same problem and must have the machinery to deal with it in capable fashion.

Aside from the imperialistic difficulty facing regions, these proposals have a third major shortcoming. They suffer from the peculiar belief that regions, like states, must have boundaries. On one side of an arbitrary line is Iowa and on the other side is South Dakota. This is necessary for citizenship and taxation purposes, and for matters pertaining to human rights, justice, equity, and certain other functions.

These guarantees are now established in federal and state constitutional proceedings. Certain major values and traditions, built up about both the federal and the state governments, are so basic that they need to be preserved. There appears to have grown up a division of labor in government that makes for both federal and state security. Under present arrangements, civil action and justice can be sought on the state level and finally on the national level. For these things it is necessary to have boundaries.

The need facing the nation at the present is not a third unit of government, namely regional government, with specific territorial boundaries and limits; rather, the need is for a unit of government, regional in character and purely administrative in function, that does not have boundaries. It is necessary to invent a unit of government, responsible to the people, that is flexible and mobile in character. This would be an administrative type of government that can function in interstate and interregional matters; one that can get the states and regions to function in co-operation with each other.

ADMINISTRATIVE REGIONALISM

Odum and Moore have developed the concept of group-of-states regions. It is a planning tool. The shortcoming is that it is not dynamic regionalism. Odum and Moore fell into the usual trap of thinking that regions must have boundaries. Therefore they conceived the idea that an entire group of states must be included in a region.

However, Odum and Moore should be given credit for taking the first step towards true regionalism. Their term, group-of-states regions, must be modified to be a system of group-of-states administrative regionalism. This and other modifications mean that administrative regionalism should be characterized by the following four things:

(1) Administrative regionalism would be purely administrative in character, without boundaries. Thus it can have flexibility.

(2) Administrative regionalism should involve a group of states or portions of states, placing the emphasis upon interstate co-operation. Part of a single state may be in one region and another part in another region. This very fact would make for co-operation between regions.

(3) Administrative regionalism would retain state boundaries and functions as they now exist, and also federal functions in much the same way as today. The regional administration would have policy and advisory functions to bring about co-operation between states within a region, between states of neighboring regions, and between a group of states and the federal government. Thus the imperialistic exploitation of one region by another would be avoided.

(4) Administrative regionalism would retain federal functions much as today but would urge that administrative activity be delegated to the states, and to state and federal agencies located in the region.

The significant aspects of administrative regionalism are that it requires no constitutional revision, is without boundary, and provides for co-operation between regions and between them and the federal government.

ORGANIZATION OF ADMINISTRATIVE REGIONALISM

It is now necessary to explain the details of administrative regionalism. The situation in the Plains will be used as a case illustration. Portions of ten states—Texas, Oklahoma, Kansas, Nebraska, South Dakota, North Dakota, Montana, Wyoming, Colorado, and New Mexico—are involved in this region. Figure 21 serves as a skeleton outline of the contents of the proposal.

367

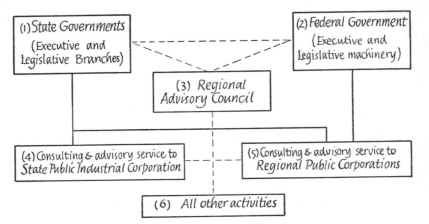

FIG. 21.   A plan for administrative regionalism.

In this plan for the administrative region, the legislatures of the various participating state governments (1) and various agencies, including the Congress, of the federal government (2) would approve proposals made by the Regional Advisory Council (3) consisting of the two United States senators from each state, the senate majority leader and the senate minority leader from each state, and a research and clerical staff. The Council would operate on a budget provided from state and federal sources.

The functions of the Regional Advisory Council would be to (a) study regional problems, sometimes in co-operation with other agencies such as planning groups; (b) make proposals for regional action, both legislative and administrative, and to transmit these proposals as reports to the U.S. Senate and to the senates of the various participating states; (c) advise the regional public corporations; (d) advise the state public industrial corporations; (e) counsel the state legislatures if requested; and (f) sit in the region at a designated place for a specific time in order to give service. The Council would be, of course, subject to state and federal authority as now constituted.

The state public industrial corporations (4), which the Regional Advisory Council would advise, would be true public corporations, analogous to TVA, financed by the separate states, and created by the states. Several of these corporations might exist in a region to perform industrial functions now left undone by private enterprise, and they might also perform some of the functions now performed by state agencies and bureaus.

Also advised by the Regional Advisory Council would be the regional public corporations (5), created by a group of states or by the federal government as public corporations, likewise analogous to TVA but more democratic. Several of these corporations might exist in a region, concerning themselves with public power, public lands, public forests, conservation of the soil, and the like. Some of

The major part of such an administrative device would be a Regional Advisory Council. This council would be made up of legislators already elected: the two federal senators, the state senate majority leader, and the state senate minority leader from each state. Four legislators would represent each state. Since there are ten states in the Plains region, this would mean a council of forty elected representatives of the people. Under these conditions, the Regional Advisory Council could not be considered dominated by federal interests. There could be no question of state versus federal rights since each of these four persons is elected by the citizens of each state.

This advisory body would have a certain stability and also a certain responsiveness to the public will. This arises from the fact that the federal senators have six year terms, while the state senators have either two or four year terms. The minority leader from each state would represent the interests of the minority party, and the majority leader would represent the majority wishes. The body would always have sufficient hold-over members to give stability.

The federal senators are suggested as members of the council because their selection involves no complex formula. There are always two from each state, while the number of representatives varies greatly and their tenure is of shorter duration. The state majority and minority leaders, besides being the selectees of fellow senators, have longer tenure than state representatives. The chances of having more states adopt the unicameral legislature, as Nebraska has already done, makes the choice of senate members obvious.

Another merit of this proposal is that these four elective positions may become stepping stones to higher offices of statesmanship, and thus these offices call for greater responsibility on the part of the citizens as an electorate. An added merit is that the council would meet in the region and, therefore, the

---

these corporations would perform the functions now performed by federal government bureaus and agencies, departments and services.

Other groups (6) which could take advantage of the Council's assistance would include state and federal agencies; private and public organizations and businesses, including co-operatives, partnerships and corporations; county and town governments; school district administrations; and agriculture and labor associations and unions.

federal senators would be required to participate in governmental affairs closer to their electorate than is now the case.

The council would need a staff for research, technical con-
sultation, and clerical purposes. A budget to finance this staff
and also the additional salary and living cost allowances for
the council members would be necessary. It should not be difficult to apportion these expenditures among the several states
and the federal government. The resulting regional budget
would serve as an example for interstate use of public funds
by states for purposes involving interstate co-operation of a
kind for which there are now no budget arrangements.

The council would have no legislative functions other than
those already attached to the present offices of the incumbents.
The major responsibility of the council would be the study of
problems requiring regional and interregional action. For this
purpose the council would be empowered to make studies of
its own and to co-operate with other agencies that carry on
research.

On the basis of the facts discovered, the council would be
empowered to formulate suggested legislation. This, of necessity, would be made public. Copies of reports and proposals
would be transmitted to the federal Senate, House, and to the
President, and to the same offices of the respective states. All
reports would be available to the citizens of the state.

Once these reports and suggestions for action have been submitted to the respective legislative bodies, they would automatically become part of the legislative agenda on both the
state and federal levels. The legislative members of the council
would be responsible for initiating their proposals.

In addition to these quasi-legislative functions, the council
would have direct consultant responsibilities for any federal
programs in the region. The council might be called upon to
consult with the respective state legislatures and also with state
agencies for such services.

In order to perform certain resource-development tasks on
a regional level, it will be necessary to have the machinery to
do these things. The need for certain multi-purpose development has become apparent. The scope of activity and capital requirement for such development is so huge, and for a time actually unprofitable, that sometimes the activity must be initiated

and operated by quasi-public rather than by purely private interests. Public power development, flood control, navigation, river and harbor development, forestry, conservation, administration of the public domain, and stimulation of the fertilizer industry are such instances.

It is worth pointing out that these semi-public multi-purpose programs, when couched in the frame of a public corporation, are not a limitation on private enterprise or a rejection of it. Upon the basis of these programs can be built numerous private enterprises, especially of the smaller individually-owned and individually-operated kind. There is room for investment of private capital, privately-owned tools and private management, along with public financing and civil service management-personnel in such programs of resource development by public corporations. The emphasis should be on multi-purpose planned and co-ordinated programs, regardless whether the operation and administration be entirely or only partially private or public.

That these multi-purpose development programs are basic necessities is illustrated by developments already under way. Examples include the following: the Tennessee Valley Authority, the Missouri Basin program, the Río Grande Basin, the Arkansas–White River project, the Red River (Texas–Oklahoma) project, the Bonneville Power Administration, the Grand Coulee development, the Taylor Grazing Service, the Forest Service program, the Federal Land Bank and Farm Credit Administration programs, the Reconstruction Finance Corporation and its successor.

The task ahead is to decentralize some of these functions and place them in the region where they belong. Many already have regional offices. But others are now so closely attached to the executive and administrative functions of the federal government that their activity depends upon and fluctuates with the rise and fall of political parties. This creates confusion and uncertainty. If these activities are worth performing for the welfare of all in the nation, their permanency should be assured. One way of doing this is to place them in the regions where they operate, subject to ordinary corporate business procedure. They should not be invested with governmental immunity.

Secondly, some of these agencies have unduly large authority and functions outside their legitimate sphere of action. They actually replace or interfere with the channels of true democratic government. This has been the by-product of their experimental nature. The fact that their survival was hazardous required that they have recourse to special immunity. Their democratic administration was often accidental rather than the product of their organization.

The TVA is such an example. It and some other agencies listed above have been so successful that their continuation should be assured. But they should be incorporated into the fabric of democratic governmental and administrative procedure. In fact, they should be made a model in this respect, and a coat hook upon which to expand private economic activity and political democracy. This is the meaning of true regionalism to which the nation has evolved.

It is, therefore, proposed that the concept of the public corporation be further improved upon, more perfectly developed, and specifically applied to those spheres of resource utilization where it can operate most beneficially. The nation has had sufficient experience to do this. The proposal here is that the pattern of the TVA be followed, with some modifications. The word "authority" should itself be removed, since the TVA is not alone characterized by authority; every group activity, to function successfully, must have authority. The word "corporation" should be substituted, for that is what TVA is, invested with public responsibilities. The public corporation should have most of the functions which TVA now has, except that it should come within the scope of the true public corporation. One of these is that it should be subjected to the right of being sued and to sue people just as any other corporate entity, and it should be removed from under the cloak of immunity against legal and judicial processes.

The public corporation, again using TVA as an example, should enjoy freedom to do business within the limits of its public charter just as any other private corporation operates under a charter. It should operate under the advisory guidance of the proposed Regional Advisory Council.

The centering of many governmental functions within the region would result in the decentralization of governmental activity and population. Such a move would contribute to the increase of communication agencies and facilities within the region. It would bring the legislative potentials closer to the people. Many other functions would be decentralized, so that there would be a concentration of activity within the region. This would mean employment, opportunities for self-expression and a chance to exert influence. The Plains region does not now have these things.

With the help of all these forces, the stage would be set for an attack on the discriminatory freight rate and transportation restrictions which now hamper the full development of the resources and the manpower in the Plains. News could originate in the region, and national and international events could be evaluated in the light of the region's needs. Newspapers and radio could then be a constructive force in the region. All these things have a place in the building of a region.

Another function of administrative regionalism would be to inject renewed vigor into state and local government. The entire machinery for administrative regionalism, as here proposed, would lay the burden upon the shoulders of the people of the region. They would be forced to do many of the things for themselves. The cry for state's rights would have to be backed up by action.

To demonstrate their sincerity, the people of each state would be expected to do certain things for themselves through the channels of state-sponsored public corporations. Such state public corporations could perform some of the duties now rendered by certain departments and agencies of the federal and state governments. Examples might include state park systems, state water-conservation activities, the administration of state land programs of various types, and the administration of a mineral resource extraction program. It may mean the initiation of production activities usually undertaken by private enterprise, if private enterprise does not do the job.

North Dakota has specific examples, namely the State Mill and Elevator and the State Bank of North Dakota. Kansas has, for example, its Industrial Commission of Kansas; Oklahoma its State Corporation Commission; and New Mexico its Conservancy District–Reclamation Contract Commission. These could all take on the form of public corporations on the state level and could venture where private enterprise has failed to do so until a climate for private investment and enterprise has been created.

Failure on the part of private enterprise to perform its duty should not be allowed to encourage the stagnation of an entire region, including the stagnation of the small private enterprises of such a region. The public corporation device, on the state level, might well lead the way and furnish an example of the opportunities that can be developed. Such activities by the state public corporations might be carried on jointly with private enterprise or with federal regional development agencies, including federal–regional public corporations.

INTERREGIONAL CO-OPERATION

The problem of interregional co-operation is an urgent one, as is also that of interstate co-operation between adjacent states which now consider themselves as belonging to different spheres of metropolitan influence. Many of the states, under this system of administrative regionalism, would belong to more than one region. For example, the Rocky Mountain portions of Montana and Colorado face in a different geographic and metropolitan direction than do the Plains portions of these states. The same is true of North Dakota, Nebraska, or Texas.

Thus, the four elected representatives of Montana and Colorado, or of North Dakota, Nebraska and Texas, for example, would also serve on the regional advisory councils of these other regions of which the state is a part. Their duties and obligations would be the same as for the Plains. Thus the legislatures of such states would receive two sets of reports and proposals for regional action. It would then fall upon the legislatures of the states involved to become informed concerning the regional diversities within their borders and shape legislation in conformity with these varied needs. The Congress, on the national level would, likewise, become informed concerning the regional differences as they apply to individual states and groups of states. Federal legislation, to allow for such differences, would then become a reality.

Administrative regionalism would, under this plan, become a truly practical system for interregional development and co-ordination. It would be a means of avoiding the provincialism and sectionalism of an earlier day. It would avoid the danger of imperialism by states and regions. It would contribute to a growth in democracy and to the decentralization of the forces of government and business which now stifle regional development. It would become an instrument in developing local responsibility and also a large measure of interregional co-operation for the benefit of the entire nation.

CHAPTER 27

Opportunities and Tools for Regionalism in the Plains

With St. Louis as focal point, the humid-area influence from the East and Midwest began to reach out, as early as the beginning of the nineteenth century, across the Plains—by water up the Missouri River, by land along the basin of the Platte River and over the Santa Fé Trail. Trade and exploration reached out across the Plains to the Rocky Mountain West, to the Pacific Coast, to Mexico. Traffic moved from east to west and back again. Later, when trade was accompanied by settlement—the cattlemen and the sheepmen came first, then the farmers—settlement, too, came from east to west bringing a humid-area culture with it. Eventually, late in the nineteenth century, the railroads came following the same routes—east to west—now through Omaha, Kansas City, St. Paul, and Minneapolis as well as through St. Louis. Quite obviously, the avenues of travel and transportation across and into the Plains have always been the same for over a century and a half, and along those east–west avenues the ideas and values of a humid-area culture have been continuously carried.

Even today these east–west avenues of travel continue to have a similar impact upon the Great Plains. The Corps of Army Engineers is moving up the main stem of the Missouri, up the Platte and the Yellowstone, up the Grand and the Republican, up the Arkansas and the Red River, up the Canadian and the Río Grande—all in the form of the Pick Plan or its modified version. In the past this branch of the army was a navy-like land operation on inland lakes, at the mouth of rivers, or along their main stems in the humid parts of the nation. Harbor and port development, navigation, flood control, dike and levee construction were the major tasks of the army engineers. In recent years this humid-area agency has extended its activities into the inland semiarid Plains. There appears to be little experience in past activities that would entitle this agency to a major role in the resource development program of the Plains.

From the West, into the Plains, comes federal reclamation, down the upper Missouri and the Yellowstone, down the Platte and the Republican, down the Río Grande and the Canadian, down the Red River and up the Arkansas, and down the branches of all these. Federal reclamation, in its historical origin, is also prejudiced in favor of humid-area ways—it came to make wet that which is dry in order to build humid-area oases in the arid and semiarid regions. The object of its works are to make it possible for the semiarid and arid lands to support a humid-area way of life. There is still much of this thinking among reclamationists and irrigationists.

The important thing is that the Great Plains are again being invaded by two giant forces along the same avenues taken by the humid-area invasion 125 years earlier. Both came as agency forces, with vested interests, to appropriate a semiarid land— one from a wet and humid-area setting; the other from the arid West and the Rocky Mountains to make wet that which is dry.

Reclamation, however, has the historical roots of organization and philosophy that can fit into conditions characterized by semiaridity. It can adapt its philosophy and techniques to such conditions, if the engineers and the technicians can be kept within bounds.

THE HISTORY OF THE
PICK-SLOAN PLAN

These two forces—the army engineers and federal reclamation—canvassed the Plains to enlist the residents in support of their respective programs, especially during the thirties and the early forties. Rufus Terral (*The Missouri Valley*), who has given the propaganda phase of this campaign detailed study, put it in these words: "The confusion engendered by the only partial readiness of the Pick and the Sloan plans, and the contradictions between them was staggering, but Pick was not staggered. The Colonel, taking his plan to the people, was soon joined by Sloan with his plan. The two men enjoyed one thing in common—a mutual detestation. Sloan liked to say that the Army Engineers didn't know any better than to design one dam to a height that would submerge another dam to a depth of some several feet. Pick regarded Sloan as getting his plan before the people only by holding tightly onto the Pickian coat-tails. . . . As the two great plans for one river were being peddled about the Valley, it became evident that instead of two incomplete and conflicting plans, one complete and harmonious plan was needed."

From the Missouri Valley came the plea for an MVA, modeled after the pattern of the TVA, a plea sponsored originally by the St. Louis Post-Dispatch and by the National Farmers' Union. This forced the army engineers to join hands with the reclamation interests. There emerged the Pick–Sloan Plan for the Missouri—"a shameless, loveless shotgun wedding!" according to James G. Patton, president of the National Farmers' Union.

That the Pick–Sloan Plan represented, at best a tragic state of tension and at worst no workable plan at all, was apparent from the beginning. In reality, it was a contest for power between two federal agencies who trampled on the people. The central issue was whether the limited and exhaustible waters of the Missouri should be used for the humid-area part of the Basin first, and primarily, or for the semiarid part first. The line of battle was drawn on the ninety-eighth meridian, and there emerged the Missouri River Compromise of 1944.

This latest "Missouri Compromise" holds that the waters of the Missouri shall first be used for irrigation west of the ninety-eighth meridian. If there is any remaining water it is to be used for down river purposes, east of the ninety-eighth meridian, in the humid-area east of the Great Plains. Unfortunately, to do this, many of the navigation and flood control sites are located west of the ninety-eighth meridian in the heart of the Plains.

To overcome the basic rift between the two agencies—the army engineers and the reclamation service—there was created the Missouri Basin Inter-agency Committee. This is an unworkable arrangement, no more than a makeshift answer to the continued pressure for a single-agency, co-ordinated approach.

378

Agriculture, other than irrigation, is largely omitted and so are the industrial possibilities of the region.

The United States Department of Agriculture claimed a decided hand in the Missouri Basin development program as the third major agent—the third leg of the stool. This program, emphasizing on-the-farm conservation, was intended to keep the snow and rainfall where it fell—to avoid runoff wherever possible and enhance production under dry-land farming and ranching conditions. Work on writing this program started in 1948. The final report was completed in 1949 and presented to formal Congressional channels on September 29. To date the plan has not been given a hearing nor has it been acted upon, but its existence has served as a pressure to include some of its recommendations in the inter-agency program for the Basin.

Neither the army nor reclamation service is enthusiastic about the agricultural program. Effective water conservation in the uplands by proper farming, contouring, and pond development would result in only partially filled main stem reservoirs and water shortage for irrigation, power, and navigation under the Pick and the Sloan parts of the plan.

After the Department of Agriculture filed its report, the Hoover Committee Report on Reorganization of the Executive Branch of Government, made in 1949, officially criticized the Pick–Sloan Plan as wasteful, expensive, and unco-ordinated. Even later, President Truman's committee on water resources made its study and recommendations in the form of a report entitled *A Water Policy for the American People*. Its recommendation was that there be a single co-ordinated river basin development for the Missouri, patterned after the fashion of TVA, with certain modifications.

Such have been the politics of the Missouri River Basin development to date. The Upper Missouri, west of Sioux City, Iowa, and west of the ninety-eighth meridian, is almost identical with the Northern Great Plains. Portions of the Upper Missouri extend westward beyond the Plains, into the Rockies. The lower Missouri reaches east of the ninety-eighth meridian, into the humid prairies of the Midwest. Thus the Missouri flows through one region and touches on two others.

But the agency battle is still on. The army engineers do not capitulate readily. Colonel Pick was promoted from the Missouri division to become Chief of the army engineers with headquarters in the nation's capital, but he has now retired. The army engineers proceed according to historical plan; it is altogether likely that they will lay claim to the entire Missouri system as their prerogative. Their authority, they will argue, is to be found in the original instructions given by President Jefferson to Captains Lewis and Clark in 1803, namely to explore the newly acquired Louisiana Territory, especially that portion tributary to the Missouri.

The report of President Truman's Water Resources Policy Commission showed that the inter-agency struggle for authority is not confined to the Missouri River. In the Southern Plains this same struggle prevails in the Río Grande, in the Red River, and in the Arkansas River basins, as well as in others throughout the West.

OPPORTUNITIES FOR REGIONALISM

What does all this mean for regionalism in the Plains? It means that the Missouri River basin, and the basins of the Río Grande, the Arkansas, the Red, the Colorado of Texas, and other rivers will be developed along multi-purpose lines. Irrigation, water power, navigation, and flood control will receive major attention. There may be industrial development, if it is included in the large plan. There may be recreational and scenic development, if it receives adequate attention. There will be a tightening up of the agricultural industry in parts of the region.

In short, many benefits will accrue to the residents of the Plains as a result of the activities that have already been undertaken, and that are in prospect for development. But the results will not be adequate. There is no administrative regionalism that will result from this activity. There will be no vehicles to enable the many minorities in the region to join hands in a common purpose. There are no provisions for the creation of a regional consciousness. There is no machinery for making democracy really workable in the region. There is no provision for the development of effective communication within the region. Much of the population of the region will not benefit from this activity because the development reaches in island-like projections into parts of the region only—into the sutland chiefly. The yonland will receive little benefit, except accidentally. And the preponderance of population and political influence in the portions of the basin outside the Plains will have the effect of orienting the development to the outside. This is especially true of the Missouri basin in which case the politically powerful part is the lower Missouri.

If there were true regionalism for the Great Plains, all these shortcomings would be overcome. The conflict between the Pick and the Sloan part of the Missouri Basin development program would be resolved. The struggle for power between the upper and lower parts of the basin would be resolved. The impact of the downstream metropolitan centers and interests could be modified by an exchange of information. Democratic forces would come into play.

Placing the development part of the Missouri or the Arkansas River basins, for example, under the controls of a regional public corporation would make the program for these basins what it should be—a mere development program, unhindered by tasks beyond its scope. A separate over-all regional organization of the administrative regionalism type would make it possible to have the over-all regional program within which the public corporation could operate. Such an over-all administrative regionalism could also deal with the basin development programs in all the river areas of the Plains.

In short, there are now tools and opportunities in the Plains for the development of regionalism. The task is to create the necessary machinery for administrative regionalism so that these tools and opportunities can be used for the fullest possible development of the resources, under the control of the people of the region. The Missouri development program would not then be one for the benefit of General L. A. Pick and the army, or for Mr. W. G. Sloan and reclamation. It would be for the benefit of the people of the Missouri Basin, for the people of the Northern Great Plains, and for the benefit of all the nation.

There is yet another aspect of the Missouri Basin development program that should be mentioned. As stated earlier, the Missouri spans the Plains, but originates in the Rockies and projects into the Midwest. The activities on the entire basin would, of necessity, call for co-operation between these three regions. The merit of the public corporation approach is that it would precipitate and encourage such co-operation between regions, and this is true of the basin development of all the rivers of the region. When several such regions become involved, the base of interest is widened and soon most people of the nation become involved in one way or another. Even Congress would find it less easy to "log roll" and operate in "pork barrel" fashion. A basic development program would not then be stopped by personal whims of an easily irritated or a largely uninformed Congressman.

MULTI-PURPOSE DEVELOPMENT

Multi-purpose development of resources is so basic that it fixes the opportunities of a region for a long time to come. It involves the use of public as well as private funds so that the public welfare of the entire nation is involved. The Plains have oil, gas, lignite coal, water power, precious minerals, and rocks that need to be placed into production for the welfare of all people. All this requires extensive capital—more than is now available from private sources. Present and future generations will be served. This means that the investment for the development must come from many sources, including future generations. A new type of bookkeeping is, therefore, necessary.

The idea of multiple-purpose development is a practical formula to accomplish all these things. This multiple-purpose approach to resource development is being put to the test in the Missouri Basin, including the Upper Missouri, and also in other basins of the region. The difficulty is that it is not now being put to its maximum use. The part that is being omitted is the industrial development of the Plains. Nevertheless, this multi-purpose concept is now a tool and an opportunity. Coupled with administrative regionalism it could be expanded to its fullest extent.

It is essential to explain the concept of multi-purpose development and reimbursement briefly at this time. It received the fullest analysis in the 1950 report of President Truman's Water Resources Policy Commission. The commission points

382

out that the test as to whether a certain construction should be undertaken or not includes the following considerations:

First, it shall be clearly demonstrated that multi-purpose development of a specific project is superior to single purpose development. Failing to be of the multi-purpose type, it should be rejected. Secondly, once accepted as a multi-purpose project, the private benefits, both direct and indirect from such development, should be identified and clearly determined. Thirdly, such private benefits shall be assessed fully against those who benefit, and a clear procedure should be worked out to recapture the full amount of such private benefits. Fourthly, capacity for reimbursement or repayment shall be the main though not the lone factor in the justification of developing a multi-purpose activity. And, finally, the reimbursement policy shall be designed to encourage the maximum of local participation in financing resource development.

This clear definition of multi-purpose development and re-payment would remove the hope of windfall gains for some people. It would permit participation of private and public interests, whether local, state, or federal. It would make it possible to remove "log rolling" and interregional "horse trading," and place emphasis on decision making based on the merits of the situation. The peculiar nature of the Regional Advisory Council would guarantee that action would follow from the will of the people.

In short, the multi-purpose resource development concept, in its fullest meaning, is a practical tool for the implementation of regionalism in the Plains. All that remains is to apply it with courage and conviction.

BASIN DEVELOPMENT IS ONLY

PARTIAL DEVELOPMENT

The pressures that shape national policy in resource development today are in the direction of unified river basin activity. This is true of all the rivers in the Plains. Without administrative regionalism this will result in partial development of the Plains and will serve to make of it a hinterland more than ever before. Via the several basin channels the region would be segmented and torn apart more than now and would be made tributary to many metropolitan centers. The conflict between the Plains and non-Plains portions of these states would be intensified because the non-Plains portions would find themselves more nearly identified with the down-river interests than even now.

This need not be the case, however. The point to remember is that basin-wide development is possible and practical as long as it is not confused with regionalism. If administrative regionalism on a Plains basis is made a reality, basin development will fall into its proper perspective. It would be no more than an efficient and businesslike development of the resources along public corporation lines. All the other decisions would be in the hands of administrative regionalism, carried out with the consent of the existing state and federal governmental machinery.

Basin development, then, as a public corporation service would be a practical tool for putting teeth into administrative regionalism for the Plains. Similar regionalism in the areas adjacent to the Plains would then mean the existence of a device for interregional co-operation, rather than interregional exploitation.

THE CO-OPERATIVE MOVEMENT

Next to river basin programs in importance as a vehicle for creating administrative regionalism in the Plains is the role of the co-operative movement. In spite of the attacks upon it, the movement is of the essence of private enterprise and stands as a bulwark against the forces of antidemocracy. It serves as a balance wheel in the affairs of state. On the one hand, co-operatives represent an organization of private individuals into a private business organization so as to offer competition and social direction to the power of corporate business. On the other hand, since it is separate and independent of government but a democratic device in its own right, it is a bar against excessive government control and regulation. The co-operative movement can do many things, as a democratic organization, for the welfare of society that the government would otherwise be forced to do.

384

The co-operative movement, therefore, is that middle road between state or corporate capitalism on the one hand, which in its extreme instances can manifest itself as a kind of Fascism or Nazism, and socialism on the other hand, which in its extreme forms becomes a kind of militant communism. The middle-of-the-road aspect of the co-operative movement is so significant that it undoubtedly will become an increasingly greater force in the economic lives of the American people.

A second function of the co-operative is that specific one of acting as a business organization. In this case it is an attempt to unite a group of private individuals into a private business enterprise. In contrast with the corporation, it is not organized for profit but for rendering services to its members at cost. In addition, it is a thoroughly democratic device. In contrast with the corporation, it operates on the principle of one-man–one-vote, regardless of the number of shares held by a member. The corporation operates on the principle of one-vote–one-share, making it possible to concentrate the control in the hands of a few individuals, at least an effective minority. It is for this reason that the co-operative is a democratic economic device that operates for the welfare of the community.

For these reasons the co-operative always carries with it the need for education. It has always used a portion of its patronage refunds for an educational program among its members. The co-operative is not, therefore, solely a business agency. It has the task of educating its membership to the nature of the problems facing the community. It cannot long tolerate discrimination of any type in matters of economics, race, religion, or any other sphere of activity. Bound by the principle of one-man–one-vote, it must operate in the interest of the welfare of all.

For these reasons the co-operative movement is especially well-suited for aiding in the solution of the problems that prevail in the Great Plains. The region, far from markets and with little control over price-making forces, cannot afford to pay the profit that usually goes outside the region. The residents must husband their earnings to have a level of living approximating parity with that found in other regions. Since there are periods when income is so low that profit-making enterprises can no longer make profit, such businesses discontinue their operations. This leaves the people of the region without services. The co-operative, if it has set aside the necessary reserves, will continue to operate under such conditions. It may be forced to curtail its services drastically, but it can continue to operate. Its membership, the people who would otherwise be without services, are the ones who make the decisions regarding these matters.

Finally, because it is oriented towards the development of the community and the general welfare, and because it carries on an educational program, the co-operative offers an opportunity to overcome the minority group characteristics that prevail in the Plains. Through the co-operative movement the residents of the region have an effective means to accomplish a measure of social solidarity that can become the "voice of the Plains." It represents the beginnings of creating a majority group, a focal point about which the several minorities can resolve some of their frustrations and fuse themselves into a working whole. In addition, the resulting controls remain in the hands of the residents of the region.

To function effectively in modern society, the local co-operatives have federated themselves and have organized regional co-operatives on a commodity basis. This phase of the movement started in the decade of the twenties. By this means the farmer co-operatives sought to achieve an orderly marketing of commodities and attempted to break the monopoly control exercised by corporations.

By means of such regional co-operatives, the agriculturalists of the Plains have obtained a measure of control over marketing and price conditions that affected their welfare. This was especially true for wheat, cotton, gasoline and oil, hardware, and groceries, and in a limited way for livestock and livestock products.

Another task of the region is to accumulate the capital necessary to build industry and processing plants and to finance enterprises of a varied type. Here, too, the co-operative can play a significant role. It is a means of accumulating capital to operate a business. Each member must purchase a share or accumulate it through his patronage refund. By democratic vote this investment may be modified and redirected, always on the basis of one-man–one-vote.

To help build the businesses and aid the members, the co-operatives have established credit unions and insurances of various types, including fire, health, and hospital insurances. More recently they have also entered the field of life insurance which gives the co-operatives an accumulated savings account, a portion of which can be wisely invested in business ventures within the region. Thus the co-operatives, through their various activities, can and do function as a constructive agency to build the region out of the small savings of many people. For the Plains, it is the National Farmers' Co-operative and Educational Union, along with its state organizations, its locals, and its regional co-operatives that is investing in the welfare of the region.

The federal government has helped to build agriculture in the nation and in the Great Plains by giving assistance to the co-operatives. The Federal Land Bank and the Farm Credit Administration operate as co-operatives. They function through their locals which are co-operatives owned and operated by the local shareholders—the Local National Farm Loan Association or the Local Production Credit Association. The original capital for these organizations was provided by the taxpayers and the private credit agencies that feared to risk investment in the agriculture of the region when times were difficult. At present the farmers and ranchers own the major share of the capital stock in these agencies, and this has added security and responsibility, as well as democracy, to the entire credit structure of the Plains and the nation.

It is apparent, then, that the co-operative movement has brought credit, production services, and consumption services to the agricultural people of the nation and the Great Plains. Through the co-operatives, people have a measure of control over the price and quality of produce they sell and buy. The movement has grown to the stage where it is now a practical instrument in building democracy and regionalism.

OTHER PROGRAMS TO BUILD THE REGION

There are other programs that are making their contribution to the building of the Plains. They are largely in agriculture, with the co-operation and sponsorship of the federal government and its agencies. In this way, the people of the entire nation are contributing to the building of the Plains. If

387

these programs were to function in the framework of administrative regionalism, their benefits would be much enhanced and still more constructive. Others of these programs are supported by the residents of the locality and region exclusively.

A mere enumeration of these services and agencies must suffice, but that does not decrease their significance. Among them are the Soil Conservation Service and its state and local variants, the Production and Marketing Administration and its local associations, the Farm Credit Administration and its locals, the Federal Land Bank and its locals, the Bank for Co-operatives and its locals, the Reclamation Service and its local projects, the State and local Water Conservation Boards and projects, the Rural Electrification Service and its local co-operatives, the Farm and Home Administration and its local associations, and the various emergency programs that have assisted in the mitigation of drought and relief needs.

It is significant that these agency services are largely confined to agriculture. There are few such services in the field of business and industry and in the sphere of industrial resource development. The gas and the oil of the region and the precious metals have been drained out of the region without any particular benefit to the people of the region. Here, too, is a need for repayment and rehabilitation. But first the businessmen and industrialists of the region must learn to know the land in which they live—the land in which they are a minority and which they have exploited and helped to keep in a minority status.

To incorporate the Main Street businessmen, the professional persons, and the industrialists into a Great Plains majority, along with the farmer and the rancher, will not be an easy task. To look for constructive leadership from these urban people at this time is expecting too much. But they must be educated and nursed along for a time, until they are finally ready to make their full and necessary contributions.

The agriculturalists of the Plains cannot afford to allow the Main Streeters to continue to go in their minority ways. The task ahead is to establish communication between them and the agriculturalists. Ignorance concerning the problems of the region and the tools to solve them is no longer an excuse for waiting to solve the problems of the region.

That the Great Plains are able and should someday function as a region is clear. Whether they will acquire administrative regionalism and be a truly self-respecting part of the nation is now the issue. The Plains can achieve their rightful regional status if the minorities can be joined together by the vehicle of administrative regionalism, and if the region, by the same device, can ward off all past forms of exploitation.

An experiment in administrative regionalism for the Plains would serve to create a model that could eventually be emulated by Greater New York, Greater Chicago, and other regions of the nation. By means of administrative regionalism, matters of international concern—in this case Mexico, Canada, and the United States at least—could be handled.

The only question that remains is whether there is the will on the part of the people in the region and in the nation to do these things now.

Bibliographical Notes

CHAPTER I—

The Great Plains in National and Global Perspective

THE CANADIAN PLAINS: Jean Burnett, *Next-Year Country* (Toronto, University of Toronto Press, 1951), provides an economic and social treatment of the Plains of Canada; Alfred Leroy Burt, *A Short History of Canada for Americans* (Minneapolis, University of Minnesota Press, 1942), gives a brief history of the Canadian Plains in Chapters 8, 9, and 11.

THE GREAT PLAINS IN THE UNITED STATES: R. S. Kifer and H. L. Stewart, *Farming Hazards in the Drought Area*, W.P.A. Research Monograph XVI (Washington, U.S. Government Printing Office, 1938); Carl F. Kraenzel, Watson Thomson, and Glenn H. Craig, *The Northern Plains in a World of Change* (Canada, Gregory-Cartwright, Ltd., 1942); C. Warren Thornthwaite, "The Climates of the Earth," *The Geographical Review*, Vol. XXIII, No. 3 (July, 1933), 433–40, map is attached.

SEMIARID AREAS OF MEXICO: Nathan L. Whetten, *Rural Mexico* (Chicago, University of Chicago Press, 1948), gives a survey of Mexico from the standpoint of semiaridity and aridity in Chapter 1.

CHAPTER II—

The Climate of the Great Plains

CLIMATE IN THE GREAT PLAINS: *Atlas of American Agriculture* (Washington, U.S. Department of Agriculture, 1936), 6–9, 13–15, 22–23, 26–29, with maps and charts on precipitation and temperature; Alvin T. Burrows, "The Chinook Winds," *Yearbook of the Department of Agriculture* (1901), 555–66; J. Sullivan Gibson and Douglas C. Ridgley, *Climate of the Earth* (Chicago, A. J. Nystrom and Co., 1937), 28–29, 40–41, chart; Willard D. Johnson, "The High Plains and Their Utilization," *United States Geological Survey, 21st Annual Report*, Vol. IV (1900), 457–79, 660–62, 678; J. B. Kincer, "The Climate of the Great Plains and Their Utilization," *Annals of the Association of American Geographers,* Vol. XIII (June, 1923), 67–80; C. Warren Thornthwaite, "Climate and Settlement in the Great Plains," *Yearbook of the Department of Agriculture* (1941), 177–87; Harry E. Weakly, "A Tree-Ring Record of Precipitation in Western Nebraska," *Journal of Forestry,* Vol. XLI, No. 11 (Nov., 1943), 816–19; George F. Will, *Tree Ring Studies in North Dakota,* North Dakota State College Agricultural and Experimental Station *Bulletin No. 338* (April, 1946).

CHAPTER III—

The Soils, Plants, and Animals Native to the Plains

GENERAL ECOLOGY OF THE GREAT PLAINS: Johnson, "The High Plains and Their Utilization," *United States Geological Survey, 21st Annual Report,* Vol. IV (1900),612–52; Walter Prescott Webb, *The Great Plains* (Boston, Ginn and Co., 1931), 10–11, 35–36, 41–44, 52ff., 54–57, 58–60, 62–64, 66, 115–26, 209, 253, 492–94; *The Western Range,* 74 Cong., 2 sess., *Sen. Doc. 199.*

ANIMAL LIFE IN THE GREAT PLAINS: W. C. Allee, *et al., Principles of Animal Ecology* (Philadelphia, W. B. Saunders, 1949) presents pertinent information in Chapters 30 and 33, pp. 466–76, 656ff., and 110, 209, 277–78, 330, 338, 468, 470, 650, 685, 686, 697; V. Baily, *Biological Survey of North Dakota,* United States Department of Agriculture, Bureau of Biological Survey *Bulletin No. 49* (1926), 19–31, 156–60; Frederic E. Clements and Victor E. Shelford, *Bio-Ecology* (New York, John Wiley and Sons, 1939), Chapter VIII; Lee R. Dice, *The Biotic Provinces of North America* (Ann Arbor, University of Michigan Press, 1943) gives a delineation of biotic provinces of North America; J. Frank Dobie, "The Magic of Don Coyote," *Southwest Review,* Vol. XXXIII, No. 3 (Summer, 1948), 247; Arthur Skogman Einarsen, *The Pronghorn Antelope and Its Management* (Washington, Wildlife Management Institute, 1948); W. J. Hamilton, *American Mammals* (New York, McGraw-Hill, 1939), 71–74, 77–83, 83ff., 135–37, 335–36, 411–14, 416, and Chapters IV, XIII; R. Hesse, W. C. Allee and Karl P. Schmidt, *Ecological Animal Geography* (New York, John Wiley and Sons, 1937), 23–24, 443–69; N. Hollister, *A Systematic Account of the Prairie-Dogs,* U.S. Department of Agriculture, Bureau of Biological Survey, *North American Fauna Bulletin No. 40* (1916); William T. Hornady, *The Extermination of the American Bison, Report* of the United States National Museum (1887); D. C. Lantz, "The Relation of Coyotes to Stockraising in the West," U.S. Department of Agriculture *Farmer's Bulletin No. 266* (1905); C. Hart Merriam, "The Prairie-Dog of the Great Plains," *Yearbook of the Department of Agriculture* (1901), 257–70; E. W. Nelson, *The Rabbits of North America,* U. S. Department of Agriculture, Bureau of Biological Survey, *North American Fauna Bulletin No. 29* (1909);

T. S. Palmer, *Jack-Rabbits of the United States*, U. S. Department of Agriculture, Bureau of Biological Survey *Bulletin No. 8* (1897); C. V. Terrell, "Echoes of the Old West, Texas Buffalo Hunt: 1876," *Southwest Review*, Vol. XXXIII, No. 3 (Summer, 1948), 233-37.

VEGETATION IN THE GREAT PLAINS: *Atlas of American Agriculture* has a section on natural vegetation, especially pp. 4-5; Charles E. Kellogg, *Development and Significance of the Great Soil Groups of the United States*, U.S. Department of Agriculture *Misc. Publications No. 229* (April, 1936), 29ff. especially; C. F. Marbut, "Soils of the Great Plains," *Annals of the Association of American Geographers*, Vol. XIII (June, 1923), 42-66, is still a standard and classic classification of the major soil areas of the Plains; H. L. Shantz, "The Natural Vegetation of the Great Plains Region," *Annals of the Association of American Geographers*, Vol. XIII (June, 1923), 81-107; *Yearbook of the Department of Agriculture* (1938), 948, 958, 970-72; James Thorp, B. H. Williams, and W. I. Watkins, "Soil Zones of the Great Plains—Kansas to Canada," *Soil Science Society of America Proceedings*, Vol. XIII (1948), 438-45; John E. Weaver and Frederic E. Clements, *Plant Ecology* (New York, McGraw-Hill, 1929), 212-55, 350-77, 400-16, 458-68.

CHAPTERS IV & V—

An Old and Forbidding Land; Plains History Immediately Following Louisiana Purchase

HISTORICAL BACKGROUND OF THE PLAINS AREA: Charles A. and Mary R. Beard, *The Rise of American Civilization* (New edition, New York, Macmillan, 1935), 87; Ray A. Billington, *Westward Expansion* (New York, Macmillan, 1949), 58, 423-25, 427-28, 436, 459, especially; Lt. J. Henry Carleton, *The Prairie Logbooks, Dragoon Campaigns to the Pawnee Villages in 1844 and to the Rocky Mountains in 1845*, ed. by Louis Pelzer (Chicago, Caxton Club, 1943), 9, especially for remark by Pelzer; Hiram Martin Chittenden, *The American Fur Trade of the Far West* (New ed., New York, Press of the Pioneers, Inc., 1935, 2 vols.) I, Chap. 2, pp. 38-39, 48; II, 547-48, 565-74; Bernard De Voto, *The Year of Decision: 1846* (Boston, Little, Brown, and Co., 1943) contains much information of background nature for the latter part of the period dealt with in these two chapters; *Encyclopedia Americana* (1940), XV, 610; XXIV, 122, 281; LeRoy R. Hafen and Carl C. Rister, *Western America* (2nd. ed., New York, Prentice-Hall, Inc., 1950), 4-17, 17-20, 25-26, 34, 41, 42, 43-44, 45-46, 58, 149-51, 153-54, 155, 156-57, 185-88, 190, 211, 212-13, 216-17, 217-21, 221-22, 225, and Chapters 4, 5, 12, 13, 15, 16; F. L. Paxson, *History of the American Frontier* (New York, Houghton Mifflin Co., 1924), 304, 331; J. W. Powell, *Lands of the Arid Region* (Washington, U.S. Government Printing Office, 1879), is the report of the geologist in charge of the U.S. Geographical and Geological Survey of the Rocky

Mountain region upon the lands of the arid region of the United States; Frederick Jackson Turner, *The Significance of Sections in American History* (New York, Henry Holt, 1932), especially the second essay; Stanley Vestal, *Kit Carson, the Happy Warrior of the Old West* (New York, Houghton Mifflin Co.; Cambridge, Riverside Press, 1928); Webb, *The Great Plains,* 99–111, 115, 146–47, 156–57, and Chapters 1, 4.

THE SOUTHERN PLAINS: R. L. Duffus, *The Santa Fé Trail* (New York, Longmans, Green, 1930), 7–15, 19–20, 21–22, 26–28, 55, 61ff., 65–66, and Chapters, 5, 7, 12; Leah Carter Johnston, *San Antonio* (San Antonio, Naylor Press, 1947), 1, 3ff., 4, 5, 6ff.

THE MISSOURI RIVER: Bernard De Voto, *Across the Wide Missouri* (New York, Houghton Mifflin Co., 1947), 239–40, 372, 387, and Chapter 10; Stanley Vestal, *The Missouri* (New York, Farrar & Rinehart, Inc., 1945), 61, 67.

THE NORTHERN PLAINS: Struthers Burt, *Powder River, Let 'er Buck* (New York, Farrar & Rinehart Inc., 1938), 25–26, 53–54, 62, and Chapters 5, 6; W. J. Ghent, *The Road to Oregon* (New York, Tudor, 1934), 11; Bruce Nelson, *Land of the Dacotahs* (Minneapolis, University of Minnesota Press, 1946), 35–37, 78, 110; *South Dakota Legislative Manual* (Pierre, State Publishing Co., 1941), 350ff.; Catherine M. White (ed.), *David Thompson's Journals Relating to Montana and Adjacent Regions, 1808–1817* (Missoula, Montana State University Press, 1950), xxxiii, xxxviff., xliff.

CHAPTER VI—
The Adapted Ways of the Plains Indian and the Texans

HISTORICAL BACKGROUND OF ADAPTATION IN THE PLAINS: De Voto, *Across the Wide Missouri,* 42–43; Paxson, *History of the American Frontier,* 515; Webb, *The Great Plains,* 52, 68, 90–94, 95–98, 114–26, 160–79, 387, 425–26, 426ff.

ADAPTATION OF THE PLAINS INDIANS: Carleton, *The Prairie Logbooks,* 56–152; Nelson, *The Land of the Dacotahs, Chapters* 2, 14, and pp. 37–39; Clark Wissler, *The American Indian* (New York, Oxford University Press, 1922), contains a map in Chapter 2 showing the location of the Plains tribes; Clark Wissler, *North American Indians of the Plains* (New York, American Museum of Natural History, 1927).

THE CONQUEST OF THE PLAINS INDIANS: George Catlin, *North American Indians* (Edinburgh, John Grant, 1926); Hafen and Rister, *Western America,* Chapter 28 and especially their bibliography, 495–96; Nelson, *Land of the Dacotahs;* Paxson, *History of the American Frontier,* 425–26, 485–93 especially, and Chapter 53; Standing Bear, *My People, The Sioux* (New York, Houghton Mifflin Co., 1928); Wissler, *The American Indian;* Wissler, *North American Indians of the Plains.*

LAND POLICY IN THE PLAINS: B. H. Hibbard, *A History of Public*

Land Policies (New York, Macmillan, 1924), Chapter 28 and pp. 565–67; Elword Mead, *Irrigation Institutions* (New York, Macmillan, 1903), 15; B. Youngblood and A. B. Cox, *An Economic Survey of a Typical Ranching Area,* Texas Agricultural and Experimental Station *Bulletin No. 297* (n.d.), 123, 126.

CHAPTER VII—

"The American Desert," A Land to Cross

THE CONQUEST OF THE PLAINS: Billington, *Westward Expansion,* 351, 452, 524, 528, 529–31, 537, 539, 543, 579–80, 591–92, 595–96, 636, 638–40, 646–48; De Voto, *The Year of Decision,* Chapters 4, 5, 13, and pp. 40, 159–63, 233–44, 249–50, 252, 254–55, 465–66; Hafen and Rister, *Western America* (1941), Chapters 15, 17, 20, 22, and pp. 239–42, 243–44, 249–50, 252, 256–57, 294–96, 327–28, 330–37, 372, 374, 375, 479, 480–81, 484–86, 551–52, 562; Paxson, *The History of the American Frontier,* Chapter 52, and pp. 426, 430, 452, 460, 469–71, 548; W. B. Hennessy, *History of North Dakota* (Bismarck, *Bismarck Tribune,* 1910), 203.

THE SANTA FÉ TRAIL: Duffus, *The Santa Fé Trail,* gives an account of the Santa Fé Trail and the Mexican War in Chapters 13, 14, and on pp. 67–84, 204ff.; Josiah Gregg, *Commerce of the Prairies* (New York, H. G. Langley, 1844, 2 vols.); also vols. XIX and XX of *Early Western Travels,* ed. by Reuben Gold Thwaites (Cleveland, Arthur H. Clark Co., 1905); also ed. by Max L. Moorhead (Norman, University of Oklahoma Press, 1954).

THE MISSOURI RIVER ROUTE: Eleanor Banks, *Wandersong* (Caldwell, Idaho, Caxton Printers, Ltd., 1950), contains a description in Chapter 10, of early life at Fort Benton, Montana; "Steamboat Arrivals at Fort Benton, Montana, and Vicinity," *Historical Society of Montana Publications,* Vol. III (1900), 351–54; James Stuart, "Adventures on the Upper Missouri," *Historical Society of Montana Publications,* Vol. I (1876), 80–89, 82, and 23; Vestal, *The Missouri,* Chapter 10, and pp. 18–33, 106–107, 112, 114.

THE OREGON TRAIL AND THE NORTHWEST: Ghent, *The Road to Oregon,* 86, 91, 162, 163, 164–73, 241–46; Joseph Kinsey Howard, *Strange Empire, A Narrative of the Northwest* (New York, William Morrow and Co., 1952); Robert Stuart, *On the Oregon Trail,* ed. by Kenneth A. Spaulding (Norman, University of Oklahoma Press, 1953).

CHAPTER VIII—

The Adapted Ways of the Early Cattlemen

THE RANGE CATTLE INDUSTRY: Ramon F. Adams, *Western Words: A Dictionary of the Range, Cow Camp, and Trail* (Norman, University of Oklahoma Press, 1946); *Annual Report of the United States Commissioner of Agriculture* (1870), 303–309; E. E. Dale, *The Range*

Cattle Industry (Norman, University of Oklahoma Press, 1930); Bernard De Voto, "The West against Itself," *Harper's* Magazine, Vol. XCCIV, No. 1160 (Jan., 1947), 1–13, and also other articles in later issues; Duffus, *The Santa Fé Trail*, 258–59, 261–62; Horace Greeley, *Overland Journey* (New York, C. M. Saxton, Barber & Co.; San Francisco, H. H. Bancroft & Co., 1860), 72, 115; Hafen and Rister, *Western America*, 545–47, 548–53, 553–54; Henry Latham, *Trans-Missouri Stock Raising: The Pasture Lands of North America* (Omaha, Daily Herald Steam Printing House, 1871), 41; E. S. Osgood, *The Day of the Cattleman* (Minneapolis, University of Minnesota Press, 1929), Chapters 1, 2, 5, 7, and pp. 11–14, 18, 21–23, 30, 37–39, 42–43, 46–48, 97–98, 105, 113, 117ff., 216; Mont Saunderson, *Western Stock Ranching* (Minneapolis, University of Minnesota Press, 1950), 3–11, 26–32, 40–55, 61–65, 68–79, 82–108, 152–53, 186–208, and Chapter 8; Granville Stuart, *Forty Years on the Frontier* (Glendale, California, Arthur H. Clark, 1925), 95, 195; Webb, *The Great Plains*, 216ff., 217, 217–218, 219, 219–20, 223, 224, 227, 227–28, 239–40.

IN THE NORTHERN PLAINS: Joseph Kinsey Howard, *Montana: High, Wide, and Handsome* (New Haven, Yale University Press, 1943), Chapters 11, 16–19; Vance Johnson, *Heaven's Tableland* (New York, Farrar, Straus, 1947), Chapters 3, 4, 5–10, and pp. 24–29, 31–38, 44; Nelson, *The Land of the Dacotahs*, Chapters 11, 13, 16, and pp. 190, 196; Paul C. Phillips, *The Journals and Letters of Major John Owen* (Historical Society of Montana *Publications,* 1925).

CHAPTER IX—
Sheepman Days and Ways

THE PLAINS SHEEP INDUSTRY: Banks, *Wandersong,* gives a biographical treatment of the origin of the sheep industry in the Judith Basin country of Montana in Chapters 17, 18, 19, 21, 22; Hughie Call, *The Golden Fleece* (New York, Houghton Mifflin Co., 1942), is a novel about sheep in Montana; Hafen and Rister, *Western America* (1941), 554–58; D. A. Spencer, *et al.,* "The Sheep Industry," *Yearbook of the Department of Agriculture* (1923), 234–62; Saunderson, *Western Stock Ranching,* 10–11, 28–29, 31, 46, 51, 58–61, 65–68, 79–83, 84–108, 151–52, 186–208; Charles Wayland Towne and Edward Norris Wentworth, *Shepherd's Empire* (Norman, University of Oklahoma Press, 1945); E. N. Wentworth, *America's Sheep Trails* (Ames, Iowa State College Press, 1948), 24–26, 27, 36, 75–78, 112, 113, 113–15, 165, 309, 330, 399–400.

CHAPTER X—
Hesitation along the Ninety-eighth Meridian

PIONEER LIFE ON THE PLAINS: Billington, *Westward Expansion,* 469, 643–50, 711–12, 713–14; Everett Dick, *The Sod-House Frontier,*

1854–1890 (New York, D. Appleton-Century Co., 1937), Chapters 5, 8, 18, and pp. 57–59, 112, 289–90, 291–94, 294–95, 296; E. E. Edwards, "American Agriculture—The First 300 Years," *Yearbook of the Department of Agriculture* (1940), 229–30; Hafen and Rister, *Western America* (1941), 360, 566; Hennessy, "History of North Dakota," 133, 199–201; Howard, *Montana: High, Wide, and Handsome,* 172; John Ise, *Sod and Stubble* (New York, Barnes and Noble, Inc., 1940), Chapters 10, 18, and pp. 7–9, 11; John Ise (ed.), *Sod House Days: Letters from a Homesteader, 1877–78* (New York, Columbia University Press, 1937), 27–28, 34, 40, 43, 49, 91–92, 234–39; Osgood, *The Day of the Cattleman,* 211; Paxson, *History of the American Frontier,* Chapters 52, 56, 57, and pp. 430, 449, 477, 494–96, 514–15, 544–48; *Report of the United States Department of Agriculture* (1871), 497; *South Dakota State Legislative Manual* (Pierre, State Publishing Co., 1944), 352, 353; Webb, *The Great Plains,* Chapter 8, and pp. 279, 290–95, 341, 348, with reference to barbed wire, 296–318, and to the windmill, 336–41.

CHAPTERS XI & XII—

The Settlement Era; The Testing of Civilization

THE PLAINS PROBLEM: *The Future of the Great Plains,* The President's Report, 75 Cong., 1 sess., *House Doc. 144; Fergus County Democrat* (March 22, 1910), 1; *Fergus County Argus* (March 18, 1910), 1; William Allen White, *The Autobiography of William Allen White* (New York, Macmillan, 1946), Chapters 26–43 inclusive.

SETTLEMENT AND HOMESTEADING IN THE PLAINS: Dick, *The Sod-House Frontier,* Chapters 15, 31, 32, and pp. 185, 221, 230, 316; Hennessy, *History of North Dakota,* 211, 213–17, 222–26; David J. Hilger, "Montana Homestead Days" (Unpublished article, Montana Historical Society, 1936).

AGRICULTURAL PRODUCTION IN THE PLAINS: E. R. Ahrendes and R. J. Doll, *Alternate Use of Excess Wheat Acreage,* Kansas State Experiment Station *Agriculture Economics Bulletin No. 39* (December, 1949); R. S. Dunbar, "Agricultural Adjustments in Eastern Colorado in the Eighteen-Nineties," *Agricultural History,* Vol. XVIII (Jan., 1944), 41–52; Edwards, "American Agriculture—The First 300 Years," *Yearbook of the Department of Agriculture* (1940), 227–28; Howard, *Montana,* Chapters 17, 18, 19, and pp. 168, 169–70, 172–73, 177, 207, 228, 230; Johnson, *Heaven's Tableland,* Chapters 8, 10, 11–12, 13–22, and pp. 45–56, 56–57, 58ff., 75ff., 82–83, 84, 119–20, 214, 229–30; *Journal of Farm Economics,* Vol. XXXII, No. 3 (August, 1950) includes several articles indicative of an understanding of flexibility; Nelson, *Land of the Dacotahs,* Chapters 16, 17 and pp. 244, 257, 309–10, 310–11, 312–13; Eric Thane, *High Border Country* (New York, Duell, Sloan, and Pearce Inc., 1942), Chapters 9, 10; Robert F. Wallace,

"Western Farm Areas in Two World Wars," *Journal of Farm Economics*, Vol. XXXII, No. 1 (Feb., 1950), 82–94.

LIVESTOCK PRODUCTION IN THE PLAINS: F. E. Mollin, *The Stockman's View of the Range Question* (American National Livestock Association, 1938); *The Western Range*, 7–60; *Shifts in the Trade in Western Slaughter Livestock*, Agricultural Experiment Station of Western States *Information Bulletin No. 14* (1950).

CHAPTER XIII—

Unsuitable Governmental Institutions for the Plains

STATE GOVERNMENT: F. G. Bates and Oliver P. Field, *State Government* (New York, Harper and Brothers, 1938), 439ff., 450–51; Paxson, *History of the American Frontier*, Chapter 58, and pp. 561–63; F. N. Thorpe, "Recent Constitution Making in the United States," *Annals of the American Academy*, Vol. II (Sept., 1891), 145ff., 191ff., 153, 153–58.

GOVERNMENT IN THE NORTHERN PLAINS: N. C. Abbott, *Montana Government* (Billings, Gazette Printing Co., 1937), 150; R. M. Black, *History of the State [North Dakota] Constitutional Convention of 1889, Collections* of the State Historical Society of North Dakota, Vol. III (1910), 111ff.; Hennessy, *History of North Dakota*, 251–52; J. D. Hicks, *Constitutions of the Northwest States*, University of Nebraska *Studies*, Vol. XXIII (1923), 90ff., 141, 21n.; Howard, *Montana*, Chapter 12; Clement A. Lounsberry, *Early History of North Dakota* (Washington, D. C., Liberty Press, 1919), 392–98, 399, 413–14, 466; *Proceedings and Debates of the Montana Constitutional Convention, 1889* (Helena, State Publishing Co., 1921), 12–14, 47, 52, 61, 63, 75, 89, 137–39, 148–49, 156–58, 218, 246, 253–54, 376–77, 472–78, 496–512, 520–29, 533, 551–71, 509–92, 628–29, 675–79, 675–81, 803ff., 820–54, 865, 878, 895–901; *Proceedings and Debates at the First Constitutional Convention of North Dakota, 1889* (Bismarck, State Printers and Binders, 1889), 85–98, 128–33, 410–12, 610–14, and the preface; *South Dakota Manual* (Pierre, State Publishing Co., 1941), 36; H. H. Swain, *Montana Civics* (New York, Scott, Foresman, and Co., 1903), 70; E. A. Willson, *Migration of Farm Families to Town* (Bozeman, Montana Agricultural Experiment Station, 1949).

KANSAS SCHOOL QUESTION: *Closed Schools in Kansas*, Kansas Legislative Council *Public Bulletin No. 113* (Sept., 1942); *School District Reorganization*, Kansas Legislative Council *Public Bulletin No. 130* (Oct., 1944).

GOVERNMENT IN THE SOUTHERN PLAINS: Edwin C. McReynolds, *Oklahoma: A History of the Sooner State* (Norman, University of Oklahoma Press, 1954).

JAMES BRADLEY THAYER: *Who Was Who in America* (New York, A. N. Marquis, 1943), 1226; J. B. Thayer, *A Western Journey with Mr. Emerson* (Boston, Little, Brown and Co., 1884), is the record Thayer kept of his experiences when he took a trip across the Plains to California with a small party including Ralph Waldo Emerson, and a study of this treatise warrants the conclusion that Thayer did not understand the semiarid Plains and the arid West.

CHAPTER XIV—
Unadapted Land and Finance Policies for the Plains

THE LAND QUESTION: Charles Abrams, *Revolution in Land* (New York, Harper and Brothers, 1939), Chapters 1 and 2 have a discussion of problems related to land ownership and control; *Constitution of the State of Montana, Article XVII; Proceedings and Debates of the Montana Constitutional Convention,* 75–89, 218, 520–29, 590–92, 628–29, 878; B. J. Hibbard, *A History of the Public Land Policies* (New York, MacMillan, 1924), 409; Hicks, *Constitutions of the Northwest States,* 76ff.; Paxson, *History of the American Frontier,* 220–24, 381–91, 417–21, 480; *Proceedings and Debates of the First Constitutional Convention of North Dakota,* 159–82, 288–93, 512–30, 604–10; *Improving Farm and Ranch Tenure in the Northern Great Plains,* Montana Agricultural and Experiment Station *Bulletin No. 436* (July, 1946), is a report of the Tenure Committee of the Northern Great Plains Agricultural Advisory Council; M. H. Saunderson and N. W. Monte, *Grazing Districts in Montana: Their Purpose and Organization Procedure,* Montana Agricultural and Experiment Station *Bulletin No. 326* (Sept., 1936); Thorpe, "Recent Constitution Making in the United States," *Annals of the American Academy,* Vol. II (Sept., 1891), 172ff., especially 178ff.; *Report of the Special Committee on Farm Tenancy,* 75 Cong., 1 sess., *House Doc. 149,* especially p. 20, R. B. Tootell, *Grazing Districts,* Montana Extension Service *Bulletin No. 127* (Dec., 1932).

PUBLIC DOMAIN: *Federal Rural Lands* (Washington, U.S. Department of Agriculture, 1947); De Voto, "The West against Itself," *Harper's* Magazine, Vol. XCCIV, No. 1160 (Jan., 1947), 1ff.; Bernard De Voto, "The Easy Chair," *Harper's* Magazine, Vol. XCCIV, No. 1165 (June, 1947), 543ff.; *Padlocking Western Lands, Public Domain Issue* (Washington, D. C., U.S. Chamber of Commerce Natural Resources Department, 1943), is the testimony of Frederick P. Champ and J. Elmer Brock at Senate hearings in Jackson, Wyoming.

CREDIT AND FINANCING: Harold Hoffsommer, *et al., The Social and Economic Significance of Land Tenure in the Southwestern States* (Chapel Hill, University of North Carolina Press, 1950), gives a discussion of sources of credit in the Southwestern states in Chapter 8, and for related legal and other aspects see Chapters 7, 9, 10; *Farm Credit Administration* (American Institute of Banking, 1943), gives in Chapter 13 a definition of credit, especially as related to agriculture, and shows on pp. 21–42, 422–23 the difference between industrial and commercial credit needs on the one hand and agricultural credit needs on the other, on pp. 34–40, 58–96, 420–21 the sources of agricultural credit, in Chapter 14 and on p. 425 the development of Federal Land Banks, in Chapter 14 a description of German and Danish credit associations, and on pp. 164–67, 208–209, 216–19, 369, 458–68, and in Chapter 15 a description of variable and flexible repayment plans; *Encyclopedia of Social Sciences* (1937), IV, gives a historical analysis of credit and its control; Abrams, *Revolution in Land*, Chapters 1–4, 7 for a broader treatment of credit and its origin, especially in relation to land; William G. Murray, *Agricultural Credit* (Ames, Iowa State College Press, 1941), gives a description of agricultural credit agencies in Chapters 14–28; Earl S. Sparks, *History and Theory of Agricultural Credit in the United States* (New York, Thomas Y. Crowell Co., 1932), presents a historical treatment of rural credit facilities and their urban origin prior to the Farm Loan Act of 1916 in Chapter 1–6 and 19–24 inclusive, and from the data presented in these chapters and in the introduction it is clear that the American rural credit experience prior to the Farm Loan Act was also linked up with the urban and commercial sources of the humid East and Midwest; James B. Morman, *Principles of Rural Credit* (New York, Macmillan, 1915); Donald D. Horton, "Adaptations of the Farm Capital Structure to Uncertainty," *Journal of Farm Economics*, Vol. XXXI, No. 1 (Feb., 1949), 76–100, points out the contrast of credit uncertainty in the Great Plains to that in the Midwest; I. W. Duggan and U. Battles, *Financing the Farm Business* (New York, John Wiley and Sons, Inc., 1950), 136–39; F. F. Hill, "Flexibile Repayment Plans for Farm Mortgage Loans," *Journal of Farm Economics*, Vol. XX, No. 1 (Feb., 1938), 257–81, defines the problem of variable and flexible repayment plans clearly, but his conclusions are not very sympathetic toward such plans; I. S. Falk and Wilbur J. Cohn, "Social Security for Farm People," *Journal of Farm Economics*, Vol. XXVIII, No. 1 (Feb., 1946), 84–96; Kenneth H. Parsons, "Social Security for Farm People," *Journal of Farm Economics*, Vol. XXVIII, No. 1 (Feb., 1946), 97–109; Daniel K. Andrews, "Old-Age Security for the American Farm Population," *Journal of Farm Economics*, Vol. XXVII, No. 3 (Aug., 1945), 634–49.

CHAPTER XV—
Sutland and Yonland Communities

COUNTY-WIDE SOCIAL ORGANIZATION: Frank Alexander and Carl F. Kraenzel, *Social Organization in Sweet Grass County, Montana,* Montana State Experiment Station *Bulletin No. 490* (Nov., 1953); Frank Alexander and Lowry Nelson, *Rural Social Organization in Goodhue County, Minnesota,* University of Minnesota Agriculture Experiment Station *Bulletin No. 401* (1949).

POPULATION DISTRIBUTION IN THE PLAINS: A. H. Anderson, "Space as a Social Cost," *Journal of Agricultural Economics*, Vol. XXXII, No.

3 (August, 1950), 417, 419, points out that the ten Plains states, including the humid and mountainous areas, had 11,960 villages, towns, and cities, and of this total, 9,841 had less than 500 people, and 4,504 had 50 or fewer people; W. D. Brogan, *The American Character* (New York, Alfred A. Knopf, 1944), 14–15, 115.

TEXAS: *The Texas Almanac, 1947–48 (Dallas Morning News)*, is the only state almanac in publication, and Texas is the only state that was granted the privilege of administering its own land policy separate from the policy followed by the federal government; John Gunther, *Inside U.S.A.* (New York, Harper and Brothers, 1946) brings out the originality and peculiarity of Texas in Chapters 47, 48, 49.

URBAN POPULATION IN THE PLAINS: Gunther, *Inside U.S.A.*, 159–63, 832–35, 835–38 for a description of the cities of the Plains, and for a description of cities outside the region but projecting their influence into the region see pp. 214–15, 220–26, 251, 255, 259, 266–67, 271ff., 296, 318, 337, 343, 345–48, 350–56, 358, 536, 827–32, 877–79.

RURAL LIFE AND COMMUNITY ORGANIZATION: C. C. Taylor, *et al., Rural Life in the United States* (New York, Alfred A. Knopf., Inc., 1949), 386–87, 403–404, and Chapters 19, 20, 22, 23; A. H. Anderson and Glen V. Vergeront, *Rural Communities and Organization*, North Dakota Agricultural Experiment Station *Bulletin No. 351* (1948); A. H. Anderson, "Space as a Social Cost," *Journal of Farm Economics,* Vol. XXXII, No. 3 (August, 1950).

CHAPTER XVI—
The Hinterland Role of the Great Plains

PLAINS ECONOMICS: Wendell Berge, *Economic Freedom for the West* (Lincoln, University of Nebraska Press, 1946), 98, 99–106, 109; A. W. Currie, "Freight Rates and Regionalism," *Canadian Journal of Economics and Political Science*, Vol. XIV, No. 4 (Nov., 1948), 427ff.; Joseph Kinsey Howard, "Montana Twins in Trouble," *Harper's* Magazine, Vol. CLXXXIX, No. 1132 (Sept., 1944), 334ff.; Vernon H. Jensen, *Heritage of Conflict* (Ithaca, Cornell University Press, 1950), 17, and Chapters 16, 17; A. G. Mezerik, *The Revolt of the South and West* (New York, Duell, Sloan and Pearce, Inc., 1946); A. G. Mezerik, *Pursuit of Plenty* (New York, Harper and Brothers, 1950); Rufus Terral, *The Missouri Valley* (New Haven, Yale University Press, 1947), Chapter 17, p. 165; Walter Prescott Webb, *Divided We Stand* (New York, Farrar and Rinehart, 1937); "The Basing Points: The Great Muddle," *Fortune* Magazine, Vol. XXXVIII, No. 3 (Sept., 1948).

THE MOUNTAIN STATES: M. E. Garnsey, *Americas New Frontier— The Mountain West* (New York, Alfred A. Knopf., Inc., 1950), Chapter 13, pp. 181–89; M. E. Garnsey, "The Future of the Mountain States," *Harper's* Magazine, Vol. CXCI, No. 1145 (Oct., 1945), 329ff.

URBAN AREAS: Gunther, *Inside U.S.A.*, gives a reasonable account of cities in the Plains; Mildred L. Hartsough, "The Development of the Twin Cities as a Metropolitan Market" (Graduate thesis, University of Minnesota, 1924), gives an analysis of influence of the Twin Cities of Minnesota on the Northern Great Plains; Howard, *Strange Empire*, gives a historical treatment of the influence of the Twin Cities on the Red River Valley of the North and the Plains area immediately to the west; R. I. McKenzie, *The Metropolitan Community* (New York, McGraw-Hill, 1933).

FEDERAL AGENCIES: *Regional Factors in National Planning*, National Resources Planning Committee *Report* (December, 1935), 206ff.

PLAINS AGRICULTURE: Taylor, *Rural Life in the United States*, Chapters 20, 21, 23; W. D. Goodsell, *et al.*, "Typical Family-Operated Farms, 1930–45, Adjustments, Costs and Returns," U.S. Department of Agriculture, Bureau of Agricultural Economics *Bulletin No. 55* (April, 1946) W. D. Goodsell, "Farm Costs and Returns, 1945–47," U.S. Department of Agriculture, Bureau of Agricultural Economics *Bulletin No. 70* (Sept., 1948); H. R. Hockmuth and W. D. Goodsell, "Commercial Family-Operator Cattle Ranches, Intermountain Region, 1930–47, Organization, Costs, and Returns," U.S. Department of Agriculture, Bureau of Agricultural Economics, *Bulletin No. 71* (Nov., 1948); Hoffsommer, *The Economic and Social Significance of Land Tenure;* Glenn T. Trewartha, "Some Regional Characteristics of American Farmsteads," *Annals of the Association of American Geographers*, Vol. XXXVIII, No. 3 (Sept., 1948), 469ff.

CHAPTER XVII—
The Minority Status of the People

KANSAS: White, *Autobiography*, gives an analysis of the Populist movement in the Plains in Chapters 26–28, 30–33, 40–42, and Chapter 40 contains a reproduction of White's famous editorial "What Is Wrong with Kansas?"; Debs Myers, "The Exciting Story of Kansas," *Holiday* Magazine, Vol.IX, No. 6 (June, 1951), 52–63.

AGRARIAN REVOLT: John D. Barnhart, "Rainfall and the Populist Party in Nebraska," *American Political Science Review*, Vol. XIX, No. 3 (Aug., 1925), 527–40, has a discussion of farmer revolts; De Voto, "The West against Itself," *Harper's* Magazine, Vol. XCCIV, No. 1160 (Jan., 1947); Paul F. Sharp, *The Agrarian Revolt in Western Canada* (Minneapolis, University of Minnesota Press, 1948); Nelson, *The Land of the Dacotahs*, Chapters 17, 18; F. B. Tracy, "Rise and Doom of the Populist Party," *Forum*, Vol. XVI (Oct., 1893), 240–50.

MINORITY BEHAVIOR: John Dollard, *et al.*, *Frustration and Aggression* (New Haven, Yale University Press, 1939); Alfred R. Lindesmith and Anselm L. Strauss, *Social Psychology* (New York, Dryden Press, Inc., 1949), 318–25, and on p. 307 the statement, "One is driven to the conclusion that experimental psychology has not yet made a major contribution to these problems. . . . The studies of aggression, displacement, repression and projection serve no more than to give crude confirmation of phenomena that do not require it"; Karl A. Menninger, *Man against Himself* (New York, Harcourt Brace, 1938), gives an analysis of the pathological aspects associated with frustration; Kimball Young, *Social Psychology* (New York, D. Appleton-Century Co., 1944), 45, 70–74, 84–85, 130, 146, 340, 379–83; Gunnar Myrdal, *et al.*, *An American Dilemma* (New York, Harper and Brothers, 1944, 2 vols.), II, 50, and all of that section gives an analysis of the meaning of minority; R. A. Schermerhorn, *These Our People—Minorities in American Culture* (New York, D. C. Heath & Co., 1949) gives a discussion of minorities in Chapters 1, 18, 19, 20, 21, 22; Saul Rosensweig, "Types of Reaction to Frustration," *Journal of Abnormal and Social Psychology*, Vol. XXIX, No. 3 (Oct.–Dec., 1934), 298–300, is an early attempt at classification of frustrations; J. McVicker Hunt, *Personality and the Behavior Disorders*, (New York, Ronald Press, 1944, 2 vols.), I, Chapters 8–14 inclusive; F. J. Brown and J. S. Roucek, *One America: Our Racial and National Minorities*, (New York, Prentice–Hall, 1945), Chapters 1, 17, 20, 22; Hu Shih, *et al.*, *Studies in Political Science and Sociology* (Philadelphia, University of Pennsylvania Press, 1941), 148–49, and sections by Louis Wirth, Arthur Cole, and Carl Kelsey; W. L. Warner and Leo Srole, *The Social Systems of American Ethnic Groups* (New Haven, Yale University Press, 1945), Chapter 1.

CITY DOMINATION: Garnsey, *America's New Frontier;* Mezerick, *The Pursuit of Plenty*, gives a discussion of big city domination of the West.

WATER RESOURCES: Gunther, *Inside U.S.A.*, 147, 188, 215, 245, has a discussion of the Missouri River Basin development issue; *Bozeman* [Montana] *Chronicle*, March 20, 1949, p. 2; *Great Falls* [Montana] *Tribune* March 20, 1949, p. 8; *Great Falls Tribune*, March 26, 1949, p. 1; *Great Falls Tribune*, March 31, 1949, p. 2; *Great Falls Tribune*, April 5, 1949, p. 4; *New York Tribune*, March 20, 1949, p. 65; *Ten Rivers in America's Future* (Report of the President's Water Resources Policy Commission, 1950, Vol. II), 295, 825–26, and for Texas water-use law see 318–19, 323–44, 325–26; *Water Resources Law* (Report of the President's Water Resources Policy Commission, 1950, Vol. III), 746–47, 761–62, 765.

CHAPTER XVIII—

Traditional Minorities in the Plains

THE PLAINS INDIAN MINORITY: Gunther, *Inside U.S.A.*, 325, 869–75, 891–95, and Chapter 50 distinguishes between the Five Civilized Tribes, moved from the humid East and relocated in the humid part of Oklahoma, and the Plains Indians, called "blanket Indians" in Oklahoma, living in the Plains part of that state as they do in many of the other Plains states; Wissler, *North American Indians of the Plains;* Brown and Roucek, *One America,* (bibliography), 662–63 and Chapters 3, 18; Nelson, *The Land of the Dacotahs,* Chapters 14, 15; E. E. Edwards and Wayne D. Resmussen, *A Bibliography on the Agriculture of the American Indian,* U.S. Department of Agriculture *Misc. Publication 447* (1942), 35–36, 64ff.; William C. MacLeod, *The American Indian Frontier* (New York, Alfred A. Knopf, 1928), especially Part 5; Clarence S. Runyan, "Utilization of Indian Land on the Crow Reservation" (Unpublished thesis, Montana State College Library, 1939), 41.

THE SPANISH-AMERICAN MINORITY: Sigurd Johansen, "Rural Social Organization in a Spanish American Culture Area," *University of New Mexico Publications in Social Sciences and Philosophy, No. 1* (1948); Merrill Jensen, *Regionalism in America* (Madison, University of Wisconsin Press, 1951), Chapter 5; Brown and Roucek, *One America,* 346ff.; H. E. Bolton, "Defensive Spanish Expansion and the Significance of the Borderlands," *The Trans-Mississippi West* (Boulder, University of Colorado Publications, 1930); Johnston, *San Antonio;* Duffus, *The Santa Fé Trail;* Gunther, *Inside U.S.A.,* 822–24, 832–35, 887, 891–95, and Chapter 51; D. Leonard and C. P. Loomis, *Culture of a Contemporary Rural Community, El Cerrito, New Mexico,* U. S. Department of Agriculture, Bureau of Agricultural Economics *Rural Life Studies* (Nov. 1, 1941); Taylor, *Rural Life,* 399, 400, 409–10; *Migratory Labor in American Agriculture,* Report of the President's Commission on Migratory Labor (1951), Chapter 4; *Migrant Labor, A Human Problem,* U. S. Department of Agriculture, Report of Federal Interagency Committee on Migrant Labor (March, 1947); S. C. Menefee and John N. Webb, *Mexican Migratory Workers of South Texas,* W.P.A. Research Division *Bulletin* (1941).

THE NEGRO MINORITY: Gunnar, *et al., The American Dilemma,* II; Brown and Roucek, *One America,* Chapters 19, 29, and bibliography, pp. 664–65, 690; Gunther, *Inside U.S.A.,* 825, 834, 865–68, 876, 881–82, 897; Hoffsommer, *et al., The Social and Economic Significance of Land Tenure,* 50, 378–84; Taylor, *Rural Life,* 354–55, 358–59; Harold Hoffsommer, *Land Tenure in the Southwestern States,* University of Arkansas College of Agriculture *Bulletin No. 482* (1948), 16–17, 30–31; T. J. Woofter, *Landlord and Tenant on the Cotton Plantation,* W.P.A. *Research Monograph V* (1936), 31.

NATIONALITY MINORITIES: Brown and Roucek, *One America,* Chapters 5, 6, 7, 8; Earl H. Bell, *The Culture of a Contemporary Rural Community, Sublette, Kansas,* U.S. Department of Agriculture, Bureau of Agricultural Economics *Rural Life Studies* (Sept., 1942); R. W. Lynch, *Czech Farmers in Oklahoma,* Oklahoma Agricultural and Mechanical College, *Bulletin No. 13* Vol. XXXIX (June, 1942); Vera Lysenko, *Men in Sheepskin Coats* (Toronto, Ryerson Press, 1947), is a study of Ukranian settlements in the Plains of Canada; Paul De Kruif, *Hunger Fighters* (New York, Harcourt Brace, 1928), Chapter

1 is a portrayal of the Mennonites; Gunther, *Inside U.S.A.*, 259–60, 824; Samuel Lubell, "Who Votes Isolationist and Why," *Harper's Magazine*, Vol. CCII, No. 1211 (April, 1951), refers to the voting record of nationality groups in selected areas of the Plains and other areas of the nation; Howard, *Montana*, Chapters 16–18; Nelson, *The Land of the Dacotahs, Chapters* 17, 18; Johnson, *Heaven's Tableland*, Chapters 6–17; John Steinbeck, *The Grapes of Wrath* (New York, Viking Press, 1939); F. D. Cronin and H. W. Beers, *Areas of Intense Drought Distress, 1930–36*, W.P.A. Division of Social Research, Series V, No. 1.

CHAPTER XIX
Minorities in the Rural Areas

ECONOMICS OF RANCHING: W. H. Nicholls, *Imperfect Competition within Agricultural Industries* (Ames, Iowa State College Press, 1941), 334, gives a discussion of the financial influence on ranching; Nelson, *The Land of the Dacotahs*, Chapter 12; *Large-Scale Organization in the Food Industries*, 76 Cong., 3 sess., Senate Temporary National Economic Committee, *Monograph No. 35* (1940), is an investigation of concentration of economic power—see especially pp. 16–17, 20, 107–16; Sparks, *History and Theory of Agricultural Credit*, Chapter 25, gives a history of the sources of credit for the stockman; H. L. Purdy, M. L. Lindahl, and W. A. Carter, *Corporate Concentration and Public Policy* (New York, Prentice Hall, 1946), gives a discussion in Chapter 23 of concentration and control in and by the meat industry, especially pp. 497–504, 505–509; Harry W. Laidler, *Concentration of Control in American Industry* (New York, Thomas Y. Crowell, 1931), 197, 213; A. J. Heidenheimer, "Behind the Meat Strike," *The New Republic*, Vol. CXXIV, No. 26 (June 25, 1951), 18–21; F. E. Mollin, *If and When It Rains* (American National Livestock Association) depicts the stockman's view of the range question; Hochmuth and Goodsell, *Commercial Family-Operated Cattle Ranches;* Wentworth, *America's Sheep Trails*, Chapter 22, is on the public domain and deals with one of the most obviously controversial issues in historical scholarship, but it is well worth a reading.

SUBSIDY AND RELIEF: Purdy, Lindahl, and Carter, *Corporate Concentration and Public Policy*, 501; Nicholls, *Imperfect Competition within Agricultural Industries*, Chapter 4, especially pp. 69–71, 78, 178–79; *Large-Scale Organization in the Food Industries*, 19–24.

CONFLICT WITHIN THE RANCHING INDUSTRY: Wayne Gard, "Rivals for Grass," *Southwest Review*, Vol. XXXIII, No. 3 (Summer, 1948), 266–73 for a discussion of the conflict between sheepmen and cattlemen; Burt, *Powder River*, Chapter 45; *Padlocking Western Lands;* De Voto, "The West against Itself," *Harper's* Magazine, Vol. XCCIV, No. 1160 (Jan., 1947).

PROBLEMS OF DRY-LAND FARMING: Nicholls, *Imperfect Compe-*

tition within Agricultural Industries, 75–76, 77; W. E. Blackmore, *Farm to Retail Margins for White Flour and White Bread,* U.S. Department of Agriculture, Bureau of Agricultural Economics *Bulletin* (Dec., 1948); Laidler, *Concentration of Control in American Industry,* 221–43, and Chapter 20; Bob Faulds, "Dakota Points the Way," *The New Republic,* Vol. CXIX, No. 7 (Aug. 16, 1948), 9; Nelson, *The Land of the Dacotahs,* Chapters 17, 18; *Large-Scale Organization in the Food Industries,* Chapter 5, especially pp. 43–44; Goodsell, *et al., Typical Family-Operated Farms, 1940–45;* Goodsell, *et al., Farm Costs and Returns;* "Farmers Owning More of F.C.A.," *Co-ops in Action, News for Farmers Co-operatives* (Dec., 1948), 2.

IRRIGATION AND RECLAMATION: Michael W. Straus, "Take Reclamation off the Merry-Go-Round," *Reclamation Era,* Vol. XXXIII, No. 11 (Nov., 1947), 235, includes the statement, "And we might add that Congress did that [appropriate more money for reclamation than in any previous year] in the face of a lot of divided counsel from the West itself"; M. W. Straus, "Reclamation Revelations—1948–49," *Reclamation Era,* Vol. XXXIV, No. 12 (Dec., 1948), 223ff.; "Railroads and Irrigation," *Reclamation Era,* Vol. XXXIV, No. 7 (July, 1948), 140; William E. Warne, "Land Speculation," *Reclamation Era,* Vol. XXXIII, No. 8 (Aug., 1947), 176ff.; Remarks by Adolph J. Sabath, *Congressional Record Appendix,* Vol. XCII, Part 11, p. A2916, contains a statement by Secretary of the Interior Harold L. Ickes; "Ickes Challenged," *Business Week,* Dec. 2, 1944, p. 34; Purdy, Lindahl, and Carter, *Corporate Concentration and Public Policy,* Chapter 25, especially pp. 526–29; George W. Stocking and Myron W. Watkins, *Cartels in Action* (Twentieth Century Fund, 1946), Chapter 2; W. R. Nelson, "What Multiple Purpose Means," *Reclamation Era,* Vol. XXXIII, No. 7 (July, 1947), 145ff.; A statement by E. Polk, *New York Times,* Nov. 19, 1948, p. 22; Roy E. Huffman and D. C. Myrick, *Farm Organization and Production Requirements in Selected Irrigation Areas,* Montana Agricultural Experiment Station *Bulletin No. 453* (1948), gives information about the integration of irrigated and dry land and points out the high proportion of operators also using dry land in the farm or ranch unit, though this illustration may be distorted because the data were actually selected for another use; *Irrigation Agriculture in the West,* U.S. Department of Agriculture, *Misc. Publication No. 670,* (1948), 4–8; *Landownership Survey on Federal Reclamation Projects,* U.S. Department of Interior, Bureau of Reclamation *Bulletin* (1946); *H. H. Johnson,* "Forty-three Years on the Shoshone Project," *Reclamation Era,* Vol. XXXIII, No. 6 (June, 1947), 124ff.; P. L. Slagsvold, *Agriculture on the Huntley Project,* Montana Agricultural Experiment Station, *Bulletin No. 342* (1937); W. C. Brady, "Kansas Pioneers in Irrigation," *Reclamation Era,* Vol. XXXIV, No. 6 (June, 1948), 109ff.; W. C. McKain and H. O. Dahlke, *Turnover of Farm Operators, Vale and Owyhee Irrigation Projects,* U.S. Departmentment of Agriculture, Bureau of Agricultural Economics *Bulletin* (1946); William E. Warne, "Land Speculation," *Reclamation Era*, Vol. XXXIII, No. 8 (Aug., 1947), 176ff.; Garford L. Wilkinson, "The People," *Reclamation Era*, Vol. XXXIII, No. 4, (April, 1947), 73ff.

COMMODITY SPLIT: Nicholls, *Imperfect Competition within Agricultural Industries*, 76–81; *Large-Scale Organization in the Food Industries*, Chapter 6; E. H. Wiegand, "Agriculture and Food Processing in Oregon," *Reclamation Era*, Vol. XXXIV, No. 10 (Oct., 1948), 194–96.

SUGAR BEET INDUSTRY: Carl F. Kraenzel, "The Montana Sugar Beet Industry, with Special Emphasis upon the Agricultural Labor Phase" (Unpublished manuscript, Montana State College); *Migrant Labor—A Human Problem*.

COTTON INDUSTRY: Hoffsommer, *et al.*, *The Social and Economic Significance of Land Tenure*, Chapters 7, 10, and pp. 30–32, 34, 65, 78, 88–90, 96, 102–103, 378–84, 404–406, 432; Goodsell *et al.*, *Typical Family-Operated Farms, 1930–45*, 66–78; C. A. Bonnen and B. H. Thibedeaux, *A Description of the Agriculture and Type-of-Farming Areas of Texas*, Texas A. & M. Agricultural Experiment Station *Bulletin No. 544* (June, 1937), 74–83; E. L. Langsford, "Overall Adjustment in Southern Agriculture," *Journal of Farm Economics*, Vol. XXXII, No. 4, Part 2 (Nov., 1950), 773–76, and also see other articles on the cotton farming situation in this same issue.

SORGHUM DEVELOPMENT: Terral, *The Missouri Valley*, Chapter 9, and pp. 169–71.

FARM HOLIDAY ACTIVITIES AND THE ROLE OF AGRICULTURE IN POLITICS: J. Herbst, "Feet in the Grass Roots," *Scribner's*, Vol. XCIII, No. 1 (Jan., 1933), 46ff.; "The Corn Belt Cracks Down," *New Republic*, Vol. LXXVII, No. 990 (Nov. 22, 1933), 36; "Milo Reno and His Farmers," *New Republic*, Vol. LXXVII, No. 991 (Nov. 29, 1933), 63; T. N. Darling, "The Farmers Holiday," *New Outlook*, Vol. CLXI (Oct., 1932), 18; W. Gard, "The Farmers' Rebellion," *Nation*, Vol. CXXXV, No. 3505 (Sept. 7, 1932), 207; B. H. Hibbard, "The Farmers in Revolt," *Nation*, Vol. CXXXVII, No. 3568 (Nov. 22, 1933), 589; Samuel Lubell, "Who Really Elected Truman," *Saturday Evening Post*, Vol. CCXXI, No. 30 (Jan. 22, 1949), 15ff.; "Why Farmers Swung to Truman," *U.S. News and World Report*, Vol. XXV, No. 21 (Nov. 19, 1948), 23–24; "Congress Goes to the Country," *Hoard's Dairyman*, (Sept., 10, 1948), 658.

CHAPTER XX—

Minorities in the Towns

CITIES PERIPHERAL TO THE PLAINS: Gunther, *Inside U.S.A.*, 214–15, 220–26, 251, 259, 266–67, 271ff., 296, 318, 337, 343, 345–48, 350–56, 358, 536, 827–32, 877–79.

EXPLOITATION OF PLAINS RESOURCES: Gunther, *Inside U.S.A.*,

147-48, 151-54, 185, 214-15, 220-21, 223-26, 244-47, 259, 266-67, 814-15, 842, 880; Garnsey, *America's New Frontier*, Chapter 15.

RAILROADS IN THE PLAINS: Nelson, *The Land of the Dacotahs*, Chapter 8, especially references to Alec McKenzie, pp. 127-36, and the description of Jim Hill's vision in Chapter 16; Garnsey, *America's New Frontier*, Chapter 13 deals with freight rates and railroad policy; Mezerik, *The Pursuit of Plenty*, 70-71, and Chapter 9; Terral, *The Missouri Valley*, Chapter 16.

OIL AND NATURAL GAS: Mezerik, *The Pursuit of Plenty*, Chapters 5 and 55, pp. 72-75; Terral, *The Missouri Valley*, Chapter 18; *Great Falls* [Montana] *Tribune*, July 21, 1951, p. 6, for the role of oil in the Williston Basin; *Time* Magazine, Vol. LVIII, No. 5, (July 30, 1951), 76; *Bozeman* [Montana] *Chronicle*, February 23, 1951, p. 1; Harold L. Ickes' column, *New Republic*, Vol. CXXV, No. 8 (Aug. 20, 1951), 17, and in subsequent issues.

LANDOWNERSHIP IN THE PLAINS: R. R. Renne, *Montana Land Ownership*, Montana Agricultural Experiment Station *Bulletin No. 322* (1936); R. R. Renne, *Montana Farm Foreclosures*, Montana Agricultural Experiment Station *Bulletin No. 368* (1939); G. H. Lambrecht and L. S. Wallin, *Farm Tenancy in Box Butte, Nebraska*, Agriculture Experiment Station of Nebraska *Bulletin No. 336* (1942), especially pp. 27-28; M. L. Wilson, *Dry Farming in the North Central Montana Triangle*, Montana Extension Service and Agriculture Experiment Station *Bulletin No. 66* (June, 1923), 27-29.

PLAINS LABOR SUPPLY: Alston P. Waring and Clinton S. Golden, *Soil and Steel* (New York, Harper and Brothers, 1947), Chapters 2, 7, 8, 9, 11, 12, and pp. 117-18; Gunther, *Inside U.S.A.*, 178-79, 234-35, 253ff., 831, 881; *The Program of the National Farmers Union*, 40th Annual Convention (1946), 15-17; *Truth about Subsidies* (National Farmers Union, 1944).

MEDICAL SERVICE IN THE PLAINS: Carl F. Kraenzel, *The Hospitals of Montana, Existing Facilities and Attendant Problems*, Montana Agricultural Experiment Station *Bulletin No. 438* (Oct., 1946); *The Hospitals of Montana, A Basis for a Co-ordinated Hospital-Health-Medical Care Program*, Montana Agricultural Experiment Station *Bulletin No. 456* (Jan., 1949); *Medical Care and Health Services for Farm Families of the Northern Great Plains*, Proceedings of the Subcommittee on Health of the Northern Great Plains Council, University of Nebraska (1945); *Medical Care and Health Services for Rural People* (Farm Foundation, 1944), 19-29, 82-85, 86-88, 153-169; Ross E. Thomas, "A.M.A. *vs.* Country Doctor," *New Republic*, Vol. 124, No. 7 (Feb., 12, 1951), 13; *Information Letters of the Co-operative Health Federation of America*, Vol. V, No. 1 (Jan.-Feb., 1951), 1; The Michael A. Shadid Collection in the University of Oklahoma Archives, Norman.

INDUSTRY COMMERCE AND AGRICULTURE IN THE PLAINS—THEIR INTERRELATIONSHIPS: Terral, *The Missouri Valley*, Chapter 17, pp.

165–66, 168; Gunther, *Inside U.S.A.*, 218 and Chapters 11, 12, 14, 15–17, 47–50; Garnsey, *America's New Frontier*, Chapters 10–14; James E. Murray and Dewey Anderson, "The Force of Social Organizations in Regional Development," *Social Forces*, Vol. XXV, No. 4 (May, 1947), 367–73; O. B. Jesness, "What the Farmer Thinks of Business," an address given at the Association of National Advertisers, New York, Nov. 18, 1943; Stuart Chase, *Democracy under Pressure* (Twentieth Century Fund, 1945), Chapters 4, 5, 6; John Ise, *Economics* (New York, Harper and Brothers, 1946), 247; Eugene Holman, "The Public Responsibilities of Big Business," an address given at the Economic Club of Detroit, Nov. 8, 1948; J. H. Kolb and E. de S. Brunner, *A Study of Rural Society* (New York, Houghton Mifflin, 1946), Chapters 13, 14, 15, especially p. 321.

MISSOURI RIVER BASIN DEVELOPMENT: Straus, "Reclamation Revelations," 223ff.; Gunther, *Inside U.S.A.*, Chapter 12, Terral, *The Missouri Valley*, Chapters 19–21; Nelson, *Land of the Dacotahs*, Chapter 19; *Great Falls Tribune*, March 20, 1949, p. 8; *New York Times*, March 20, 1949.

CO-OPERATIVES: F. H. Hollands, *Montana Farmers Co-operatives, 1941–46*, Montana Agricultural Experiment Station *Bulletin No. 449* (1948); *The Competition of Co-operatives with Other Forms of Business Enterprise, First Interim Report* from the Committee on Small Business of the House of Representatives pursuant of H. Res. 64 (April 9, 1946), 9ff.; James West, *Plainville, U.S.A.*, (New York, Columbia University Press, 1945), 51–53; Gunther, *Inside U.S.A.*, 32, 95, 178–81, 226, 242–44, 336, 881; Taylor, *et al., Rural Life in the United States*, 390–91, 295; *The Program of the National Farmers Union*, 18–19; The various publications and bulletins of the National Tax Equality League; W. L. Bradley, "The Way of Co-op Taxes," *Farm Policy Forum* July, 1948, p. 70ff.; "Racket on Main Street," *Co-op Grain Quarterly*, Vol. IX, No. 2 (June, 1951), 3–5; A speech by the Hon. Daniel A. Reed of New York, *Congressional Record*, 82 Cong., 1 sess. (March 20, 1951); Faulds, "Dakota Points the Way," *New Republic*, Vol. CXIX, No. 7 (Aug. 16, 1948), 9–10; H. Wallace, "Report on the Farmers," *New Republic*, Vol. CXVI, No. 26 (June 30, 1947), 12ff.; Nelson, *Land of the Dacotahs*, 309–13.

CHAPTER XXI—

The Need to Adapt or Get Out

WATER RESOURCES: Bernard Frank and Anthony Netboy, *Water, Land and People* (New York, Alfred A. Knopf, 1950) gives a discussion of many of the problems related to a balance between natural resources and the way of living in the United States; Arthur Maass, *Muddy Waters: The Army Engineers and the Nation's Rivers* (Cambridge, Harvard University Press, 1951) gives an analysis of the army engineer role in the matter of building structures to control floods and permit navigation on the nation's rivers.

GEOGRAPHIC DETERMINISM: *Encyclopedia of Social Sciences*, V, 110–14 gives a partial inventory of geographic determinism—see also VI, 621–24; Friederick Ratzel, *Anthropogeographie* (2nd ed., Stuttgart, 1899–1912, 2 vols.); Henry Thomas Buckle, *History of Civilization in England* (London, 1857–61, 2 vols.); (New York, D. Appleton-Century Co., 1874) and the revised new edition with introduction by J. M. Robertson (New York, Dutton, 1951); Ellen Churchill Semple, *Influences of Geographic Environment* (New York, Henry Holt, 1911); Ellsworth Huntington, *Civilization and Climate* (New Haven, Yale University Press, 1915).

CULTURAL DETERMINISM: *Encyclopedia of Social Sciences*, V, 110–14, VI, 621–29; St. Augustine's *City of God* is an example of determinism and absolutism in religion; E. Durkheim, *Les règles de la méthode sociologique* (Paris, 1895); E. Durkheim, *De la division du travail social* (Paris, 1893); Max Weber, *Gesammelte Aufsätze zur Wissenschaftslehre* (Tübingen, 1922); Emroy S. Bogardus, *The Development of Social Thought* (New York, Longman's, Green and Co. 1947), gives a general treatment of the many points of view concerning cultural determinism.

CHAPTER XXII—

New Ways for Water, Land, and Plow

IRRIGATION AND WATER PROBLEMS: *Appleton's Annual Encyclopedia and the Register of Important Events for the Year 1889* (New series, New York, Appleton and Co., 1891), XIV, 452ff., on irrigation; R. G. Dunbar, "Water Conflict and Controls in Colorado," *Agricultural History*, Vol. XXII (July, 1948), 127ff., 180–68; R. G. Dunbar, *Colorado and Its People*, ed. by LeRoy R. Hafen (New York, Lewis Historical Publishing Co., 1948), 122, 445–46; *Preliminary Examinations of Reservoir Sites in Wyoming and Colorado*, 55 Cong., 2 sess. *House Doc. No. 144*, Serial No. 3666; Wells A. Hutchins, *Selected Problems in the Law of Water Rights in the West*, U. S. Department of Agriculture *Misc. Publication No. 418* (1942), Chapter 2, pp. 38–109; C. S. Kinney, *Law of Irrigation and Water Rights and the Arid Region Doctrine of Appropriation of Waters* (San Francisco, Bender-Moss, 1912, 4 vols.), I, Sections 455, 487, 507, 587, 600, 611, 622; *Missouri River Basin*, 78 Cong., 2 sess., *Senate Doc. No. 191*, 23, 28, 54, 69, 89, 106; J. W. Powell, "Report on the Lands of the Arid Region of the United States," *U.S. Geographical and Geological Survey of the Rocky Mountains* (1879), 3; William E. Smythe, *The Conquest of Arid America* (New York, Macmillan, 1911), 261ff.

DRY-LAND FARMING AND OTHER ASPECTS OF PLAINS AGRICULTURE: J. L. Coulter, *Bonanza Farms and the One Crop System of Agriculture*, *Collections* of the State [North Dakota] Historical Society, (1910), III, 569ff., 577ff.; Dick, *Sod-House Frontier*, 291, 300ff.; Edwards, "American Agriculture," *Yearbook of the Department of Agriculture* (1940), 230–31; Roy E. Huffman, *Production Costs on Selected Dry-land Grain Farms*, Montana State Agricultural Experiment Station, *Circular No. 52* (Sept., 1949), gives costs and expense items for typical farms; R. S. Kifer, "Influence of Technical Progress on Agricultural Production," *Yearbook of the Department of Agriculture* (1940), 513, 515; *Montana Agricultural Statistics* (Montana Department of Agriculture, Labor, and Statistics, 1950), III; Osgood, *Day of the Cattleman*, 195; Webb, *The Great Plains*, 357–66, 412, 414, 423, 424–25, 431–52, 434, 435, 437, 442–49; John A. Widtsoe, *Dry-Farming—A System of Agriculture* (New York, Macmillan, 1911), 228, 230, 413; James L. Krall, *A Blade Drill for Seeding Trashy Fallow*, Montana Agricultural Experiment Station *Circular No. 194* (June, 1951).

CHAPTER XXIII—

Specially Suitable Institutions

DRY-LAND FARMING: Alfred Atkinson and J. B. Nelson, *Dry Farming Investigations in Montana*, Montana Agricultural Experiment Station *Bulletin No. 83* (Jan., 1911); Alfred Atkinson and N. C. Donaldson, *Dry Farm Grain Tests in Montana*, Montana Agricultural Experiment Station *Bulletin No. 110* (Feb., 1916); E. Lloyd Barber and Philip J. Thair, "Institutional Methods of Meeting Weather Uncertainty in the Great Plains," *Journal of Farm Economics*, Vol. XXXII No. 3 (Aug., 1950), 391ff.; L. J. Briggs, and J. O. Beltz, *Dry-Farming in Relation to Rainfall and Evaporation*, U. S. Department of Agriculture, Bureau of Plant Industry *Bulletin No. 188* (Nov., 1910); H. W. Campbell, *Campbell's 1907 Soil Culture Manual* (Lincoln, Campbell Soil Culture, Inc., 1909); E. C. Chilcott, *A Study of Cultivation Methods and Crop Rotations for the Great Plains Area*, U. S. Department of Agriculture, Bureau of Plant Industry *Bulletin No. 187* (Nov., 1910), 8–9, 18–20, 67–72; John S. Cole and O. R. Mathews, "Tillage," *Yearbook of the Department of Agriculture* (1938), 324, 327; Coulter, *Bonanza Farms*, 571–72, 607; De Kruif, *Hunger Fighters*, Chapter 2; Howard, *Montana*, 172–73; Roy I. Kimmel, "Unit Reorganization Program for the Southern Great Plains," *Journal of Farm Economics*, Vol. XXII, No. 1 (Feb., 1940), 264–70; O. R. Mathews and John S. Cole, "Special Dry Farming Problems," *Yearbook of the Department of Agriculture* (1938), 683–87; Nelson, *Land of the Dacotahs*, 244 and Chapter 16; *Report of the Secretary of Agriculture for 1906*, 40–41; Rainer Schickele, "Farmers' Adaptations to Income Uncertainty," *Journal of Farm Economics*, Vol. XXXII, No. 3, (Aug., 1950), 356ff.; J. M. Stephens, *et al.*, *Report of the Northern Great Plains Field Station for the 10-Year Period, 1913–22 Inclusive*, U. S. Department of Agriculture *Bulletin No. 1301* (March, 1925); F. B. Linfield and Alfred Atkinson, *Dry Farming in Montana*, Montana Agricultural Experiment Station *Bulletin No. 63* (1907); J. A. Widtsoe, *Dry-Farming* (New York, Macmillan, 1920), 74–78, 194, 355–58, 361–63, 366, 368, 374–77, 563, and Chapter 17.

EARLIER TECHNIQUES OF DRY-LAND FARMING: Alfred Atkinson and J. B. Nelson, *Dry Farming Investigations in Montana*, Montana Agricultural Experiment Station *Bulletin No. 74* (Dec., 1908); Alfred Atkinson, *et al.*, *Dry Farm Moisture Studies*, Montana Agricultural Experiment Station *Bulletin No. 87* (Sept., 1911); Alfred Atkinson, *et al.*, *Dry Farm Crop Rotations and Cultural Methods*, Montana Agricultural Experiment Station *Bulletin No. 116* (Mar., 1917); Wilson, *Dry Farming in the North Central Montana Triangle*.

MORE RECENT TECHNIQUES OF DRY-LAND FARMING: Torlief S. Aasheim, *The Effect of Tillage Methods on Soil and Moisture Conservation and on Yield and Quality of Spring Wheat in the Plains Area of Northern Montana*, Montana Agricultural Experiment Station *Bulletin No. 468* (Dec. 1949); S. Barnes, *Soil Moisture and Crop Production under Dry Land Conditions in Western Canada*, Dominion of Canada Department of Agriculture, *Publication No. 595* (Jan., 1938.)

GRAIN ADAPTATIONS: De Kruif, *Hunger Fighters*, Chapter 1 contains information about Carleton; Edward Jerome Dies, *Titans of the Soil* (Chapel Hill, University of North Carolina Press, 1949), 141–49, information on Carleton; "Fifty Years of Work as Agricultural Explorer and Plant Breeder," *Transactions of the Iowa State Historical Society*, Vol. LXXIX (1944), 28ff., gives information on Hansen; N. E. Hansen, *Plant Introductions*, South Dakota Agricultural Experiment Station *Bulletin No. 224* (May, 1927).

FARM MECHANIZATION: Martin R. Cooper, Glen T. Barton, and Albert P. Brodell, *Progress of Farm Mechanization*, U. S. Department of Agriculture *Misc. Publication No. 630* (Oct., 1947); Sherman E. Johnson, "Technological Changes and the Future of Rural Life," *Journal of Farm Economics*, Vol. XXXII, No. 2 (May, 1950), 225–40; John C. Ellickson and John M. Brewster, "Technological Advance and the Structure of American Agriculture," *Journal of Farm Economics*, Vol. XXIX, No. 4 (Nov., 1947), 827–47; M. L. Wilson, *Big Teams in Montana*, Montana Extension Service *Bulletin No. 70* (April, 1925).

IRRIGATION AND RECLAMATION: Walter U. Fuhriman, "Federal Aid to Irrigation Development," *Journal of Farm Economics*, Vol. XXXI, No. 4, Part 2 (Nov., 1949), 965–75; Huffman and Myrick, *Farm Organization and Production Requirements; Irrigation Agriculture of the West*, 4–7, 8–11, 12–21, 39; H. E. Selby, "The Importance of Irrigation in the Economy of the West," *Journal of Farm Economics*, Vol. XXXI, No. 4, Part 2 (Nov., 1949), 955–64; Ray P. Teele, *The Economics of Land Reclamation in the United States* (London, A. W. Shaw & Co., Ltd. 1927); R. E. Ward and M. M.

Kelso, *Irrigation Farmers Reach out into the Dry Land,* Montana Agricultural Experiment Station *Bulletin No. 464* (Sept., 1949).

INTEGRATED LAND USE: Elco S. Greenshields and Stanley W. Voelker, *Integration of Irrigated and Dry Land Farming in the North Platte Valley in 1946,* (Washington, U.S. Department of Agriculture, 1947); Ned O. Thompson and Robert L. Berger, *From Dry-Land Farming to Irrigation* (Washington, U.S. Department of Agriculture, 1946).

AREA DIVERSIFICATION: E. A. Starch, "Type of Farming Modifications Needed in the Great Plains," *Journal of Farm Economics,* Vol. XXI, No. 1 (Feb., 1939), 117–20; J. L. Paschal and P. L. Slagsvold, "Irrigation Development and Area Adjustment in the Great Plains," *Journal of Farm Economics,* Vol. XXV, No. 2 (May, 1943), 433–44; Roy E. Huffman and J. L. Paschal, "Integrating the Use of Irrigated and Grazing Land in the Northern Plains," *Journal of Land and Public Utility Economics,* Vol. XVIII, No. 1 (Feb., 1942).

CREDIT REQUIREMENTS IN THE PLAINS: *Improving Farm and Ranch Tenure in the Northern Plains,* Montana Agricultural Experiment Station *Bulletin No. 436* (July, 1946), 23–27; I. W. Duggan and Ralph U. Battles, *Financing the Farm Business* (New York, Wiley and Sons, 1950), 139.

CHAPTER XXIV—

Keys for Survival

FARM INCOME AND FINANCING: Lloyd E. Barber, "Modifying the Federal Income Tax to Promote Greater Stability of Farm Income," *Journal of Farm Economics,* Vol. XXX, No. 2 (May, 1948), 331–39; Barber and Thair, "Institutional Methods of Meeting Weather Uncertainty," *Journal of Farm Economics,* Vol. XXXII, No. 3 (Aug., 1950), 401n., and pp. 391–410; Duggan and Battles, *Financing the Farm Business,* 139; H. G. Halcrow, "Actuarial Structure for Crop Insurance," *Journal of Farm Economics,* Vol .XXXI, No. 3 (May, 1949), 418–43; H. G. Halcrow and Roy E. Huffman, "Great Plains Agriculture and Brannan's Farm Program," *Journal of Farm Economics,* Vol. XXXI, No. 3 (Aug., 1949), 497–508; Carl P. Heisig, "Income Stability in High Risk Farming Areas," *Journal of Farm Economics,* Vol. XXVIII, No. 4 (Nov., 1946), 961–72; D. Gale Johnson, *Forward Prices for Agriculture* (Chicago, University of Chicago Press, 1947), Chapter 10; T. K. Pavlychenko and J. B. Harrington, "Root Development of Weeds and Crops in Competition under Dry Farming," *Scientific Agriculture,* Vol. XVI, No. 3 (Nov., 1935), 153–56; Rainer Schickele, "Farm Business Survival under Extreme Weather Risks," *Journal of Farm Economics,* Vol. XXXI, No. 4, Part 2 (Nov., 1949), 917–30, 931–43; Theodore W. Schultz, *Production and Welfare of Agriculture* (New York, Macmillan, 1950), Chapters 14, 15, and pp. 24,

141–45, 145–49, 175–80, 245–47; Theodore W. Schultz, *Agriculture in an Unstable Economy* (New York, McGraw-Hill, 1945), Chapters 8, 10, 11, 12; A. E. Seamans, *Recommended Practices for Soil Erosion,* Montana Agricultural Experiment Station *Circular No. 190* (July, 1948), 3; Starch, "Type of Farming Modifications," 114–17 and the rejoinder of E. C. Johnson, pp. 121–22; Layton S. Thompson, *Bulging Bins—Blessing or Menace,* a release of the Great Plains Tenure Committee of the Agriculture Committee of the National Planning Committee, jointly with the Department of Agriculture Economics and Rural Sociology, Montana Stage College, Sept., 1950.

MEDICAL CARE IN THE PLAINS: Frank G. Dickinson, "Fundamental Requirements of Insurance Applied to Voluntary Prepayment Medical Care Plans," *Journal of American Medical Association,* Vol. CXXXIII (Feb. 15, 1947), 483–84, 487; *Medical Care and Health Services for Rural People; Hearings on Hospital Construction Act,* 79 Cong., 1 sess., *Senate Bill 191;* Jon L. Indries, *Flynn of the Inland* (Sydney, Angus and Robertson, 1948); *Airdoctor, 14th Annual Report* of the Flying Doctors Service of Australia (Sept., 1950); Kraenzel, *The Hospitals of Montana: Existing Facilities;* Kraenzel, *The Hospitals of Montana: A Basis;* Frederick D. Mott and Milton I. Roemer, *Rural Health and Medical Care* (New York, McGraw-Hill, 1948), Chapters 8–16, 19–25, and p. 505; Joseph W. Mountain, *et al., Health Service Areas,* U.S. Public Health Services, Federal Security Agency *Bulletin No. 292* (1945); Mendel C. Sheps, "Saskatchewan Plans Health Services," *Canadian Journal of Public Health,* May, 1945; Bill Wolf, "Here Comes the Flying Ambulance," *Saturday Evening Post,* Vol. CCXXIV, No. 26 (Dec. 29, 1951).

CHAPTER XXV—
Growth of Regionalism in America

POLITICAL AND ADMINISTRATIVE REGIONALISM: Donald Davidson, "Political Economy of Regionalism," *American Review,* Vol. VI (Feb., 1936), 430–32; Donald Davidson, "Political Regionalism and Administrative Regionalism," *Annals of the Academy of American Political and Social Science* (1940), 138–43; James W. Fesler, "Federal Use of Administrative Areas," *Annals of the American Academy of Political and Social Science* (1940), 111–15; Robert H. Jackson, "The Supreme Court and Interstate Barriers," *Annals of the American Academy of Political and Social Science* (1940), 70–78; W. Kollmorgan, "Political Regionalism in the U.S., Factor Myth," *Social Forces,* Vol. XV, No. 1 (Oct., 1936), 111–22; Rodney L. Matt, "Uniform Legislation in the United States," *Annals of the American Academy of Political and Social Science* (1940), 79–92; Elwin A. Mauch, "Interregional Relations," *Annals of the American Academy of Political and Social Science* (1940), 124–29; William B. Munro, "Regional Government for Regional Problems," *Annals of the American Academy of Political and*

Social Science (1936), 124–28; William B. Munro, "The New Deal and a New Constitution," *Atlantic Monthly,* Vol. CLVI, No. 5 (Nov., 1935), 617–24; Murray and Anderson, "The Forces of Social Organization in Regional Development"; *Regional Factors in National Planning,* National Resources Committee *Report* (1935), Chapters 6, 7, and pp. 36–44; Howard W. Odum, *Southern Regions of the United States* (Chapel Hill, University of North Carolina Press, 1936), 235–61, gives a clear distinction between regionalism and sectionalism; Howard W. Odum and H. E. Moore, *American Regionalism* (New York, Henry Holt, 1938), Chapters 2, 5, 6, 7, 9, 10, 12–17, 25, and pp. 3–5, 9–10, 10–12, 12–14, 16, 18, 105, 110–12, 115–26, 143–50, 188–99, 202–207; Arthur Pound, "The U. S. Redrawn," *Review of Reviews, Vol.* XCIV (Oct., 1936), 28–31; C. Herman Pritchett, "Regional Authorities through Interstate Compact," *Social Forces,* Vol. XIV, No. 2 (Dec., 1935), 200–10; C. Herman Pritchett, "Tennessee Valley Authority as a Government Corporation," *Social Forces,* Vol. XVI, No. 1 (Oct., 1937), 120–30; Garland C. Routt, "Interstate Compacts and Administrative Co-operation," *Annals of American Academy of Political and Social Science* (1940), 93–102.

REGIONAL ECONOMY: Lucien Brocard, "Regional Economy and Economic Regionalism," *Annals of the American Academy of Political and Social Science* (1932), 81–92; Peter Drucker, "The Insecurity of Labor Unions," *Harper's* Magazine, Vol. 199, No. 1195 (Nov., 1949); Joseph P. Harris, "The Future of Grants-in-Aid," *Annals of the American Academy of Political and Social Science* (1940), 14–26; Fred Rogers Fairchild, *et al., Elementary Economics* (Revised edition, New York, Macmillan, 1935, 2 vols.), II, Chapter 27; A. T. Hadley, *Railroad Transportation: Its History and Its Laws* (New York, Putnam's 1885), justifies the existing pattern of railroad rate discrimination; Carl J. Friedrich, *Alfred Weber's Theory of the Location of Industries* (Chicago, University of Chicago Press, 1929), translates Weber's principles justifying the higher cost of the long haul; F. Eugene Milder, "Trade Barriers between States," *Annals of the American Academy of Political and Social Science* (1940), 54–61; M. V. Howard, *Authority in TVA Land* (Kansas City, Frank Glenn Publishing Co., 1948); Ellis F. Hartford, *Our Common Mooring* (Athens, University of Georgia Press, 1941); Joe S. Ransmeier, *The Tennessee Valley Authority* (Nashville, Vanderbilt Press, 1942).

THE URBAN REGION: "Building the Future City," *Annals of the American Academy of Political and Social Science* (1945); R. E. Dickinson, *City Region and Regionalism* (New York, Oxford University Press, 1947), Chapters 7, 9, and pp. 3, 4, 6, 105–107, 210, 249–53, 297, 297–98; William T. R. Fox and Annette Baker Fox, "Municipal Government and Special Purpose Authorities," *Annals of the American Academy of Political and Social Science* (1940), 176–84; Victor Jones, "Politics of Integration in Metropolitan Areas," *Annals of the American Academy of Political and Social Science* (1940), 161–

67; Victor Jones, "Government in the Future City," *Annals of the American Academy of Political and Social Science* (1945), 79–87; R. D. McKenzie, *The Metropolitan Community* (New York, McGraw-Hill, 1933); *Regional Survey of New York and Environs: The Regional Plan of New York and Its Environs* (1929, 2 vols.)I, 133; Charles P. Taft, *City Management: The Cincinnati Experiment* (New York, Farrar & Rinehart, 1933); John K. Wright, "Summary of Property Inventory of Greater New York," *Geographical Review*, Vol. XXVI (1936), 620–39; Lewis Mumford, *The Culture of Cities* (New York, Harcourt, Brace, and Company, 1938).

SECTIONALISM: Frederick Jackson Turner, "The Significance of the Section in American History," *Selected Readings in Economics*, comp. by C. J. Bullock (Boston, Ginn & Co., 1907).

LITERARY REGIONALISM: Melvin J. Vincent, "Regionalism and Fiction," *Social Forces*, Vol. XIV, No. 3 (March, 1936), 335–40.

CHAPTER XXVI—
A Practical Test of Regionalism in the Plains

REGIONAL GOVERNMENT: E. M. Barrows, "United Regions of America: A New American Nation," *New Outlook*, Vol. CLXI (May, 1933), 17; Berge, *Economic Freedom;* Lewis G. Burdette, "Regionalism, A Plan for Uniting the States More Effectively," *Forum*, Vol. LXXXIX, No. 3 (March, 1933), 136–41; Davidson, "Political Economy of Regionalism," *American Review*, Vol. VI (Feb., 1936), 424–25, 426, 429, 431–32; Davidson, "Political Regionalism and Administrative Regionalism," *Annals of the American Academy* (1940), 138–43; De Voto, "The West against Itself," *Harper's* Magazine, Vol. XCCIV, No. 1160 (Jan., 1947); G. Homer Durham, "Politics and Administration in Intergovernmental Relations," *Annals of the American Academy of Political and Social Science* (1940), 1–6; W. Y. Elliott, *The Need for Constitutional Reform* (New York, McGraw-Hill, 1935); Harris, "The Future of Federal Grants-in-Aid," 14–16; Howard, *Authority in TVA Land;* V. O. Key, "State Legislation Facilitative of Federal Action," *Annals of the American Academy of Political and Social Science* (1940), 7–13; 69 Cong., 1 sess., *House Doc.* 398 (Library of Congress Documents, *The United States—Formation of the Union*, 1927), 1066–67; W. Lissner, "Regulating the Mixed and Public Corporations," *American Journal of Economics and Sociology*, Vol. VIII, No. 9 (Jan., 1949), 144; Munro, "Regional Government for Regional Problems," *Annals of the American Academy* (1936), 123–32, 245; Munro, "The New Deal and a New Constitution," *Atlantic Monthly*, Vol. CLVI, No. 5 (Nov., 1935), 619; William B. Munro, "Do We Need Regional Government?" *Forum*, Vol. LXXIX, No. 1 (Jan., 1928), 108–12; *Regional Factors in National Planning*, 34ff.; Odum and Moore, *American Regionalism*, Chapters 10, 11, 18, 19–24, 25; Pritchett, "Regional Authorities through Interstate Compact," *Social Forces,* Vol. XIV, No. 2 (Dec., 1935), 200–10; Pritchett, "Tennessee Valley Authority as a Government Corporation," *Social Forces,* Vol.XVI, No. 1 (Oct., 1937), 120–30; Pound, "The U.S. Redrawn," *Review of Reviews,* Vol. XCIV (Oct., 1936), 28–31.

CHAPTER XXVII—
Opportunities and Tools for Regionalism in the Plains

Co-operatives and Co-operation: M. Childs, *Co-operation: The Middle Way* (Rev. ed., New Haven, Yale University Press, 1947); Chris L. Christensen, *Agricultural Co-operation in Denmark* (Washington, U.S. Department of Agriculture, 1924); Ellis Cowling, *Co-operatives in America* (New York, Coward-McCann, Inc., 1938); Robert de Roos and Arthur A. Maass, "The Lobby That Can't Be Licked," *Harper's* Magazine, Vol. 199, No. 1192 (Aug., 1949), 15–30; *Encyclopedia of Social Sciences,* IV, 285ff., 359ff.; Ward W. Fetrow and R. H. Elsworth, *Agricultural Co-operation in the United States,* U.S. Department of Agriculture, Farm Credit Administration *Bulletin No. 54* (April, 1947), 2–3, 10–12; Bertram B. Fowler, *The Co-operative Challenge,* (Boston, Little, Brown and Co., 1947), Chapters 2, 6, 10, 12, 14; *Hoover Commission Report on Organization of the Executive Branch of Government* (New York, McGraw-Hill, 1949),276–90 and 282–83, contains the statement, "The [interagency] Committees have failed to solve any important aspects of the problem . . . because dominant members, the Corps and the Bureau, have been unwilling to permit interagency committees to settle their differences. The result has been neglect and avoidance by the committees of virtually all major areas of interagency conflict . . ."; Andren Kress, *et al., Introduction to the Co-operative Movement* (New York, Harper and Brothers, 1941); Benson Y. Landis, *A Co-operative Economy* (New York, Harper and Brothers, 1943), Chapter 2; *A Statistical Handbook of Farmers' Co-operatives,* U.S. Department of Agriculture, *Bulletin No. 26* (Nov., 1938), 1–19.

Missouri River Basin Project and Water Resources: Elliott Coues, *History of the Expedition under the Command of Lewis & Clark* (New York, Francis P. Harper, 1893), I, *xiii–xxxiii; Hoover Commission Report on Organization of the Executive Branch of Government; Irrigation Agriculture in the West,* 26, 29; Maass, *Muddy Waters; Missouri Basin Agricultural Program, Report* of the U.S. Department of Agriculture (Washington, U.S. Government Printing Office, 1949), 32, 48, 49, 54, 58, 63; *A Water Policy for the American People (Report* of the President's Water Resources Policy Commission, 1950, Vol. I), Chapters 1–4, 5, and pp. 9–17, 21–23, 26–29, 69, 74–75, 76–86, 116–17; *Ten Rivers in America's Future,* 285–355; *Natural Resources,* a report to the Hoover Commission (Washington, U.S. Government Printing Office, 1949), 22–39, 107–49; Terral, *The Missouri Valley,* Chapter 21, pp. 201, 207–208; 78 Cong., 2 sess., *Public*

Law 534, the O'Mahoney Amendment to the Flood Control Act of 1944; 79 Cong., 1 sess., *Public Law 14*, Rivers and Harbors Improvement Act.; J. K. Howard, *Golden Rivers* (New York, Harper and Brothers, 1945), 515; *The Big Missouri: Hope of Our West*, Public Affairs Institute, *Report No. 2* (June, 1948).

REGIONAL FINANCES: F. F. Burtchett and C. M. Hicks, *Corporation Finance* (2nd ed., New York, Harper and Brothers, 1948), 697–98; P. H. Nystrom, *Marketing Handbook* (New York, Ronald Press, 1949), Section 14, especially pp. 588–98; "Smoot-Hawley Returns," *New Republic*, Vol. 124, No. 8 (Feb., 19, 1951), 7; "G. O. P. Tariff Binge," *New Republic*, Vol. 124 No. 7 (Feb., 12, 1951), 7.

Index

The Great Plains in Transition

has been composed in Linotype Caledonia and printed directly
from type. The maps in the text were printed along with the
type from photoengravings, which were made from drawings
prepared for this book. The folding map facing page 2 was produced the same way except that it was printed separately on
special map paper and tipped into the book at the binding stage,
as was the frontispiece. The long narrow format of the book was
used in order to retain a readable length of line but not to increase the number of pages beyond comfortable proportions.
The shape might also suggest the shape of the area of the Great
Plains.

University of Oklahoma Press

NORMAN